An Outline of
Financial Economics

An Outline of Financial Economics

Satya R. Chakravarty

ANTHEM PRESS
LONDON · NEW YORK · DELHI

Anthem Press
An imprint of Wimbledon Publishing Company
www.anthempress.com

This edition first published in UK and USA 2013
by ANTHEM PRESS
75-76 Blackfriars Road, London SE1 8HA, UK
or PO Box 9779, London SW19 7ZG, UK
and
244 Madison Ave. #116, New York, NY 10016, USA

British Library Cataloguing-in-Publication Data
A catalogue record for this book is available from the British Library.

Library of Congress Cataloging-in-Publication Data
A catalog record for this book has been requested.

ISBN-13: 978 0 85728 507 2 (Hbk)
ISBN-10: 0 85728 507 6 (Hbk)

This title is also available as an eBook.

To Ananyo and Sumita

Contents

Preface   xi

Part I: Introduction and Basic Concepts

1. Basic Concepts   3
   1.1.   Introduction   3
   1.2.   Financial Institutions, Financial Markets and Financial Instruments   3
   1.3.   Portfolio Management   7

2. Intertemporal Decision-Making and Time Value of Money   8
   2.1.   Introduction   8
   2.2.   Consumer's Time Preferences   8
   2.3.   Discounted Present Value and Fisher's Proposition   12

3. Risk and Uncertainty   16
   3.1.   Introduction   16
   3.2.   Von Neumann–Morgenstern Utility Function   17
   3.3.   Risk Aversion   22
   3.4.   Certainty Equivalent   28
   3.5.   Mean-Variance Analysis: A Special Case of the Expected   33
          Utility Approach
   3.6.   Prospect Theory: A Brief Analysis   36
   Appendix   39

Part II: Firm Valuation and Capital Structure

4. Valuation of Stocks   51
   4.1.   Introduction   51

4.2. Stock Transactions   52
4.3. Valuation of Stocks: A Simple Structure   54
4.4. Valuation of Stocks: A General Framework   56
4.5. Price-to-Earnings Ratio   58

5. Valuation of Cash Flows and Capital Budget Allocation   62

5.1. Introduction   62
5.2. Net Present Value   64
5.3. Internal Rate of Return   65
5.4. Benefit–Cost Ratio and Profitability Index   67
5.5. Some Additional Issues   68
Appendix   72

6. Financial Structure of a Firm   75

6.1. Introduction   75
6.2. The Modigliani–Miller Theorem   75
6.3. Discussion   80

Part III: Fixed Income Securities and Options

7. Valuation of Bonds and Interest Rates   87

7.1. Introduction   87
7.2. Discounted Present Values and Constant Earnings Streams   87
7.3. Special Case of a Bond   88
7.4. Yield to Maturity of Bonds   89
7.5. Duration of Bonds   94
7.6. Duration and Convexity of a Bond   97
7.7. Immunization of Interest Rate Risk   98
7.8. Forward Interest Rate   99
7.9. Forward Rate Agreement   101

8. Markets for Options   105

8.1. Introduction   105
8.2. Types of Options   106
8.3. Payoff Functions for Options   109
8.4. Profit Functions for Options   114
8.5. Boundaries for Option Values   117
8.6. Forward and Futures Contracts   126

9. Arbitrage and Binomial Model   134

9.1. Introduction   134
9.2. Conditions for Non-arbitrage: A Simple Model   135

9.3.   Conditions for Non-arbitrage: A More General Model   138
9.4.   The Binomial Model   143
Appendix   150

10. Brownian Motion and Itō's Lemma   154
10.1. Introduction   154
10.2. Random Walk   154
10.3. Weiner Process (Brownian Motion)   156
10.4. Itō's Lemma   158
10.5. Applications   159
Appendix   162

11. The Black–Scholes–Merton Model   164
11.1. Introduction   164
11.2. The Black–Scholes–Merton Partial Differential Equation 164
11.3. The Black–Scholes Pricing Formulae   170
11.4. Comparative Statics: The Greek Letters   171
11.5. Implied Volatility   175
Appendix   177

12. Exotic Options   181
12.1. Introduction   181
12.2. Digital Options   182
12.3. Asian Options   184
12.4. Barrier Options   186
12.5. Gap Options   190
12.6. Discussion   192
Appendix   194

13. Risk-Neutral Valuation and Martingales   204
13.1. Introduction   204
13.2. Martingale: Background and Interpretation   205
13.3. Equivalent Martingale Measure: Discrete-Time Models   210
13.4. Equivalent Martingale Measure: Continuous-Time Models   212
13.5. Equivalent Martingale Measure: Continuous-Time Path and 213
       Stochastic Interest Rate

Part IV: Portfolio Management Theory

14. Portfolio Management: The Mean-Variance Approach   221
14.1. Introduction   221
14.2. Preliminaries   222

14.3.	Construction of a Portfolio: The Two-Asset Case and a Diagrammatic Exposition	224
14.4.	Construction of a Portfolio: The Multi-Asset Case	231
14.5.	Two-Fund Separation Theorem	235
14.6.	Capital Asset Pricing Model	236
	Appendix	245
15.	**Stochastic Dominance**	**253**
15.1.	Introduction	253
15.2.	First Order Stochastic Dominance	254
15.3.	Second Order Stochastic Dominance	256
15.4.	Lorenz Ordering, Generalized Lorenz Ordering and Stochastic Dominance	259
15.5.	Ranking Portfolios	263
	Appendix	265
16.	**Portfolio Management: The Mean-Gini Approach**	**272**
16.1.	Introduction	272
16.2.	Gini Evaluation Function and Stochastic Dominance	273
16.3.	Efficient Set	276
16.4.	Portfolio Analysis	278
16.5.	Gini Capital Asset Pricing Model	280
	Appendix	282
Bibliography		287
Index		293

Preface

There has been a revolution in financial economics, particularly in the theory of trading of derivative securities, in the past few decades. This book on mathematical finance deals with the study of pricing models of financial derivatives and some other highly relevant issues: choice under uncertainty, security analysis, capital structure and investment theory. The fundamental objective of the book is that in order to get a correct idea of the issues, first it is necessary to understand their economics (that is, potential cash flows) and then to do the mathematical analysis.

The book is divided into four parts. Part I is composed of Chapters 1–3. The first chapter provides a preliminary discussion on (i) financial institutions, (ii) markets and instruments, (iii) derivatives products, and (iv) portfolio management. Chapter 2 contains a relatively simple treatment of time value of money and intertemporal decision-making. Since financial decisions are intertemporal, they are generally characterized by uncertainty. We, therefore, present in Chapter 3 the relevant basic theoretical structure, which describes how individual investors behave in an uncertain situation. Concepts, such as attitudes towards risk, certainty equivalent and cost of risk, are also analyzed. Prospect theory, which incorporates psychology into the analysis of choice under uncertainty, is briefly discussed in the chapter.

The second part of the book, which consists of Chapters 4–6, is concerned with firm valuation and capital structure. A stock is a security that represents ownership share in the issuing company. Stocks are examples of financial instruments. They are important ingredients of option valuation. Stock certificates are issued by a company for financing its expenditures. An analysis of stock transactions and valuations is presented in Chapter 4. Chapter 5 provides a discussion on alternative criteria for judging whether a project should be undertaken by a firm. The subject of Chapter 6 is the financial structure of a firm. The Modigliani–Miller theorem concerning the irrelevance of the method of financing a firm is presented.

The subjects of Part III of this book, which contains seven chapters (Chapters 7–13), are fixed income securities and options. A bond is a debt security issued to raise capital. This financial instrument, which plays an important role in option valuation, is an example of a fixed income security. Chapter 7 presents a relatively complete treatment of a bond. It also covers the important concepts of duration and convexity. Chapters 8–13 provide a detailed approach to the valuation of financial derivative instruments over a wide range of financial assets. Chapter 8 is about standard call and put options, futures and forward contracts, their uses in hedging risks, and basic properties related to option pricing, such as the put-call parity relations and boundaries of option values. Chapter 9 tries to give an insight into the non-arbitrage argument and presents option pricing under the discrete-time binomial option pricing model. We show how the absence of arbitrage becomes equivalent to the existence of a risk-neutral measure. In order to price options accurately, it is necessary to understand the underlying mathematics. Chapter 10 is concerned with the Brownian motion and Itō's process. Concepts such as volatility, random walks and Markovian processes are also exposed and given interpretation in this chapter. The materials discussed in this chapter prepare the background for the celebrated Black–Scholes–Merton option pricing model, which we present in Chapter 11. We show how the modern asset valuation principles rely on hedging and dynamic replication. The concern of Chapter 12 is pricing of non-standard options. Chapter 13 covers risk-neutral valuation and martingale pricing.

Finally, Part IV is concerned with portfolio management theory. The subject of Chapter 14 is the problem of choosing assets in a portfolio and risk management. The basic finance theory results, including the Markowitz mean-variance analysis and the Sharpe–Lintner capital asset pricing model, are analyzed. While in this chapter the variance is taken as an indicator of risk, an alternative indicator of risk is the well-known Gini index. The portfolio choice problem, using the Gini index as a measure of risk, is discussed in detail in Chapter 16. Chapter 15 (which forms the basis of Chapter 16) is concerned with ranking of two securities, using the stochastic dominance criteria, on the basis of their returns. Last but not the least, in the Appendix sections, the reader will find technical analyses of many results reported in different chapters of the book.

There are several innovative features of the book that are worth noting. The methodology adopted in the book is analytical and geometric. I have tried to keep mathematics mostly out of the main body of the text. Most of the chapters are, therefore, supplemented by necessary mathematical appendices. Attempts have been made to explain the technical terms and mathematical operations employed for discussing the results in non-technical language, and intuitive explanations of the mathematical results are given. Wide coverage of the topics and their analytical and informative presentation will make the book theoretically and methodologically quite contemporary and inclusive and highly responsive to the problems of recent concern. In each chapter there are analytical examples. Each chapter contains at least one applied example directly related to the theory presented in the text. Combination of theory and practice helps students understand the theoretical issues first, and then see their practical applications. Each chapter contains different types of problems. They can be solved using the materials presented in the text and have been designed to enhance students' understanding of the subject. Each prove-disprove question, which involves a sequence of logical reasoning, is designed to test students' understanding of the subject.

I have used several sections of this book for giving a graduate course on mathematical finance to the master of statistics and master of science in quantitative economics students at the Indian Statistical Institute, Kolkata, India. So most of the materials covered in the book have been classroom-tested. The book will be suitable for students in: economics/finance, economics/finance/econometrics, economics/finance/statistics and mathematics/economics/finance. Rigorous demonstration of the results in the appendices to different chapters, along with the main text materials, will make the book highly suitable as a graduate text. The mathematical techniques employed in demonstrating the results in the appendices will be helpful for those who wish to learn application of mathematics for solving problems in economics/finance. The proofs of all the results considered in the book are quite explicit. Given that the book presents a systematic treatment of theory and methodology, it will also be very useful to researchers working in this very active area. The materials presented in the text and their diagrammatic expositions should be sufficient to design a course on finance at the undergraduate level.

It is a pleasure to acknowledge comments and suggestions that I received from students. My gratitude goes to Pradip Maiti who went through one section of Chapter 14 and offered many suggestions. Thanks are due to Luigi Guiso, Campbell R. Harvey and Yue K. Kwok for the help and advice I received from them. Thanks are also due to an anonymous reviewer for constructive suggestions. I am grateful to the members of the Advisory Board of Anthem Press for their suggestions on re-organization of the chapters. I have worked jointly with Debkumar Chakrabarti and Claudio Zoli on the theory of risk and uncertainty. My gratitude goes to them as well for the benefit I derived from direct interactions with them. The library staff of the Indian Statistical Institute has always been very helpful in getting me the books and journals I requested. I thank them for their helpful cooperation. My wife Sumita sat through some sessions of proofreading. Debasmita Basu, Srikanta Kundu, Satyajit Malakar, Sattwik Santra and Sandip Sarkar have drawn all the figures. Chaiti Sharma Biswas and Chunu Ram Saren were always available for computer advice. I am happy to thank them all for their support. Finally, of course, I must also thank my son Ananyo and wife Sumita, without whose cooperation this book could not possibly have been written.

PART I

Introduction and Basic Concepts

CHAPTER 1

Basic Concepts

1.1 INTRODUCTION

Financial markets have been growing rapidly over the last 30 years or so. They provide a wide range of financial instruments for different purposes. The objective of this chapter is to present a gentle introduction to financial institutions, financial markets, financial instruments and portfolio management.

1.2 FINANCIAL INSTITUTIONS, FINANCIAL MARKETS AND FINANCIAL INSTRUMENTS

A growing and prosperous economy is characterized by a strong financial system. Well-functioning financial markets and institutions are necessary for enabling companies to raise funds for financing capital expenditures and for individuals to save funds for future use. There will be an efficient flow of funds from suppliers to demanders in an economy with well-organized financial markets and institutions.

Often it may be necessary for businesses, individuals and governments to raise money. Individuals and organizations currently possessing surplus funds can accumulate funds for future use. In order to make some future investments as a part of its expansion activities, a business house may need to raise money. A firm desiring to establish a new plant may need money to meet its fund requirements. A government may have to borrow funds for providing a public good. A family might have to take loans from banks to bear its children's education expenses or to purchase a home. A young graduate may need to raise funds to start a new business. There is definitely a cost associated with this and this cost is the return that a saver expects to receive on his surplus funds. While a business organization might save today for future investments, an individual's objective for saving in the current period might be to finance family expenditure after retirement.

Financial institutions are those organizations that operate as a channel between savers and borrowers of funds. Broadly speaking, there are two major types of financial institutions: depository and non-depository institutions. A depository financial institution is one that collects funds from savers in the form of deposits and pays them interest from the interest earned on loans taken by the borrowers. Examples of such organizations are banks and credit unions. Non-depository financial institutions like insurance companies, mutual fund companies and brokerage firms sell their policies and shares/units to the public, and returns are provided in the form of benefits, as per agreement. Thus, the objective of a financial institution is to provide financial services to its depositors and borrowers. For instance, banks accept deposits from those who have money to save, and lend money in the form of loans and mortgages. This is essentially a transfer of funds from a lender to a borrower with a bank working as a financial intermediary.

Financial markets provide a link between buyers and sellers for trading different types of financial products or securities. Often a financial product is referred to as a financial instrument. A financial instrument is a particular type of legal contract. Financial markets give participants opportunities for short- and long-term exchange of assets and risk transfer. If the purpose of trade is not immediate consumption of a product, rather delaying consumption over time, then the market for the product under consideration can as well be regarded as a financial market. Financial markets are affected by supply–demand forces, and resources are allocated over time through a price mechanism, such as an interest rate. The objectives of financial markets are many: for instance, to raise capital (in the capital market), to transfer risk (in the derivatives market) and to trade at international level (in the currency market). These markets are the coming together of buyers and sellers of financial products for the purpose of the desired type of trade.

Without financial markets it would be difficult for borrowers to find lenders on their own. Lending activities may take many forms, including: (i) depositing money with a bank, (ii) contribution to a provident fund, (iii) payment of insurance premiums, (iv) buying government bonds and (v) buying company shares. Borrowers can be individuals, companies, governments, public corporations and municipalities. As we have argued, individuals may have to borrow from banks in order to fulfill their needs. More complex financial transactions may take place between two parties, where the borrowing party is the borrower and its agent and the lending party is the lender and its agent.

The branch of economics that deals with the workings of the financial markets is known as financial economics. The typical questions that are addressed in this subject are generally formulated in terms of uncertainty, risks, time, options, securities, interest rates, information, etc.

Financial markets can be subdivided into different categories: (1) capital markets, (2) money markets, (3) derivatives markets, (4) insurance markets, (5) foreign exchange markets, (6) commodity markets and (7) futures markets.

One common component of all financial markets is risk. As we will note, there can be asset risks (security), foreign exchange risks, credit risks, commodity risks, interest rate risks, etc. Risks can bring unforeseen losses. They can give rise to unexpected gains as well. Situations like replacing uncertainty with certainty and increasing the desirability to invest in risky assets in order to reap profits from frequent changes in asset prices call for specific risk-management instruments. Willingness to take risks with the objective of making profits resulting from predictions of future price movements is called speculation. It is risky and different from arbitrage, which is a situation to make profits from price differences existing in reality and is, consequently, riskless. All discussions in this book rely on the assumption that arbitrage opportunities do not exist.

Capital markets consist of stock markets (which facilitate the trading of shares of stocks) and bond markets (which enable the buying and selling of bonds and debentures). A share of a stock (often also referred to as an equity security) is an entitlement that provides the holder a part of the ownership of the issuing company. Companies may borrow money for short- and long-term cash flows, modernization and expansion of business. Companies issue stock certificates to raise capital for financing their activities. A company is then owned by its shareholders. Examples of stock markets are those in London, New York City and Tokyo. It also becomes necessary to understand the capital composition of a firm—that is, how the financing of the firm takes place in terms of a combination of debt and equity.

A bond is a debt security issued by companies and governments to raise capital, and the holder receives coupons periodically and the principal amount (the initial investment) from the issuing authority when the investment matures. Thus, while in the case of a stock the financial instrument conveys ownership, for a bond it conveys credit. Governments may have to borrow to fill in the gap between expenditure requirements and tax revenues. Government borrowings take place through the issuance of bonds. Public corporations—which typically include railways, postal services and nationalized industries—raise loans through bond sales. Municipalities may borrow from the government.

Money markets provide facilities for short-term debt financing and investment. Short-term debts are generally priced using an annual rate of interest. A derivative is a financial instrument whose value depends on that of other financial securities. In this case the latter security is referred to as the underlying security or asset. Derivative products, or simply derivatives, are financial instruments for managing financial risks. Frequent fluctuations of share prices, interest rates, bond prices, currency exchange rates and dividends in the financial markets create risk. Derivatives are financial securities used for hedging financial risks—that is, to protect, or at least reduce, a risk. In other words, financial derivatives are one type of risk management instrument and the basic strategy is hedging. In hedging the trader holds two positions of equal amounts simultaneously, one in the underlying asset market and the other in the derivatives market. These positions are in opposite directions and it is expected that normally the prices of the underlying assets and derivatives move along the same direction with roughly the same magnitude so that the losses (or gains) in the asset market get offset by gains (or losses) in the derivatives markets. The most well known example of a derivative is a stock option. A stock option is an agreement that provides the buyer with the right, but not obligation, to purchase (a call option) or sell (a put option) the underlying asset at a future date.

Insurance markets are helpful for redistribution of risks of various types. As is evident from the name, foreign exchange markets facilitate trading of foreign exchanges. In such markets standard buyers and sellers are importers and exporters, governments (for example, spending on diplomats abroad), tourists, and banks and institutions. A commodity market is a mechanism that facilitates the trading of physical assets like oil, wheat, gold, silver, copper etc.

In a futures market trading of futures contracts takes place. A futures contract is an exchange-traded agreement in which the holder has the obligation to buy or sell an asset on a future date at a pre-determined price. In futures markets, agreements in the form of contracts (implying the promise for future exchanges) are made. A forward contract, which is an over-the-counter contract—for example, settled through telephone—that obligates the holder to deliver an asset on a pre-determined date at a pre-determined price. A swap is an over-the-counter financial contract between two parties to exchange in the future one cash flow for another according to some prearranged formula. An interest rate swap can be used to convert a floating-rate borrowing into a fixed-rate borrowing or vice versa. Under a currency swap, a loan in one currency can be converted into a loan in another currency. Swaps are used for the purpose of reduction of financing costs or hedging. Interest rate swaps constitute an important derivative holding of banks.

In view of their wide applications, derivatives by now have become so popular that many of them are based on financial entities, which are different from standard financial securities. For example, an interest rate derivative is a financial instrument whose value depends on the structure of evolution of interest rates. In a foreign currency option, the underlying asset is a foreign currency. Companies use foreign currency derivatives as a mechanism to alter their response to fluctuations in foreign currency. Credit derivatives can be used to manage a company's exposure to credit risks, such as supplier default. These non-standard derivatives are referred to as exotic options. Just as one pays an insurance premium for obtaining protection against a particular event, there are some derivative products which have payoffs contingent on the occurrence of some event for which an advance premium has to be paid. One of the major objectives of financial economics is the determination of the price of a derivative as a function of the price of the underlying asset.

The valuation of derivatives makes use of advanced statistical mathematics of uncertainty. Fisher Black, Myron Scholes and Robert C. Merton revolutionized the option pricing theory using continuous hedging as a risk management strategy.

A major part of the financial market involves variation of price. The scale of asset price changes per some unit of time is known as volatility. There are unpredictable price fluctuations in a volatile market. A key factor in making money in options is to understand the nature of volatility clearly.

1.3 PORTFOLIO MANAGEMENT

Portfolio analysis provides a framework for identifying and measuring risk and assigning returns for bearing risk. Since the future return on an asset may be uncertain, an asset's return in such a case is a random variable. The first problem here is quantification of the risk of an asset. Investors prefer a higher expected return to a lower expected return and dislike risks. Two different stocks generally have different expected returns and risks. This theory enables us to understand why expected returns and risks change over time. The problem of ranking stocks on the basis of their returns and risks is a major issue in financial economics.

Portfolio management theory helps us understand the risk of acquisition of a new project by a firm. The theory helps the investor characterize the risk associated with a portfolio. In a portfolio investment setting, it is necessary to understand the interactions of two different assets. The variance of an asset return, which is a measure of the spread of possible values from the average, is taken as an indicator of risk. The risk of a portfolio is its variance. Investors like portfolios with higher expected return and lower variance. This is the framework advanced by Harry Markowitz. The interaction of an asset with another asset is measured by the covariance or the correlation coefficient. The capital asset pricing model (CAPM) of William Sharpe and John Lintner suggests that investors prefer to hold well-diversified portfolios. While standard asset pricing theory relies on the mean and variance, an alternative framework can be one where the Gini index is taken as an indicator of risk.

BIBLIOGRAPHICAL NOTES

An introduction to various financial markets and a description of functions of financial institutions can be found in Saunders and Cornett (2001). The structure of financial institutions and markets is investigated in Kohn (2003). For a comprehensive overview of financial markets, a good reference is Bailey (2005).

CHAPTER 2

Intertemporal Decision-Making and Time Value of Money

2.1 INTRODUCTION

Often decisions made by consumers, firms etc take into account consequences not only for the current period, but also for the future periods. This is because future payoffs are often determined by current decision-making. Some goods are durable; they can last and contribute to a consumer's satisfaction for years. Examples are a refrigerator and an air conditioner. Likewise, capital expenditures by a firm involve purchases of equipment that is likely to last for several years. In such cases decisions may involve comparison of an outflow today with inflows in the future. Thus, "time" becomes an important ingredient of analysis in such a situation. It is, therefore, necessary to understand the structure of markets that links current decision-making with future payoffs. It becomes essential to note that lending and borrowing will be an important aspect of a decision-maker's behavior. Consumer's preference ranking over consumption bundles are now defined on the amounts of goods to be consumed in the current period and the amounts to be consumed in the future periods. This is discussed in Section 2.2 of this chapter.

A natural question that arises in an intertemporal set up is: how much are future payoffs worth now? To answer a question of this type we need to calculate the current value of future flows of money. Section 2.3 presents a discussion on this.

2.2 CONSUMER'S TIME PREFERENCES

For simplicity of exposition, we assume that a consumer's preference relation is now over amounts of goods to be consumed in period 0 (today) and amounts to be consumed in period 1 (next period or future). Let c_i be the units of a normal composite good consumed in period i, where $i = 0, 1$. We assume that the good cannot be stored. Consequently, number of units purchased in period equals consumption in the period. The price per unit of the composite good in period i is denoted by χ_i, where $i = 0, 1$. The ratio $(\chi_1 - \chi_0)/ \chi_0$ gives the proportionate rate of increase in price of the good between the two periods. The consumer knows with certainty that his income from supply of factor services in period i is, M_i, where $i = 0, 1$. For instance, his current period income may be salary income and the next period income will be pension. Let $\varsigma = M_0 - \chi_0 c_0$ be the consumer's saving—the difference between his income and expenditure—in period 0. If ς is negative then the consumer is a borrower in period 0.

To determine the expenditure in period 1, it is necessary to take into the account the interest on the amount saved. The rate of interest is the rate of return received per unit of time by lending money to borrowers, for use in the current period, to be repaid at a future date. In other words, this is the rate of return earned by the lender for waiting to get back the money that has been lent. Therefore, it can be regarded as an indicator, which can convert the current period funds into funds at a future date. We assume here the existence of a rate of return λ at which lending and borrowing are possible. While it tells the investors (lenders) how much they can expect on their investment (lending), for borrowers, it determines the amount to be paid as interest. It plays an important role in the trade off between period 0 and period 1 consumptions. It is the opportunity cost of consumption in the current period; it reflects the cost of waiting.

Given the interest rate λ, the consumer earns a gross interest of $\lambda\varsigma$ on his saving in period 1. Therefore, his expenditure in period 1 becomes $\chi_1 c_1 = M_1 + \varsigma + \varsigma\lambda = M_1 + \varsigma(1 + \lambda)$. If ς is negative, then $\varsigma(1 + \lambda)$ gives the amount to be paid in period 1 to repay borrowings ς and gross interest $\lambda\varsigma$. Plugging $\varsigma = M_0 - \chi_0 c_0$ into the equation for expenditure in period 1, we get the consumer's intertemporal budget constraint: $\chi_1 c_1 = M_1 + (M_0 - \chi_0 c_0)(1 + \lambda)$, which on rearrangement becomes

$$\chi_0 c_0 + \frac{\chi_1 c_1}{1+\lambda} = M_0 + \frac{M_1}{1+\lambda}.$$

(2.1)

Now, 1 dollar at period 0 will grow into $(1 + \lambda)$ dollars at period 1. That is, the value of $(1 + \lambda)$ dollars at period 1 is 1 dollar at period 0. Hence the value of 1 dollar received at period 1 is $1/(1 + \lambda)$ dollars at period 0. Thus, the price of 1 unit of the good at time 1 in terms of the good at time 0 is $\chi_1/(1 + \lambda)$ dollars. The left-hand side of the budget constraint gives the discounted present value of the consumption bundle (c_0, c_1), whereas the right-hand side is the present value of the income stream (M_0, M_1) (see Section 2.3).

The consumer's intertemporal preferences are represented by a utility $U(c_0, c_1)$ function defined on the bundle (c_0, c_1). For simplicity of exposition, we assume the $U(c_0, c_1)$ has the following additive form

$$U(c_0, c_1) = h(c_0) + \tau\, h(c_1),$$

(2.2)

where $0 < \tau < 1$ is a psychological discount factor (see Varian 1992; Mas-Colell et al. 1995; and Demange and Laroque 2006). The restriction $0 < \tau < 1$ shows that there is preference for current period consumption (since the weight assigned to $h(c_0)$ in the aggregation is 1, which is higher than τ). The function h is assumed to be differentiable, increasing and strictly concave. Increasingness of h means that more is preferred to less. Strict concavity means that the rate of increase in utility from additional consumptions is decreasing. (See Chapter 3 for definitions of increasingness and strict concavity of a function.)

Along an indifference curve the marginal rate of substitution between c_0 and c_1, which we refer to as the marginal rate of time preference, is defined by $-dc_1/dc_0$. It indicates the consumer's willingness to forgo future consumption for current consumption, given that the level of utility is fixed. Diminishing marginal rate of time preference means that along an indifference curve the consumer's willingness to give up consumption in period 1 to increase consumption in period 0 decreases as the amount of current consumption increases.

A consumption bundle (c_0, c_1) is called optimal when it maximizes $U(c_0, c_1)$, subject to the budget constraint. At the point of optimal consumption, we have the usual tangency condition for utility maximization, that is, the marginal rate of time preference will be equal to the ratio between the two prices. Differentiating the utility function $U(c_0, c_1)$ totally, we have $dU = (\partial U(c_0, c_1)/\partial c_0)dc_0 + (\partial U(c_0, c_1)/\partial c_1) dc_1$. From (2.2) it follows that $\partial U(c_0, c_1)/\partial c_0 = h'(c_0)$ and $\partial U(c_0, c_1)/\partial c_1 = \tau h'(c_1)$, where h' is the first derivative of the function h. Note that $h'(c_0)$ and $\tau h'(c_1)$ are the marginal utilities of $U(c_0, c_1)$ in (2.2) with respect to c_0 and c_1. Since along an indifference curve, $dU = 0$, it follows that for the utility function in (2.2) $[-dc_1/dc_0 = h'(c_0)/(\tau h'(c_1))]$. From (2.1) we have $[-dc_1/dc_0 = (\chi_0(1 + \lambda))/\chi_1]$. This is the ratio between the prices of the composite good in the two periods 0 and 1. Thus, the tangency condition for utility maximization becomes

$$\frac{h'(c_0)}{\tau h'(c_1)} = \frac{\chi_0(1+\lambda)}{\chi_1}.$$

$$(2.3)$$

With a perfect lending and borrowing market, all consumers face the same interest rate. Prices are also the same for all consumers. Hence the utility maximizing tangency condition in (2.3) implies that the marginal rate of time preference will be the same for every consumer. That is, each consumer will adjust his consumption stream (c_0, c_1) to satisfy (2.3).

A consumer is impatient or myopic if he allocates a higher proportion of his income to the current consumption, that is, he is a borrower in the current period. A patient consumer is a lender in the current period. Suppose a consumer is a lender in the current period and his consumption is represented by the point C^0 (see Figure 2.1). Since for any interest rate the initial endowment $\left(\dfrac{M_0}{\chi_0}, \dfrac{M_1}{\chi_1}\right)$ is available, as the rate of interest rate increases from λ^0 to λ^1, the budget line rotates around the endowment point in the clockwise direction. This increase in interest rate will motivate the consumer to remain a lender because he can move to a higher indifference curve if he continues his lending position. His consumption bundle in the changed scenario will be a point like C^1 (see Figure 2.1). The actual level of consumption will depend on the strengths of the substitution and income effects. With an increase in the interest rate, saving increases and the person would like to consume less in the current period and more in the future period, that is, he wishes to substitute his current consumption by future consumption. But the increased interest rate increases his income as well, and since both the goods are normal, the income effect acts to increase their consumptions. If the substitution effect dominates the income effect, then current consumption will reduce and future consumption will increase. The opposite happens if the substitution effect is dominated by the income effect. If he becomes a borrower under this change, then he becomes worse off because his consumption bundle will be a point like C^2, which corresponds to a lower indifference curve. Hence this possibility is ruled out.

Figure 2.1   Change in the Rate of Interest and Consumer's Time Preference

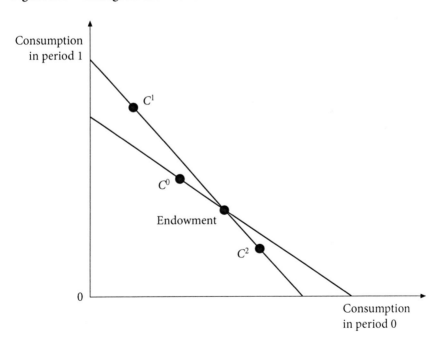

If a person is a borrower initially, then as the increase in the interest rate decreases his income, the substitution effect forces him to consume less in the current period and more in the next period and the income effect decreases his consumptions in both the periods. Finally, note that if a person is a borrower initially, then with a reduction in the interest rate, he continues to be a borrower.

For our analysis in this section we have assumed the existence of an interest rate at which it is possible to lend and borrow money. Since households, governments and firms borrow and lend under different terms and conditions, a variety of interest rates exist in practical situations. We conclude this section with a very brief discussion on this. A London Interbank Offered Rate (LIBOR) is the rate of interest at which a bank is willing to lend money to other banks in the London wholesale money market or interbank market. The Mumbai Interbank Offered Rate is the Mumbai counterpart to LIBOR, that is, it is based on the Mumbai interbank market. The interest rate that the Bank of England charges the banks for secured overnight lending is called the Bank of England Base Rate. The interest rate charged to banks for short-period borrowings from Federal Reserves is known as the discount rate. For instance, in India this is the rate at which the commercial banks borrow short-term funds from the Reserve Bank of India. Call money rate (or call rate) in India is the interest rate charged on one-day loans (call money) at which banks and corporate entities can borrow from other banks. This rate may vary from day to day. (See also Chapter 7 and Hull and Basu 2010.)

2.3 DISCOUNTED PRESENT VALUE AND FISHER'S PROPOSITION

The discounted present value refers to evaluation of future cash flows in terms of today's dollars. Our presentation on this issue will be brief and analytical. For detailed discussion on this, the reader is referred to Damodaran (2010).

Assume, for simplicity, that the length of a period is one year. Suppose a person is offered the following stream of payments: B_1 dollars after one year from now, B_2 dollars after two years from now, and in general B_t dollars after t years from now. The final payment he receives is B_T dollars T years from now. Given the annual interest rate λ, it becomes necessary for the person to determine the value of such a stream at present.

Note that 1 dollar at present becomes $(1 + \lambda)$ dollars after one year from now. Hence at present the value of 1 dollar received after a year from now is $1/(1 + \lambda)$ dollars. Since B_1 dollars are received after one year from now, the present value of B_1 dollars is $B_1/(1 + \lambda)$ dollars. Alternatively, we can say that in order to receive B_1 dollars after a year from now, it is necessary to invest $B_1/(1 + \lambda)$ dollars at present. Likewise, an investment of $B_2/(1 + \lambda)^2$ is required at present to obtain B_2 dollars after two years from now, and in general to obtain B_t dollars after t years from now, the person has to invest $B_t/(1 + \lambda)^t$ now.

Thus, the amount that the person has to invest now to receive the stream of payments considered above is $\sum_{t=1}^{T} \left(B_t / (1+\lambda)^t \right)$. We call this sum the discounted present value (DPV) of the income stream B_1, B_2,..., B_T and denote this sum by DPV. Thus,

$$DPV = \sum_{t=1}^{T} \frac{B_t}{(1+\lambda)^t}. \qquad (2.4)$$

The DPV is the amount that the person is willing to pay now in return for a promise to receive the income stream B_1, B_2,...,B_T. This DPV is the price of the asset that promises to pay the stream B_1, B_2,...,B_T. To understand this, consider two assets, where they have the same cash flows but one has higher price than the other. Then a person would sell the higher priced asset and invest the proceeds in the lower priced asset to earn profit without investing any money. Thus, selling some of an asset and buying some of a different asset enables him to realize a sure return without making any additional investment. This practice is known as arbitrage. There will be excess supply of the higher priced asset, but at the high price it will not have any demand. Thus, supply exceeds demand and hence price will fall until the two prices coincide. Consequently, there does not exist any scope for arbitrage. If there is no opportunity for arbitrage, then all assets must sell for their DPVs.

Given $B_i's$, an increase in the interest rate λ reduces the DPV. The reason is that when the interest rate goes up, the amount that must be invested now to receive 1 dollar at a future date decreases. Also the marginal product of the rate of interest as a driver of the measured DPV increases as the rate of interest increases.

Fisher (1930) argued that a consumer's choice among income streams should be guided by their DPVs. His proposition can be stated as follows: "Any two assets with the same discounted present value must sell for the same price, given a perfect lending market." In a perfect lending market, which is synonymous with a perfect capital market, a person can borrow or lend as much as he desires at the on going market rate of interest. By the principle of non-arbitrage, the DPV of an asset equals its price. Therefore, Fisher's proposition is essentially a restatement of the non-arbitrage principle.

Example 2.1: An individual borrows a certain amount of money from a bank at an annual interest rate λ for financing the purchase of a house. The number of years to pay back the loan is T and his annual payment to the bank is m. The price of the borrowing P is the DPV of these payments:

$$P = \sum_{t=1}^{T'} \frac{m}{(1+\lambda)^t} = \frac{m\left(1-(1+\lambda)^{-T}\right)}{\lambda}.$$

Applied Example 2.1: The State Bank of India, which has branches in many countries of the world, offers house building loans for purchase/construction of a new house, purchase of an existing house, purchase of land for the construction of a new house and similar purposes, under certain conditions about the eligibility of the persons asking for loans, quantum of loan amount, and repayment of loans etc. Depending on the amount of loan taken and period of repayment, fixed and floating interest rates are charged. For instance, it was notified on 28 October 2010 that for loans in between Rupees 2000000 and Rupees 3000000 if the tenure of repayment varies from 15 years to 20 years, then the floating annual interest rate is 8 percent for the first year, 9 percent for the next two years and 10 percent for the remaining years.

BIBLIOGRAPHICAL NOTES

For deeper discussion on consumer's time preference, the reader can refer to Varian (1992), Mas-Colell et al. (1995), Demange and Laroque (2006) and Chakravarty (2010). Damodaran (2010) is superb for an overview of discounted present value.

EXERCISES

1. Each of the following statements is either true or false. If the statement is true prove it. If it is false, give a counter-example or justify your answer by logical reasoning.
    (a) A reduction in the interest rate makes the intertemporal budget line flatter.
    (b) The interest rate is an indicator of the opportunity cost of current period consumption.
    (c) A person borrows 2000 dollars and pays in 12 equal annual installments of 200 dollars. The underlying interest rate is 10 percent.
    (d) A consumer in a two-period horizon, who is a lender initially, will unambiguously become a borrower if the interest rate decreases.
    (e) An individual can invest 100 dollars for a year at an annual interest of 10.3 percent or at a quarterly interest of 10 percent. Then former is a better option for him.
2. Assume that the interest rate is given and both current and future period consumptions are normal. Demonstrate graphically that an increase in the current period income induces increments in both current and future period consumptions.
3. Consider a consumer who pays the interest rate λ_1 for borrowing and earns the interest rate λ_2 for saving, where $\lambda_2 < \lambda_1$. Draw the budget line for this consumer.
4. A forester has to decide when to cut down a tree. The value of the tree at time t is given by $V(t)$ and the initial expenditure for plantation of the tree

is M. The continuous market interest is λ. Determine the first and second order conditions for choosing the (optimal) harvest date that will maximize the discounted present value of the forester's profits. What will be the impact of an increase in the interest rate on the optimal harvest date?

5. Demonstrate the Fisher Proposition using the principle of non-arbitrage.

CHAPTER 3

Risk and Uncertainty

3.1 INTRODUCTION

Uncertainty plays an important role in many real world situations. As we have seen in the earlier chapters, financial decisions are often intertemporal decisions. Such decisions involve choices whose consequences extend into the future. Since the future is unknown, it is often likely that the financial decisions are inevitably taken under conditions of uncertainty. For instance, a stock may not pay a constant dividend and may not grow at a constant rate (see Chapter 4 for a detailed discussion). In such a case buying and selling of stocks takes place in an uncertain environment. Thus, buying a stock here is taking the form of playing a game or lottery whose outcome is not known with certainty. Uncertainty often arises because of lack of necessary information, so that an uncertain set-up cannot be converted into a certain framework. If we do not have sufficient information on expected growth rate of a company, then it is not possible to make a conclusive statement on expected output on equity. In many economic situations outcome depends on what others do. Thus, an individual may not be able to predict the outcome of the corresponding situation with certainty. An example is the diplomatic behavior.

The objective of this chapter is to look at the consumption and investment decisions under uncertainty and their implications for the valuation of uncertain prospects. A well-accepted theory of prospect choice under uncertainty is the expected utility hypothesis. Under this hypothesis an individual's consumption and investment decisions are guided by maximization of expected utility. A utility function, satisfying this hypothesis, is called a von Neumann–Morgenstern (1944) utility function. We discuss such utility functions in the next section of the chapter. The Arrow (1963)–Pratt (1964) measures of risk aversion for von Neumann–Morgenstern utility functions have been employed extensively for analyzing problems on uncertainty. For instance, they have been used to investigate the properties of demand in asset and insurance markets, interactions between risk and life-cycle savings, behavior of individuals in risky choice situations and properties of risk taking in taxation models. Section 3.3 analyses properties of these measures. The certainty equivalent of a prospect is the output that an individual would have to receive to be indifferent between that output and the prospect. It has a negative monotonic relationship with the cost of risk in the prospect. This cost is an indicator of the amount of premium that an individual would like to pay to avoid facing the prospect. We investigate properties of the certainty equivalent in Section 3.4. Characterizations of the utility functions with constant levels of the Arrow–Pratt measures of risk aversion are developed in this section. These characterizations give us insight of the underlying utility functions through the postulates employed in the characterization exercises. In Section 3.5 we examine the possibility of using the quadratic utility function as a utility function that fulfills the expected utility hypothesis. Finally, Section 3.6 briefly analyzes prospect theory, a viable alternative to expected utility theory.

3.2 VON NEUMANN–MORGENSTERN UTILITY FUNCTION

A person chooses economic actions on the basis of consequences produced by them. However, actions alone may not be sufficient to determine alternative consequences. Some additional factors may interact with an action to produce a particular consequence. These factors, which are beyond the control of the person taking actions, are referred to as "states of the world." Thus, actions along with states generate consequences. Choosing an action will determine a consequence corresponding to each state of the world. If the state of the world does not influence the consequence at all, the decision is made in a situation of certainty. On the other hand, if different states lead to different consequences, then the decision is said to be made under uncertainty. To illustrate this, consider a competitive profit maximizing firm whose input use depends on weather conditions (states). If there is uncertainty about future weather conditions, the issue of choice of inputs (actions) becomes a problem of a decision made under uncertainty.

There is an induced probability distribution on the set of consequences for each action. In other words, given a particular action, the probability of a particular consequence is equal to the probability of the state of the world, which gives rise to this consequence. Since the probability of a consequence depends on the choice of an action, we can also say that the choice of an action amounts to the choice of a probability distribution on consequences. In other words, the choice of an action in an uncertain world amounts to the choice of probability distribution over outcomes. Thus, if we consider an uncertain prospect A there is a probability distribution on the different levels of output of the prospect. We refer to outputs of a prospect as state-contingent outputs. Contingent here means depending on something not yet certain, so that a state-contingent output is an output that depends on the outcome of the state. Unless specified, we assume throughout this chapter that all prospects under consideration are characterized by uncertainty.

Assume that the individual assigns a probability p_i to the state i, $1 \le i \le k$. We denote the vector of probabilities by $(p_1, p_2,..., p_k)$ by $\underline{p}$, while $\underline{R} = (R_1, R_2,..., R_k)$ is the vector of state-contingent outputs on the prospect A. In other words, the individual assumes that p_i is the probability that the output on the prospect will be R_i. Evidently, $0 \le p_i \le 1$ for all $1 \le i \le k$ and $\sum_{i=1}^{k} p_i = 1$. We assume the existence of a minimum and a maximum value of output and denote them by R_l and R_u respectively. Assume that $-\infty < R_l < R_u < \infty$. For each $1 \le i \le k$, $R_l \le R_i \le R_u$. Thus each R_i is taken from the non-degenerate interval $[R_l, R_u]$ in the real line. In other words, each element of $[R_l, R_u]$ is not less than the real number R_l (lower bound) and not greater than the real number R_u (upper bound). Equivalently, we say that the set $[R_l, R_u]$ is a bounded set. By non-degeneracy of $[R_l, R_u]$ we mean that it contains at least two different elements. Since the interval $[R_l, R_u]$ includes its boundaries R_l and R_u, it is a closed set. We use the compact notation $A = \left(\underline{p}, \underline{R} \right)$ to indicate the outputs on the prospect and the corresponding probabilities.

For a choice between alternative prospects, it is necessary to have a preference ordering on the set of prospects. If between any two prospects A^1 and A^2, the individual regards A^1 to be at least as good as A^2, we denote this by $A^1 \succeq A^2$. If both $A^1 \succeq A^2$ and $A^2 \succeq A^1$ hold, then the individual is indifferent between A^1 and A^2, and we use the notation $A^1 \sim A^2$ to indicate this. If $A^1 \succeq A^2$ holds but $A^2 \succeq A^1$ does not hold, we say that the individual prefers A^1 to A^2 and this is denoted by $A^1 \succ A^2$.

Since an individual's preferences over prospects are defined in an environment characterized by uncertainty, the average utility expected from a risky situation may be regarded a yardstick. More precisely, maximizing expected utility is something that a decision-maker should do. Since only one of the many possible outcomes will occur, only one of the outputs will be realized. Average of utilities of many possible outputs can be taken as a representative utility. We say that a decision-maker's preferences over uncertain prospects satisfy the expected utility hypothesis if there exists a real-valued function U defined on $[R_l, R_u]$ such that for any two prospects $A = \left(\underline{p}, \underline{R} \right) \succeq A' = \left(\underline{p}', \underline{R}' \right)$ if and only if $\sum_{i=1}^{k} p_i U(R_i) \ge \sum_{i=1}^{k} p_i' U(R_i')$.

Likewise, $\left(\underline{p}, \underline{R} \right) \succ \left(\underline{p}', \underline{R}' \right)$ if and only if $\sum_{i=1}^{k} p_i U(R_i) > \sum_{i=1}^{k} p_i' U(R_i')$. The function U here is called a von Neumann–Morgenstern utility function. In other words, the individual will choose one prospect over another if and only if there exists a von Neumann–Morgenstern utility function such that the expected utility of the former exceeds that of the latter. Thus, the decision-maker's choice variable is the expected utility from the prospect not the expected value of the prospect; that is, the individual maximizes not the expected value but rather the expected utility.

The function $U : [R_l, R_u] \to \Re$ is said to be non-decreasing if for any R_1, R_2 $\in [R_l, R_u]$, $R_1 \le R_2$, $U(R_1) \le U(R_2)$, where $\Re$ is the real line. For an increasing function, the defining inequality is $U(R_1) < U(R_2)$, $R_1, R_2 \in [R_l, R_u]$, with $R_1 < R_2$. If U is differentiable, then non-decreasingness (increasingness) of U is same as the condition that $U' \ge 0(U' > 0)$, where U' is the derivative of U. That is, for a non-decreasing (an increasing) utility function U, the marginal utility U' is non-negative (positive).

A natural question that arises at this stage is: why should the preferences over uncertain outcomes have the particular structure implied by the expected utility hypothesis? There are compelling reasons to believe that maximization of expected utility can be a reasonable objective for problems of choice of outputs in the context of uncertainty. An individual's preference $\succ$ on the set of prospects is assumed to satisfy certain axioms. They are necessary to set up a formal analysis in the present context. We follow mostly Gravelle and Rees (2004) in presenting the first five of these axioms and representing the decision-maker's preference ordering.

Axiom 1: (Ordering): (i) For any two prospects A^1 and A^2, exactly one of the statements, $A^1 \succ A^2$, $A^2 \succ A^1$ and $A^1 \sim A^2$ holds. (ii) For any three prospects A^1, A^2 and A^3, if $A^1 \succ A^2$, $A^2 \succ A^3$ hold, then $A^1 \succ A^3$ holds.

Statement (i) of this axiom says that $\succ$ is a complete relation; any two prospects are comparable under $\succ$. The individual does not withhold his judgment for comparing any two prospects. Statement (ii) means transitivity. That is, if the individual thinks that A^1 is better than A^2 and A^2 is better than A^3, then A^1 must be better than A^3. Transitivity represents consistency in individual behavior in a particular way.

In order to state the next axiom, let us define a standard prospect A_s as one in which the only outcomes are R_u and R_l, and chances of their occurrences are p_u and $(1 - p_u)$ respectively. We write a specific standard prospect A_s^1, using a compact notation, as $A_s^1 = \left(p_u^1, R_u, R_l \right)$. The following axiom can now be stated.

Axiom 2: (Preference for higher output under higher probability): For any two standard prospects $A_s^1 = \left(p_u^1, R_u, R_l \right)$ and $A_s^2 = \left(p_u^2, R_u, R_l \right)$, (i) $A_s^1 \succ A_s^2$ if and only if $p_u^1 > p_u^2$, (ii) $A_s^1 \sim A_s^2$ if and only if $p_u^1 = p_u^2$.

According to condition (i) of Axiom 2, one standard prospect is regarded as better than another standard prospect if the probability of occurrence of the higher output under the former is larger than the corresponding probability under the latter. The converse is also true. Likewise, the individual is indifferent between two such prospects if and only if the corresponding probabilities for higher prospects coincide. This axiom may be treated as a non-satiation condition of individual behavior.

The next axiom also deals with standard prospects. To understand this, suppose the output R_u occurs with certainty. We can represent this situation as

$A_s^u = (1, R_u, R_l)$. Since an individual is ultimately interested in output from a prospect and R_u arises under $A_s^u = (1, R_u, R_l)$, it is evident that $R_u \sim A_s^u = (1, R_u, R_l)$. Following Gravelle and Rees (2004) we can say that $A_s^u = (1, R_u, R_l)$ is the equivalent standard prospect for R_u. Likewise, $A_s^l = (0, R_u, R_l)$ is the equivalent standard prospect for R_l. More generally, we have Axiom 3.

Axiom 3: (Equivalent standard prospect): Given any certain or risk-free level of output $R_f \in [R_l, R_u]$, there exists one and only one probability p_f for the output R_u such that $R_f \sim A_s^f = (p_f, R_u, R_l)$.

This axiom demands that given any certain level of output R_f in the interval $[R_l, R_u]$, it is possible to find a unique probability p_f for the outcome R_u such that the individual becomes indifferent between getting R_f with certainty and the standard prospect having p_f as the appropriate probability. Note the explicit dependence of p_f on R_f.

The statement of the next axiom relies on the notion of compound prospect, which is constructed using a finite sequence of standard prospects. Let $A_s^1 = (p_u^1, R_u, R_l)$, $A_s^2 = (p_u^2, R_u, R_l),..., A_s^v = (p_u^v, R_u, R_l)$ be a finite sequence of standard prospects. Let π_j^1 be the probability of getting the standard prospect j in which the probability of occurrence of higher output R_u is p_u^j, $1 \le j \le v$. We denote the vector of probabilities $(\pi_1^1, \pi_2^1,..., \pi_v^1)$ by $\underline{\pi}^1$. Then the compound prospect associated with this sequence of standard prospects and the probability vector $\underline{\pi}^1$ is $A_c^1 = (\underline{\pi}^1, A_s^1, A_s^2,..., A_s^v)$. If there is only one prospect which arises with certainty so that $\pi_j^1 = 1$, say for $j = 1$, then the definition of the compound prospect A_c^1 reduces to that of the single standard prospect $A_s^1 = (p_u^1, R_u, R_l)$.

We may illustrate the concept by an example. Suppose a person with an initial income of e_1 is participating in a two-stage gamble. At the first stage he is betting an amount $e_2 \le e_1$ under the *a priori* condition that if the gamble is won, then the gross payoff $e_2 + e_3$ will be put as bet at the second stage. He may lose the initial amount e_2 with probability $(1 - \pi_1)$. Equivalently, we can say that the chance of participation at the second stage is π_1. At the second stage the person may lose the bet with probability $(1 - \pi_2)$ and his net payoff will be $e_1 + e_3 - e_2 - e_3$. In the opposite situation the net payoff is e_4. We can then present this sequential gamble as a compound prospect as follows:

$$[1 - \pi_1, e_1 - e_2, (1 - \pi_2, e_1 - e_2, e_1 + e_4)] = (1 - \pi_1, e_1 - e_2, A^1), \quad (3.1)$$

where $A^1 = (1 - \pi_2, e_1 - e_2, e_1 + e_4)$ is the second-stage gamble.

In our general case, there are k different ways of arising R_u or R_l in the compound prospect A_c^1. The chance of occurrence of the standard prospect j is π_j^1 and the probability of outcome R_u in this standard prospect is p_u^j. Consequently, the probability of arising R_u in this specific way is $\pi_j^1 p_u^j$. Thus, the overall probability that R_u arises in the compound prospect is

$$\pi_1^1 p_u^1 + \pi_2^1 p_u^2 + \ldots\ldots + \pi_v^1 p_u^v = \sum_{i=1}^{v} \pi_i^1 p_u^i = \overline{p}_u. \tag{3.2}$$

Since $\overline{p}_u$ gives us the probability of achieving R_u in a particular framework, we can define a standard prospect $A_{cs}^1 = (\overline{p}_u, R_u, R_l)$ using this probability. A_{cs}^1 can be treated as rational equivalent of A_c^1. This enables us to state the following axiom.

Axiom 4: (Rational equivalence): For any compound prospect A_c^1 with outcomes only standard prospects and its rational equivalent A_{cs}^1, $A_c^1 \sim A_{cs}^1$.

This axiom represents the decision-maker's view in a rational way for evaluating the probabilities of ultimately obtaining the two outcomes R_l and R_u. Evaluation is independent of the number of standard prospects considered in the sequence.

To understand the next axiom, consider a sequence of prospects $A^j = (\underline{p}^j, \underline{R}^j)$, $j = 1, 2, \ldots, v$, where $\underline{p}^j = (p_1^j, p_2^j, \ldots, p_k^j)$ is the vector of probabilities and $\underline{R}^j = (R_1^j, R_2^j, \ldots, R_k^j)$ is the vector of state-contingent outputs corresponding to prospect j. For each R_i^j, we can find the equivalent standard prospect $R_i^j \sim A_s^{ij} = (p_u^{ij}, R_u, R_l)$, where $1 \leq j \leq v$ and $1 \leq i \leq k$. Since $R_i^j \sim A_s^{ij}$, we may replace R_i^j in the vector $\underline{R}^j$ in A^j by A_s^{ij} to get the compound prospect $A_c^j = (\underline{\pi}, (A_s^{1j}, A_s^{2j}, \ldots, A_s^{kj}))$. The following axiom can now be stated.

Axiom 5: (Context independence): $A^j \sim A_c^j$ for any prospect j.

This axiom indicates that the basic relation of indifference works between the state-contingent outputs and their equivalent standard prospects. Since state-contingent outputs and standard prospects are two different context-based concepts, the term "context independence" appears quite sensible here. Loosely speaking, state-contingent outputs and their equivalent standard prospects play the same role for the ordering of prospects.

Since the output R_f of a risk-free prospect A_f is received with certainty (probability 1), we can identify A_f uniquely by R_f. The following axiom reflects the view that in an environment characterized by certainty more is preferred to less. This is quite plausible.

Axiom 6: (Preference for higher output under certainty): For any two risk-free outputs R_f and R'_f, $R_f \succ R'_f$ if and only if $R_f > R'_f$.

We are now in a position to demonstrate that these six axioms lead to a representation of an individual's preferences on the set of prospects.

Theorem 3.1: If $\succeq$ satisfy Axioms 1–6, then there is an increasing utility function U that satisfies the expected utility hypothesis.

Proof: See Appendix.

We will assume throughout the chapter that U is increasing. Now, if a utility function U satisfying the expected utility hypothesis is subjected to a transformation of the type $\hat{U} = a + bU$, where $b > 0$ and a are constants, then $\hat{U}$ also possesses the expected utility property. This is because there is no directional change if we convert the inequality $\sum_{i=1}^{k} p_i U(R_i) \ge \sum_{i=1}^{k} p_i' U(R_i')$ into $ak + b\sum_{i=1}^{k} p_i U(R_i) \ge ak + b\sum_{i=1}^{k} p_i' U(R_i')$. The transformation that takes us from U to $\hat{U}$ here is called an affine transformation. However, any arbitrary increasing transformation of U may not preserve the expected utility property.

3.3 RISK AVERSION

Suppose a person's current level of wealth is 100 dollars, which he is investing in an even prospect in which there is a 50–50 chance of wining or losing 1 dollar. In an even prospect there is a 50–50 chance of losing or receiving the same amount. The expected payoff from the investment is $((100-1)\,0.5 + (100 + 1)\,0.5)$ dollars $= 100$ dollars. He may also invest in a second prospect in which there is a 50–50 chance of getting or losing 50 dollars. The expected payoff from this investment is here also 100 dollars. Note that the individual's level of wealth reduces or increases to 50 dollars or 150 dollars according as he loses or gains money from the second investment, whereas for the first investment the corresponding amounts are 99 dollars and 101 dollars respectively. Thus, deviations of outcomes from the expected value are higher for the latter investment than for the former. In other words, variability of output associated with the second investment is higher. If the variability is high then the outcome of an uncertain activity is regarded as risky. If the variability is quite low, then the outcome is almost certain.

In order to illustrate the above idea graphically, suppose an individual with initial level of wealth M_0 contemplates to invest in two even prospects: a 50–50 chance of losing or receiving an amount ε from the first and a 50–50 chance of losing or receiving an amount 2ε. Evidently, $2\varepsilon \le M_0$. In both cases the expected payoff is M_0. Then the expected utility from these two investments are $U^1(M_0) = 0.5U(M_0 - \varepsilon) + 0.5U(M_0 + \varepsilon)$ and $U^2(M_0) = 0.5U(M_0 - 2\varepsilon) + 0.5U(M_0 + 2\varepsilon)$ respectively, where U is the individual's von Neumann–Morgenstern utility function.

If the individual is risk averse, he dislikes variability of output around expected wealth. The individual will prefer expected wealth to investment in the prospects and since preferences are represented by U, it must be the case that $U(M_0) > U^1(M_0) > U^2(M_0)$. This is shown graphically in panel (a) of Figure 3.1. We note from the figure that expected utility decreases as variability increases.

From the figure it turns out that the line joining any two points on the curve lies below the curve. This is known as strict concavity. Formally, a utility function $U : [0, \infty) \to \Re$ is concave if for all $\xi \in [0, 1]$ and for all $R, R' \in [0, \infty)$, $U(\xi R + (1 - \xi) R') \ge \xi U(R) + (1 - \xi) U(R')$. For a strictly concave function, the defining inequality is $U(\xi R + (1 - \xi)R') > \xi U(R) + (1 - \xi) U(R')$ for all $\xi \in (0, 1)$ and for all $R, R' \in [0, \infty)$ with $R \ne R'$.

Figure 3.1   Attitudes towards Risk

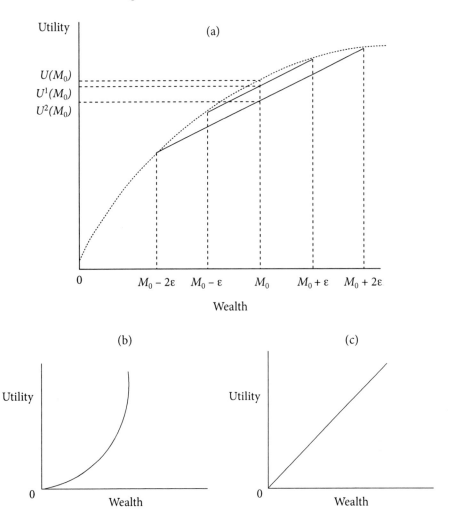

If an individual prefers a random distribution of wealth to its expected value, then he is a risk-lover and the utility function for such a person is strictly convex. For a strictly convex function, the line joining any two points on the curve lies above the curve (See panel (b) of Figure 3.1). A function $U : [0, \infty) \to \Re$ is called convex (strictly convex) if $-U$ is concave (strictly concave). For a strictly convex utility function the slope becomes steeper as the level of wealth increases, whereas for a strictly concave utility function the slope becomes flatter with increase in the level of wealth. A person may not care about the extent of risk involved in a prospect, the only consideration may be the expected payoff from the investment in a prospect. This intermediate situation between risk aversion and risk loving is known as risk neutrality. In this case the utility function is linear, that is, for all $R \in [0, \infty)$, $U(R) = a + bR$, where $b > 0$ and a are constants. The assumption $b > 0$ is necessary to ensure increasingness of U. Panel (c) of Figure 3.1 represents a function of this type.

For a twice-differentiable utility function U, concavity (strict concavity) is same as the condition that $U'' \leq (<)0$ where U'' is the second derivative U. Thus, for a concave (strictly concave) utility function U, the marginal utility function U' is non-increasing (decreasing). Likewise, convexity (strict convexity) of U means that $U'' \geq (>)0$. We assume throughout the chapter that U is twice differentiable. Existence of U' implies that U is continuous.

It often becomes useful to have a measure of risk aversion. A risk aversion indicator enables us to judge to what extent an individual is risk averse. It also becomes helpful to make a comparison between two individuals in terms of their attitudes toward risk. One may argue that we may regard U'' as a risk aversion measure. But if $\hat{U} = a + bU$, where $b > 0$ and a are constants, then $\hat{U}'' = bU''$, which means that this measure of risk aversion does not remain invariant under affine transformations. But a von Neumann–Morgenstern utility function and its affine transformations essentially convey us the same information in terms of ranking of uncertain prospects. That is, U'' does not fulfill the information invariance requirement. One measure of risk aversion that satisfies the information invariance assumption is the Arrow–Pratt measure of absolute risk aversion $AP_A(M)$, which for a person with utility function U and level of wealth M, is defined as

$$AP_A(M) = -\frac{U''(M)}{U'(M)}. \qquad (3.3)$$

The indicator $AP_A(M)$ takes on a positive, zero or negative value accordingly if the individual is risk averse, risk neutral or risk lover. A higher value of AP_A shows that the individual's aversion toward risk is higher. However, often an individual's risk tolerance may increase with his or her level of wealth. Since AP_A indicates risk aversion, the reciprocal $1/AP_A(M)$ can be taken as an absolute risk tolerance measure.

To provide further rationale for this measure, let us consider an even prospect denoted by the random variable $\tilde{\varepsilon}$ so that $\Xi(\tilde{\varepsilon}) = 0$, where $\Xi(\tilde{\varepsilon})$ stands for the expected value of $\tilde{\varepsilon}$. Let $h(\tilde{\varepsilon})$ be the amount of premium that an individual with utility function U and current level of wealth M would be willing to pay to avoid investment in the even prospect. Formally, $\Xi(U(M + \tilde{\varepsilon})) = U(M - h(\tilde{\varepsilon}))$. The left-hand side is the expected utility from investment in the prospect, and the right-hand side gives the utility when the level of wealth reduces to $(M - h(\tilde{\varepsilon}))$ after payment of the premium $h(\tilde{\varepsilon})$. Thus, $h(\tilde{\varepsilon})$ is the maximum amount the individual would like to forego to avoid investment in the even prospect.

Expanding each side of $\Xi(U(M + \tilde{\varepsilon})) = U(M - h(\tilde{\varepsilon}))$ by Taylor's series around M, for small $\tilde{\varepsilon}$ we get

$$\Xi\left(U(M)+\tilde{\varepsilon}U'(M)+\frac{(\tilde{\varepsilon})^2}{2}U''(M)+higher\ order\ terms\right)$$

$$=U(M)-h(\tilde{\varepsilon})+higher\ order\ terms. \tag{3.4}$$

Taking expectation on the left-hand side, using the fact that $\Xi(\tilde{\varepsilon})=0$ and ignoring higher order terms we have

$$U(M)+\frac{\Xi(\tilde{\varepsilon})^2}{2}U''(M)=U(M)-h(\tilde{\varepsilon})U'(M). \tag{3.5}$$

Using the constant q^* to denote $\Xi(\tilde{\varepsilon})^2/2$, from (3.5) it follows that $h(\tilde{\varepsilon})=q^*AP_A(M)$. That is, the amount of premium to be paid to avoid investment in an uncertain prospect is directly proportional to the Arrow–Pratt absolute risk aversion measure. The premium amount increases, as the person becomes more risk averse, which is quite sensible. We summarize the above observations in the following proposition.

Proposition 3.1: The maximum amount of wealth that a person would be willing to pay in order to avoid investment in an even uncertain prospect is directly proportional to the Arrow–Pratt absolute measure of risk aversion.

It often becomes necessary to investigate whether one person is more risk averse than another for all levels of wealth. Evidently, one plausible way to formalize this notion is to say that the Arrow–Pratt absolute risk aversion measure for one person is higher than that of the other everywhere. Formally, person 1 with utility function $U_1(M)$ is more risk averse than person 2 with utility function $U_2(M)$ if and only if $-(U_1''(M))/(U_1'(M))>-(U_2''(M))/(U_2'(M))$ for all levels of wealth M. This definition of "more risk averse," which is quite reasonable intuitively, becomes equivalent to two other plausible conditions. This is demonstrated formally in the following theorem.

Theorem 3.2 (Pratt 1960): Let $U_1(M)$ and $U_2(M)$ be twice differentiable, increasing and strictly concave utility functions. Then the following conditions are equivalent.

(i) $-\dfrac{U_1''(M)}{U_1'(M)}>-\dfrac{U_2''(M)}{U_2'(M)}$ for all M.

(ii) $U_1(M)=g(U_2(M))$ for some increasing and strictly concave function g.

(iii) $h_1(\tilde{\varepsilon})>h_2(\tilde{\varepsilon})$, where $h_1(\tilde{\varepsilon})(h_2(\tilde{\varepsilon}))$ is the maximum amount that the person with utility function $U_1(M)$ $(U_2(M))$ would be willing to pay to avoid investment in the even prospect $\tilde{\varepsilon}$.

Proof: See Appendix.

What this theorem says is the following. Of two individuals 1 and 2, individual 1 would like to pay more premium to avoid investment in an even prospect than individual 2 if and only if the former person has a higher level of absolute Arrow–Pratt measure of risk aversion than that of the latter person. This is also equivalent to the condition that the utility function of person 1 is an increasing and strictly concave transformation of that of person 2. That is, the utility function of person 1 is obtained by concavifying the utility function of person 2.

Example 3.1: Consider an individual with the exponential utility function

$$U_\alpha(M) = -\bar{q}\,exp(-\alpha\,M), \qquad (3.6)$$

where $\bar{q}, \alpha > 0$ are constants and "exp" is the exponential transformation. Then $U'_\alpha(M) = \bar{q}\alpha\left(exp(-\alpha\,M)\right) > 0$ and $U''_\alpha(M) = -\bar{q}\alpha^2\left(exp(-\alpha\,M)\right) < 0$. Consequently, for the exponential utility function $U_\alpha(M)$, $AP_A(M) = \alpha > 0$. Thus, the absolute risk aversion is constant. Conversely, suppose that $AP_A(M) = \dfrac{-U''(M)}{U'(M)} = \alpha$, where $\alpha > 0$ is a constant and we assume that $U'(M) > 0$ and $U''(M) < 0$. Then integrating both sides, we get $ln\left(U'(M)\right) = -\alpha M + \tilde{q}$, where $\tilde{q}$ is constant of integration and "ln" represents natural logarithm. This gives $U'(M) = exp(-\alpha\,M + \tilde{q})$, which we can rewrite as $U'(M) = \hat{q}\,exp(-\alpha\,M)$, with $\hat{q} = exp(\tilde{q})$. Integrating the latter form of U' and ignoring the constant of integration, we derive that $U(M) = -\bar{q}\,exp(-\alpha\,M)$, where $\bar{q} = \hat{q}/\alpha > 0.$. Thus, absolute risk aversion is a constant if and only if the underlying utility function is of the exponential type.

It is often possible to explain the behavior of demand for prospects using properties of risk aversion measures. To understand this, following Demange and Laroque (2006), we consider the following problem of the portfolio choice of an individual with wealth holdings M_0. By a portfolio, we mean here a list of financial securities or prospects held by the individual. We assume, for simplicity, that there are two prospects, one risk-free and one risky. Thus, the individual invests his wealth M_0 in two prospects, one risk-free and one risky. There are two periods, $t = 0$, when the decisions are taken, and $t = 1$, when uncertainty is completely resolved. There is no source of income in period 1.

Each unit of the risk-free prospect yields one unit of currency. Its price is $1/(1 + \lambda)$, where λ is the risk-free interest rate. This is because at the interest rate λ, 1 dollar at $t = 0$ will grow into $(1 + \lambda)$ dollars at $t = 1$. That is, $(1 + \lambda)$ dollars is the future equivalent of 1 dollar. In other words, $(1 + \lambda)$ dollars at $t = 1$ is equivalent to 1 dollar. Hence 1 dollar at $t = 1$ is equivalent to $1/(1 + \lambda)$ dollars at $t = 0$. The risky prospect can be traded at price χ at $t = 0$. There corresponds a stochastic payoff a_1 to each unit of the risky prospect. Realization of the payoff occurs at $t = 1$. If the individual purchases z_1 units of the risky prospect, then the corresponding expenditure is χz_1 and the payoff is $a_1 z_1$. If the individual possesses z_f units of the risk-free prospect, then the corresponding expenditure and payoff are respectively $z_f/(1 + \lambda)$ and z_f. Therefore, the individual maximizes the expected value of the utility function

$U(z_f + a_1 z_1)$, subject to the budget constraint $(z_f/(1 + \lambda)) + \chi z_1 = M_0$, where U is increasing and strictly concave.

Eliminating z_f from the objective function using the budget constraint, the problem then reduces to maximization of expected value of $U(M_0(1 + \lambda) + z_1 (a_1 - \chi(1 + \lambda)))$ with respect to z_1. The first order condition for this maximization problem is

$$\Xi\left(U'(\hat{c})\left(a_1 - \chi(1+\lambda)\right)\right) = 0, \tag{3.7}$$

where $\hat{c} = M_0(1+\lambda) + z_1\left(a_1 - \chi(1+\lambda)\right)$ and Ξ stands for expectation. This condition characterizes an optimal solution. Since $U' > 0$, the optimal solution will not exist if $(a_1 - \chi(1 + \lambda)) > 0$ always holds. Therefore, for the optimal solution to exist, the probability that $(a_1 - \chi(1 + \lambda)) > 0$ must lie in the interval $(0, 1)$. If $(a_1 - \chi(1 + \lambda))$ is always positive the individual will be willing to buy an infinite number of units of the risky prospect by borrowing.

We can now state the following theorem, which demonstrates that for the amount invested in the risky prospect to increase as initial wealth increases, a sufficient condition is that the absolute measure of risk aversion should decrease.

Theorem 3.3: Suppose an individual's optimal portfolio consists of positive quantities of two prospects, one risky and one risk-free, and the amount invested in the risky prospect is less than the invested wealth M_0. Then the amount invested in the risky prospect increases with M_0 if the absolute risk aversion measure is decreasing.

Proof: See Appendix.

The theorem indicates that as a person becomes less risk averse with increase in the level of wealth, his demand for risky asset increases. This means that the risky prospect is a normal good (Arrow 1970). A necessary condition for decreasing absolute risk aversion is that the marginal utility function U' is a strictly convex function $(U''' > 0)$, where U''' is the third derivative of U. Increasing absolute risk aversion implies that the risky prospect is an inferior good and constant absolute risk aversion implies that the individual's demand for the risky prospect is independent of his initial wealth.

The Arrow–Pratt absolute measure of risk aversion indicates an individual's aversion to gambles of absolute size. Alternatively, we can consider aversion to gambles of a size which is a proportion of individual's wealth. This is because outputs are generally expressed as percentages of investment. An appropriate measure that indicates attitudes toward risk in this case is the Arrow-Pratt relative risk aversion measure defined as

$$AP_R(M) = -\frac{MU''(M)}{U'(M)}. \tag{3.8}$$

The measure AP_R takes on positive, zero or negative values depending on whether an individual is risk averse, risk neutral or a risk-lover. Clearly, this measure also remains invariant under affine transformations of U. The individual becomes more risk averse, as the value of AP_R increases with W. The inverse indicator $1/AP_R$ is a measure of relative risk tolerance.

The following theorem, which parallels Theorem 3.3, shows how the demand for risky prospect changes under increasingness of AP_R.

Theorem 3.4: Suppose an individual's optimal portfolio consists of positive quantities of two prospects, one risky and one risk-free, and the amount invested in the risky prospect is less than the invested wealth M_0. If the relative risk aversion measure is increasing, then the share of wealth invested in the risky prospect decreases with M_0, that is, the wealth elasticity of demand for risky prospect is less than one.

Proof: See Appendix.

The theorem indicates that under increasingness of the relative risk aversion measure, the proportion of the individual's original wealth declines as the level of wealth increases. However, Theorems 3.3 and 3.4 do not generalize to the case of several risky prospects.

Suppose that an individual holds the same portfolio of risky prospects and only changes the mixture between the portfolio and the risk-free prospect for differing levels of initial wealth. Then the individual's optimal portfolios for different levels of initial wealth are linear combinations of the risk-free prospect and a risky prospect mutual fund (Cass and Stiglitz 1970). This phenomenon is known as two fund monetary separation. Cass and Stiglitz (1970) identified the increasing and risk-averse von Neumann–Morgenstern utility functions for two fund monetary separation. These utility functions have the marginals (i) $U'_\alpha(M) = \bar{k}\alpha\,exp(-\alpha M) > 0$ (see Example 3.1) and (ii) $U'(M) = (a + bM)^c$, where either $b > 0$, $c < 0$ and $M \geq max[0 -(a/b)]$, or, $a > 0$, $b < 0$, $c > 0$ and $0 \leq M \leq -(a/b)$. These conditions are necessary to ensure that the utility function, corresponding to the marginal in (ii), is increasing and strictly concave.

3.4 CERTAINTY EQUIVALENT

We have noted in Section 3.3 that two standard questions that generally arise in the context of revelation of a decision-maker's attitude toward risks are: (i) would he prefer to receive the expected output on a prospect with certainty rather than facing the prospect? (ii) What sum would the individual be willing to pay to avoid the risk involved in the prospect? We can also look at the issue in terms of the certainty equivalent of a prospect.

The certainty equivalent of a prospect is that level of output, which if received from each state of the prospect, will generate the same level of expected utility as that produced by the actual prospect. Formally, for any individual with a utility function U and given any prospect $A = (\underline{p}, \underline{R})$, the following implicit relation defines the certainty equivalent R_e associated with $A = (\underline{p}, \underline{R})$:

$$\sum_{i=1}^{k} p_i U(R_e) = \sum_{i=1}^{k} p_i U(R_i). \tag{3.9}$$

The certainty equivalent aggregates the state-contingent outputs in a particular way. We may illustrate the concept graphically. The individual's expected utility from a prospect with two states is $\sum_{i=1}^{2} p_i U(R_i)$. We assume that the individual is risk averse so that U is strictly concave. In Figure 3.2, state 1 and 2 outputs are plotted along the horizontal and vertical axes respectively. A contour in the (R_1, R_2)-space is the set of all (R_1, R_2) values that generate the same level of expected utility $\sum_{i=1}^{2} p_i U(R_i) = U^0$, say. Total differentiation gives $p_1 U'(R_1) + p_2 U'(R_2) \, (dR_2/dR_1) = 0$, from which we get $(dR_2/dR_1) = -(p_1 U'(R_1)/p_2 U'(R_2))$. This is the slope of the indifference curve, which in view of the facts that probabilities are positive and $U' > 0$, is negative. Since U is strictly concave, the indifference curve is strictly convex to the origin.

Figure 3.2 Certainty Equivalent

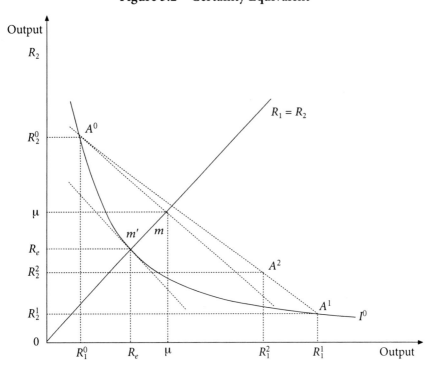

In the figure, we interpret the 45^0 line, as the line of certainty since along this line the individual will receive the same output irrespective of the state. The certainty equivalent is the certain output, which the individual would treat as equivalent, in terms of expected utility, to the prospect A^0, that is, receiving outputs R_1^0 and R_2^0 with probabilities p_1 and p_2 respectively. Consequently, the certainty equivalent corresponding to the prospect A^0 will be the point of intersection of the 45^0 line and the indifference curve I^0 that passes through A^0. The person is indifferent between R_e in each state and the prospect A^0. In Figure 3.2, R_e is given by the length of the side $0R_e$ of the triangle $0m'R_e$.

In the figure, combinations of R_1 and R_2 that have the same expected value $\bar{\mu}$, say, satisfy the equation $p_1R_1 + p_2R_2 = \bar{\mu}$. This is the equation of the iso-expected output line. Differentiating this expression totally, we get $(dR_2/dR_1) = -(p_1/p_2)$. Given positivity of probabilities, an iso-expected output line is negatively sloped. The expected output on the prospect A^0 is the point of intersection m of the 45^0 line and the iso-expected output line with slope $-(p_1/p_2)$ that passes through A^0. At m the output corresponding to each state is the same.

Often state-contingent outputs are subject to fluctuations. For instance, they may depend on the performance of the market. If the utility function is a continuous function of outputs, then minor changes in outputs will generate minor changes in the functional value of utility. Consequently, the certainty equivalent should also be a continuous function. That is, for minor changes in one, or more outputs, the certainty equivalent should not change abruptly. Thus, for small observational errors in outputs a continuous certainty equivalent will not show a big jump. This is a sensible property. We show this formally in the following theorem (see Chakravarty and Chakrabarti 2010).

Theorem 3.5: Given the probability vector $\underline{p}$, continuity and increasingness of the utility function, the certainty equivalent R_e is an increasing and continuous function of state-contingent outputs.

Proof: See Appendix.

Thus, given other things, if a state-contingent output increases the certainty equivalent also increases.

From Figure 3.2, it appears that for a risk-averse person, the deviation between the expected output and the certainty equivalent may be regarded as an indicator of cost of risk in the sense that in the absence of uncertainty this cost is zero and it becomes positive only when the situation is characterized by uncertainty. The deviation may be measured in proportional or difference form. The risky prospect is costly because it reduces expected utility compared to that obtained under certainty. In order to measure the cost of risk in difference form, we consider the vector of outputs $\underline{R} = (R_1, R_2, ..., R_k)$. Since the level of cost depends on the unit of the outputs, we refer to it as absolute cost. Formally, the measure of absolute cost of risk is defined as

$$C_A\left(\underline{p}, \underline{R}\right) = \sum_{i=1}^{k} p_i R_i - R_e = \Xi\left(\underline{p}, \underline{R}\right) - R_e, \tag{3.10}$$

where $\Xi\left(\underline{p},\underline{R}\right) = \sum_{i=1}^{k} p_i R_i = \mu$ is the expected output. In terms of Figure 3.2, the cost measure $C_A\left(\underline{p},\underline{R}\right)$ becomes the distance $R_e\mu = 0\mu - 0R_e$. Given the expected output, an increase in certainty equivalent is equivalent to a reduction in the cost of risk and vice versa.

If $\Xi\left(\underline{p},\underline{R}\right) > R_e$, then the decision-maker's valuation of the prospect is less than its expected value. The individual in such a case is risk averse. The difference $\Xi\left(\underline{p},\underline{R}\right) - R_e$ can be treated as the maximum amount that the individual would be willing to pay to avoid risk in the prospect. That is, this measure of risk premium or the cost of risk shows how much the individual would be willing to give up instead of facing the risky prospect. On the other hand, if $\Xi\left(\underline{p},\underline{R}\right) < R_e$, the valuation of the prospect is more than its expected output and the individual is risk attracted. In this case the risk premium becomes negative because the individual would be willing to pay more for the risky prospect than its expected value. Risk neutrality arises if the valuation of the prospect coincides with its expected value, that is, if $\Xi\left(\underline{p},\underline{R}\right) = R_e$.

In the following theorem, we demonstrate non-negativity of the cost measure under certain assumptions.

Theorem 3.6: Given that the utility function U is continuous, increasing and strictly concave, the absolute cost of risk is positive. This cost is of zero value if the prospect is a degenerate one in the sense that outputs in all the states are the same, that is, there is no uncertainty.

Proof: See Appendix.

One particular type of change that may take place in all state-contingent outputs on an uncertain prospect is that they increase or decrease by the same absolute amount. Formally, the state-contingent output vector $\underline{R} = \left(R_1, R_2, ..., R_k\right)$ changes to $(R_1 + c, R_2 + c, ..., R_k + c)$, where c is a constant and $(p_1, p_2, ..., p_k)$ remains unaltered. Then the mean output on the prospect changes by c. A cost indicator C is called translation invariant if it remains invariant under a change of this type, that is, $C\left(\underline{p},\underline{R}\right) = C\left(\underline{p}, R_1 + c, R_2 + c, ..., R_k + c\right)$ for all permissible values of c. A natural question that arises now is the following: How is an individual's attitude toward risk related to the condition that the cost of the risk satisfies the translation invariance property? The following theorem, which is based on Chakravarty and Chakrabarti (2010), provides an answer to this question.

Theorem 3.7: Let U be a continuous, increasing and strictly concave utility function. Then the following conditions are equivalent:

(i) The cost of risk C_A is translation invariant.

(ii) The Arrow–Pratt absolute risk aversion measure AP_A is a constant.

Proof: See Appendix.

This theorem thus provides a characterization of the utility function with a constant absolute risk aversion in the sense that it is the only utility function for which the absolute cost of risk is translation invariant. This characterization exercise specifies necessary and sufficient condition, that is, translation invariance of cost of risk, for identifying the utility function uniquely.

While C_A expresses cost of risk in absolute terms, we can also measure the cost in relative terms, more precisely, as a proportion of expected output. Hence we can consider the following as an alternative measure of the cost of risk:

$$C_R\left(\underline{p},\underline{R}\right) = 1 - \frac{R_e}{\Xi\left(\underline{p},\underline{R}\right)}. \tag{3.11}$$

Since C_R is stated in a ratio form, we call it a relative measure. It gives us the premium, as a proportion of the expected output on the prospect, that the person is ready to pay to avoid risk in the prospect. If the utility function is strictly concave, C_R is bounded between zero and one, where the lower bound is attained whenever state-contingent outputs are the same. In terms of Figure 3.2, C_R is given by $R_e\mu/0\mu$.

For illustrative purpose, assume that the outputs are measured in currency units. Now, suppose that the currency unit changes from dollar to cents. Then since the outputs are essentially unchanged and their probabilities also remain the same, one might argue that the cost of risk should not change. A cost measure satisfying this condition is called a scale invariant measure. Formally, a cost indicator C is scale invariant if $C\left(\underline{p},\underline{R}\right) = C\left(\underline{p},c\underline{R}\right)$, where $c > 0$ is a constant. In the following theorem, we show that C_R satisfies this condition if AP_R is constant. The converse is also true.

Theorem 3.8: Assume that all state-contingent outputs are positive. Let U be a continuous, increasing and strictly concave utility function. Then the following conditions are equivalent

(i) The cost of risk C_R is scale invariant.

(ii) The Arrow–Pratt relative risk aversion measure AP_R is a constant.

Proof: See Appendix.

Thus, the theorem characterizes the utility function with constant relative risk aversion using the scale invariance property of the cost of risk (see also Chakravarty and Chakrabarti 2010). That is, relative risk aversion is a constant if and only if the relative cost of the risk involving the underlying utility function is scale invariant. "Assuming constant relative risk aversion is probably not too bad an assumption, at least for small changes in wealth" (Varian 1992, 189).

Figure 3.2 can be used to demonstrate a second aspect of risk aversion: preference for diversification. In the figure the prospects A^0 and A^1, with state-contingent output vectors $\left(R_1^0, R_2^0\right)$ and $\left(R_1^1, R_2^1\right)$ respectively, are on the same indifference curve I^0. Now, a prospect A^2 formed by combining a fraction $\xi \in (0, 1)$

of A^0 and a fraction $(1 - \xi) \in (0, 1)$ of A^1 will give the state-contingent output vector $\left(\xi R_1^0 + (1-\xi) R_1^1 = R_1^2, \xi R_2^0 + (1-\xi) R_2^1 = R_2^2 \right)$. The new prospect A^2 is a portfolio of the prospects A^0 and A^1. From the figure, it follows that A^2 lies on a higher indifference curve than I^0, which passes through A^0 and A^1. That is, A^2 has a higher expected utility than that of A^0 or A^1. Thus, a diversified portfolio consisting of a combination of any two initial prospects with the same expected utility would generate a higher expected utility than the portfolio consisting of either of the two prospects (see Gravelle and Rees 2004).

3.5 MEAN-VARIANCE ANALYSIS: A SPECIAL CASE OF THE EXPECTED UTILITY APPROACH

The expected utility from a prospect depends explicitly on the state-contingent probabilities and corresponding outputs. However, in some situations it may be possible to summarize the expected utility from a prospect in terms of some summary statistics of the distribution of the outputs. A well-known example is the quadratic utility function given by $U_a(M) = aM^2 + M$, where M denotes wealth and a is a constant. The inequality $a > 0$ implies a risk-loving attitude, $a = 0$ displays risk neutrality and $a < 0$ represents risk aversion. For $a < 0$, $U_a(M)$ is decreasing in M if $M > -0.5a.^{-1}$ This is an undesirable characteristic of the quadratic utility function since this goes against non-satiation principle. Therefore, it becomes necessary to assume that the wealth distribution is concentrated in the interval $[0, -0.5a^{-1}]$. The absolute risk aversion measure for the quadratic utility function has the form $-2a/(1 + 2aM)$ and its derivative is $(4a^2/(1 + 2aM)^2) > 0$. This implies that the risky prospect is an inferior good (see Section 3.3). This is also an undesirable feature of the quadratic utility function.

Now, $\Xi(U_a(M)) = \Xi(M) + a\Xi(M^2) = \Xi(M) + a(\Xi(M))^2 + a\sigma_M^2$, where σ_M^2 is the variance of the wealth distribution. Thus, the expected utility depends only on the mean and variance of the wealth distribution. That is why this expected utility is also referred to as the mean-variance utility function. Unfortunately, the normal distribution is the only distribution, which is completely characterized by its first two moments, the mean and the variance. Thus, a useful situation where the mean-variance analysis can be justified is the case when the prospect follows a normal distribution. Consequently, the problem of choice among normally distributed prospects is equivalent to the problem of comparison among corresponding means and variances. However, the support of this distribution is the entire real line, which makes it unsuitable for many economic applications.

We now provide an application of the mean-variance analysis to the portfolio choice problem with two prospects; one of them is risk-free and the other is risky. The portfolio choice problem with two prospects is a special case of the more general approach studied in Chapter 14. The objective is to choose the portfolio weights optimally, that is, to find how much wealth a person should invest in each prospect. An optimal set of weights is the one that ensures an acceptable expected output with minimal risks. We assume here that the risk of the portfolio is measured by the variance. Since the standard deviation, the positive square root of the variance, is directly related to the variance, it can as well be taken as an indicator of risk. Thus, the investors control risks through an allocation between a risky asset and a risk-free asset. Assume also that all assets are tradable and there is zero transaction cost.

The proportions of total wealth M, invested in the risk-free and risky prospects in the portfolio, are $(1 - x)$ and x respectively. The risk-free asset generates a fixed output R_f. The expected gross output on risky prospect $A = \left(\underline{p}, \underline{R}\right)$ is $\Xi\left(\underline{p}, \underline{R}\right) = \sum_{i=1}^{k} p_i R_i$ and the variance of A is $\sigma^2\left(\underline{p}, \underline{R}\right) = \sum_{i=1}^{k} p_i \left(R_i - \Xi\left(\underline{p}, \underline{R}\right)\right)^2$. The expected output on the portfolio is then given by $\mu_x = (1 - x)R_f + x\Xi\left(\underline{p}, \underline{R}\right)$. The variance of the portfolio is $\sigma_x^2 = x^2 \sigma^2\left(\underline{p}, \underline{R}\right)$, which gives $x = \sigma_x / \sigma\left(\underline{p}, \underline{R}\right)$, where σ is the standard deviation.

Substituting $x = \sigma_x / \sigma\left(\underline{p}, \underline{R}\right)$ in the equation for μ_x and simplifying the resulting expression we get,

$$\mu_x = (1 - x)R_f + \left[\frac{\Xi\left(\underline{p}, \underline{R}\right) - R_f}{\sigma\left(\underline{p}, \underline{R}\right)}\right]\sigma_x. \tag{3.12}$$

It is natural to assume that $\Xi\left(\underline{p}, \underline{R}\right) - R_f > 0$, otherwise a risk-averse individual would never hold a risky asset. The numerator of the third bracketed term on the right-hand side of equation (3.12) is the expected excess output, which is also known as the market premium. The denominator is a measure of risk. The ratio between the two terms is a measure of reward to risk. In other words, it is a tool for comparing output with risk. It indicates how well the output of an asset compensates the investor for the risk taken. The higher the ratio, the better the individual's output is relative to risk from the portfolio. Equation (3.12) thus says that expected output on a portfolio of risky and risk-free prospects is the sum of the return on the risk-free prospect and the reward-to-risk ratio multiplied by the risk of the portfolio.

For every combination of (μ_x, σ_x) there is exactly one portfolio. Choosing a portfolio is, therefore, equivalent to choosing a pair (μ_x, σ_x) of the desired mean and standard deviation of portfolio output, where the expected output of a portfolio exceeds the risk-free output. For $x = 1$, the investor puts all of his wealth in the risky asset and for $x = 0$ entire wealth is invested in the sure prospect. Under the assumption that $\Xi\left(\underline{p}, \underline{R}\right) - R_f > 0$, a plot of μ_x against σ_x gives us an upward sloping

straight line whose slope is given by $\left[\dfrac{\Xi\left(p,\underline{R}\right)-R_f}{\sigma\left(p,\underline{R}\right)}\right]$. As we move up along the line,
it turns out that a larger expected output has to be accompanied by an increased standard deviation. This line can be treated as a budget line, indicating the trade off between risk and output. We can also refer to this as a risk–reward line.

A natural question here is: which risk-output combination should be chosen along the risk–reward line? We need an expected utility function that depends on (μ_x, σ_x) in order to describe the portfolio choice. Assume that an investor's utility from the risky prospect is of quadratic type, considered in the section. Thus, the expected utility from the portfolio is given by $\Xi(U_x)=\mu_x+a(\mu_x)^2+a\sigma_x^2$. If an individual is risk averse, a higher expected output makes him better off, whereas a higher standard deviation makes him worse off. This means that standard deviation, which characterizes risk, is a bad. Consequently, the indifference curve will have a positive slope.

An indifference curve in the (μ_x, σ_x) space is the set of all (μ_x, σ_x) values that generate the same level of expected utility $\Xi(U_x)=\mu_x+a(\mu_x)^2+a\sigma_x^2=U^0$ say. Differentiating totally we get $d\mu_x + 2a\mu_x\,d\mu_x + 2a\sigma_x d\sigma_x = 0$, from which we get $(d\mu_x/d\sigma_x) = -(2a\sigma_x/(1 + 2a\mu_x))$. This is the slope of the indifference curve. Since $a < 0, 2a\sigma_x < 0$, Therefore, for the slope of the indifference curve to be positive, we need the condition that $(1 + 2a\mu_x) > 0$, which is same as the requirement that $\mu_x < -1/2a$. The converse is also true. That is, $\mu_x < -1/2a$ is necessary and sufficient for the indifference curve to be positively sloped.

In terms of indifference curve, the investor will choose that point where there is a tangency between the highest attainable upward sloping indifference curve and the risk–reward line. The utility maximizing investor adjusts his investment in the risky asset relative to that in the risk-free asset so as to reach the highest possible indifference curve. The point of tangency between the risk–reward line and the investor's indifference curve shows this. Since the risk–reward line has a constant

slope of $\left[\dfrac{\Xi\left(p,\underline{R}\right)-R_f}{\sigma\left(p,\underline{R}\right)}\right]$, it is also the common slope at the point of tangency of
the indifference curve and the risk–reward line. We call it "price of risk," since it equals the investor's marginal rate of substitution between risk and output and hence measures how risk and output are traded off in making portfolio choices. The optimal portfolio choice problem between a risk-free and a risky prospect can now be characterized by claiming that the marginal rate of substitution between

risk and output must be equal to the price of risk $\left[\dfrac{\Xi\left(p,\underline{R}\right)-R_f}{\sigma\left(p,\underline{R}\right)}\right]$.

In order to ensure that the individual's portfolio choice is unique, we require that the indifference curve be strictly convex, that is, $\left(d^2\mu_x/d\sigma_x^2\right) > 0$. Now, $\left(d^2\mu_x/d\sigma_x^2\right) = -\left(2a + 8a^2\mu_x + 8a^3\mu_x^2 + 8a^3\sigma_x^2\right)/\left(1 + 2a\mu_x\right)^3$. Given that $\left(1 + 2a\mu_x\right)^3 > 0$, the condition $\left(d^2\mu_x/d\sigma_x^2\right) > 0$ holds if and only if $-\left(2a + 8a^2\mu_x + 8a^3\mu_x^2 + 8a^3\sigma_x^2\right) > 0$. This implies and is implied by the inequality, $\left(\mu_x + a\mu_x^2 + a\sigma_x^2\right) < -1/4a$. This inequality along with $\mu_x < -1/2a$ should hold for the mean-variance expected utility function to be upward sloping and strictly convex (see Figure 3.3).

Figure 3.3   Risk and Output

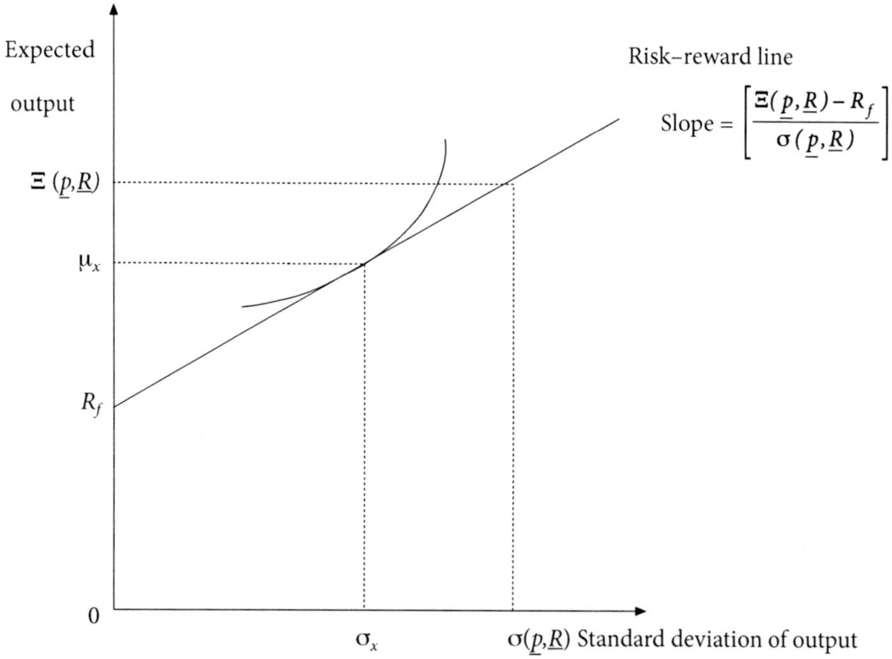

Now, if many individuals are choosing between these two prospects, for each of them the marginal rate of substitution must be equal to the price of the risk. In equilibrium, the marginal rate of substitution is the same across individuals and this is same as the price of the risk.

3.6 PROSPECT THEORY: A BRIEF ANALYSIS

Prospect theory, which was developed by Kahneman and Tversky (1979), has brought psychology into the analysis of decision-making under uncertainty. The central idea is that value is assigned to gains and losses rather than to final positions in asset holding. Also the decision weights are used in place of probabilities. Thus, while in expected utility theory, utility depends on final wealth position, in prospect theory value is defined in terms of gains and losses, relative to some reference point or status quo, which may vary depending on the situation. This idea goes back to Markowitz (1952), who argued that utility should be defined by gains and losses rather than by final asset holdings (see also Mosteller and Nogee 1931 and Davidson et al. 1937). Furthermore, utility is linear in probabilities, but value need not satisfy this condition. The idea of replacing probabilities by more general weights was suggested by Edwards (1962) (see also Tversky 1967 and Anderson and Shanteau 1970).

The value function increases over the entire domain. It is strictly concave for gains and strictly convex for losses, which means that the decision-maker is risk averse in the domain of gains and risk loving in the domain of losses. The curve is steeper for losses than for gains. The magnitude of pain from losses is much higher than the magnitude of pleasure one derives from gains. Decision weights are such that, except for small probabilities, these weights are generally not higher than corresponding probabilities. Small probabilities are over-weighted. Such a situation arises when an individual is participating in a lottery. Generally, illiterate and poor people play the lottery and assign importance to it. On the other hand, large probabilities are under-weighted.

Formally, let us consider a prospect with potential outputs $R_1, R_2, ..., R_k$ and $p_1, p_2, ..., p_k$, are respective probabilities. Then the prospect theory says that the value of the prospect is $V = \sum_{i=1}^{k} w(p_i) v(R_i)$, where $w : [0,1] \rightarrow [0,1]$ is a probability weighting function. It is increasing in its argument and satisfies the normalization conditions $w(0) = 0$ and $w(1) = 1$. Also $w(q) > q$ for small q and $w(q) < q$ for q close to 1. A weighting function w is concave first and then convex. On the other hand, v is a value function that assigns a value to an outcome.

A hypothetical weighting function is shown in panel (a) of Figure 3.4. Kahneman and Tversky (1979) gave an example to justify the non-linearity of the weighting function. Suppose that a person is compelled to play Russian roulette, but he is also given the opportunity of purchasing the removal of one bullet from the loaded gun. Then most people feel that they would be willing to pay less for the reduction of probability of death from 4/6 to 3/6 than for the reduction of probability of death from 1/6 to 0. But economic consideration would lead a person to pay more in the former situation. This is because in the former case the value of money is reduced considerably by the probability that the person will not survive to enjoy that. An example of a weighting function is $w(q) = q^{.8} / \left(q^{.8} + (1-q)^{.8} \right)$.

Given a reference point R_0, $R_i < R_0$, indicates a loss, whereas $R_i > R_0$ represents a gain. The value function passes through the reference point and because of its

Figure 3.4   Hypothetical Weighting and Value Functions

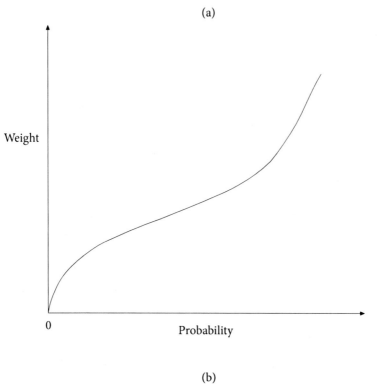

(a)

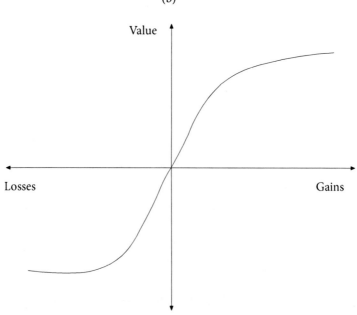

(b)

asymmetry around this point it is s-shaped. For instance, if we take zero as the reference point, then $v : (-\infty, \infty) \to \Re$ is increasing, strictly convex on $(-\infty, 0)$ and strictly concave on $(0, \infty)$. We represent a typical value function graphically in panel (b) of Figure 3.4.

Suppose the probability that fire may damage a person's house is 0.25 and the cost of the damage is 1000 dollars. He can buy a fire insurance policy for a premium of 50 dollars against the damage. Prospect theory value from payment of premium is $v(-50)$ and the value from purchase of the policy is $w(25)v(1000)+w(.75)v(0)$, which equals $w(.25)v(1000)$ if 0 is taken as the reference point.

Example 3.2: The following function is an example of a plausible value function with zero as the reference point:

$$v_\alpha(z) = \begin{cases} 1 - exp(-\alpha z), & z > 0, \\ -c(1 - exp(-\alpha|z|)), & z \le 0, \end{cases} \tag{3.13}$$

where $\alpha, c > 0$ are constants. This function takes on the value 0 at $z = 0$. It is increasing on $(-\infty, \infty)$, strictly convex on $(-\infty, 0)$ and strictly concave on $(0, \infty)$.

Applied Example 10.1: Agricultural production in low-income developing countries is generally dependent on rainfall. Production decisions made by households are therefore often made within risky environments. Since credit and insurance markets are generally not well developed in such countries, it becomes difficult to pass on these risks to another party. As a result, households are reluctant to adapt new technologies involving more risk. Using Ethiopian data, Yusuf and Randy (2007) found that more than 50 percent of the households are extremely risk averse. However, it was found that most households in Asia are moderate to intermediate risk averse. It was also noted that the households that are financially better off are willing to accept more risks in exchange for higher output. This is consistent with decreasing absolute risk aversion.

APPENDIX

Proof of Theorem 3.1: By Axiom 3 we can choose any output R^c in the interval $[R_l, R_u]$ and unambiguously determine a unique probability p^c for defining an equivalent standard prospect. That is, the axiom defines a function explicitly from the output domain $[R_l, R_u]$ to the range of probability values $[0,1]$. We denote this function by U. Now consider two risk-free outputs R_f and R'_f, where $R_f > R'_f$. By Axiom 6, $R_f \succ R'_f$. Now, by Axiom 3 there exists one and only one probability p_f for the output level R_f. The corresponding probability for R'_f is denoted by p'_f. Since $R_f \sim A_s^f = (p_f, R_u, R_l)$, $R_{f'} \sim A_s^{f'} = (p'_f, R_u, R_l)$ and $R_f \succ R'_f$, it must be the case that $(p_f, R_u, R_l) \succ (p'_f, R_u, R_l)$. By Axiom 2 we then have $p_f > p'_f$. This shows that the function U is increasing in its argument. Given R_l and R_u, by Axiom 3, the function is uniquely defined.

By Axiom 3, given any sequence of prospects $\left\{A^j\right\}_{j=1}^{v}$, it is possible to replace A^j by the corresponding compound prospect A_c^j, where $A_c^j = \left(\underline{\pi}, \left(A_s^{1j}, A_s^{2j}, ..., A_s^{kj}\right)\right)$, where $A_s^{ij} = \left(p_u^{ij}, R_u, R_l\right)$. By Axiom 4, A_c^j is indifferent to its rational equivalent A_{cs}^j. Thus, we have $A^j \sim A_c^j \sim A_{cs}^j$. More precisely,

$$\left(\underline{p}^j, \underline{R}^j\right) \sim \left(\underline{\pi}, \left(A_s^{1j}, A_s^{2j}, ..., A_s^{kj}\right)\right) \sim \left(\overline{p}_u^j, R_u, R_l\right), \tag{3.14}$$

where $R_i^j \sim A_s^{ij} = \left(p_u^{ij}, R_u, R_l\right)$ and $\overline{p}_u^j = \sum_{i=1}^{v} \pi_i^j p_u^{ij}$. In view of our earlier observation, $U\left(R_i^j\right) = p_u^{ij}$. Using (3.2) we then have

$$\overline{p}_u^j = \sum_{i=1}^{v} \pi_i^j U\left(R_i^j\right). \tag{3.15}$$

Now, from Axiom 2 it follows that $A_{cs}^j \succ A_{cs}^q$ if and only if $\overline{p}_u^j > \overline{p}_u^q$ and that $A_{cs}^j \sim A_{cs}^q$ if and only if $\overline{p}_u^j = \overline{p}_u^q$. This means that the rational equivalent standard prospect A_{cs}^j can be completely ordered by the corresponding $\overline{p}_u^j$ values, where $1 \le j \le v$. The most preferred rational equivalent standard prospect will be the one with the highest $\overline{p}_u^j$ value. But from (3.15) it follows that $\overline{p}_u^j$ is the expected value of $U\left(R_i^j\right)$ values associated with the rational equivalent standard prospects A_s^{ij}. Consequently, U satisfies the expected utility hypothesis for rational equivalent standard prospects.

Now, by Axiom 1 the preference ordering over all possible prospects, including the standard prospects, is transitive. Thus, $A^j \sim A_{cs}^j, A^q \sim A_{cs}^q$ and $A_{cs}^j \succ A_{cs}^q$ imply that $A^j \succ A^q$. Consequently, because of $A^j \sim A_c^j \sim A_{cs}^j$, the preference ordering over the rational equivalent standard prospects A_{cs}^j, represented by $\overline{p}_u^j$, coincides with that over the initial prospects, A^j, $1 \le j \le v$. Thus, the choice among the original prospects can be modeled as if the objective of the decision-maker is to maximize $\overline{p}_u$. Since $\overline{p}_u$ corresponds to the expected value of U, we can treat U as a von Neumann–Morgenstern utility function for initial prospects. This completes the proof of the theorem.

Proof of Theorem 3.2: $(i) \Rightarrow (ii)$. Since $U_2(M)$ is increasing, we can define g implicitly by $U_1(M) = g(U_2(M))$. Since $U_1(M)$ and $U_2(M)$ are increasing, we have $U_1' > 0$ and $U_2' > 0$. Then $U_1'(M) = g'(U_2(M))U_2'(M)$ establishes that $g' > 0$, that is, g is increasing. Next, $U_1''(M) = g''(U_2(M))(U_2'(M))^2 + g'(U_2(M))U''(M)$. Then condition (i) becomes

$$-\frac{g''(U_2(M))U_2'(M)}{g'(U_2(M))} - \frac{U_2''(M)}{U_2'(M)} > -\frac{U_2''(M)}{U_2'(M)}. \tag{3.16}$$

For $-\dfrac{U_1''(M)}{U_1'(M)} > -\dfrac{U_2''(M)}{U_2'(M)}$ to hold, we need $-\dfrac{g''(U_2(M))U_2'(M)}{g'(U_2(M))} > 0.$ Since

$U_2' > 0$ and $g' > 0$, it must be the case that $g'' < 0$, that is, g is strictly concave.

$(ii) \Rightarrow (iii)$ From the definition of $h_1(\tilde{\varepsilon})$ and the condition (ii) it follows that

$$U_1(M - h_1(\tilde{\varepsilon})) = \Xi(U_1(M + \tilde{\varepsilon})) = \Xi(g(U_2(M + \tilde{\varepsilon}))). \tag{3.17}$$

Now, Jensen's inequality demands that for any random variable X and any strictly concave function f of X, $\Xi(f(X)) < f(\Xi(X))$. The inequality $\Xi(f(X)) < f(\Xi(X))$ becomes an equality if the random variable is degenerate in the sense that it is a constant (see Marshall and Olkin 1979, 434). By Jensen's inequality we then have

$$\Xi(g(U_2(M + \tilde{\varepsilon}))) < g(\Xi(U_2(M + \tilde{\varepsilon}))). \tag{3.18}$$

In view of the definition of $h_2(\tilde{\varepsilon})$ and condition (ii) we get,

$$g(\Xi(U_2(M + \tilde{\varepsilon}))) = g(U_2(M - h_2(\tilde{\varepsilon}))) = U_1(M - h_2(\tilde{\varepsilon})). \tag{3.19}$$

Combining (3.17)–(3.19), we derive that $U_1(M - h_1(\tilde{\varepsilon})) < U_1(M - h_2(\tilde{\varepsilon}))$. By increasingness of U_1, it then follows that $M - h_1(\tilde{\varepsilon}) < M - h_2(\tilde{\varepsilon})$, from which we get $h_1(\tilde{\varepsilon}) > h_2(\tilde{\varepsilon})$.

$(iii) \Rightarrow (i)$ We assume, for simplicity, that the prospect is such that there is a 50–50 chance of losing or receiving an amount $\tilde{\varepsilon}$. Then an individual's net wealth will be $(M - \tilde{\varepsilon})$ or $(M + \tilde{\varepsilon})$ depending on whether he loses or gains $\tilde{\varepsilon}$. Expected utilities of the two persons from the prospect are $0.5U_1(M - \tilde{\varepsilon}) + 0.5U_1(M + \tilde{\varepsilon})$ and $0.5U_2(M - \tilde{\varepsilon}) + 0.5U_2(M + \tilde{\varepsilon})$ respectively. By definition, $U_1(M - h_1(\tilde{\varepsilon})) = 0.5U_1(M - \tilde{\varepsilon}) + 0.5U_1(M + \tilde{\varepsilon})$. Expanding each side of this expression by Taylor's series around M, for small $\tilde{\varepsilon}$ we get $U_1(M) - h_1(\tilde{\varepsilon})U_1'(M) + higher\ order\ terms =$

$$0.5\left(U_1(M) + \tilde{\varepsilon}U_1'(M) + \frac{(\tilde{\varepsilon})^2}{2}U_1''(M) + higher\ order\ terms\right) +$$

$$0.5\left(U_1(M) - \tilde{\varepsilon}U_1'(M) + \frac{\tilde{\varepsilon}^2}{2}U_1''(M) + higher\ order\ terms\right). \tag{3.20}$$

Ignoring the higher order terms and rearranging the resulting expression we get $h_1(\tilde{\varepsilon}) = -\dfrac{U_1''(M)}{U_1'(M)}\dfrac{\tilde{\varepsilon}^2}{2}$. By a similar argument, $h_2(\tilde{\varepsilon}) = -\dfrac{U_2''(M)}{U_2'(M)}\dfrac{\tilde{\varepsilon}^2}{2}$. Then

$h_1(\tilde{\varepsilon}) > h_2(\tilde{\varepsilon})$ implies that $-\dfrac{U_1''(M)}{U_1'(M)} > -\dfrac{U_2''(M)}{U_2'(M)}$. This completes the proof of the theorem.

Proof of Theorem 3.3: The idea of the proof is taken from Demange and Laroque (2006). The optimality condition (3.7) determines z_1 implicitly as a function of M_0. In order to see how in the optimal portfolio z_1 changes with M_0, we differentiate both sides of (3.7) with respect to M_0 to get

$$\Xi\Big(U''(\hat{c})(a_1 - \chi(1+\lambda))^2\Big)\frac{dz_1}{dM_0} + \Xi\Big(U''(\hat{c})(a_1 - \chi(1+\lambda))(1+\lambda)\Big) = 0, \quad (3.21)$$

where $\hat{c} = M_0(1+\lambda) + z_1(a_1 - \chi(1+\lambda))$. Due to strict concavity of U, the coefficient of dz_1/dM_0 is negative. Consequently, the sign of dz_1/dM_0 is same as that of $\Xi\Big(U''(\hat{c})(a_1 - \chi(1+\lambda))\Big)$. To prove that this expression is positive, let us invoke the assumption that the absolute risk aversion measure is decreasing. Then under the assumption that $(a_1 - \chi(1+\lambda)) < 0$, we have $-\big(U''(\hat{c})/U'(\hat{c})\big) = AP_A(\hat{c}) > AP_A(M_0(1+\lambda))$. It then follows that $-U''(\hat{c}) > AP_A(M_0(1+\lambda))U'(\hat{c})$. Multiplying both sides of this inequality by the positive quantity $\big(\chi(1+\lambda) - a_1\big)$, we get

$$-\big(\chi(1+\lambda) - a_1\big)U''(\hat{c}) > AP_A\big(M_0(1+\lambda)\big)U'(\hat{c})\big(\chi(1+\lambda) - a_1\big),$$

which we can rewrite as

$$\big(a_1 - \chi(1+\lambda)\big)U''(\hat{c}) > AP_A\big(M_0(1+\lambda)\big)U'(\hat{c})\big(\chi(1+\lambda) - a_1\big).$$

Now, by positivity of $\big(\chi(1+\lambda) - a_1\big)$ it follows that

$$AP_A\big(M_0(1+\lambda)\big)U'(\hat{c})\big(\chi(1+\lambda) - a_1\big) > AP_A\big(M_0(1+\lambda)\big)U'(\hat{c})\big(a_1 - \chi(1+\lambda)\big).$$

Therefore,

$$U''(\hat{c})\big(a_1 - \chi(1+\lambda)\big) > AP_A\big(M_0(1+\lambda)\big)U'(\hat{c})\big(a_1 - \chi(1+\lambda)\big). \quad (3.22)$$

A similar calculation will give rise to the same result if we assume that $\big(\chi(1+\lambda) - a_1\big) < 0$. Then taking mathematical expectation on both hand sides, we note, in view of condition (3.7), that the right-hand of the expression is zero. Thus, the left-hand side is positive. Hence dz_1/dM_0 is positive. In other words, demand for risky prospect increases as initial wealth holding increases. This completes the proof of the theorem.

Proof of Theorem 3.4: For proving this theorem also we follow Demange and Laroque (2006). The share of wealth in the risky prospect is given by $\chi z_1/M_0$. Since this share is decreasing in M_0, we have $d(\chi z_1/M_0)/dM_0 < 0$, that is,

$\dfrac{\big(\chi M_0\left(dz_1/dM_0\right)\big)-\chi z_1}{M_0^2}<0.$ Since the denominator is positive, the numerator must

be negative, that is, $\big(\chi M_0\left(dz_1/dM_0\right)\big)<\chi z_1$. Dividing both sides of this inequality by $\chi>0$, we get $\big(M_0\left(dz_1/dM_0\right)\big)<z_1$. We can rewrite the latter inequality as $\left(M_0 dz_1\right)/\left(z_1 dM_0\right)<1$. This means that the wealth elasticity of demand for the risky prospect is less than unity.

Now, we can rewrite equation (3.21) as

$$-\Xi\Big(U''(\hat{c})\big(a_1-\chi(1+\lambda)\big)^2\Big)\frac{dz_1}{dM_0}=\Xi\Big(U''(\hat{c})\big(a_1-\chi(1+\lambda)\big)(1+\lambda)\Big). \quad (3.23)$$

Note that the coefficient of dz_1/dM_0 in (3.23) is positive and since $\left(dz_1/dM_0\right)<\left(z_1/M_0\right)$ is a positive quantity, from (3.23) it follows that

$$-\Xi\Big(U''(\hat{c})\big(a_1-\chi(1+\lambda)\big)^2\Big)\frac{z_1}{M_0}>\Xi\Big(U''(\hat{c})\big(a_1-\chi(1+\lambda)\big)(1+\lambda)\Big). \quad (3.24)$$

From the above inequality we get

$$-\frac{M_0}{z_1}\Xi\Big(U''(\hat{c})\big(a_1-\chi(1+\lambda)\big)(1+\lambda)\Big)>\Xi\Big(U''(\hat{c})\big(a_1-\chi(1+\lambda)\big)^2\Big), \quad (3.25)$$

which gives $-M_0\Xi\Big(U''(\hat{c})\big(a_1-\chi(1+\lambda)\big)(1+\lambda)\Big)>z_1\Xi\Big(U''(\hat{c})\big(a_1-\chi(1+\lambda)\big)^2\Big)$. This is same as the condition $\Xi\Big(U''(\hat{c})\big(a_1-\chi(1+\lambda)\big)\big(M_0(1+\lambda)+z_1\left(a_1-\chi(1+\lambda)\right)\big)\Big)<0$, which can be written in more compact form as $\Xi\Big(U''(\hat{c})\big(a_1-\chi(1+\lambda)\big)\hat{c}\Big)<0$.

Increasing relative risk aversion along with the supposition that $\big(a_1-\chi(1+\lambda)\big)<0$ gives $-\big(\hat{c}U''(\hat{c})/U'(\hat{c})\big)=AP_R(\hat{c})<AP_R\big(M_0(1+\lambda)\big)$. Multiply both sides by $\big(\chi(1+\lambda)-a_1\big)>0$ and simplify to get

$$-\hat{c}U''(\hat{c})\big(\chi(1+\lambda)-a_1\big)$$
$$<\Big[-\big(M_0(1+\lambda)\big)\big(U''\big(M_0(1+\lambda)\big)/U'\big(M_0(1+\lambda)\big)\big)\Big]\big(\chi(1+\lambda)-a_1\big)U'(\hat{c}).$$

From this we get the inequality

$$\hat{c}U''(\hat{c})\big(a_1-\chi(1+\lambda)\big)<\big(M_0(1+\lambda)\big)\big(U''\big(M_0(1+\lambda)\big)/U'\big(M_0(1+\lambda)\big)\big) \quad (3.26)$$
$$\big(a_1-\chi(1+\lambda)U'(\hat{c}).$$

An analogous calculation will yield the same result for $\big(a_1-\chi(1+\lambda)\big)>0$. We then take expectation on both hand sides of (3.26) and use condition (3.7) to conclude that $\Xi\Big(U''(\hat{c})\big(a_1-\chi(1+\lambda)\big)\hat{c}\Big)<0$.

Before we demonstrate Theorem 3.5, note that since U is increasing, for each R_i in $[R_l, R_u]$ there is exactly one u_i such that $U(R_i) = u_i$, the image of R_i under U. Hence the inverse of U exists (Rudin 1976, 90). The u_i's are elements in the domain of the inverse function of U, which we denote by U^{-1}. The inverse function U^{-1} is defined by $U^{-1}(u_i) = U^{-1}(U(R_i)) = R_i$.

Proof of Theorem 3.5: Given that U is increasing, U^{-1} exists. Then note that R_e can be written explicitly as $R_e = U^{-1}\left(\sum_{i=1}^{k} p_i U(R_i)\right)$. Now, each R_i is drawn from the compact set $[R_l, R_u]$, where a set is called compact if it is closed and bounded. Hence the domain of the function $U(R_i)$ is $[R_l, R_u]$. Given that U is increasing and the continuous image of a compact set is compact (Rudin 1976, 89), $U(R_i)$ must take values in the compact set $[U(R_l), U(R_u)]$. For a given p, continuity and increasingness of the function U show that the average function $\sum_{i=1}^{k} p_i U(R_i)$ is continuous in its arguments and takes on values in the compact set $[U(R_l), U(R_u)]$. Now, if f is an increasing and continuous function on a compact interval $[a, b]$, then the inverse function f^{-1} is increasing and continuous on the interval $[f(a), f(b)]$ (Apostol 1973, 93). A direct application of this result demonstrates that U^{-1} is continuous and increasing. This, therefore, establishes that R_e is increasing and continuous.

Proof of Theorem 3.6: The inequality $C_A > 0$ can be written as $\sum_{i=1}^{k} p_i R_i > R_e$. Evidently, R_e can be written as $U^{-1}\left(\sum_{i=1}^{k} p_i U(R_i)\right)$. Therefore, $\sum_{i=1}^{k} p_i R_i > R_e$ becomes $U\left(\sum_{i=1}^{k} p_i R_i\right) > \left(\sum_{i=1}^{k} p_i U(R_i)\right)$. Since this is Jensen's inequality for a strictly concave function, it follows that $C_A > 0$. Given strict concavity of U, C_A becomes zero if output associated with each state is the same.

Proof of Theorem 3.7: (i) $\Rightarrow$ (ii) When R_i's increase by the same absolute amount c, expected output also increases by c. Consequently, translation invariance of C_A of requires that it should as well increase by c. Using the expression for C_A from the proof of Theorem 3.6, we can write this condition as

$$U^{-1}\left(\sum_{i=1}^{k} p_i U(R_i + c)\right) = U^{-1}\left(\sum_{i=1}^{k} p_i U(R_i)\right) + c. \qquad (3.27)$$

The only continuous solution to the functional equation (3.27) is given by $U(R_i) = -a\exp(-bR_i)$, where a and b are constants (Aczel 1966, 133). Increasingness and strict concavity of U demand that $a > 0$ and $b > 0$. This utility function and the exponential utility function in Example 3.1, have the same constant absolute risk aversion measure, since without loss of generality we can set $\bar{q} = a$ and $\alpha = b$.

(ii) $\Rightarrow$ (i). The utility function in Example 3.1 has a constant absolute risk aversion and its associated absolute cost of risk is given by $\left(\ln\left(\sum_{i=1}^{k}p_i\exp\left(\alpha\Xi\left(\underline{p},\underline{R}\right)-\alpha R_i\right)\right)\right)\Big/\alpha$. This cost measure satisfies translation invariance property.

Proof of Theorem 3.8: (i) $\Rightarrow$ (ii) Observe that $\Xi\left(\underline{p},c\underline{R}\right)=c\Xi\left(\underline{p},\underline{R}\right)$, where $c>0$. Therefore C_R will be a relative measure if $R_e\left(\underline{p},c\underline{R}\right)=cR_e\left(\underline{p},\underline{R}\right)$, where $c>0$. Using the expression for R_e we can write the latter condition as

$$cU^{-1}\left(\sum_{i=1}^{k}p_iU\left(R_i\right)\right)=U^{-1}\left(\sum_{i=1}^{k}p_iU\left(cR_i\right)\right), \tag{3.28}$$

where $c>0$ is a scalar. The only continuous solution to the functional equation (3.28) is given by

$$U\left(R_i\right)=\begin{cases}\hat{a}+\hat{b}\dfrac{R_i^{1-\beta}}{1-\beta},\beta\neq1,\\[2mm]\hat{a}+\hat{b}ln\left(R_i\right),\beta=1,\end{cases} \tag{3.29}$$

where $\hat{a}$ and $\hat{b}$ are constants (Aczel 1966, 133). Increasingness and strict concavity of U demand that $\hat{b}>0$ and $\beta>0$ in the first expression for $U(R_i)$ in (3.29). The relative risk aversion measure AP_R for this utility function is β, a positive constant (see Exercise 10 of this chapter).

(ii) $\Rightarrow$ (i). The utility function given by (3.29) is the only utility with constant relative risk aversion (see Exercise 10 of this chapter). The corresponding C_R measure is

$$C_R\left(\underline{p},\underline{R}\right)=\begin{cases}1-\dfrac{\left(\sum\limits_{i=1}^{k}p_iR_i^{1-\beta}\right)^{\frac{1}{(1-\beta)}}}{\Xi\left(\underline{p},\underline{R}\right)},\beta>0,\beta\neq1,\\[6mm]1-\dfrac{\prod\limits_{i=1}^{k}(R_i)^{p_i}}{\Xi\left(\underline{p},\underline{R}\right)},\beta=1.\end{cases} \tag{3.30}$$

This C_R function satisfies scale invariance.

BIBLIOGRAPHICAL NOTES

Varian (1992), Mas-Colell et al. (1995), Gravelle and Rees (2004) and Chakravarty (2010) provide in-depth presentation of axioms of expected utility. Rigorous analysis of risk aversion measures and their behaviors are available in the first two books and also in Pratt (1964) and Demange and Laroque (2006). The interested reader may refer to Gravelle and Rees (2004) and Chakravarty and Chakrabarti (2010) for analytical discussion on certainty equivalent. Axiomatic characterizations of the cost of risk can be found in Chakravarty and Chakrabarti (2010). The presentation of the portfolio choice problem for the quadratic utility function relies on Eichberger and Harper (1997). Prospect theory was pioneered by Kahneman and Tversky (1979).

EXERCISES

1. Each of the following statements is either true or false. If the statement is true, prove it. If it is false, give a counter-example or justify your answer by logical reasoning.

   (a) If the Arrow–Pratt relative risk aversion measure is a decreasing function of investment in the quantities of risky asset, then the wealth elasticity of the asset is greater than unity.

   (b) Assume that a decision-maker ranks prospects using the mean-variance expected utility function $\mu(10 - \sigma)$, where μ stands for expected output on the prospect and σ denotes standard deviation. Then the decision-maker prefers a prospect, which pays 10 with probability 1 to the one that pays 20 with probability 0.5 and 10 with probability 0.5.

   (c) If the risk-free output is 5, and if there is a risky prospect with an output of 8 and a standard deviation of 2, then the price of risk is 1.

   (d) Curvature of a utility function represents an individual's attitude toward risk.

   (e) The expected utility property remains preserved under any increasing transformation.

   (f) An individual's utility function is given by $U(W) = \sqrt{W}$. His current level of wealth is 500 dollars, which he decides to invest in a prospect in which the chances of gaining 284 dollars or losing 400 dollars are respectively 1/3 and 2/3. The certainty equivalent of this investment is 16 dollars.

   (g) For an individual with utility function U, a sufficient condition for decreasing absolute risk aversion is that the second derivative of U has an increasing marginal.

2. We say that $\hat{U}$ is affinely related to U if $\hat{U}$ can be obtained from U by an affine transformation. Demonstrate rigorously that the relationship "affinely related" is an equivalence relation.

3. An individual is considering the possibility of insuring his house, which has a current market valuation of 10000 dollars against fire. The probability

that the house gets partly damaged by fire is 0.25 and he assumes that it will be necessary to spend 1000 dollars to repair the damage. Determine the maximum amount that the individual would be willing to pay as a premium to insure the repairing cost of 1000 dollars.

4. Consider the utility functions associated with the two-fund monetary separation. Show that these utility functions exhibit linear absolute risk tolerance.

5. Explicitly derive the condition for strict convexity of the indifference curve of the mean-variance expected utility function considered in Section 3. 4.

6. A person is indifferent between receiving 100 dollars with probability 1 and (20 dollars with probability 0.5 and 200 dollars with probability 0.5). He is also indifferent between receiving 120 dollars with probability 1 and (20 dollars with probability 1/3 and 200 dollars with probability 2/3). The individual's utility function U satisfies the condition that $U(200) = 1$ and $U(20) = 0$. Then what can you say about the individual's choices in the following situations? (i) Between 120 dollars with probability 1 and (100 dollars with probability 0.25 and 200 dollars with probability 0.75) and (120 dollars with probability 0.5 and 200 dollars with probability 0.5).

7. Person 1 is said to be at least as risk averse as person 2 in the sense of Ross (1981) if $\inf\limits_{z} \dfrac{U_1''(z)}{U_2''(z)} \geq \sup\limits_{z} \dfrac{U_1'(z)}{U_2'(z)}$. Show that this condition implies that person 1 is at least as risk averse as person 2 in the Arrow–Pratt absolute sense. Is the converse true? Also show that if person 1 is at least as risk averse as person 2 in the Ross sense, then there exists a decreasing concave function g and a positive constant c such that $U_1(z) = cU_2(z) + g(z)$ for all z.

8. Stochastic outputs on two prospects are denoted respectively by a_1 and a_2. They have equal mean and equal variance. Assuming that the variance can be taken as an indicator of risk, show that a risk-averse individual will invest his wealth in these two prospects equally.

9. An individual's von Neumann–Morgenstern utility, as a function of wealth W, is given by $U(W) = -W^{-1}$. He can invest this amount in a prospect, which gives him a wealth of W_1 with probability p and a wealth of W_2 with probability $(1-p)$. Determine W as a function of W_1 and W_2 that will make him indifferent between retaining the current wealth and investing in the prospect.

10. Show that the Arrow–Pratt measure of relative risk aversion is a constant if and only if the utility function is of the following form:

$$U(R_i) = \begin{cases} \hat{a} + \hat{b}\dfrac{R_i^{1-\beta}}{1-\beta}, & \beta > 0, \beta \neq 1, \\[2mm] \hat{a} + \hat{b}\ln(R_i), & \beta = 0, \end{cases}$$

where $\hat{b} > 0$ is a constant. The parameter β is the absolute value of the constant elasticity of the marginal utility function U'. That is why this utility function is often referred to as the iso-elastic utility function.

11. Consider an individual with the utility function $U(W) = W(1 - exp(- W))$, where the domain of W is $(0, \infty)$. Identify the sub-domains of W over which the individual is a risk-lover and risk averse respectively.

12. An individual's utility function is characterized by constant absolute Arrow–Pratt risk aversion. The individual has an initial wealth of W, which he decides to invest in a prospect. The chance of gaining 100 dollars from the investment is p and the chance of losing 90 dollars is $(1 - p)$. Then show that the individual's decision to invest in the prospect is independent of W.

13. Demonstrate rigorously that the certainty equivalent of a prospect remains unaltered under an affine transformation of the utility function.

14. An individual can gain a very small amount ε from a gamble with a probability p and the chance of losing ε amount is $(1 - p)$. Will he participate in the gamble if $p > (1 - p)$?

15. (a) Show that the following function is a plausible value function with zero as the reference point:

$$v_\beta (z) = \begin{cases} z^\beta & , z > 0, \\ -c|z|^\beta & , z \leq 0, \end{cases}$$

where $0 < \beta < 1$ and $c > 0$ are constants (Hastie and Dawes 2001, 216).

(b) There is a 50–50 chance of receiving or losing ε from investment in an even prospect. What risk premium would a person pay to avoid investment if we use prospect theory with the value function given by (a) and the weight function is $w(q) = q$?

16. A person is called infinitely risk averse if he is concerned with the minimum output on a prospect: $\min_i \{R_1, R_2, ..., R_k\}$. Suppose that the absolute value of the elasticity of his marginal utility function is $\beta > 0$. How does his indifference curve look as $\beta \to \infty$? Determine the certainty equivalent in this limiting case.

PART II

Firm Valuation and Capital Structure

CHAPTER 4

Valuation of Stocks

4.1 INTRODUCTION

Stocks are ownership certificates in a company. In the theory of finance often "stocks" and "shares" are used synonymously. To understand this, consider the following example. One share of stock in a company with 2000 shares outstanding entitles the owner of the share to (1/2000) of the dividends paid by the company. If the company gets liquidated, then this ownership establishes a claim for (1/2000) of the net assets (assets minus liabilities) of the company. There are many reasons for issuing stock certificates by a company. For instance, for a new investment a firm may need some financial support to pay the bills until the cash inflows start coming. One way of raising money for the new investment is to issue stock certificates. Likewise, an entrepreneur can start a new company with the support of some financial backers. Once the company is established, the stockholders are entitled to the relevant shares of the profit that the company will generate in the future. Thus, there will be a stream of future payments. Another reason why a company may be interested in issuing shares in it is that this spreads the risk of the company among a large number of stockholders.

An owner of shares in a company may be interested in selling these shares and purchasing others. A market where such trading of shares takes place is called the stock market. We present a discussion on stock transactions in Section 4.2 of this chapter. Since the ownership of a company establishes a claim for a stream of future payments, stocks can be evaluated using the discounted present value of future dividends. We discuss this issue in Sections 4.3 and 4.4 under alternative structural assumptions. Price-to-earnings ratio is the ratio between the price of a share and the earning of the firm per share. This ratio is employed to judge whether one share in a company is more expensive than that in a different company. It is analyzed in Section 4.5 of this chapter.

4.2 STOCK TRANSACTIONS

Stocks confer ownership rights in the issuing company on their owners. Generally, there are two types of stocks: (i) common stock and (ii) preferred stock. In the case of common stock the shareholders possess voting rights that can be exercised in corporate decisions. Holders also get dividends on the stocks. A preferred stock holder does not have the voting right in the company decisions but has the claim to receive certain level of dividends before any dividend is paid to a common stock holder (see Bodie et al. 2008).

At the outset stocks are purchased from the originating company. Later they can be traded in the stock market, which is also referred to as the stock exchange. Returns on the stocks possessed by an investor come in the form of dividends and capital gains (see Brav et al. 1999b). When a person purchases a share we say that he has a long position in the share. Generally, transactions of stocks in the market take place as follows. A specialist, known as a broker, receives orders to purchase and sell a particular stock from other brokers on the floor of the exchange. A broker is a representative of a brokerage-firm. His job is to execute these orders according to the instructions received from the other brokers. Some of these orders ask the broker to buy or sell a particular number of shares at the maximum price he can get. Some orders mention the price at which a particular number of shares are to be traded. Thus, at any time a broker has an order book that will list the number of orders received. A broker gets a brokerage charge for executing the orders. In the recent period, the method of transaction has undergone some changes. For instance, in the London Stock Exchange deals are entered into a computer known as CREST and buying and selling bids are matched automatically. Much of the private purchase and sale are carried out by e-brokers and a brokerage charge still has to be paid. In the New York Stock Exchange, stocks can be bought and sold via its electronic hybrid market. Customers can place orders for immediate execution electronically or send orders to the floor.

Selling of stocks may often take the form of short selling. This case arises when the broker borrows the stocks from another organization to fulfill a purchase order. Short selling is done under the belief that the stock price will go down. The short seller delivers the borrowed security to the purchaser who will then start receiving dividends paid by the company. The short seller is obliged to pay dividends to the original owner from which the stocks were borrowed as long as the borrowing remains outstanding. In order to close the short sale, the short seller must purchase the stocks and return them to the original owner. We may take an example to illustrate this situation. Suppose that a broker receives an order for delivering 300 shares of a company, where the price of each share is 100 dollars. The broker borrows these shares and delivers them to the purchaser. He receives a sum of $100 \times 300 = 30000$ dollars from this deal. However, he has to pay a dividend of

1 dollar per share, that is, 300 dollars to the party from which they were borrowed. Now, suppose the share price has gone down and each share costs 80 dollars. He can buy 300 shares at an aggregate cost of 80 × 300 dollars = 24000 dollars and return the shares to the party from which they were originally borrowed to close the short selling. This shows that the net profit of the short seller from this deal is (30000 − 300 − 24000) dollars = 5700 dollars. However, if he originally purchases the shares from the market at a total cost of 30000 dollars for delivering to the purchaser, then he has to incur a net loss of (30000 − 300 − 24000) dollars = 5700 dollars, since now he receives a dividend of 300 dollars.

In a stock market when a purchase order arrives, there is a positive excess demand at the old or existing price, and the purchase order will be executed at a new price, higher than the old price. Likewise, when a sell order arrives, there is excess supply at the old price, and the execution of the order will take place at a new price, lower than the old price. Thus, there is an upward or a downward movement of price depending on whether there is a positive excess demand or supply. In other words, price rises if there is positive excess demand and it falls if there is negative excess demand. Thus, the order book has similar characteristics as the market supply and demand schedules in a perfectly competitive framework. Price adjustments in a stock exchange are instantaneous. Often a stock market is referred to as a "frictionless market" in the sense that there are many specialists on the floor (many buyers and sellers), adjustment cost is quite low and there are quick responses to changes in demand and supply. Note that a stock market uses the publicly available information and no investor can make money by using this information personally. This reflects the view that the resulting equilibrium in the market has a flavor of rational expectations equilibrium (see Quirk 1986).

To understand the relationship between the prices of bonds and stocks, note that a bond is an alternative way of investing money to earn income and from this perspective bonds and stocks are substitutes. With an increase in the price of stocks, given that the prospective dividends on stocks remain unchanged, a bond purchase becomes a more lucrative purchase. Similarly, given other factors, as the price of bonds becomes higher, the lower the yields of bonds and hence stocks become a better buy.

Investors keep watch on stock indices to decide on their investments in the stock market. A stock index is a summary measure of the performance of the market. The index is calculated as an average of prices of a list of companies. An index may be an equally weighted index or a value-weighted index. An increase in the value of a stock index over some specified short interval, say one day, is taken as an indication of an increase in the value of the companies considered. Hence a high value of an index is desirable. Examples of such indices are: the Nasdaq 100 index, the Dow Jones Industrial Average index, the Toronto Stock Exchange 400 index, the Swiss Market index, the Amsterdam Exchanges index and the Sensex index.

4.3 VALUATION OF STOCKS: A SIMPLE STRUCTURE

The theory of finance stock valuation involves a method of determining the values of companies and their stocks. The valuation of stocks is important for a stockholder because ownership of stocks generates income in terms of dividends and the valuation of a company is related to the valuation of its stocks. Stock valuation is more complicated than valuation of bonds because there is no finite period of maturity and dividends may not be specified. Some structural assumptions are necessary regarding dividends. Our presentation in this section is mostly based on Brav et al. (1999b). Suppose an individual buys a company share at $t = 0$ with a price P_0. At the end of the year, that is, at $t = 1$ it can be traded on the stock exchange at an expected price P_1. The ownership entitles the individual to get the first year's expected dividend D_1. That is, D_1 is the dividend that the person expects for holding the share for a year. The expected rate of discount or the required rate of return, for the share, is a constant and equals λ_s. More generally, we can assume variability of λ_s over time. The constancy assumption makes the analysis simple. Thus, after one year from today ($t = 0$), the holder receives two cash flows: P_1 and D_1. Then the discounted present value (DPV) of the share is $(D_1 + P_1)/(1 + \lambda_s)$ (see Chapter 2). But the current price of the share is P_0. Hence

$$P_0 = \frac{D_1 + P_1}{1 + \lambda_s}. \tag{4.1}$$

Solving equation (4.1) for λ_s, we get

$$\lambda_s = \frac{D_1}{P_0} + \frac{P_1 - P_0}{P_0}. \tag{4.2}$$

Since D_1 is an expected figure, the first term on the right-hand side of (4.2) is the prospective dividend and the second term is the expected capital gain, both expressed as fractions of the current stock price. The left-hand side is the expected rate of return of a share. The financial ratio D_1/P_0 is popularly known as the prospective dividend yield. Practitioners generally refer to the historic dividend yield D_0/P_0 as the dividend yield. Clearly, there are important differences between the two financial ratios. On the other hand, the financial ratio $((P_1 - P_0)/P_0)$ is the rate of growth of the share price over the 0–1 period.

Denoting the expected price of the share at $t = 2$ by P_2 and the second year's expected dividend by D_2, we have $P_1 = (D_2 + P_2)/(1 + \lambda_s)$, which on substitution into (4.1) yields

$$P_0 = \frac{D_1}{1 + \lambda_s} + \frac{D_2 + P_2}{(1 + \lambda_s)^2}. \tag{4.3}$$

Continuing this way for a time horizon of length T we get

$$P_0 = \sum_{i=1}^{T-1} \frac{D_i}{(1+\lambda_s)^i} + \frac{D_T + P_T}{(1+\lambda_s)^T}, \tag{4.4}$$

where D_i expected dividend at the end of period i and P_T is the expected price of the share at time T. Now, for a large T, if $\dfrac{P_T}{(1+\lambda_s)^T}$ is significantly small, that is, given constancy of λ_s if P_T does not increase much, then we can neglect the term $\dfrac{P_T}{(1+\lambda_s)^T}$ on the right-hand side of (4.4). Then the current price of the share can be approximated by

$$P_0 = \sum_{i=1}^{T} \frac{D_i}{(1+\lambda_s)^i}. \tag{4.5}$$

That is, the price of a share is the DPV of the stream of dividends that an individual expects to receive from the company. This formula can be applied when we have information on all future dividends and the rate of return. The total stock market value of the company is the DPV of the stream of profits that the company expects to receive. In a world of certainty the DPV of the company is the DPV of the flow of profits, which is publicly known. In an uncertain world the company's objective should be maximization of the total stock market value. In a world of certainty, profit maximization and stock market value maximization amount the same thing.

In order to make use of (4.5) we need to make some assumptions about future dividends. The simplest possible assumption is that D_i's are constant over time, so that $D_i = D$, say, for all i. Then (4.5) becomes , $P_0 = D \Big/ \sum_{i=1}^{T}(1+\lambda_s)^{-i} = cD \sum_{i=0}^{T-1} c^i$, where $c = 1/(1 + \lambda_s)$. This, on simplification, gives $P_0 = cD(1 - c^T)/(1 - c)$. As $T \to \infty$, $c^T \to 0$ (since $0 < c < 1$). Therefore, in this limiting case we have $P_0 = cD/(1 - c)$. Substituting the value of c, we write this equation more explicitly as

$$P_0 = \frac{D}{\lambda_s}. \tag{4.6}$$

Thus, if expected dividend stays constant over time, then for an indefinite future a share can be evaluated like a consol or a perpetuity (see Chapter 7). Also from (4.6) we have $\lambda_s = D/P_0$, which indicates that in this case the expected rate of return on a share equals the constant dividend amount as a fraction of the current share price.

4.4 VALUATION OF STOCKS: A GENERAL FRAMEWORK

Constancy of dividends across time is an unrealistic assumption. A more general assumption is that the company has a steady position and dividends are expected to grow at a constant rate, that is, $(D_{i+1} - D_i)/D_i = g$, where g is the constant rate of growth and $i \geq 1$ is an integer (see Gordon 1959 and 1962 and Brav et al. 1999b). A growth of this type may result when a firm has launched a new product or introduced a new technology. That is, $D_1, D_2, D_3, \ldots\ldots$ constitute a geometric series with the common ratio $D_{i+1}/D_i = (1 + g)$, $i \geq 1$, being any integer. This gives $D_i = D_1 (1 + g)^{i-1}$ for all positive integers i. Equation (4.5) then becomes

$$P_0 = D_1 \sum_{i=1}^{T} \frac{(1+g)^{i-1}}{(1+\lambda_s)^i} = \frac{D_1}{(1+\lambda_s)} \sum_{i=0}^{T-1} \left(\frac{1+g}{1+\lambda_s} \right)^i. \tag{4.7}$$

Let us denote $(1 + g)/(1 + \lambda_s)$ by a. Then (4.7) can be rewritten as $P_0 = \left(D_1/(1+\lambda_s) \right) \sum_{i=0}^{T-1} a^i$, which on simplification becomes $P_0 = (D_1/(1 + \lambda_s))((1 - a^T)/(1 - a))$. Now, assume that $0 < a < 1$, that is, $g < \lambda_s$. If $a > 1$, then under *ceteris paribus* assumption, that is, under the assumption that other things are given, as the value of T increases P_0 increases and as $T \to \infty$, $P_0 \to \infty$. This, in view of equation (4.4), then leads to the violation of the assumption that $\dfrac{P_T}{(1+\lambda_s)^T}$ is significantly small for a large T. Therefore, we must have $0 < a < 1$, so that $g < \lambda_s$. Then as $T \to \infty$, we have $P_0 = D_1/\left((1-a)(1+\lambda_s)\right) = D_1/(\lambda_s - g)$ (since $a^T \to 0$ as $T \to \infty$). Clearly, if we know a current year's dividend, and have estimates for constant growth rate and rate of return, we can use this formula for valuation of a share. If $g = 0$, equation (4.6) drops out as a special case of this equation. From the equation $P_0 = D_1/(\lambda_s - g)$ it follows immediately that

$$\lambda_s = \frac{D_1}{P_0} + g. \tag{4.8}$$

This means that under the constant growth assumption the expected rate of return on a share equals the sum of the prospective dividend yield (expected dividend as a fraction of the current price of the share) and the growth rate.

We can now equate equation (4.2) with equation (4.8) and simplify the resulting expression to get

$$P_1 = P_0 (1+g). \tag{4.9}$$

That is, given that the dividends are expected to grow at a constant rate, the share price is also expected to grow at the same constant rate.

The constancy assumption of growth rate is a strong assumption. For firms, which are not in a steady state, this is an unrealistic assumption. For instance, for a relatively new firm it is unlikely that the dividends will grow at a constant rate at the outset. The constant growth assumption can probably be made once the firm has established its position steadily. In this case it is necessary to modify the constant growth model and identify the sub-periods with different growths. To illustrate this, suppose we have dividend forecasts up to period $T - 1$ and then from the next period onward a constant growth formula can be assumed. Thus, $D_T = D_{T-1}(1+g)$, $D_{T+1} = D_{T-1}(1+g)^2$, $D_{T+2} = D_{T-1}(1+g)^3$ and so on. The for any $j > T - 1$ formula (4.4) will be modified as

$$P_0 = \sum_{i=1}^{T-1} \frac{D_i}{(1+\lambda_s)^i} + D_{T-1} \sum_{i=T}^{j} \frac{(1+g)^{i-T+1}}{(1+\lambda_s)^i} + \frac{P_j}{(1+\lambda_s)^j}. \tag{4.10}$$

That is,

$$P_0 = \sum_{i=1}^{T-1} \frac{D_i}{(1+\lambda_s)^i} + D_{T-1} \frac{(1+g)}{(1+\lambda_s)^T} \sum_{i=T}^{j} \frac{(1+g)^{i-T}}{(1+\lambda_s)^{i-T}} + \frac{P_j}{(1+\lambda_s)^j}, \tag{4.11}$$

which we can rewrite as

$$P_0 = \sum_{i=1}^{T-1} \frac{D_i}{(1+\lambda_s)^i} + D_{T-1} \frac{(1+g)}{(1+\lambda_s)^T} \sum_{i=0}^{j-T} \frac{(1+g)^i}{(1+\lambda_s)^i} + \frac{P_j}{(1+\lambda_s)^j}. \tag{4.12}$$

As before, we assume that $\dfrac{P_j}{(1+\lambda_s)^j}$ is significantly small and hence the third term on the right-hand side of (4.12) can be neglected. Then

$$P_0 = \sum_{i=1}^{T-1} \frac{D_i}{(1+\lambda_s)^i} + D_{T-1} \frac{(1+g)}{(1+\lambda_s)^T} \sum_{i=0}^{j-T} a^i$$

$$= \sum_{i=1}^{T-1} \frac{D_i}{(1+\lambda_s)^i} + D_{T-1} \frac{(1+g)}{(1+\lambda_s)^T} \sum_{i=0}^{j-T} a^i = \sum_{i=1}^{T-1} \frac{D_i}{(1+\lambda_s)^i} + D_{T-1} \frac{(1+g)}{(1+\lambda_s)^T} \frac{(1-a^{j-T+1})}{(1-a)}, \tag{4.13}$$

where $a = (1 + g)/(1 + \lambda_s)$ and it is assumed that $0 < a < 1$ and hence $g < \lambda_s$. Now, for any finite T, as $j \to \infty$, $j - T + 1 \to \infty$, which in turn implies that $(1 - a^{j-T+1}) \to 1$. Hence in the limiting case P_0 in (4.13) becomes

$$P_0 = \sum_{i=1}^{T-1} \frac{D_i}{(1+\lambda_s)^i} + D_{T-1} \frac{(1+g)}{(1+\lambda_s)^T (1-a)} = \sum_{i=1}^{T-1} \frac{D_i}{(1+\lambda_s)^i} + D_{T-1} \frac{(1+g)}{(1+\lambda_s)^{T-1} (\lambda_s - g)}. \tag{4.14}$$

Formula (4.14) is quite general in the sense that T is arbitrary. This formula for valuation of a share can be applied if we have information on dividends up to period $T-1$, rate of return and constant growth rate with effect from period T. For any value of T, we can employ formula (4.14).

Formula (4.14) gives one modification of (4.7). We can also make other assumptions. For instance, dividends may increase and then become constant. Another possibility is that the dividend increases then goes down. In each case we can develop the corresponding stock valuation formula under certain plausible assumptions. The estimation of the growth rate can be based on analysts' forecasts of future growth rates (for a discussion see Vander Weide and Carleton 1988).

4.5 PRICE-TO-EARNINGS RATIO

Valuation of stocks presented in Sections 4.3 and 4.4 are based on cash flows. The bases of an alternative valuation can be an investor's willingness to pay per share of stock and the company's earnings per share. Formally, we combine the share price and the company's earnings per share in the following ratio form measure

$$PE = \frac{P_0}{E_1}, \tag{4.15}$$

where E_1 denotes earnings per share. This financial ratio, which is a well-known metric of stock evaluation, is an indicator of the extent to which the market is willing to pay for the company's earnings. For a firm with high PE, investors have high hopes of the firm's future. A higher value of PE indicates that the investors are ready to pay more for each unit of annual earning. A low PE firm is stated as having low growth and this could also mean that the share is undervalued (see Graham et al. 1962).

The PE is the reciprocal of the earnings yield E_1/P_0. It is a measure of a normalized expected return that can be earned from holding a share. More precisely, it can be interpreted as the amount of earnings that the holder of a share buys for one dollar.

In order to relate PE to a company's payout policy, we consider the company's dividend payout ratio DPR, defined as the ratio between dividends per share and earnings per share, that is

$$DPR = \frac{D_1}{E_1}. \tag{4.16}$$

The financial ratio DPR is bounded between 0 and 1, where the lower bound is achieved when the company does not pay any dividend. On the other hand, DPR attains its upper bound 1 if the company pays its entire earnings as dividends. A high DPR of a firm indicates that it pays more in dividends. Hence shares of a firm with high DPR will attract investors desiring higher income and the firm will have little left for future investment. Often investments are necessary to foster growth and in such a case a firm may not be willing to pay high dividends. For a firm of this type DPR will be low. The difference 1 − DPR is known as retention ratio. A higher value of the retention ratio means that the DPR is low.

From (4.16) it follows that $D_1 = (DPR)E_1$, which when plugged into (4.8), gives

$$\lambda_s = \frac{E_1}{P_0} DPR + g. \tag{4.17}$$

Equation (4.17) when rearranged, gives

$$\frac{P_0}{E_1} = \frac{DPR}{\lambda_s - g}. \tag{4.18}$$

Thus, (4.18) shows given λ_s and g, an increase in DPR is equivalent to an increase in PE and vice versa. From equation (4.18) it also follows that for any two firms with the same dividend-payout ratio, rate of return, and growth rate, the price-to-earnings ratio will be the same (see also Brav et al. 1999b). Equation (4.17) specifies a relationship between the rate of return and the earnings yield.

Equation (4.17) relies on prospective dividends and earnings. Often historical values are used for empirical purposes. For instance, in his empirical work, Abidin (2008) used trailing PE for Malaysian companies. In order to use the formula for practical purposes, we may assume that dividends and earnings grow at a constant rate g, so that $D_1 = D_0 (1 + g)$ and $E_1 = E_0 (1 + g)$. This ensures that the DPR is constant over time. Then (4.8) becomes

$$\lambda_s = \frac{D_0 (1+g)}{P_0} + g. \tag{4.19}$$

The ratio D_0/P_0 is the historical dividends yield. We can solve (4. 19) for g to get

$$g = \frac{\lambda_s - (D_0/P_0)}{1 + (D_0/P_0)}. \tag{4.20}$$

Equation (4.20) expresses growth rate as a function of the required rate of return and historical dividends yield. Given D_0/P_0, an increase in λ_s increases g. Likewise, given λ_s, a reduction in D_0/P_0 increases the growth rate.

According to Beaver and Morse (1978) "differences in expected growth are commonly offered as a major explanation for differences in PE" (Beaver and Morse 1978, 65). Penman (2001) stated that "PE indicates a firm's ability to earnings" (Penman 2001, 527). The relation between historical growth and PE is not quite clear. Several studies along this line report conflicting results (see for example,

Zarowin 1990 and Alford 1992). However, forecasted rates of growth are important (Zarowin 1990).

Example 4.1: A firm has just paid a dividend of 2 dollars per share and the current price of a share is 50 dollars. Determine the required rate of return if it is forecasted that the dividend will grow at 5 percent indefinitely.

We apply equation (4.8) to determine the required rate of return. We know that $D_1 = D_0 (1 + g) = 2 \times 1.05$ dollars $= 2.1$ dollars. Then $\lambda_s = (2.1/50) + .05 = .092$. Thus, the required rate of return is 9.2 percent.

BIBLIOGRAPHICAL NOTES

Important sources of overview of valuations of stocks under alternative assumptions are Graham et al. (1962), Gordon (1962) and Brav et al. (1999b). An elegant discussion on trading of securities is available in Bodie et al. (2008).

EXERCISES

1. Each of the following statements is either true or false. If the statement is true, prove it. If it is false, give a counter-example or justify your answer by logical reasoning.
    (a) Since the dividends paid by a company are not growing, a share of the company is not a good buy.
    (b) For a given level of dividends, a higher required rate of return has to be compensated by a higher growth rate in order for the price of a share to remain unchanged.
    (c) Suppose the future dividends grow at a constant rate and the required rate of return is also constant. Then the price of the share is independent of the number of periods for holding the share.
    (d) A company share without price appreciation is not a good buy.
    (e) If dividends remain constant over time, there is essentially no difference between a share and an annuity.
2. Interpret the difference $gP_0 - (1 - DPR)E_1$, where the symbols have their usual meanings.
3. Assume that the dividend of a company grows at a constant rate for an indefinite period of time. Graphically explain the relationship between the required rate of return and prospective dividend yield.
4. A company's dividends for years 1 and 2 are 2 dollars and 3 dollars respectively. Then dividend payments grow by 5 percent indefinitely. Determine the price of a share if the required rate of return is 10 percent.

5. It is possible to make a forecast about the dividend for only one period. After that the dividends are expected to grow at a constant rate. Determine the price of a share in a situation of this type.

6. Given that the dividends of a company grow at a constant rate for an indefinite period, what will be the percentage change in prospective dividend yield if the required rate of return changes from 5 percent to 7 percent after 5 years?

7. A firm has just paid a dividend of 1 dollar per share. Then dividends are expected to grow at a constant rate of 5 percent. If the required rate of return is 10 percent, what will be the share price after a year from now?

8. A company has a required rate of return of 8 percent and an expected growth rate of 4 percent. Determine the prospective dividend yield. What will be the dividend yield if the expected growth rate reduces to 4 percent? Explain the direction of change intuitively.

9. Given the constant rate of growth and required rate of return, graphically show the relationship between the earnings yield and the dividend-payout ratio.

10. An investor buys a company share for 20 dollars and expects dividends of 1.05 dollars and 1.1025 dollars in years 1 and 2 respectively. The implicit growth rate in dividends is expected to continue indefinitely. Determine the required rate of return.

11. Clearly examine the relationship between the price-to-earnings ratio and the retention ratio.

CHAPTER 5

Valuation of Cash Flows and Capital Budget Allocation

5.1 INTRODUCTION

Capital budgeting is an investment decision to be taken by a firm or a company as to whether a project should be undertaken or not. Every capital budgeting decision that a firm takes will change the volume of the cash receipts and payments of the firm. For instance, suppose a firm is considering introducing a new product. Then in order to ensure that the new product occupies a significant position in the market, it is necessary that the product is advertised and distributed properly. This will involve a sequence of cash outflows from the firm in terms of payment for advertising, service for distribution, transportation cost etc. If the product is a substitute of an already available product in the market, then there may be additional expenditures like the one for quality packaging. The firm, of course, will start receiving cash inflows from the sale of the product after a certain period. A bank loan is one way of financing the expenditure of the project. Alternatively, a highly significant number of stocks can be issued to finance the expenditure partly or fully. This will mean that the same amount of equity is to be distributed among an increased number of shareholders. The organization would need to consider the impact of an additional loan on the overall cost of financing the projects.

As a second example, suppose a hotel has decided to purchase ski areas for its boarders. The hotel will then have a regular cash outflow for paying the interest on the bank loan taken, but it may now charge higher rents to boarders for the additional service provided. Next, consider the example where an upstream firm, firm I, dumps its wastes into a river and a downstream firm, firm II, uses river water to process its output. With an increase in output (and hence wastes) of firm I, firm II needs more chemical and labor to produce the same output. If in order to resolve this externality problem, firm II decides to purchase firm I, then the necessary expenditure is a cash outflow from firm II. But as a merged entity firm II can now dump optimal level of wastes into the river for producing the output that firm I was producing. Because of optimal dumping of wastes, the merged entity will now require less chemicals and less labor for producing the same level of output that firm II was producing. This reduction in expenditure may be treated as a cash inflow to the merged firm. Finally, suppose two firms are vertically related, that is, one produces for another. A merger of these two firms saves payment to the firm whose output is used as input in the other firm, but there may be an initial expenditure for purchasing the input-producing firm. Merger of a steel firm with a firm producing pig iron is an example of vertical merger. Many other decisions—like buying or leasing land, building, equipments, choosing distributional channels of products, employing sales managers and/or travelling sales persons etc.—affect the firm's cash flows.

Typically, projects yield a stream of costs (outflows) and benefits (inflows) that stretch over a period of time. It is worthwhile to have a general decision rule which enables us to aggregate the various inflows and outflows to arrive at an indicator of net benefits and hence at a decision as to whether or not to proceed. In order to obtain a single indicator of the net social benefit of a project, it is necessary to aggregate monetary benefits and costs over time. At each time point, all benefits and costs can be added together under the assumption that one dollar is judged to have the same value, no matter to whom it accrues. But as we have noted, one dollar received now is not necessarily worth the same as a dollar received next year. Thus, what we need is the net present value of the project. We analyze this in details in Section 5.2 of the chapter.

An alternative criterion, often used to judge the viability of a project, is the internal rate of return—the rate of return for which the present value of outflows equals that of inflows. In other words, the internal rate of return is that level of rate of return for which the net present value of the project equals zero. The net present value criterion and the internal rate of return are related and often lead to the same conclusion. This is discussed in Section 5.3.

A third rule for judging the suitability of a project is the benefit–cost ratio, defined as the ratio between the discounted present values of benefits and costs. It is related to the net present value criterion. It has been suggested that the profitability index, the ratio between the present value of the future cash flows and initial investment, can also be used as a decisive criterion for undertaking a project. An analysis of these two ratio-form indices is presented in Section 5.4.

The net present value is an aggregate figure and it cannot be used when the projects have unequal lifespans. The internal rate of return is also based on an aggregate. "It is important to realize the limitations of these aggregates and to analyze the nature of their construction" (Samuelson 1983, 155). In Section 5.5 we therefore consider the equivalent annual index, a measure that can be employed when the projects have unequal lifespans. This section also analyzes some additional issues, like the relationship between the net present value and the internal rate of return criteria and some inconsistency problems.

5.2 NET PRESENT VALUE

When a firm undertakes a project, direct and indirect effects can occur for several periods. The management must first decide whether the project is worth undertaking. The firm is required to obtain an aggregate measure that will measure the extent to which the firm is better or worse off with the project in place. The management may have to choose intelligently between two mutually exclusive projects in the sense that with its limited budget only one project can be funded. The choice of developing a golf course or ski areas by a hotel may be a case in point.

The investment appraisal indicator, we discuss in this section, is the net present value (NPV). Assume that the capital market is perfect yielding an interest rate λ per period of time, say, a year. Assume that it is now year zero. Let B_t and C_t respectively be the money inflows (benefits) and outflows (costs) occurring in year t, where $t = 0, 1,..., T$; T being the last year that the project affects benefits and costs. Then, as observed in Chapter 2, the discounted present value of the inflows is given by $\sum_{t=0}^{T} \left(B_t / (1+\lambda)^t \right)$. Likewise, the discounted present value of the outflows is $\sum_{t=0}^{T} \left(C_t / (1+\lambda)^t \right)$. Then the NPV of the project is defined as

$$NPV = \sum_{t=0}^{T} \frac{B_t - C_t}{(1+\lambda)^t}. \tag{5.1}$$

It may be worthwhile to mention here that the reliability of the NPV depends on that of the discount rate. It gives the aggregate value in terms of current year dollars of all cash inflows and outflows induced by the project, both now and in the future. The indicator NPV is an appropriate yardstick with which we can judge the desirability of the project (see also Damodaran 2010).

If $NPV < 0$, that is, if discounted benefit is less than discounted cost, the project should be rejected, since it incurs loss to the firm. On the other hand, if $NPV > 0$, that is, if discounted benefit exceeds discounted cost, the project can be undertaken since it would increase the firm's profit. The positive magnitude of the NPV indicates the amount by which the firm becomes better off in terms of the present value. The management can, therefore, rank alternative projects in terms of their contributions to the firm's financial position. Thus, from a policy point of view, if alternative and mutually exclusive projects are available, the optimal policy is to choose the one that yields the highest NPV. If for any two projects the NPV is equal, the management is indifferent between the two. Some caution has to be exercised while using the NPV rule. There may be a choice regarding the scale or size of a project and in such case the chosen scale should be the one that maximizes the NPV. Also if a project can be undertaken at different time points, then the management should introduce it at the time at which its NPV is maximized.

Following our discussion in Chapter 2 again, if the discount rate is time dependent, which we denote by λ_s, then the NPV is $\sum_{t=0}^{T}\left((B_t - C_t)/(1+\lambda_t)^t\right)$. However, for simplicity, we assume that the discount rate is fixed since there is no essential difference between the evaluation procedures, using constant and non-constant discount rates. A second issue is concerning valuation of stream of returns in terms of present year's dollars. We can definitely measure the value in terms of any arbitrary year's dollars. For instance, the NPV of the stream of returns B_t and C_t in terms of year j dollars is $\sum_{t=0}^{T}\left((B_t - C_t)/(1+\lambda_t)^{t-j}\right)$. Some of the cash flows B_t and C_t may be subject to uncertainty. In Chapter 3 we discuss the issue of risk and uncertainty in details. Using the tools developed in the chapter we can calculate the expected values of uncertain cash flows.

Example 5.1: Consider two mutually exclusive projects, I and II, with four respective cash flows –2400 dollars and 800 dollars, 800 dollars, 800 dollars and 800 dollars; and –1800 dollars, 600 dollars, 600 dollars, 600 dollars, 600 dollars. The discount rate is 10 percent. We wish to identify the preferred alternative.

For project I the NPV is $NPV_I = \left((1-1.1^{-4})/.1\right)800 - 2400 = 2480 - 2400 = 80$. On the other hand, $NPV_{II} = \left((1-1.1^{-4})/.1\right)600 - 1800 = 1860 - 1800 = 60$. Hence the first project should be chosen.

5.3 INTERNAL RATE OF RETURN

While the NPV is a correct measure of a project's contribution to a firm's financial position, a second criterion, the internal rate of return (IRR), is often used to judge the viability of a project. The IRR of a project is defined as the rate of return for which its net present value is zero. That is, the IRR on an investment is the number, which when used as the rate of return, makes the discounted present value of benefits from the project equal to its discounted costs. More precisely, the IRR is implicitly defined by

$$\sum_{t=0}^{T} \frac{B_t - C_t}{(1 + IRR)^t} = 0. \tag{5.2}$$

Thus, while the NPV assumes that the rate of return is given and recommends acceptance of a project if its NPV is positive, the IRR rule looks for the rate of return for which the NPV is zero. Consequently, in a sense the IRR rule uses the reverse logic employed for determining the NPV.

Since equation (5.2) is a polynomial of degree T, it may have T solutions. For instance, if $T = 2$, we have

$$B_0 - C_0 + \frac{B_1 - C_1}{1 + IRR} + \frac{B_2 - C_2}{(1 + IRR)^2} = 0, \tag{5.3}$$

or,

$$(1 + IRR)^2 (B_0 - C_0) + (1 + IRR)(B_1 - C_1) + (B_2 - C_2) = 0,$$

which can be rewritten as

$$a(IRR)^2 + b(IRR) + c = 0, \tag{5.4}$$

where, and $a = (B_0 - C_0)$, $b = 2(B_0 - C_0) + (B_1 - C_1)$ and $c = (B_0 - C_0) + (B_1 - C_1) + (B_2 - C_2)$. This is a quadratic equation in IRR and it has two solutions. In fact, the number of solutions will depend on the number of times $B_t - C_t$ changes sign over time. Thus, in the above example, if $B_0 - C_0 = -7270$, $B_1 - C_1 = 17100$ and $B_2 - C_2 = -10000$, then $B_t - C_t$ changes sign twice in going from one year to the next, so there are two solutions ($IRR = 0.10, 0.25$) (see Boadway and Wildasin 1985).

Since equation (5.2) has in general T roots, this can be a significant obstacle to using the IRR notion for general net benefit streams. It is possible to rule out the existence of more than one IRR under certain realistic assumptions. In many cases the projects incur net costs in initial years ($B_t - C_t < 0$) and benefits in later years ($B_t - C_t > 0$). For instance, a bank that provides a loan to an organization has a cash outflow initially, which is followed by a sequence of cash inflows. In such a case the sign changes only once and the IRR is uniquely determined. This is shown more formally in the following theorem.

Theorem 5.1: Assume that the net benefit stream $\left\{ B_0 - C_0, \dfrac{B_1 - C_1}{(1 + \lambda)}, \ldots\ldots, \dfrac{B_T - C_T}{((1 + \lambda)^T}\right\}$

has $(B_0 - C_0) < 0$ and $B_t - C_t \geq 0$ for all $t = 1, 2 \ldots T$. Suppose also that $\displaystyle\sum_{t=0}^{T}(B_t - C_t) > 0$.

Then there exists a unique positive internal rate of return.

Proof: See Appendix.

Theorem 5.1 gives us sufficient conditions for existence of a unique IRR and its positivity. It says that the net benefit of a project is negative at the initial year. This is reasonable since at the outset the firm has an investment cost. From next year onwards its cash flows are nonnegative, which is again a sensible assumption. Positivity of the sum of all net benefits is a natural condition. It then follows that the positive IRR is unique. Note that the condition $\displaystyle\sum_{t=0}^{T}(B_t - C_t) > 0$ demands that

$B_t - C_t > 0$ for at least one t, $1 \leq t \leq T$. If it is possible to determine an IRR, then one can use it as an indicator of valuation of a stream of net benefits if IRR $> \lambda$.

This implies that the NPV is positive at the discount rate λ and vice versa. The IRR criterion thus involves a comparison with the discount rate λ, given that the IRR is unique. The IRR does not incorporate the scales of the projects. If there are mutually exclusive projects, then the management should choose the one with the highest IRR. If the discount rate changes over time, the IRR criterion may not be useful. For instance, if there are two discount rates λ_1 and λ_2, and if the inequality $\lambda_1 < IRR < \lambda_2$ prevails, then the required comparison between the IRR and the discount rate is not defined here. This is irrespective of whether the NPV is positive or not.

We may now illustrate Theorem 5.1 by an example.

Example 5.2: Consider a project with the stream of cash flows: -1000 dollars, 550 dollars and 635 dollars. The discount rate yielded by the perfect capital market is 5 percent. We wish to check whether the sufficient conditions specified in Theorem 5.1 are satisfied. Also, it is necessary to verify whether the investment is worthwhile by the IRR criterion. Note that $(B_0 - C_o) = -1000\, dollars < 0, B_1 - C_1 = 550\ dollars > 0$ and $B_2 - C_2 = 634\, dollars > 0$. Further, $\sum_{t=0}^{2}(B_t - C_t) = 184\, dollars > 0$. Hence all the three sufficient conditions of the theorem are satisfied. Consequently, there exists a unique positive IRR. It is easy to see that the value of the IRR is 12 percent and the NPV is 100 dollars. Since the IRR is greater than the discount rate, the project should be undertaken.

5.4 BENEFIT–COST RATIO AND PROFITABILITY INDEX

The management can also use the benefit–cost ratio of a project to check whether the financial position of a firm improves by undertaking the project. It is defined as

$$\frac{B}{C} = \frac{\sum_{t=0}^{T} B_t / (1+\lambda)^t}{\sum_{t=0}^{T} C_t / (1+\lambda)^t}. \tag{5.5}$$

Thus, while the NPV is the difference between the discounted present values of benefits and costs, the B/C measure is simply their ratio. Clearly, the ratio B/C is greater (less) than unity if the NPV is positive (negative). The converse is also true. That is, if the NPV is positive (negative) then the ratio B/C is greater (less) than unity. Hence for a specific project the measures essentially convey the same information. Higher values of both the NPV and the B/C criteria are regarded as better. But they can rank alternative projects in different directions. For instance, suppose the discounted present values of benefits and costs of project I are respectively 340 dollars and 160 dollars and for project II the corresponding figures are 400 dollars and 200 dollars. Then the NPV criterion prefers II to I $\big((400-200)\text{dollars} > (340-160)\text{dollars}\big)$, whereas according to the B/C criterion I is better than II $\big((340/160) > (400/200)\big)$.

Another measure that has been employed to judge viability of a project is the profitability index (PI) defined as the ratio between the present value of the future cash flows and initial investment. Formally,

$$PI = \frac{\sum_{t=1}^{T}(B_t - C_t)/(1+\lambda)^t}{C_0}. \tag{5.6}$$

Thus, the PI has a structure similar to that of the measure B/C. Both are expressed in ratio form, but while the former uses the discounted future cash flows and the initial investment, the latter uses the discounted cash inflows and outflows. If the PI takes on a value greater than unity, acceptance of the project is recommended. A value of the PI less than unity indicates that the discounted present value of the future cash flow is less than initial investment and hence the project should be turned down. If $PI > 1$, then $NPV > 0$ and vice versa. The PI is generally applied when the firm has a limited supply of the capital budget. Therefore, the objective of the firm will be to rank the projects in descending order of their PI values and recommend acceptance of all those projects from the top until the limited budget is exhausted. In case of a tie between two PI values, the tie should be broken arbitrarily.

Example 5.3: From Example 5.1 it follows that for project I, $PI_I = 2480/2400 = 1.03$. Likewise, $PI_{II} = 1860/1800 = 1.03$. The firm has a limited budget of 2500 dollars. Its budget allows it to select either of the two projects but not both simultaneously. However, by the PI criterion the firm is indifferent between the two projects. Probably it should choose project II because the saving in this case is $(2500-1800)\text{dollars} = 700\text{dollars}$, which is higher than 100 dollars, the corresponding saving when project II is selected. The common B/C value for these two projects is also 1.03. Thus, the projects are ranked indifferently by the B/C criterion as well. But Example 5.1 clearly indicates that by the NPV criterion, project I should be undertaken. This clearly establishes inconsistency between the NPV and the PI and B/C criteria.

5.5 SOME ADDITIONAL ISSUES

Section 5.3 provides a brief discussion on the relationship between the NPV and the IRR. In this section, we first analyze this issue further. Following Boadway and Wildasin (1984), we consider two projects, I and II. Their stream of net benefits $B_t - C_t$ in three consecutive years, the IRRs and the NPVs for three different rates of return are shown below.

Table 5.1 Net Benefits and Net Present Values

Project	Benefit in Year (in dollars)			Net Present Values (NPV) at the Rate of Return (in percent)			
	0	1	2	IRR	2 percent	5.2 percent	7 percent
I	−1000	0	1210	0.10	163	93	57
II	−1000	1150	0	0.15	127	93	75

The IRR for I is 10 percent and for II is 15 percent, thus this criterion would rank II above I. Now, if $\lambda = 2$ percent, the NPV for I exceeds that for II. If funds can be borrowed and lent at 2 percent, then the stream of net benefits of I can be converted into a stream of benefits through capital market transactions that will Pareto dominate the stream of net benefits of II. Of two streams of net benefits $\{u_t\}_0^T = (u_0, u_1, \ldots u_T)$ and $\{z_t\}_0^T = (z_0, z_1, \ldots z_T)$ over the same lifespan, the former is said to Pareto dominate the latter if $u_i \geq z_i$ for all i, with strict inequality for some i, $0 \leq i \leq T$. For example, if 1150 dollars is borrowed in year one, a total of 1173 (= 1150 × 1.02) dollars will have to be repaid in period two, leaving (1210–1173) dollars = 37 dollars for investment elsewhere or for consumption. Therefore, a net stream of (−1000, 1150, 37) can be generated by combining this borrowing transaction with the net benefit stream of project I. Obviously; this benefit stream Pareto dominates that of II. However, it should be noted that the Pareto dominance rule is an incomplete relation. That is, there may exist net benefit streams that may not be comparable by this criterion. For example, the net benefit streams of projects I and II are non-comparable by the Pareto dominance principle. However, Pareto dominance is a transitive relation. That is, given any three net benefit streams $\{u_t\}_0^T, \{y_t\}_0^T$ and $\{z_t\}_0^T$, if the first Pareto dominates the second and the second Pareto dominates the third, then the first Pareto dominates the third.

In general, we can use capital market transactions to convert the net benefits of one project into some other net benefit stream, which Pareto dominates the net benefit stream of another project that has lower NPV. This clearly indicates that the NPV criterion implicitly takes into consideration the cost of financing, whereas the IRR criterion does not. This example illustrates inconsistencies of the IRR rule.

Figure 5.1 shows that for this example the NPVs are decreasing functions of the rate of interest λ. The IRR is that value of the interest rate at which the NPV curve intersects the horizontal axis. Note that the NPVs of the two projects are equal at $\lambda = 5.2$ percent and II has a higher NPV than I at $\lambda = 7$ percent. In fact, for any interest rate below 5.2 percent, the NPV of II is lower than that of I and the opposite happens for all interest rates above 5.2 percent. The value of λ plays an

Figure 5.1 Net Present Value and Internal Rate of Return

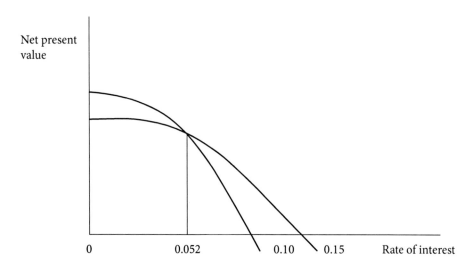

important role in arriving at the inconsistency of the IRR we discussed here.

While using the *NPV* criterion for selecting projects, we must exercise some caution in case there is a fixed capital budget. For instance, suppose an organization has a fixed capital budget of 1000 dollars and there is a choice among four projects I, II, III and IV whose net benefits in two years and the NPVs at the rate of return 5 percent are shown below (see Boadway and Wildasin, 1985). The NPV rule ranks the projects in terms of decreasing preference as I, III, II and IV. If I is chosen, limited funds would not permit undertaking of II or III. However, funds would permit joint undertaking of II and III. Alternatively, IV and I can be undertaken jointly. Since the combined NPVs of II and III exceed that of I and IV, the former pair should be chosen.

Table 5.2 Net Benefits and Net Present Values

Project	Net Benefit in Year (in dollars) 0	1	Net Present Value at $\lambda = 5$ percent
I	−800	950	105
II	−500	600	71
III	−400	500	76
IV	−200	240	28

Thus, in case a capital budget constraint exists, the relevant comparison should be made between the NPVs of alternative combinations of the projects.

Use of the NPV and the IRR for comparing projects with different scale, size and lifespan is not desirable. For instance, the comparison between a 20-year project with an initial investment of 200000 dollars with a 5-year project having an initial investment of 20000 dollars does not seem quite plausible. In fact, the first project can be treated as equivalent to ten second projects. For comparing projects with different lives, NPV and IRR rules are inappropriate. The reason is that they are based on aggregate figures. Consequently, a comparison between two projects with different lives using these rules is improper. One appropriate criterion here can be the annual equivalent, which is defined as the ratio between the NPV and an annuity factor. An annuity is a promise to pay N dollars in each period for T periods. The discounted present value of such a promise is $N\left(\left(1-(1+\lambda)^{-T}\right)/\lambda\right)$ (see Chapter 7). The inverse $\dfrac{1}{\left(\left(1-(1+\lambda)^{-T}\right)/\lambda\right)}$ of the multiplicative factor of N in this expression is called the loan repayment factor, the inverse of the discounted present value $\left(\left(1-(1+\lambda)^{-T}\right)/\lambda\right)$ of the income stream that pays one dollar of income in each period for T periods. The inverse $\left(\left(1-(1+\lambda)^{-T}\right)/\lambda\right)$ of the loan repayment factor is called the annuity factor. Then the annual equivalent of a project is defined as

$$AE = \frac{NPV}{\left(\dfrac{1-(1+\lambda)^{-T}}{\lambda}\right)}. \tag{5.7}$$

Thus, we can as well say that the AE is obtained by multiplying the NPV by the loan repayment factor.

To understand the issue better, let us consider an organization, which can use two machines I and II independently to produce an output. Suppose machine I needs replacement after every 5 years and machine II should be replaced after every 4 years. Thus, the two machines, although they have different lives, are substitutes. The NPV of the cash flow over the lifespan of Machine I is higher than the corresponding figure associated with machine II. An example can be two varieties of computer with different lives. The organization plans on continuing this production process for T years. Then machine I should be replaced $\left[\dfrac{T}{5}\right]$ times, where $\left[\dfrac{T}{5}\right]$ stands for the integral part of $\dfrac{T}{5}$. For instance, if $T = 22$, then $\left[\dfrac{T}{5}\right] = 4$. Likewise, machine II needs $\left[\dfrac{T}{4}\right]$ replacements. Now, the use of the AE implies that the project can be replaced by an exactly identical project. As argued above, the use of the NPV rule is inappropriate here because it gives an aggregate figure and is related to the decision for a one-time investment without any consideration for repetition. Hence comparison between the two aggregate figures that are based respectively on 5 and 4 years is not correct. If the aggregate is transformed into an average or an annual figure, then the comparison between the transformed figures is quite appropriate. The annual equivalent cash flow AE, the normalized NPV, obtained by dividing the NPV by the annuity factor, is an annual figure and hence is a suitable measure in this context. For mutually exclusive projects, the one with the highest AE, should be undertaken. Thus, for a choice between two types of machines that can be replaced any arbitrary number of times, the firm should select the one with higher AE.

Applied Example 5.1: The IRR is an important measure of profitability. Laitinen (1997) considered a method of estimation of the IRR, which is based on the model assumptions that the lifespan of investment projects is infinite and that the distribution of the relative cash inflow (the cash inflow of a specific variable divided by the total cash inflow) is constant and geometric. The model was applied to three different samples of Finish firms. The estimated results provide information on current profitability and a prediction about its future changes.

Applied Example 5.2: Traditional calculations of net present values do not incorporate uncertainty into the variables concerned. Dimakos et al (2006) considered a stochastic model to describe simultaneous behavior of risk factors that have high influence on the uncertainty of the NPV of the considered project. London Metal Exchange Zinc time series data were used for estimation purpose. The probability distribution of the underlying risk factors over the time horizon of the project was obtained by simulation from this model. They then obtained the probability distribution of the NPV by incorporating this distribution in the NPV calculation.

APPENDIX

Proof of Theorem 5.1: Letting $\dfrac{1}{(1+\lambda)} = k$, we can rewrite the equation $\sum_{t=0}^{T} \dfrac{B_t - C_t}{(1+\lambda)^t} = 0$

as $\sum_{t=0}^{T}(B_t - C_t)k^t = 0$. Note that for the polynomial $f(k) = \sum_{t=0}^{T}(B_t - C_t)k^t$, we

have $f(0) = B_0 - C_0 < 0, f(1) = \sum_{t=0}^{T}(B_t - C_t) > 0$. Since we have $f(0) < 0$ and

$f(1) > 0, f(0) < 0 < f(1)$. We can now apply the intermediate value theorem to the real valued continuous function f defined on the interval $[0, 1]$. The intermediate value theorem says that if g is a continuous real valued function defined on the interval $[a, b]$ where $g(a) < g(b)$ and if c is such that $g(a) < c < g(b)$, then there exists a point $z \in (a, b)$ such that $g(z) = c$ (Rudin, 1976, p.93). Thus, in our case there must be a number $\bar{k}$, where $0 < \bar{k} < 1$, such that $f(\bar{k}) = 0$. That is, there is a root of the equation $f(k)=0$ lying between zero and one.

Now, the derivative of $f(k)$ with respect k is $\sum_{t=1}^{T} t(B_t - C_t)k^{t-1}$. In view of our

assumption that $B_t - C_t \geq 0$ for all $t = 1, 2, T$ and $\sum_{t=0}^{T}(B_t - C_t) > 0$, it must be the

case that $B_t - C_t > 0$ for at least one t, $1 \leq t \leq T$. Consequently, by positivity of

$k \in (0, 1)$ and t, $\sum_{t=1}^{T} t(B_t - C_t)k^{t-1}$ is positive for all $0 < k < 1$. Now, a function with a

positive derivative on its domain is increasing. This means that the function $f(k)$ is increasing over the interval $[0, 1]$. Hence it cannot change sign more than once as k moves from 0 to 1. In other words, the graph of $f(k)$ as k goes from 0 to 1 intersects the horizontal axis exactly once. That is, the value of k that solves the equation

$f(k) = 0$ is unique. This implies that the positive internal rate of return $\lambda = \frac{1}{k} - 1$ is

unique. This completes the proof of the theorem.

BIBLIOGRAPHICAL NOTES

An illuminating discussion on net present value is available in Damodaran (2010). Internal rate of return and related issues are presented quite elegantly in Boadway and Wildasin (1984).

EXERCISES

1. Each of the following statements is either true or false. If the statement is true prove it. If it is false, give a counter-example or justify your answer by logical reasoning.
   (a) Since positivity of the net present value is necessary and sufficient for the condition that the benefit–cost ratio is greater than unity, the two rules will rank all projects in the same way.
   (b) The benefit–cost ratio and the profitability index of a project can never coincide.
   (c) The net present value decreases monotonically as the rate of interest rises.
   (d) The annuity factor is a monotonically non-decreasing function of the rate of interest.

(e) Assuming that the initial inflow is zero, the profitability index is greater than the unity if and only if the benefit–cost ratio is greater than unity.

2. Suppose the market rate of interest is 5 percent. Consider two projects, I and II, with the following stream of benefits.

	Benefit in Year (in dollars)		
Project	0	1	2
I	−1000	550	634
II	−1000	1150	0

(a) Calculate their internal rates of return and rank them in terms of decreasing preference.
(b) Then show that I is preferred to II by the NPV criterion. Are the rankings by the NPV and IRR criteria consistent?
(c) Show that through capital market transactions the stream of net benefits of I can be converted into a stream of benefits that Pareto dominates the stream of net benefits of II.

3. Demonstrate Theorem 5.1 graphically.

4. Give explicit reasoning for using the annual equivalent rule for ranking two projects when their lives differ.

5. Consider two machines whose lifespans are respectively 4 years and 5 years. The net present values of cash flows over the lives of the machines are respectively 3000 dollars and 4000 dollars. Assume that the rate of interest yielded by the perfect capital market is 10 percent. Calculate the annual equivalent of the two cash flows.

6. Provide two sufficient conditions for the benefit–cost ratio and the net present value criteria to rank two mutually exclusive projects in the same direction.

CHAPTER 6

Financial Structure of a Firm

6.1 INTRODUCTION

A firm's financial or capital structure is a composition of its liabilities. More precisely, it refers to the way in which the financing of the firm takes place through a combination of debt and equity. In order to determine the value of a firm, it is necessary to evaluate the inflows and outflows over time. The Modigliani–Miller (1958, 1961, 1963) theorem is concerned with the process of determination of the value of a firm. No single result has been more important than the Modigliani–Miller theorem of capital structure in the development of the field of corporate finance. The theorem says that if the capital market is perfect, then the value of a firm is independent of the method by which a firm finances its asset. This result forms the basis for examining the reason why in reality the method of financing or capital structure may affect a firm's value. It can be useful to investigate in what respects actual valuation may deviate from the valuation that arises when the method of financing is assumed to be irrelevant. We, therefore, analyze the Modigliani–Miller theorem in Section 6.2 of this chapter. Section 6.3 provides a discussion on the assumptions of the theorem.

6.2 THE MODIGLIANI–MILLER THEOREM

The Modigliani–Miller theorem specifies the conditions under which the value of a firm remains unaffected by how it is financed. It forms the basis of modern thinking of capital structure. It relies on the assumptions that investors care only about risks and returns, about whom such views are common, and that there is competitiveness in the capital market—that is, the capital market is perfect in the sense that all individuals and corporations can borrow and lend at the same rate, there is equal access to all relevant information, and there are no transaction costs, default risks and market imperfections such as taxes. It consists of two theorems, which can be extended to the case with taxes.

The approach to the problem is as follows. There can be a categorization of firms in terms of the income classes to which they belong. Firms belonging to a given income class have the characteristic that the corresponding random time stream of net incomes are perfectly positively correlated. In other words, for any two firms belonging to the same income class, income of one will be a positive multiple of that of another. The beliefs of all investors about the probability distributions of income streams are assumed to be the same.

We write V_u for the value of an unlevered firm—that is, the price of buying a firm composed only of equity—and V_l for the value of a levered firm—that is, the price of buying a firm composed of debt and equity. The values of debt and equity are respectively the discounted present values of payments to debt and equity holders. Leverage is defined as *debt/(debt + equity)*. If a firm is 25 percent equity-financed and 75 percent debt-financed, then the firm's ratio of debt to total financing (75 percent) is firm's leverage. The levered firm is assumed to be otherwise identical to the unlevered firm. Then the first theorem without taxes says that $V_u = V_l$.

The first Modigliani–Miller theorem can be formally sated as follows:

Theorem 6.1 Modigliani–Miller Theorem I (without taxes): If V_u is the value of an unlevered firm and V_l is the value of a levered firm, and the two firms are identical except for their financial structures, then $V_u = V_l$.

This theorem thus says that the value of a firm is independent of its capital structure. That is, it is a "law of conservation of value" (Brealey and Myers 2003, 468). To understand why this should hold, suppose an investor plans on buying one of the two firms u and l. Instead of buying shares of l, he could buy shares of u and borrow the same amount of money as firm l borrows. The returns to either of these two investments would be equal. Hence the price of l must be equal to the price of u minus the amount borrowed, which is same as l's debt.

To see the implication of $V_u \neq V_l$, suppose $V_u < V_l$ holds. Then an investor could get something for nothing by borrowing and selling stock in the levered firm, and buying stock in the unlevered firm. A similar conclusion holds if we have $V_u > V_l$. That is, arbitrage opportunities would exist if $V_u = V_l$ does not hold. In financial economics, arbitrage is a transaction or portfolio that offers profits without any risk. For instance, if a contract is offered at 40 dollars on one exchange and bid at 41 dollars on another, then a trader can make a risk-free profit of 1 dollar by buying it at one price and selling it at the other. In this case arbitrage opportunities exist.

Proof of Theorem 6.1: Let E_u and E_l denote the market values of equity (shares) in firms u and l. Then we have the following relations: $V_u = E_u$ and $V_l = E_l + D_l$, with D_l denoting the debt outstanding in firm l. Because the two firms have identical income streams, we can denote the income for any firm in any period simply by y.

Let m_u and m_l denote the incomes available for the stockholders in u and l, which are given by $m_l = y - \lambda D_l$ and $m_u = y$, where λ is the risk-free interest rate.

Suppose now $V_u < V_l$. Consider an individual who owns a percent of firm l's stock so that he receives $a(y - \lambda D_l)$ from his holdings. Suppose he sells his stock obtaining aE_l and borrows additional aD_l (at λ percent interest), using all this to buy shares in u. The fraction of firm u's shares that he can buy is $a(E_l + D_l)/V_u = aV_l/V_u$. Therefore, the income he will earn is given by $a(V_l/V_u)y - \lambda a D_l = a((V_l/V_u)y - \lambda D_l) > a(y - \lambda D_l)$, since $V_u < V_l$. Thus, if $V_u < V_l$, then every stockholder in l will sell his shares and buy firm u's shares, which forces up the market value of firm u and lowers the market value of firm l. This riskless arbitrage operation will continue as long as $V_u < V_l$.

If $V_u > V_l$, then firm u is overvalued. Consider an individual who owns b percent of firm u's stock so that he receives the amount by from his holdings. Suppose that he sells his stock obtaining bE_u, which he invests in firm l's stocks and bonds as follows: he buys bE_u/V_l percent of l's stocks and bE_u/V_l percent of l's bonds. Then his new income is $(bE_u/V_l)(y - \lambda D_l) + (bE_u/V_l)(\lambda D_l) = (bV_u/V_l)y > by$, since $V_u > V_l$ by assumption. Thus, if $V_u > V_l$, stockholders in firm u will sell their shares and buy shares and bonds in firm l and this continues until $V_u = V_l$. Riskless arbitrage ensures that both firms will have the same market value whatever is their capital structure. This completes the proof of the theorem.

Example 6.1: We may illustrate the theorem using an example. Suppose firm A is an all-equity firm with 2000 shares, the value of each share being 15 dollars. Therefore, the value of firm A is 30000 (= 15 × 2000) dollars. Firm B is a levered firm, which is identical to firm A except its capital structure has a debt of 10000 dollars. Therefore, by the Modigliani–Miller theorem 1 (without taxes), the market value of Firm B's equity is (30000–10000) dollars = 20000 dollars.

Suppose firm A's expected income in the year is 9000 dollars. Therefore, expected return for an investor who owns 20 percent of the firm's equity is 1800 (= 9000 × 0.20) dollars. In contrast, while firm B also expects to earn 9000 dollars, it has to pay 10 percent interest on its debt. Since the market value of Firm B's debt is 10000 dollars, its interest payment against debt is 1000 (= 10000 × 0.10) dollars. Therefore, the amount of the firm's earnings available for equity holders is (9000–1000) = 8000 dollars. Hence return for an investor who owns 20 percent of firm B's equity is1600 (= 8000 × 0.20) dollars. Since the value of firm A is 30000, it will cost 6000 (=30000 × 0.20) dollars to buy 20 percent of the firm's equity and the cost for buying 20 percent of firm B's equity is 4000 (=20000 × 0.20) dollars. To purchase 20 percent of firm A's equity, an investor using 4000 dollars of his money has to borrow 2000 (= 6000 – 4000) dollars and pay an annual interest of 10 percent on this borrowing. His income now from 20 percent equity of firm A is 1800 dollars and his interest payment is 200 (= 2000 × 0.10) dollars. Therefore, the cash flow to the investor is 1600 (1800–200) dollars. This exactly matches the amount the investor receives from 20 percent ownership of firm B.

The second Modigliani–Miller theorem (without taxes) is stated involving the expected rate of return on the firm. Formally,

Theorem 6.2 Modigliani–Miller Theorem II (without taxes): Under the assumptions of the Modigliani–Miller theorem I, the expected rate of return on the firm and the firm's cost of capital financing do not depend on leverage.

To understand this theorem, we consider two time periods, 0 (now) and 1 (future). Let E_l^0 be the market value of equity in the levered firm under consideration in period 0 and its expected value in period 1 is denoted by E_l^1. Suppose D_l^0 and D_l^1 stand for the corresponding debt figures. Then letting V_l^j be the value of the firm l in period j, we have $V_l^j = E_l^j + D_l^j$, where $j = 0, 1$. The expected rates of return on the firm, debt and equity are given respectively by $\lambda_V = \left(V_l^1 - V_l^0\right)/V_l^0, \lambda_D = \left(D_l^1 - D_l^0\right)/D_l^0$ and $\lambda_E = \left(E_l^1 - E_l^0\right)/E_l^0$. Substituting $V_l^0 = E_l^0 + D_l^0$ and $V_l^1 = E_l^1 + D_l^1$ in the definition of λ_V, we can easily derive that $\lambda_V = \left(D_l^0/V_l^0\right)\lambda_D + \left(E_l^0/V_l^0\right)\lambda_E$. That is, the expected rate of return on the firm is the weighted average of expected rates of return on debt and equity, where the weights are the proportions of the market value of debt and equity in the value of the firm. Expected return on the firm depends on the values of the firm in periods 0 and 1. But in view of Theorem 6.1, which follows from our assumptions, the value of firm is independent of leverage. Consequently, the expected return on the firm and the firm's cost of capital financing are independent of leverage. This formally demonstrates the theorem.

To understand the theorem in greater details, we may restate it in terms of the debt-to-equity ratio. The debt-to-equity ratio of a firm is given by its total liabilities divided by the shareholders' equity. This ratio is used for measuring how solvent the firm is financially. A high value of the ratio (greater than one) will indicate that the firm has been financing its growth with too much debt. As a result, additional interest payments may make the firm's earnings volatile. A value of this ratio that is less than one indicates that the majority of financing takes place through equity. Lenders are sensitive about this ratio because a high value of the ratio may put the money they lend at the risk of non-repayment. It is, therefore, natural to look for the debt-to-equity ratio that maximizes the value of the firm in a given income class.

Now, note that we can rewrite leverage *debt/(debt + equity)* of a firm as $\left(\dfrac{1}{1+\left(equity/debt\right)}\right)$. The ratio *(equity/debt)* is the inverse of the debt-to-equity ratio. As leverage increases, the ratio *(equity/debt)* in its denominator must decrease and hence the debt-to-equity ratio will increase. Conversely, if the debt-to-equity ratio increases, *(equity/debt)* decreases, which in turn implies that leverage increases. Thus, because of monotonic relationship between leverage and debt-to-equity ratio, we can replace leverage in the statement of Theorem 6.2 by debt-to-equity ratio. Formally, the Modigliani–Miller theorem II (without taxes) may be restated as: Under the assumptions of the Modigliani–Miller theorem I, the expected rate of return on the firm and the firm's cost of capital financing do not depend the debt-to-equity ratio.

Solving the equation $\lambda_V = \left(D_I^0/V_I^0\right)\lambda_D + \left(E_I^0/V_I^0\right)\lambda_E$ for λ_E we get

$$\lambda_E = \lambda_V + \frac{D_I^0}{E_I^0}(\lambda_V - \lambda_D). \tag{6.1}$$

This equation shows that the cost of equity (the rate of return λ_E on the equity of a levered firm) equals the sum of the cost of capital for an otherwise identical all equity firm (the rate of return λ_V on the capital of an unlevered firm, which is identical in all other respects) and the excess of the cost of capital over the cost of debt (the interest rate λ_D on debt finance) multiplied by the ratio $\left(D_I^0/V_I^0\right)$. If leverage is zero, which implies that $\left(D_I^0/V_I^0\right)$ is zero, the cost of capital and the cost of equity are the same. If debt is risk free, then λ_D is the constant risk-free rate of return λ. Since λ_V is independent of leverage, in a situation with a risk-free rate of return the cost of equity is linearly and increasingly related to the ratio $\left(D_I^0/V_I^0\right)$.

A very high debt-to-equity ratio (leverage) makes debt very risky. In such a case the cost of debt is likely to increase, that is, after a certain level of the debt-to-equity ratio the rate of return on debt will exceed the risk-free rate λ and is likely to increase gradually. A high debt-to-equity ratio may also lead to a high required return on equity. This is because with high debt, higher risks are involved for equity holders and therefore there may be a demand for a higher rate of return.

Example 6.2: Suppose firm A has an outstanding debt of 40000 dollars and the firm's debt to its equity ratio is 0.4. Then the market value of its equity is 100000 $(=\dfrac{40000}{0.4})$ dollars. Thus, the value of firm A is (100000 + 40000) dollars = 140000 dollars. Suppose $\lambda_D = 10$ percent. Then the firm's interest payment on debt is 4000 (= 40000 × 0.10) dollars. The firm expects to generate an earning of 30000 dollars. Hence its annual earning net of debt is 26000 (= 30000 – 4000) dollars. Given that the market value of the firm's equity is 100000 dollars, the expected return on the firm's equity (λ_e) is 26 percent $(=\dfrac{26000}{100000} \times 100)$. Then by the Modigliani–Miller theorem II (without taxes), the expected rate of return λ_V on the assets of an all equity firm is given by $0.26 = \lambda_V + 0.4(\lambda_V - 0.10)$, from which we get $\lambda_V \approx 0.21$.

The Modigliani–Miller theorems with taxes are reformulations of their theorems without taxes. Firms have to pay corporate tax on their income, but interest expenses can be deducted as a cost, so that tax is payable only on net income (income less interest). For instance, in the US interest payments on debt are excluded from corporate taxes (see Vilamil 2008). However, the income of equity holders is taxable. Thus, debt and equity are treated asymmetrically in terms of taxes. Since the levered firm and the unlevered firm are identical in all other respects, we denote the common earning before tax by I_{BT}. Then the unlevered firm's earning after tax is $I_{BT}(1 - t_{co})$, where t_{co} is the corporate tax rate. The levered firm's earning after tax is $(1 - t_{co})(I_{BT} - \lambda_D D_l) + \lambda_D D_l = (1 - t_{co})I_{BT} + t_{co}\lambda_D D_l$, where, as before, D_l is the debt outstanding in the firm. The amount $t_{co}\lambda_D D_l$ is referred to as the interest tax shield. Observe that this is the amount by which the post-tax earnings of the two firms differ. Assume that the cash flows are perpetual (see Chapter 7). Then the discounted present value of the tax shield is $(t_{co}\lambda_D D_l/\lambda_D) = t_{co}D_l$. Now, under taxation, the value of the unlevered firm is $V_u = I_{BT}(1 - t_{co})/\lambda_E$. Likewise, $V_l = I_{BT}(1 - t_{co})/\lambda_E + t_{co}D_l$. Hence $V_l = V_u + t_{co}D_l$.

The above discussion enables us to state the following:

Theorem 6.3. Modigliani–Miller Theorem I (with taxes): Under the assumptions, except non-taxability, of the Modigliani–Miller theorem I, the value of a levered firm equals the sum of the value of an unlevered firm and the discounted present value of the interest tax shield, that is, $V_l = V_u + t_{co}D_l$, where t_{co} is the corporate tax rate.

Theorem 6.3 is a modification of the Modigliani–Miller leverage irrelevance theorem (Theorem 6.1) in the sense that the value of the levered firm is now higher than the value of the unlevered firm. The difference between the two values arises because in the present case the splitting of the cash flow takes place among shareholders, bondholders and the government (recipient of tax). Clearly, the value of the firm increases as leverage increases. The value of the levered firm is an increasing function of debt. This means that a firm can increase its value by increasing the level of borrowings. But investors are payers of personal taxes as well and they will value a company if it can minimize the combination of corporate and personal taxes (see Brav and Maug 1999 and Brealey and Myers 2003).

The tax counterpart to Theorem 6.2 can be stated as:

Theorem 6.4 Modigliani–Miller Theorem II (with taxes):

$$\lambda_E = \lambda_V + \frac{D_l^0}{E_l^0}(\lambda_V - \lambda_D)(1 - t_{co}). \tag{6.2}$$

As in the case of Theorem 6.3, the firm is taxed at the rate t_{co} on earnings after interest cost. Theorem 6.4, like its non-tax counterpart, shows that the cost of equity λ_E rises with leverage because the role of risk still remains.

6.3 DISCUSSION

One critical assumption of the Modigliani–Miller result is that there is no risk of default. Default occurs when the firm is unable to pay the interest on its debt and losses occur to the bondholders. The market value of the firm's assets is less than the face amount of the debt. If the probability of debt-to-equity ratio increases the probability of default, there will be an impact on the value of the firm. Bonds issued by a firm when it has a high debt-to-equity ratio are different from the bonds it issues when the debt-to-equity ratio is low.

Another problem concerns the common belief of all investors about the probability distributions of income streams. The equity holders care not only for their incomes but also for market valuation of their shares. It is not sufficient to assume that all the individuals agree as to the income class for any given firm. We also need to assume that all the individuals know that all the individuals agree and that all the individuals know that all the individuals know that all the individuals agree and so on. That is, the knowledge of income class for any given firm is a common knowledge. The common knowledge assumption plays crucial role in the non-arbitrage argument (see Aumann 1966 for a formal treatment of common knowledge).

The result is based on a partial equilibrium framework. Stiglitz (1969) showed in the context of a general equilibrium that the validity of the theorem does not depend on the competitiveness of the capital market or on the agreement of the individuals about the probability distributions of the income streams (see Vilamil 2008 for a discussion).

Consider a firm with value V and debt with a face value of Q. Equity can be regarded as a European call option with strike price Q. The price at maturity is the value of the firm V. Consequently, the payoff to shareholders is $max(V - Q, 0)$ (see Chapter 8). With an increase in the value of V, the payoff to shareholders increases. But this as well increases the risk involved in payments. Thus, an increase in risk in payment is advantageous for shareholders. The creditors claim is given by

$$Q \ if \ V > Q, \qquad\qquad (6.3)$$
$$V \ if \ V \leq Q,$$

which we can write as $min(Q, V)$. This claim decreases with an increase in the value of V and hence with an increase in risk. In order to protect their payment, the creditors might try to introduce some clause, like asset sales must be used to pay down debt, into the contract (see Brav and Maug 1999)

Applied Example 6.1: Agency cost in corporate finance refers to the cost that arises because of information asymmetry existing between the agents (the managers of the firm) and the shareholders (the principals). More generally, this can be treated as a consequence of a principal–agent problem. In a principal–agent relationship the principal's welfare depends on the action of agent. A principal-agent problem arises when the agent pursues his own objectives rather than the goal of the principal. In India it is difficult for most of the stockholders of large firms to receive information on the performance of the managers. Managers are often more interested in growth rather than profit of the firm. With more rapid growth and larger market share, managers enjoy more perks. This is a principal-agent problem because of the agents' objectives to pursue their own goals.

Berger and Patti (2002) employed the data on the US commercial banks from 1990 to 1995 to test the agency cost hypothesis that increasing leverage or decreasing equity-to-asset ratio is associated with a decrease in agency costs of outside equity. The study used detailed financial data for a large number of banks. As pointed out by the authors, although the banking industry is regulated, there are agency costs in banks. Their findings report that the hypothesis is statistically and economically significant.

BIBLIOGRAPHICAL NOTES

For the Modigliani–Miller theorems, the bible in the industry is Brealey and Myers (2003). Quirk (1986) is also a good reference for these theorems. Highly innovative discussions on the assumptions of the theorems can be found in Stiglitz (1969), Brav and Maug (1999) and Vilamil (2008).

EXERCISES

1. Each of the following statements is either true or false. If the statement is true prove it. If it is false, give a counter-example or justify your answer by logical reasoning.
   (a) In the absence of corporate tax, as the debt-to-equity ratio of a firm increases, the rate of return on the firm as a whole decreases.
   (b) In a world with corporate tax borrowing is always preferable.
   (c) The required return on a firm is independent of its capital structure.
   (d) In the absence of corporate tax, the plot of the value of a levered firm against debt-to-equity ratio is upward sloping.
   (e) In a risk-free world, in the absence of corporate tax, the cost of equity is increasingly related to leverage when debt is not too high.
2. How does the graph of the value of a levered firm against the debt-to-equity ratio in a world with corporate tax look? Show the discounted present value of the tax shield in the same graph.
3. Critically examine the assumptions of the Modigliani–Miller theorem.
4. Consider an unlevered firm that pays out 2000 dollars to equity holders. The corporate tax rate is 0.3. A levered firm pays out 1900 dollars and 100 dollars respectively to equity holders and bondholders. The cost of equity is 10 percent. Determine the present value of the tax shield of the debt.
5. Establish the equation showing the required rate of return demanded by equity holders, assuming that there is no corporate tax.
6. Clearly explain why in a world with corporate tax the value of a levered firm is higher than that of an unlevered firm.

7. Does the Modigliani–Miller theorem provide some guidelines about the optimal amount of borrowing that a firm should have?
8. Consider the levered firm of Exercise 4 in a world with no corporate tax. If the cost of debt is 5 percent and the rate of return on the firm is 10 percent, what must be the required rate of return on equity?

PART III

Fixed Income Securities and Options

CHAPTER 7

Valuation of Bonds and Interest Rates

7.1 INTRODUCTION

A bond is a financial instrument that establishes a relationship between the purchaser (creditor) and the issuer (debtor). It is a promise to pay a certain amount of money by the issuer to the purchaser each period until a certain date, at which point the principal is also returned. Thus, a bond is a particular type of constant earning security.

The next section of this chapter presents a short discussion on the discounted present value of a constant earning scheme. Issues related to bonds are analyzed in detail in Sections 7.3–7.7. These sections cover bond pricing, yield curves, duration and the convexity of bonds, and use of a bond portfolio for immunization of interest rate risk. Section 7.8 deals with forward interest rate, the rate of interest for a future period implied by the interest rates existing currently. The concern of Section 7.9 is the forward rate agreement, an agreement indicating that a particular rate of interest will be effective on a certain principal amount at a certain period of time in the future.

7.2 DISCOUNTED PRESENT VALUES AND CONSTANT EARNINGS STREAMS

Some financial instruments promise to pay a fixed amount per year until a certain period T. An example is an annuity that promises to pay N dollars each year for T years. The DPV of such an instrument is

$$DPV = \sum_{t=1}^{T} \frac{N}{(1+\lambda)^t} = N \sum_{t=1}^{T} \frac{1}{(1+\lambda)^t}, \qquad (7.1)$$

where λ is the annual risk-free interest rate (see Chapter 2). Let $D = 1/(1 + \lambda)$. Then

$$DPV = N\sum_{t=1}^{T}D^t = ND\sum_{t=0}^{T-1}D^t = ND\left(\frac{1-D^T}{1-D}\right). \tag{7.2}$$

We can rewrite the DPV in (7.2) as $DPV = N((1 - (1 + \lambda)^{-T})/\lambda)$. We refer to the factor $\left(1-(1+\lambda)^{-T}\right)\Big/\lambda$ in this expression as the annuity factor. It is the DPV of the instrument that promises to pay one dollar of income each year for T years. An example of an annuity can be a mortgage loan where the borrower repays the loan in equal installments for a certain period.

If an annuity promises to pay an annual income of N dollars for an infinite period, then it is called perpetuity or a consol. Now, $\lim_{T\to\infty} D^T = 0$. Therefore, $\lim_{T\to\infty} DPV = ND\frac{1}{1-D}$ Substituting $D = 1/(1 + \lambda)$ in this limiting expression, for a consol, we have

$$\lim_{T\to\infty} DPV = ND\frac{1}{1-D} = \frac{N}{\lambda}. \tag{7.3}$$

Thus, an instrument that promises to pay N dollars per year for an infinite period has a DPV equal to N/λ. It also says that in order to get N dollars per year forever one has to invest N/λ dollars now at the interest rate λ. To see this, write $\hat{N} = N / \lambda$, which gives $\hat{N}\lambda = N$. Thus, $\hat{N}\lambda$, which equals N, is the annual interest that the person receives for an indefinite period. As the interest rate λ increases, the DPV of a consol decreases. Infinite period annuities are quite common in Canada and the United Kingdom.

7.3 SPECIAL CASE OF A BOND

Governments and corporations issue bonds to borrow money. The bond issuer, the borrower, promises to pay a fixed amount of money, say N dollars (the coupon) for a certain number of years, say T. The terminal period T is referred as the maturity period of the bond. Bonds can be purchased from the issuers or other bondholders from the bond market. On maturity, the borrower also returns the principal (face value) of the bond, which we denote by Q, to its holder. Then the DPV of such a promise is

$$DPV = \sum_{t=1}^{T}\frac{N}{(1+\lambda)^t} + \frac{Q}{(1+\lambda)^T} = ND\left(\frac{1-D^T}{1-D}\right) + QD^T. \tag{7.4}$$

The term $\sum_{t=1}^{T}\frac{N}{(1+\lambda)^t}$ is the DPV of the annual payment N for T years. On the other hand, $\dfrac{Q}{(1+\lambda)^T}$ is the DPV of the face value. Note that the DPV and the interest rate are inversely related. This DPV formula is referred to as the price of the bond under consideration. In view of Fisher's proposition, a buyer will not make any distinction (given that risk and other factors are the same) between old and new bonds if the existing bond is sufficiently discounted to yield the same DPV as that provided by a new bond, when both are held to the same date of maturity.

An increase in the current rate of interest relative to the fixed coupon amount depresses the market price of a bond, whereas a reduction in the interest rate exerts a positive effect on a bond price. More generally, the bond price is a decreasing and strictly convex function of the interest rate. In other words, the bond price decreases at an increasing rate as the rate of interest increases. Thus, the reduction in bond price when the interest rate increases from 8 percent to 9 percent is lower than that when the interest rate increases from 9 percent to 10 percent. For a strictly convex curve, the line joining any two points on the curve lies above the curve. (See Chapter 3, for a formal discussion.) Since, $\lim\limits_{T \to \infty} D^T = 0$ in this limiting case the DPV in (7.4) coincides with the DPV in (7.3). Thus, a consol can be regarded as a special kind of bond. Since the DPV of a stream of cash flows represents its current value, the formula for a consol can be used to calculate the approximate value of a long-term bond.

7.4 YIELD TO MATURITY OF BONDS

We can use (7.4) in an alternative way. Suppose that the bond is currently trading at price P. Given that N, Q, T and P are known with certainty, we can determine the rate of interest for which the DPV of the bond equals its price. Formally, we are looking for the single discount rate λ that solves the equation

$$P = \sum_{t=1}^{T} \frac{N}{(1+\lambda)^t} + \frac{Q}{(1+\lambda)^T}. \qquad (7.5)$$

The value of λ that solves this equation is known as the yield to maturity (yield, for short) on the bond and is an appropriate measure of the return on the bond. The yield to maturity of a bond not only represents the returns that are directly available as annual payments, it also represents the return that may arise because of any price differential between the initial price P and the maturity price Q. Since (7.5) is a polynomial of degree T, it has T solutions. Only one solution is relevant for us. The remaining roots of the equation are either irrelevant or imaginary. It is important to note that the bond price formula gives the price of the bond irrespective of how much progress has been made into the cash flow stream of the bond from the date of its issue. In determining the price of a bond we take the interest rate as given, whereas to get the yield we assume that the bond price is given and equate the bond price with the DPV of the cash flow. Thus, the procedure is reversed here. We assume that P is differentiable up to any desired degree.

If annual coupon value is given as a percentage of the face value, say, $N = \phi Q$, where $0 < \phi < 1$, formula (7.5) becomes

$$P = \sum_{t=1}^{T} \frac{\phi Q}{(1+\lambda)^t} + \frac{Q}{(1+\lambda)^T} = \phi Q D \left(\frac{1 - D^T}{1 - D} \right) + Q D^T = \frac{\phi Q}{\lambda} \left(1 - \frac{1}{(1+\lambda)^T} \right) + \frac{Q}{(1+\lambda)^T}, \quad (7.6)$$

which simplifies further to

$$\frac{P}{Q} = \frac{\phi}{\lambda} \left(1 - \frac{1}{(1+\lambda)^T} \right) + \frac{1}{(1+\lambda)^T}. \quad (7.7)$$

If the coupon rate equals the yield to maturity ($\phi = \lambda$), then the face value and the bond price coincide ($P = Q$). A bond satisfying this condition is called a par bond or the bond is said to be at par. If $\phi > \lambda$, which implies that $Q < P$, then the bond is called a premium bond. On the other hand, if $\phi < \lambda$, the price is lower than face value and the bond is called a discount bond.

A bond is called a zero coupon bond if its coupon value equals zero. From (7.5) it follows that for a zero coupon bond, $P = Q/(1 + \lambda)^T$, which implies that the corresponding yield to maturity is $\lambda = ((Q/P)^{1/T} - 1)$.

Sometimes coupon payments are made semiannually or quarterly. A semiannual bond would make half its coupon payment every six months. In such a case the price of a bond P with $2T$ coupon payments and the annual interest rate λ is

$$P = \frac{N/2}{(1+\lambda/2)} + \frac{N/2}{(1+\lambda/2)^2} + \cdots + \frac{N/2+Q}{(1+\lambda/2)^{2T}}, \quad (7.8)$$

where, as before, Q is the face value and N is the yearly coupon payment of the bond. In the case of monthly payments, $N/2$, $\lambda/2$ and $2T$ in the above equation will be replaced by $N/12$, $\lambda/12$ and $12T$ respectively. Since times of compounding are different, the yield to maturity of a bond that pays coupons annually is not comparable to that of a bond paying coupons biannually, quarterly or monthly.

Given that λ is the interest rate per year, suppose that half this rate is compounded every 6 months. Then at the end of 1 year an investment of 1 dollar will grow into $\left(1 + \frac{\lambda}{2} \right)^2$ dollars. In general, if the number of coupon payments per year is n, the interest rate is compounded n times during the year. Then 1 dollar grows into $\left(1 + \frac{\lambda}{n} \right)^n$ dollars. Now, for n times compounding the corresponding DPV becomes

$$P = \sum_{t=1}^{T} \frac{N/n}{(1+\lambda/n)^{tn}} + \frac{Q}{(1+\lambda/n)^{Tn}}.$$ For continuous compounding we have to take the limit of $\left(1 + \frac{\lambda}{n} \right)^{-tn}$ as $n \to \infty$, where $t \geq 0$ is any real number (since the time path

is continuous). As $n \to \infty, \left(1+\dfrac{\lambda}{n}\right)^{-tn} \to \exp(-\lambda t)$, where "exp" is the exponential transformation. Hence under continuous compounding $exp(-\lambda t)$ is the factor by which a cash flow received in t periods must be multiplied to determine its DPV, where $t \geq 0$ is any real number. Now, as $n \to \infty$, $N/n \to 0$ Therefore, as $n \to \infty$, all the terms corresponding to coupon payments tend to zero. Hence under continuous compounding, the bond price formula is $Q \; exp(-\lambda t)$ (Since $t \geq 0$ is any real number, without loss of generality we replace T by t).

A plot of the yields against the periods of maturity of different bonds at a particular time point is known as the yield curve (see Figure 7.1). The curve is monotonically increasing if longer-term bonds have higher yields than shorter-term bonds. If yields are the same for bonds of different maturities then the curve is flat. On the other hand, the curve is downward sloping if yields of the shorter-term bonds are higher than those of longer-term bonds. The yield curve is used to understand the bond market. Several explanations have been provided for an upward sloping yield curve. For instance, if investors expect interest rates to go up with an increase in the maturity period, then the yield curve becomes positively sloped. Another explanation is that longer maturities being more risky should accompany a rate premium (see Brav et al. 1999a).

The indicator yield to maturity is a valuable tool for making comparisons among bonds. The bond market controls it. It depends on the market expectation for the rate of return on investments that involve different levels of risks. For investments that are free from risks, the expected return (or yield) is lower in comparison to that of risky investments. Corporate bonds generally have higher yields than government

Figure 7.1   Yield Curve

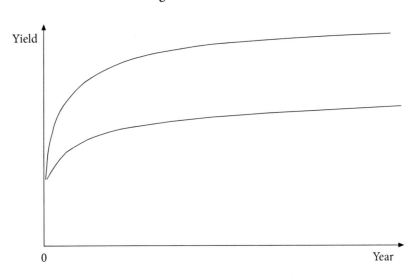

bonds. Change in the yield to maturity gives rise to changes in the price of newly issued bonds. Therefore, it becomes important to understand how bond price changes as the yield changes. For instance, if a person wishes to sell a bond before the maturity date, he should sell it at a DPV that is higher than the DPV computed using the yield on the date of purchase, because this gives him a higher effective rate of return. The sensitivity of bond price to changes in interest rate depends on many factors including time to maturity, coupon size and current yields. Changes in the yield to maturity affect the prices of some bonds more than others. As the yield to maturity of a bond increases, its purchase price decreases and vice versa. That is why the bond market is said to be up or down according as the yield goes down or up.

Figure 7.2 shows that the relationship between price of a bond (plotted on the vertical axis) and the yield to maturity (plotted on the horizontal axis) is decreasing and strictly convex. The curve intersects the vertical axis when the yield is zero.

A longer-term bond is generally more sensitive to yield changes. Figure 7.3 shows the price–yield relationship graphically for two bonds with the same yield and coupon but different maturities. In most cases a given change in yield will cause the price of a higher coupon bond to change by a larger amount.

Given the maturity period, a given change in yield will generate a higher percentage change in the price of a lower coupon bond. The reason for this is that high coupon bonds with greater cash flows provide a higher proportion of values earlier than lower coupon bonds. Thus, relatively less price adjustment is required for high coupon bonds. This also implies that, given the maturity period, a zero-coupon bond is more sensitive than a coupon bond in response to a change in the

Figure 7.2   Bond Price as a Function of Yield

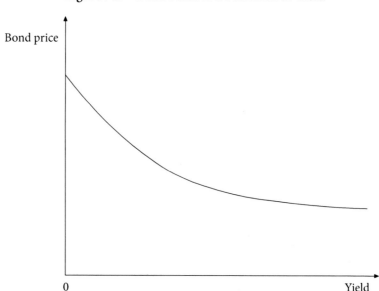

0   Yield

Figure 7.3   Bond Prices and Maturities to Yield

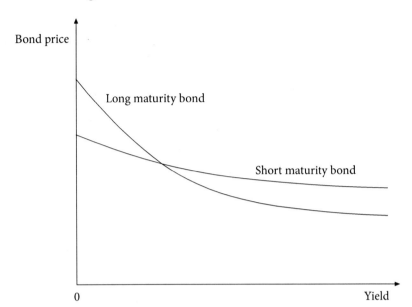

Figure 7.4   Bond Price–Yield Relationships for Different Coupon Sizes

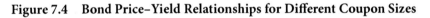
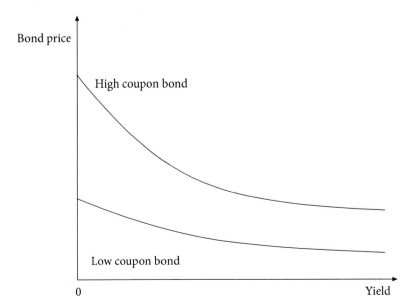

yield. Figure 7.4 compares the price–yield relationship for a high coupon bond and a low coupon bond.

Premium bonds have higher coupon rates than discount bonds. Therefore, the former type of bonds will be less sensitive to changes in the yield.

7.5 DURATION OF BONDS

Given the maturity date, higher coupon bonds provide a larger proportion of total cash flow earlier than lower coupon bonds in the bonds' lifespans. Consequently, actual maturity date is not a good indicator of the length of a coupon bond. To obtain a more meaningful indicator, it is necessary to measure the maturity of each cash flow. For this purpose, let us revisit the bond price equation in (7.5). Differentiating this equation with respect to λ we get

$$
\frac{dP}{d\lambda} = -\frac{N}{(1+\lambda)^2} - \frac{2N}{(1+\lambda)^3} - \cdots - \frac{TN}{(1+\lambda)^{T+1}} - \frac{TQ}{(1+\lambda)^{T+1}} = -\frac{1}{(1+\lambda)} \sum_{t=1}^{T} \frac{tN}{(1+\lambda)^t}
$$
$$
-\frac{TQ}{(1+\lambda)^{T+1}}. \tag{7.9}
$$

We multiply both sides of this equation by $\frac{d\lambda}{P}$ to get

$$
\frac{dP}{P} = -\frac{1}{(1+\lambda)} \left(\frac{\displaystyle\sum_{t=1}^{T} t \frac{N}{(1+\lambda)^t} + \frac{TQ}{(1+\lambda)^T}}{\displaystyle\sum_{t=1}^{T} \frac{N}{(1+\lambda)^t} + \frac{Q}{(1+\lambda)^T} \quad \sum_{t=1}^{T} \frac{N}{(1+\lambda)^t} + \frac{Q}{(1+\lambda)^t}} \right) d\lambda. \tag{7.10}
$$

The Macaulay (1938) duration, MA_d, of a bond is defined as

$$
MA_d = \left(\frac{\displaystyle\sum_{t=1}^{T} t \frac{N}{(1+\lambda)^t} + \frac{TQ}{(1+\lambda)^T}}{\displaystyle\sum_{t=1}^{T} \frac{N}{(1+\lambda)^t} + \frac{Q}{(1+\lambda)^T} \quad \sum_{t=1}^{T} \frac{N}{(1+\lambda)^t} + \frac{Q}{(1+\lambda)^t}} \right). \tag{7.11}
$$

The indicator MA_d is a measure of the sensitivity of the bond price to a change in the interest rate. The relationship between the relative change of the bond price and the relative change of the interest rate is then given by

$$
\frac{dP}{P} = -MA_d \left(\frac{d\lambda}{(1+\lambda)} \right). \tag{7.12}
$$

From this relation we can say that MA_d is simply the negative of the ratio between the relative change in bond price and the relative change in $(1 + \lambda)$. From this equation we can rewrite MA_d as

$$MA_d = -\frac{(1+\lambda)dP}{Pd\lambda} = -\frac{(1+\lambda)dP}{Pd(1+\lambda)}. \qquad (7.13)$$

That is, the Macaulay duration of a bond is the negative of the elasticity of the bond price with respect to $(1 + \lambda)$, the value of 1 dollar after one year from now.

Note that $- d\lambda/(1 + \lambda) = d \log(1/(1 + \lambda))$. But $(1/(1 + \lambda))$ is the price of a one-year zero-coupon bond with a face value of one. Then from the first expression for MA_d in (7.13) we can rewrite as MA_d

$$MA_d = \frac{d \log P}{d \log\left(\frac{1}{(1+\lambda)}\right)}. \qquad (7.14)$$

The formula for MA_d given by (7.14) is the elasticity of the bond price with respect to the price of a one-year zero-coupon bond with a face value of one. (See Bierwag 1987 for further discussion.)

Let w_i be the DPV contribution of the ith cash flow to the bond price. More precisely, assuming that there are T cash flows in a stream,

$$w_i = \frac{DPV_i}{DPV}, \qquad (7.15)$$

where $DPV_i = N/(1+\lambda)^i$ is the DPV of the ith cash flow, $1 \le i < T$, $DPV_T = (N+Q)/(1+\lambda)^T$ and $DPV = \sum_{t=1}^{T} DPV_i$. Then from (7.15) it follows that the Macaulay duration MA_d of a bond is simply the weighted average of periods of cash flows of the bond, where the weights are the DPV contributions. That is,

$$MA_d = \sum_{i=1}^{T} i w_i. \qquad (7.16)$$

We may consider the duration of a bond portfolio, which is a collection of bonds. The cash flow of a bond portfolio at a particular point in time is the sum of cash flows of the bonds in the portfolio. Therefore, the DPV of the portfolio is the sum of the DPVs of the bonds. This in turn enables us to calculate the duration of a portfolio from the durations of individual bonds.

Consider a portfolio of k bonds, where each bond has T cash flows. Let DPV_i^j be the DPV of the ith cash flow in bond j, $1 \le i \le T$, $1 \le j \le k$. Then the Macaulay duration of bond j is

$$MA_d^j = \sum_{i=1}^{T} \frac{iDPV_i^j}{DPV^j}, \qquad (7.17)$$

where $DPV^j = \sum_{i=1}^{T} DPV_i^j$ is the DPV of bond j. From (7.17) it follows that

$DPV^j\left(MA_d^j\right)=\sum_{t=1}^{T} iDPV_i^j$. Let DPV_i^{PF} be the DPV of the ith cash flow of the

portfolio, that is, $DPV_i^{PF}=\sum_{j=1}^{k} DPV_i^j$. Given that there are k bonds in the portfolio,

$$\sum_{j=1}^{k} DPV^j\left(MA_d^j\right)=\sum_{j=1}^{k}\sum_{i=1}^{T} iDPV_i^j=\sum_{i=1}^{T} i\sum_{j=1}^{k} DPV_i^j=\sum_{i=1}^{T} iDPV_i^{PF}.$$

The DPV the portfolio is $DPV^{PF}=\sum_{i=1}^{T} DPV_i^{PF}=\sum_{i=1}^{T}\sum_{j=1}^{k} DPV_i^j$. Then the Macaulay

duration of the portfolio MA_d^{PF} is defined as

$$MA_d^{PF}=\frac{\sum_{i=1}^{T} iDPV_i^{PF}}{DPV^{PF}}=\frac{\sum_{i=1}^{T} i\sum_{j=1}^{k} DPV_i^j}{DPV^{PF}}=\frac{\sum_{j=1}^{k}\sum_{i=1}^{T} iDPV_i^j}{DPV^{PF}}=\frac{\sum_{j=1}^{k} DPV^j\left(MA_d^j\right)}{DPV^{PF}}$$

$$=\sum_{j=1}^{k} w_j^{PF}\left(MA_d^j\right) \tag{7.18}$$

where the weight $w_j=\dfrac{DPV^j}{DPV^{PF}}$ on MA_d^j is the DPV of bond j as a fraction of the
DPV of the portfolio.

We may summarize the observations in the following theorem.

Theorem 7.1: The Macaulay duration of a bond portfolio is the weighted average
of durations of bonds in the portfolio, where the weights are the discounted
present values of the bonds, relative to that of the portfolio.

If we define the modified duration of the security as

$$MA_{dm}=\frac{M_d}{(1+\lambda)}, \tag{7.19}$$

then from (7.12) it follows that

$$\frac{dP}{d\lambda}=-(MA_{dm})P. \tag{7.20}$$

This gives

$$\frac{dP}{P}=-(MA_{dm})d\lambda. \tag{7.21}$$

Thus, assuming that the change in yield is very small, the corresponding
proportionate change in bond price equals the negative of the product of the
modified duration and the change in the yield. For instance, if the modified
duration of a bond is 5 and the yield per period changes by 1 percent, then the
market value of the bond changes by 5 percent. The larger the modified duration,
the more the bond is exposed to interest rate changes.

7.6 DURATION AND CONVEXITY OF A BOND

From (7.5) it follows that bond prices are non-linear functions of interest rates. For a change in the interest rate a linear approximation of the bond price in the new interest rate will generate a bias. To understand this more explicitly, let us write P as a function of λ and denote this functional representation by $P(\lambda)$. Suppose λ changes to λ_0. Let us denote the difference $(\lambda_0 - \lambda)$ by ε. Expanding P by Taylor's series around λ, we have

$$P(\lambda + \varepsilon) = P(\lambda) + \frac{dP(\lambda)}{d\lambda}\varepsilon + \frac{d^2 P(\lambda)}{d\lambda^2}\frac{\varepsilon^2}{2} + \text{higher order terms.} \qquad (7.22)$$

Neglecting higher order terms, we rewrite this expression as

$$\Delta P = \frac{dP(\lambda)}{d\lambda}\varepsilon + \frac{d^2 P(\lambda)}{d\lambda^2}\frac{\varepsilon^2}{2}, \qquad (7.23)$$

where $\Delta P = P(\lambda + \varepsilon) - P(\lambda)$. Dividing both sides of the expression in (7.23) by $P(\lambda)$ we get

$$\frac{\Delta P}{P(\lambda)} = \frac{dP(\lambda)}{P(\lambda)d\lambda}\varepsilon + \frac{d^2 P(\lambda)}{P(\lambda)d\lambda^2}\frac{\varepsilon^2}{2}, \qquad (7.24)$$

which, in view of (7.21) becomes

$$\frac{\Delta P}{P(\lambda)} = -(MA_{dm})\varepsilon + \frac{CO}{2}\varepsilon^2, \qquad (7.25)$$

where $CO = \dfrac{d^2 P(\lambda)}{P(\lambda)d\lambda^2}$ is defined as the convexity of the bond. Thus, the proportionate change in the bond price, resulting from a change in the yield, is the sum of the change in the yield multiplied by the negative of the modified Macaulay duration and convexity multiplied by half the square of the yield change. From the formula given by (7.5),

$$CO = \left(\frac{\sum\limits_{t=1}^{T} t(t+1)\dfrac{N}{(1+\lambda)^{t+2}} + \dfrac{T(T+1)Q}{(1+\lambda)^{T+2}}}{\sum\limits_{t=1}^{T}\dfrac{N}{(1+\lambda)^{t}} + \dfrac{Q}{(1+\lambda)^{T}}} \div \sum\limits_{t=1}^{T}\dfrac{N}{(1+\lambda)^{t}} + \dfrac{Q}{(1+\lambda)^{T}} \right). \qquad (7.26)$$

If we ignore the convexity, then the modified duration is a linear approximation to the sensitivity of bond prices to changes in the yield. By incorporating the convexity, the equation provides a second order approximation for sensitivity. The convexity of a bond generally increases with maturity. The reason is that as the maturity increases, because of the multiplicative factor $t(t + 1)$, the rate of increase in the numerator of (7.26) is larger than the corresponding rate in the denominator.

It is a decreasing function of the rate of interest and the coupon. We can extend these properties of the convexity of a bond to that of a bond portfolio, which is defined as the weighted average of the convexities of the bonds in the portfolio, where the weights are the proportions of investments in different bonds.

7.7 IMMUNIZATION OF INTEREST RATE RISK

An objective for construction of a portfolio that generates fixed cash inflows for a specific period is to meet certain financial obligations in the future. Suppose an investor's goal requires that an investment be used to meet a specific liability of an amount that comes due in n periods. If the investor holds a discount bond whose maturity period is n, and the face value of the bond equals this amount, then irrespective of the interest rate the future of the bond will cover the future liability. This dedicated bond is called perfectly immunized.

In general, the problem of immunization is choosing assets and liabilities in order to offset any risk that may arise. To analyze a problem of this type, let us consider an individual who has a future obligation of L to be paid back in T periods. Then the DPV of this obligation is $L_0(\lambda) = \dfrac{L}{(1+\lambda)^T}$. To meet this obligation the individual purchases a coupon bond with maturity T' and the DPV of this bond is $L_1(\lambda) = \sum_{t=1}^{T'} \dfrac{N_i}{(1+\lambda)^t}$. Note that the coupons may not be of the same value across time. The maturity periods of the bond and the financial obligations are also not the same. It is assumed that $L_0(\lambda) = L_1(\lambda)$. That is, the DPV of the bond equals the DPV of the liability so that the present value of the future liability is exactly offset by the present value of the future income stream.

Assume that the yield curve is flat and immediately after the bond purchase, the yield changes by a small amount to a new value but stays fixed there. Let us denote the change in the yield by ε. That is, there is a small parallel shift in the flat yield curve by ε. Then using Taylor's series expansion, we can approximate $L_0(\lambda + \varepsilon)$ and $L_1(\lambda + \varepsilon)$ as follows

$$L_0(\lambda+\varepsilon) = L_0(\lambda) + \frac{dL_0(\lambda)}{d\lambda}\varepsilon = L_0(\lambda) - (MA^0_{dm})L_0\varepsilon, \qquad (7.27)$$

$$L_1(\lambda+\varepsilon) = L_1(\lambda) + \frac{dL_1(\lambda)}{d\lambda}\varepsilon = L_1(\lambda) - (MA^1_{dm})L_1\varepsilon, \qquad (7.28)$$

where MA^0_{dm} and MA^1_{dm} are the modified durations associated with the DPVs $L_0(\lambda)$ and $L_1(\lambda)$, that is, $MA^0_{dm} = -\dfrac{dL_0}{L_0 d\lambda}$ and $MA^1_{dm} = -\dfrac{dL_1}{L_1 d\lambda}$.

We say that the liability is perfectly immunized by the bond with respect to interest rate risk if $L_0(\lambda + \varepsilon) = L_1(\lambda + \varepsilon)$, that is, after the change in the interest rate their market values or DPVs are equal. Consequently, if liability is perfectly immunized then under the assumption that $L_0(\lambda) = L_1(\lambda)$, we have $MA_{dm}^0 = MA_{dm}^1$ — that is, the modified durations are the same. Conversely, if $MA_{dm}^0 = MA_{dm}^1$, then given that $L_0(\lambda) = L_1(\lambda)$, we must have $L_0(\lambda + \varepsilon) = L_1(\lambda + \varepsilon)$, which means that there is perfect immunization of the liability by the bond under interest rate risks.

We are now, therefore, in a position to state the following theorem.

Theorem 7.2: Assume that the yield curve is flat and immediately after the purchase of a bond the yield changes to a new value by an infinitesimal amount and remains unaltered after that. The bondholder also has a future liability and the discounted present values of the bond and the liability are the same before the interest rate change. Then the following conditions are equivalent:

(a) The future liability can be perfectly immunized by the bond under the change in the interest rate.

(b) The modified durations of the bond and the liability are equal.

What this theorem says is the following: given that the yield curve is flat and the DPVs of a liability and coupon bond are the same, for a small parallel shift in the curve after the purchase of the bond, the liability can be matched by the bond if and only if the modified durations of the bond and the liability are the same. If the change in the yield is large, then the DPVs of the bond and liability should also take into account the corresponding convexities after the interest rate change.

Consider a bond a portfolio with k bonds. Then for neutralizing a liability with the portfolio under interest rate risk it is necessary that $\sum_{i=1}^{k} w_i \left(MA_{dm}^i \right) = MA_{dm}^L, 0 \le w_i \le 1, \sum_{i=1}^{k} w_i = 1$ where w_i is the portfolio proportion of bond i, MA_{dm}^i is its modified duration and MA_{dm}^L is the modified duration of the liability. This framework assumes that the solution is unique. If $w_i = 1$ for some i and $w_j = 0$ for all $j \ne i$, then this result reduces to the single-bond result stated in Theorem 7.2. Note that if we try to meet the financial obligations in the future with fixed income securities, then we may face the possibility of not being able to fulfill the obligations because of undesirable fluctuations in the yield. The immunization method for neutralizing this risk not only fits up the cash flow of the stream but also fits up with the duration associated with the stream.

7.8 FORWARD INTEREST RATE

An interest rate involving an agreement in the current period for investment at a later period and repayment at a further later period is referred to as a forward interest rate. To understand this in greater detail, let a "period" be one year. Let λ_{T_1} and λ_{T_2} be the annual interest rates prevailing between the current year and the next T_1 and T_2 years respectively. Assume that $T_1 < T_2$. For instance, interest rates on house building loans, offered by the banks in India, depend on the period of repayment of the loan and the level of yearly/monthly repayment. Then the annual forward rate of return λ_{T_1,T_2} between periods T_1 and T_2 is implicitly defined by the relation

$$\left(1+\lambda_{T_1}\right)^{T_1} \left(1+\lambda_{T_1,T_2}\right)^{T_2-T_1} = \left(1+\lambda_{T_2}\right)^{T_2}. \tag{7.29}$$

If a person invests 1 dollar for T_1 years then the return at the end of the T_1^{th} year is $\left(1+\lambda_{T_1}\right)^{T_1}$ dollars. Similarly, when 1 dollar is invested for T_2 years, the corresponding return after T_2 years will be $\left(1+\lambda_{T_2}\right)^{T_2}$ dollars. At the initial period the investor is indifferent between investing 1 dollar for T_2 years and investing 1 dollar for two successive periods of T_1 years and $(T_2 - T_1)$ years. The term forward interest rate is quite meaningful here because it incorporates the fact that it starts at a future period $(T_1 + 1)$ and covers an interval of length $(T_2 - T_1)$. In other words, at time 0 the investor is indifferent between investing 1 dollar for T_2 periods at the interest rate λ_{T_2} and 1 dollar for two successive periods T_1 and $(T_2 - T_1)$ at the interest rates λ_{T_1} and λ_{T_1,T_2} respectively.

We can solve equation (7.29) for λ_{T_1,T_2} to get

$$\lambda_{T_1,T_2} = \left(\frac{\left(1+\lambda_{T_1}\right)^{T_1}}{\left(1+\lambda_{T_2}\right)^{T_2}}\right)^{\frac{1}{(T_2-T_1)}} -1. \tag{7.30}$$

Suppose a person who has to borrow 1 dollar after T_1 years and return the amount along with interests after T_2 years observes that the prevailing interest rates for T_1 and T_2 years are respectively λ_{T_1} and λ_{T_2}. Then as per equation (7.30) the person makes an agreement that the interest rate λ_{T_1,T_2} will apply to the forward borrowing, which he has to pay back, along with the interest, at an even later period. Forward rates are often used to predict future levels of inflation (for further discussion see Baz and Chacko 2008).

Now, assume in (7.29) that $\lambda_i's$ are small. Expand both sides of the equation by Taylor's series and ignore terms with power 2 or more to get,

$$\left(1+T_1\lambda_{T_1}\right)\left(1+(T_2-T_1)\lambda_{T_1,T_2}\right) = \left(1+T_2\lambda_{T_2}\right). \tag{7.31}$$

Ignoring the product term $T_1(T_2-T_1)\lambda_{T_1}\lambda_{T_1,T_2}$ on the left-hand side of (7.31) and simplifying the resulting expression we have

$$(T_2 - T_1)\lambda_{T_1,T_2} + T_1\lambda_{T_1} = T_2\lambda_{T_2}, \qquad (7.32)$$

from which it follows that

$$\lambda_{T_1,T_2} = \frac{T_2\lambda_{T_2} - T_1\lambda_{T_1}}{T_2 - T_1}. \qquad (7.33)$$

We can also express (7.33) as

$$\lambda_{T_1,T_2} = \lambda_{T_2} + \left(\lambda_{T_2} - \lambda_{T_1}\right)\frac{T_1}{T_2 - T_1}. \qquad (7.34)$$

This shows how λ_{T_1,T_2} can be calculated using a linear relationship.

7.9 FORWARD RATE AGREEMENT

A forward rate agreement is an agreement between two counter parties (a buyer and a seller) at period zero on a rate of interest (pre-specified strike rate) payable on a loan (the notional principal underlying the contract) that starts at period T_1 and matures at period T_2. The borrowing and lending are normally done at LIBOR. The buyer's payoff (which may be negative) from the contract is the difference between the rate of interest prevailing at the period T_2 and the strike rate stated in the contract for a given period (typically three months), multiplied by the notional principal. If the interest rate at the period of maturity T_2 is higher than the rate agreed in the contract, then the buyer of the contract benefits from the agreement. Thus, an increase in the interest rate makes the buyer of the agreement better off. Motivation for the buyer (respectively seller) to get involved in the agreement is to make money from any increment (respectively reduction) in the interest rate that may take place between the starting period T_1 and the maturity period T_2.

Let $\bar{\lambda}$ be the rate of interest agreed on (pre-specified strike rate) in the contract and $LI(T_1, T_1, T_2)$ be the LIBOR, as of time T_1, on a loan that starts at T_1 and expires at T_2. The payments are made at the period T_2. The payments are based on the market convention that the number of days in the interest accrual period has to be divided by 360. Then the buyer's payment at period T_2 is $\left[LI(T_1,T_1,T_2) - \bar{\lambda}\right]\left(\frac{T_2-T_1}{360}\right)Q$, where Q is the notional principal mentioned in the contract. Since the agreement is settled at the period T_1, discounting of the payments are necessary. Thus, the buyer's payoff at time T_1 is

$$\frac{Q}{1 + LI(T_1,T_1,T_2)\left(\frac{T_2-T_1}{360}\right)}\left[LI(T_1,T_1,T_2) - \bar{\lambda}\right]\left(\frac{T_2-T_1}{360}\right). \qquad (7.35)$$

We can interpret $\left[LI(T_1,T_1,T_2) - \bar{\lambda}\right]\left(\frac{T_2-T_1}{360}\right)Q$ as the difference between the interest earned by the buyer on the principal Q between the periods T_1 and T_2 at a rate $LI(T_1, T_1 T_2)$ and the interest paid on the same principal over the same time period at a different rate $\bar{\lambda}$. The payoff given by (7.35) is the discounted value of this difference (see Baz and Chacko 2008).

Example 7.1: Recall from Example 2.1 that the value of a certain amount of loan which has to be paid back in T equal installments, is $P = \dfrac{m\left(1-(+\lambda)^{-T}\right)}{\lambda}$, where λ

is the annual interest rate and m annual installment. Then $\dfrac{dP}{d\lambda} = -\dfrac{P}{\lambda} + \dfrac{mT}{\lambda(1+\lambda)^{T+1}}$.

The Macaulay duration of the borrowing is $MA_d = -\dfrac{(1+\lambda)}{P}\dfrac{dP}{d\lambda} = \dfrac{1+\lambda}{\lambda} - \dfrac{T}{(1+\lambda)^T - 1}$.

Applied Example 7.1: Treasury rates are the rates of interest earned by an investor on treasury bills and bonds issued by the government. For instance, the US and the Japanese treasury rates are the rates at which the respective governments borrow in their own currencies. In India, treasury bills are discount bonds issued by the government for a period not exceeding one year. The underlying interest rate is a short-term, risk-free rate. Treasury bonds in India are issued for more than one year and generally for a period of 10–30 years. The interest rate depends on the period of maturity of the bond.

BIBLIOGRAPHICAL NOTES

For discussion on bond as a source of constant earnings the reader may refer to Quirk (1988) and Chakravarty (2010). For a nice exposition of yield to maturity of bonds two appropriate sources are Brav et al. (1999a) and Baz and Chacko (2008). A good coverage of duration of bond and interest rate risk can be found in Bierwag (1987), Baz and Chacko (2008) and Hull and Basu (2010). Forward interest rate and forward rate agreement are analyzed in Baz and Chacko (2008) and Hull and Basu (2010).

EXERCISES

1. Each of the following statements is either true or false. If the statement is true prove it. If it is false, give a counter-example or justify your answer by logical reasoning.
    (a) If the coupons of a bond with price P and face value Q are sold at par, then $P = Q$.
    (b) The relationship between the Macaulay duration MA_d of a bond and its modified duration MA_{dm} is given by $MA_{dm}(1 + \lambda) = MA_d$, where λ is the rate of interest.

(c) If a bond has a modified duration of 8 periods, and the yield per period changes by 1 percent, then its market value changes by 9 percent.

(d) The Macaulay duration of a zero coupon is independent of the rate of interest.

(e) The convexity of a zero coupon bond is an increasing function of the period of maturity.

(f) The modified duration of a par bond can be treated as an annuity factor.

(g) The coupon rate is a monotone function of the interest rate.

(h) If the rate of interest is constant, then the price of a par bond is constant.

2. A company borrows 7000 dollars by issuing a bond with an annual coupon of 700 dollars and promises to payback the principal in 20 years. If the current market rate of interest is 10 percent, what is the value of this bond?

3. Determine the Macaulay duration and modified duration of a perpetuity.

4. A person borrows 10000 dollars at an annual interest rate of 10 percent. Determine the amounts he has to pay back if the interest rate is compounded (a) annually, (b) semi-annually.

5. For a one-year bond with a current price of 103 dollars, the coupon rate is 7 percent. What is the yield to maturity?

6. What is the convexity of a perpetuity? Establish its monotonic relationship with respect to the interest rate analytically.

7. What is the discounted present value of a perpetuity, which makes an annual payment of 60 dollars, given that the annual rate of interest is 5 percent?

8. A person takes a loan of 700000 dollars by mortgaging his house at an annual interest rate of 8 percent. If the number of years to pay back the loan is 30 years, what is his monthly payment to the bank?

9. A 4-year bond paying an 8 percent coupon annually is sold at par (1000 dollars). The current rate of interest is 8 percent. Suppose the rate of interest reduces to 6 percent. Determine the percentage change in the bond price.

10. How does the Macaulay duration of a perpetuity change when interest rate increases?

11. Consider a 4-year bond paying a 9 percent coupon semiannually and the rate of interest is 9 percent. The face value of the bond is 1000 dollars. Determine the Macaulay duration of the bond.

12. Consider a four-year, 8 percent coupon bond with a principal of 1000 dollars. The current rate of interest is 6 percent, which increases first to 8 percent and then to 10 percent. Illustrate how the price of the bond decreases at an increasing rate.

13. Give an example to illustrate sensitivity of bond prices with different maturities to change in the interest rate.

14. Consider two four-year coupon bonds with a common face value of 1000 dollars. While the first has an annual coupon of 5 percent, for the second, this rate is 10 percent. The current rate of interest is 8 percent. Determine their discounted present values. Suppose now the rate of interest increases to 10 percent. Compare and interpret the percentage changes in the discounted present values of the bonds.

15. Determine the price of a 30-year 5 percent coupon bond with a face value of 1000 dollars when the annual rate of interest is 4 percent and the coupons are paid semiannually.

16. Consider a 5-year 8 percent coupon bond with a face value of 1000 dollars. If the annual rate of interest is 5 percent, determine the Macaulay duration and modified duration of the bond.

17. Determine the modified duration of a 4-year bond paying a 9 percent coupon semiannually when the rate of interest is 9 percent and the Macaulay duration is 6.89 periods.

18. Suppose the payments in an annuity grow at a constant rate. Determine the value of the annuity in terms of the growth factor, the rate of interest and the first year payment. Analytically examine the relationship of each of these factors with the annuity value.

CHAPTER 8

Markets for Options

8.1 INTRODUCTION

An option is a contract between two parties, a buyer and a seller, that allows the buyer to buy or sell a particular asset at, or before, a specified time—the expiration time or the date of maturity—at a price agreed on between the buyer and the seller. This agreed price, the price of the stock at which the contract is made, is known as the strike price or exercise price. In exchange for granting the contract, the seller obtains a premium from the buyer. This premium is known as the price of the option. The underlying asset can be a property or a security such as bond, stock etc. The premium generally depends on the strike price, the expiration time and the current price of the asset. One basic assumption in the theory of option pricing is that there is no arbitrage opportunity. An arbitrage opportunity is a trading strategy that allows the possibility of an instantaneous positive profit without any risk (see Chapter 9). The ownership of the contract entitles the buyer to exercise the right to buy or sell the asset. The essential idea is to create markets where these assets can be traded. Thus, an option is a financial derivative that connects the buyer and the seller of an asset at a reference price (the strike price) during a specified time frame (expiration time). There is no obligation on the part of the buyer to exercise the right. So, one choice for the buyer is to allow the contract to expire. However, if the buyer decides to exercise his right of buying or selling the asset under consideration, then the seller of the contract has to oblige the appropriate activity of the buyer at the strike price. The non-obligatory right on the part of the buyer of the option makes it different from a forward and futures. A forward contract is an obligatory contract between two parties, a buyer and a seller, to buy or sell an asset at a predetermined future time, at a predetermined delivery price known as the forward price. A futures contract is an obligatory contract between a buyer and a seller to buy or sell an asset at a predetermined delivery price during a specified time period in the future.

In Section 2 of this chapter we present an analysis of different types of options. The payoff and profit functions for options are discussed respectively in sections 8.3 and 8.4. We also discuss some applications of options in Sections 8.2 and 8.3. Boundaries for option values are analyzed in Section 8.5. Section 8.6 presents a discussion on forward and futures contracts.

8.2 TYPES OF OPTIONS

As stated earlier, an option is a contract between two parties that gives one party (the option holder) the right, but there is no obligation that a specified transaction has to be made with another party (option issuer) under specific conditions. There are two major types of options, call and put. The holder of a call option has the right to buy an asset by the maturity date at the strike price. On the other hand, in the case of a put option, the right for selling an asset can be exercised by the expiration date at the strike price. An option with no special characteristic is called a plain vanilla option. A plain vanilla option is either a call or a put option with a given date of expiration and strike price. An option (call or put) is said to be at-the-money if its current asset price coincides with the strike price of the option. A call option is in-the-money (or out-of-the-money) if the strike price is less (greater) than the current asset price. A put option is in-the-money (out-of-the-money) if the current asset price is below (above) the strike price.

Options can be European or American. A European option can be exercised only on the date of expiration. For buying a stock at price B and expiration date d, a European call option gives the purchaser of the option the right to buy the stock at price B on date d. In contrast, American options can be exercised at any date before expiration. For selling a stock at price B and expiration date d, an American put option gives the option holder the right to sell the stock at price B on date d or any date before d.

Clearly, there are four types of participants in the markets for options: (i) buyers of call options, (ii) sellers of call options, (iii) buyers of put options and (iv) sellers of put options. Selling an option is also referred to as writing an option. It is said that a buyer of an option has a long position, whereas a seller of the option has a short position in the market.

With an increasing number of financial contracts and corresponding derivatives traded in stock markets, the demand for rules to guide whether the current price of an asset appropriately reflects future payoffs from the asset has grown substantially. Since an option represents a claim for an underlying asset, with the price of the asset being the subject of the option contract, we can regard an option as a derivative security. Banks and non-financial institutions extensively use options for managing risks. Standard options are traded on a regulated exchange, where the terms and conditions for each option are standardized by the exchange. An example is the Chicago Board Options Exchange (www.cboe.com), the largest exchange in the world for trading stock options. Such options are referred to as exchange-traded options. Standardization of the contract enables a trader to receive complete information on the underlying asset, its quantity, the date of expiration and the strike price. The popularity of the Black–Scholes–Merton option pricing formula, which we discuss in Chapter 11, stresses the need to price options for market exchange.

Let us consider a European call option. If a trader foresees a chance of an increase in the price of a stock over the strike price, he may buy the right to purchase the stock at the strike price. Under this trading activity the individual is going to have a long position in the call option. Note that he does not have to buy the stock; he only needs to buy the right. For buying this right the trader has to pay a premium. The premium may be treated as a fixed cost. If, at the date of expiry of the option, the strike price is more than the price at maturity, then it will not be profitable for the individual to exercise the right, the contract is worthless and his loss incurred on the deal is simply the premium. If the strike price is just covered by the maturity price, then the trader's loss will be equal to the premium. It makes no difference whether the trader exercises the right or not—the loss will be equal to the premium. At a maturity price greater than the strike price but lower than the sum of the strike price and the premium, the trader should exercise the right because in this case his loss is only a part of the premium. The amount lost is simply the difference between the premium and the excess of the maturity price over the strike price. However, if the difference between the maturity price and the strike price is higher than the premium, then the trader makes a profit by the amount by which the difference exceeds the premium.

To understand this, let us consider an example. Speculating that the current price 60 dollars for a company share is likely to increase in three months, a trader purchases a call option to buy 100 shares at the strike price 50 dollars for each share and pays a premium of 10 dollars per share. The trader's initial investment is 1000(= 10 × 100) dollars. Then if after three months (the expiration date), the price of a share increases to 70 dollars, he can exercise the right to buy 100 shares at a cost of 5000 (= 50 × 100) dollars and sell them at 7000 (= 70 × 100) dollars. This gives the trader a revenue or payoff of 2000 (= 7000 – 5000) dollars and a net profit of 1000 (= 7000 – 5000 – 1000) dollars. This shows a practical application of options. With an accurate speculation, a trader may be able to make high return from a small initial outlay rather than investing directly in the underlying asset. Likewise, if a trader has a belief that a stock price will go down, he can sell or write a call option for a profitable deal.

If a trader believes that there can be a decrease in the price of a stock, he can buy a put option to sell the stock and make a profit. To see this, suppose a trader foresees a chance of a reduction in the current price 55 dollars of a stock and buys a European put option to sell 100 shares at the strike price 50 dollars per share at the date of maturity (say, three months from now) and pays a premium of 2 dollars per share. The initial investment of the trader is 200(= 2 × 100) dollars. If at the maturity date the share price reduces to 47 dollars, he can buy 100 shares at a cost of 4700 (= 47 × 100) dollars and sell them to the writer of the option at 5000(= 50 × 100) dollars. His payoff and net profit from this transaction are respectively 300 = (5000 – 4700) dollars and 100 = (5000 – 4700 – 200) dollars. Similarly, if a stock price is likely to increase, a trader can sell a put option with the expectation of deriving a profit.

In sum, a long position in a call option and a short position in a put option are optimistic (bullish) positions, in the sense that they are profitable when the stock price increases. Likewise, a long position in a put option and a short position in a call potion are pessimistic (bearish) positions.

Another practical use of options arises in the context of hedging, an investment to reduce risk. In hedging, risk involved in a portfolio is monitored by taking opposite positions in two securities that are highly negatively correlated. If it is possible to combine a risky option and the corresponding underlying asset in an appropriate proportion to form a riskless portfolio, then the situation is referred to as perfect hedging. To explain this, suppose a trader is holding 100 shares of a stock whose current price is 80 dollars per share. The trader realizes that a significant drop in the share price will cause a big loss in his portfolio. In order to hedge against this possibility, the investor buys a put option with a strike price of 85 dollars, where the date of maturity of the contract is three months from the purchase date. In the case of a tumble in the stock price, the trader can bail out the stocks at a price of 85 dollars per share. The expenditure incurred for this hedging is the price of the put option, whose current price 1 dollar. So at a total cost of 100 dollars the trader is able to provide a protection to an investment of 80000 dollars. Thus, trade in options enables individuals to insure against the risk of future price movements. We discuss this issue more explicitly in the next two sections.

Our discussion in this chapter is mostly on European options whose underlying assets are stocks. Unless specified, we assume throughout the chapter that the underlying asset is non-dividend paying. However, variants of the underlying assets are possible. For instance, the underlying asset can be a foreign currency and all prices are denominated in domestic currency. An option of this type is called a foreign currency option. Thus, a foreign currency option is a stock option whose underlying asset is a foreign currency. While European and American options are exchange-traded options, most of the foreign currency options are over-the-counter or off-exchange-traded options, for example, the ones traded over telephone, fax etc. (see Chapter 12). If the domestic currency is euro and the foreign currency is US dollar, then the spot domestic currency price of one unit of foreign currency is the value of one US dollar in euro. An option to buy US dollars is a US dollar call option and a euro put option. Suppose a trader purchases a two-month European call option of one dollar in exchange of euro with a strike price of K euro. If the dollar exchange rate at the time of expiry of the option exceeds K euro, the buyer of the option will exercise the right and earn the difference between the ongoing exchange rate and K. Thus, the motivation for buying (writing) a foreign currency call option is to derive profit from any appreciation (depreciation) in the exchange rate of the foreign currency in terms of the domestic currency at the time of exercise of the option (for further discussion see Merton 1973 and Smith 1976).

If the underlying asset of an option is an index, then it is called an index option. Since an index is based on a portfolio of stocks currently traded in the market, an index option can be regarded as betting on the movement of the underlying stocks (see Hull and Basu 2010 for a detailed analysis).

8.3 PAYOFF FUNCTIONS FOR OPTIONS

From the first numerical example considered in the earlier section it follows that the payoff from a long position in a European call option is simply the difference between the price at maturity S_T and the strike price K, if the difference $(S_T - K)$ is positive (here T stands for the date of maturity). It is zero otherwise. The option is exercised if $S_T > K$ and the corresponding payoff is $(S_T - K)$. The option will not be exercised if $S_T \le K$ and in this case the payoff is zero. Formally, the payoff function $\vartheta_{ECL}(S_T, K)$ associated with a long position in a European call option is defined as

$$\vartheta_{ECL}(S_T, K) = \begin{cases} S_T - K \ if \ S_T > K, \\ 0 \ if \ S_T \le K, \end{cases} \tag{8.1}$$

which we can rewrite in a more compact form as $\vartheta_{ECL}(S_T, K) = \max(S_T - K, 0)$. Thus, a European call option is in-the-money (out–of-the-money) if $\vartheta_{ECL}(S_T, K) > 0 (< 0)$. It is at-the-money if $\vartheta_{ECL}(S_T, K) = 0$.

Note that the strike price K is assumed to be given. Under this assumption, the payoff function $\vartheta_{ECL}(S_T, K)$ is differentiable (and hence continuous) in S_T over the interval (K, ∞). However, it is continuous but not differentiable at $S_T = K$. As S_T increases, the graph of $\vartheta_{ECL}(S_T, K)$ against S_T coincides with the horizontal axis up to K and then it increases linearly with a slope of 45 degrees (see panel (a) of Figure 8.1).

Next, we consider a trader with a short position (writer or seller) in one European call option. If $S_T \le K$, the buyer does not exercise the right at the date of expiration, hence the writer's payoff is zero. But if $S_T > K$, the right is exercised and the seller has to sell the asset at price K. In such a case, the seller has to purchase

Figure 8.1   Payoff Function of a European Option

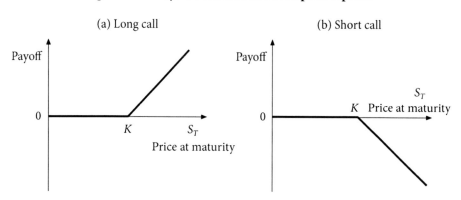

(a) Long call   (b) Short call

the asset at its current price S_T and sell it at price K to the buyer of the option. The seller's (negative) payoff from this deal is $(K - S_T)$. Thus, the payoff function associated with a short position in a European call option is defined as:

$$\vartheta_{ECS}(S_T, K) = \begin{cases} K - S_T \ if \ S_T > K, \\ 0 \ if \ S_T \le K. \end{cases} \tag{8.2}$$

We can rewrite this function in a more compact form as $\vartheta_{ECS}(S_T, K) = \min(K - S_T, 0) = - \max(S_T - K, 0)$. Panel (b) of Figure 8.1 gives a graphical representation of the function $\vartheta_{ECS}(S_T, K) = \min(K - S_T, 0)$.

From the second numerical example, considered in Section 8.2, it is clear that the holder of a European put option will exercise his right if $S_T \le K$, in which case the payoff is $K - S_T$. If $S_T > K$ he will not exercise his right and the corresponding payoff is zero. Thus, the payoff function associated with a long position in a European put option is $\vartheta_{EPL}(S_T, K) = \max(K - S_T, 0)$. By a similar argument the payoff from a short position in a European put option is $\vartheta_{EPS}(S_T, K) = \min(S_T - K, 0) = -\max (K - S_T, 0)$. Thus, a European put option is in-the-money (out-of-the-money) if $\vartheta_{EPL}(S_T, K) > 0 (< 0)$. It is at-the-money if $\vartheta_{EPL}(S_T, K) = 0$. Graphical depictions of the functions ϑ_{EPL} and ϑ_{EPS} are given respectively in panels (a) and (b) of Figure 8.2.

In order to achieve certain level of hedging, an investment aimed at reducing risk, a trader may be willing to construct a portfolio consisting of the same type of options, such as two or more put options or two or more call options, with long position in some and short position in the others. Such a strategy is known as a spread strategy. A spread strategy is called a price-spread strategy if the portfolio consists of two options of the underlying asset, of which one is bought and the other is sold, the dates of expiration are the same, but the strike prices are different. On the other hand, a spread strategy is called a calendar-spread strategy (or time-spread strategy) if of the two options bought and sold of the same underlying asset, the strike prices are the same, but the dates of expiration are different.

Figure 8.2   Payoff Function of a European Option

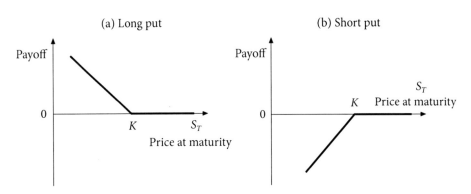

(a) Long put   (b) Short put

A price-spread strategy is referred to as bullish (bearish) if the holder of the corresponding portfolio benefits from an increase (a reduction) in the price of the underlying asset. An example of a bullish price-spread strategy is a portfolio composed of a long position in a European call option and a short position in a different European call option with a higher strike price. Let us denote the strike prices of these call options by K_1 and K_2 and their premiums by α_1^c and α_2^c respectively, where $K_1 < K_2$, $\alpha_2^c < \alpha_1^c$. Then from equations (8.1) and (8.2), it follows that the sum of the payoff functions of these options is $\vartheta_{BPS}(S_T, K_1, K_2) = \vartheta_{ECL}(S_T, K_1) + \vartheta_{ECS}(S_T, K_2) = \max(S_T - K_1, 0) - \max(S_T - K_2, 0)$, which can be written more explicitly as

$$\vartheta_{BPS}\left(S_T, K_1, K_2\right) = \begin{cases} 0 \ if \ S_T \leq K_1, \\ S_T - K_1 \ if \ K_1 \leq S_T \leq K_2, \\ K_2 - K_1 \ if \ S_T > K_2. \end{cases} \tag{8.3}$$

The payoff function in (8.3) has its maximum gain at the time of expiry when both the options expire in-the-money. The gain is minimum if, at the date of expiry, the price is not higher than the minimum of the strike prices. In this case both the options are out-of-the-money. A bullish price-spread strategy limits a trader's upward and downward risks. The payoff function of a bearish price-spread strategy with two European call options with different strike prices is simply the negative of the payoff function in (8.3) and can be used to describe either the market as a whole, or specific sectors and securities. A bearish price-spread strategy also controls a trader's upward profit potentials and downward risks.

A combination of a bullish price-spread strategy and a bearish price-spread strategy is called a butterfly price-spread strategy. Consider a portfolio consisting of a long position in two European call options with strike prices K_1 and K_3, $K_1 < K_3$, and a short position in two European call options with strike price $K_2 = (K_1 + K_3)/2$. Usually K_2 is close to the current price of the stock. Let α_i^c denote the premium of the option with strike price K_i, where $i = 1, 2, 3$ and $2\alpha_2^c < \alpha_1^c + \alpha_3^c$. The sum of payoffs from these four call options is given by $\max(S_T - K_1, 0) + \max(S_T - K_3, 0) - 2\max(S_T - K_2, 0)$, which we can write more explicitly as

$$\vartheta_{BS}\left(S_T, K_1, K_2, K_3\right) = \begin{cases} 0 \text{ if } S_T \leq K_1, \\ S_T - K_1 \text{ if } K_1 < S_T \leq K_2, \\ K_3 - S_T \text{ if } K_2 < S_T \leq K_3, \\ 0 \text{ if } S_T \geq K_3. \end{cases} \tag{8.4}$$

This payoff function achieves its maximum value at $S_T = K_2$. It decreases linearly on each side of K_2 until it achieves the value zero at $S_T = K_1$ and at $S_T = K_3$. In other words, the function $\vartheta_{BS}(S_T, K_1, K_2, K_3)$ is a linear increasing function over the interval $[K_1, K_2]$ and it decreases linearly over the interval $[K_2, K_3]$. The function is clearly continuous over $[K_1, K_2)$ and $(K_2, K_3]$. Since $K_3 - K_2 = K_2 - K_1$ it is continuous at K_2 as well. Thus, the function is everywhere continuous over $[K_1, K_3]$. Outside the interval $[K_1, K_3]$, the function takes on the value zero. Given K_1, as K_3 increases ϑ_{BS} increases. A significant movement of S_T on either side of K_2 generates a loss of small size. A butterfly hedging policy is appropriate when big movements in stock prices are unlikely.

The other popular examples of spread strategies include box and diagonal spread strategies. A box-spread strategy is a combination of a bullish price-spread strategy and a bearish price-spread strategy with the same two strike prices. In a diagonal-spread strategy the expiration and strike prices of the call options are different.

A calendar-spread strategy can be neutral, bullish or bearish. In a neutral calendar-spread hedging policy the strike price is close to the current stock price. On the other hand, a bullish (bearish) calendar-spread strategy uses a higher (lower) strike price. In a reverse calendar-spread strategy the trader has a short position in a long-maturity option and a long position in a short-maturity option. The possibility of a small amount of profit arises if the stock price at the date of expiration of the short-maturity option is significantly higher or lower than the corresponding strike price.

For the purpose of hedging it is also possible to have options of different types of the same underlying asset in a portfolio. A portfolio of this type is called a combination. An example is a bottom straddle, which consists of a European call option and a European put option with a long position, where both the options have the same strike price K and the same date of expiration. From our discussion in the section, it follows that the payoff associated with a bottom straddle is given by $\vartheta_{BOS}(S, K) = \max(S_T - K, 0) + \max(K - S_T, 0)$. This payoff function takes on the value zero only at $S_T = K$. Otherwise, it is positive everywhere. Graphically, this function resembles the letter 'V', with K being the center (see Figure 8.3). Since both the options are in long position, an initial payment of $\alpha^c + \alpha^p$ is required

Figure 8.3   Payoff Function of a Bottom Straddle

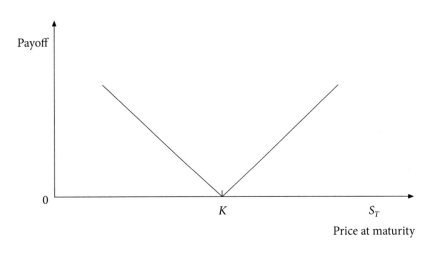

to create a bottom straddle, where $\alpha^c(\alpha^p)$ is the premium paid for acquisition of the call (put) option. As a hedging policy, a bottom straddle is appropriate if the investor expects a big movement in the stock price but is unsure about the direction of the movement.

Among other popular examples of combinations are strip, strap, strangle etc. A strip (strap) is a portfolio consisting of a long position in one European call option (two European call options) and two European put options (one European put option) with the same strike price and date of expiration. In a strip (strap) the trader's expectation is that the big movement in the price of the stock will take place in the downward (upward) direction. In a strangle, also known as bottom vertical combination, the portfolio is composed of a long position in a European put option and a European call option with the same date of expiration but different strike prices. In a strangle, the trader expects a big price movement but is not sure about the direction of the movement. For additional discussion on options and their payoff functions, see Duffe (1989), Lyuu (2002), Kwok (2008) and Hull and Basu (2010).

We now illustrate how to use the riskless hedging principle to derive the price of a European call option. Consider a two-period discrete time frame, now (the current period, period 0) and next period (period 1). Suppose a stock is currently traded at price S_0, which is expected to be equal to either S_1^1 or S_1^2 in the next period, where $S_1^1 > S_1^2$. The price S_1^i may be regarded as the future price of the stock in the next period when state i occurs in the future period, where $i = 1, 2$. That is, S_1^1 and S_1^2 are the state-contingent future prices of the stock. Assume also that there is a riskless bond currently trading at price 1 and yielding a payoff r. The European call option allows the holder to buy the stock in the next period. Given that the strike price is K, the state-contingent payoff for holding a long position in the stock is $\max\left(S_1^i - K, 0\right) = c_i$, say, $i = 1, 2$.

By non-arbitrage pricing, the hedging portfolio must have the same state-contingent payoff as the option. Let n_s and n_b be the required units of the stock and the bond in the portfolio. We therefore determine the hedging portfolio by solving the equations: $n_s S_1^1 + n_b r = c_1, n_s S_1^2 + n_b r = c_2$. These equations give $n_s = \left((c_1 - c_2)/(S_1^1 - S_1^2) \right)$ and $n_b = \left((c_2 S_1^1 - c_1 S_1^2)/(S_1^1 - S_1^2) r \right)$. This is the hedging portfolio (n_s, n_b). The price of the hedging portfolio then becomes

$$S_0 n_s + n_b = S_0 \frac{(c_1 - c_2)}{(S_1^1 - S_1^2)} + \frac{1}{r} \left[\frac{c_2 S_1^1 - c_1 S_1^2}{(S_1^1 - S_1^2)} \right] = \frac{1}{r} \left[\frac{c_1 (rS_0 - S_1^2) + c_2 (S_1^1 - rS_0)}{(S_1^1 - S_1^2)} \right]. \quad (8.5)$$

The option price must be equal to this price of the hedging portfolio. Note that a sufficient condition for positivity of this price is $S_1^1 > rS_0 > S_1^2$ (see also Eichberger and Harper 1888).

8.4 PROFIT FUNCTIONS FOR OPTIONS

In our earlier discussion we have noted that the buyer of an option has to pay a premium to the seller. The payment of this amount confers ownership of the option on the buyer. The profit function corresponding to a call option is then obtained by subtracting the premium from the payoff or revenue function. Thus, the profit function $\psi_{ECL}(\alpha^c, S_T, K)$ associated with a long position in a European call option is given by

$$\psi_{ECL}(\alpha^c, S_T, K) = \max(S_T, - K, 0) - \alpha^c$$

$$= \begin{cases} S_T - K - \alpha^c \ \text{if} \ S_T > K, \\ -\alpha^c \ \text{if} \ S_T \le K, \end{cases} \quad (8.6)$$

where α^c denotes the option premium. If the option is not exercised ($S_T \le K$), then the graph of this function is a horizontal straight line at the position $- \alpha^c$. For $S_T \ge K$, the function increases linearly as S_T increases and the graph intersects the horizontal axis at $S_T - K = \alpha^c$. At $S_T = K + \alpha^c$ the holder's profit is zero (see panel (b) Figure 8.4).

Since the seller receives the premium α^c for writing the call, the profit function $\psi_{ECS}(\alpha^c, S_T, K)$, corresponding to a short position in a European call option, is given by the sum of the seller's payoff function and premium—that is, $\psi_{ECS}(\alpha^c, S_T, K) = \min(K - S_T, 0) + \alpha^c$. The graph of this function is simply the transpose of the graph of $\psi_{ECL}(\alpha^c, S, K)$ around the horizontal axis (see panel (a) of Figure 8.4).

Likewise, the profit functions associated with long and short positions in a European put option are given respectively by $\psi_{EPL}(\alpha^p, S_T, K) = \max(K - S_T, 0) - \alpha^p$ and $\psi_{EPS}(\alpha^p, S_T, K) = \min(K - S_T, 0) + \alpha^p$, where α^p denotes the option

Figure 8.4   Profit Function of a European Call Option

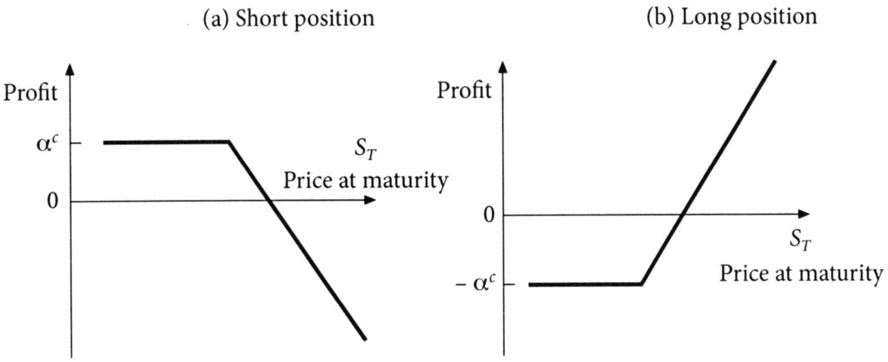

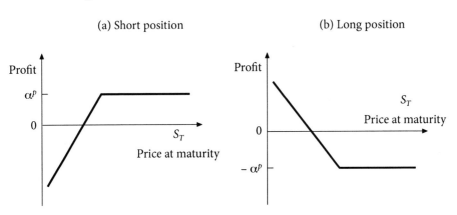

(a) Short position   (b) Long position

premium. The graph of $\psi_{EPL}(\alpha^p, S_T, K)$ decreases linearly with S_T up to $-\alpha^p$ and then it coincides with the horizontal straight line $-\alpha^p$. Since the profit of the holder becomes zero at $S_T = K - \alpha^p$, it intersects the horizontal axis at $S_T = K - \alpha^p$. The graph of $\psi_{EPS}(\alpha^p, S_T, K)$ is obtained by transposing the graph of $\psi_{EPL}(\alpha^p, S_T, K)$ around the horizontal axis (see Figure 8.5).

Figure 8.5   Profit Function of a European Put Option

(a) Short position   (b) Long position

Consider a trader with a portfolio consisting of a long position in one unit of the underlying asset and a short position in a European call option. This investment strategy is referred to as writing a covered call. The long position in the stock covers the trader from any necessary payoff on the short call that arises because of a sharp increase in the stock price. This indicates the hedging effect of the portfolio. As before, let α^c be the premium obtained for writing the call and S_0 be the asset price at the beginning of the option contract. Thus, in order to obtain a long position in one unit of the asset, the trader's initial investment on the asset is

S_0. The payoff associated with the call is $-\max(S_T, - K, 0)$, where, as before, K and S_T are respectively the strike price and the asset price at the date of expiry. At the date of expiry, the trader's revenue from the sale of one unit of the asset is S_T. Therefore, the trader's profit function at the date of expiry is

$$\psi_{CLW}(\alpha^c, S_0, S_T, K) = S_T - S_0 - \max(S_T, - K, 0) + \alpha^c$$
$$= \begin{cases} \alpha^c - S_0 + K \ if \ S_T \geq K, \\ \alpha^c - S_0 + S_T \ if \ S_T < K. \end{cases} \tag{8.7}$$

For $S_T = 0$, $\psi_{CLW}(\alpha^c, S_0, S_T, K) = \alpha^c - S_0$ and then it increases linearly as S_T increases. For $S_T \geq K$ it coincides with the horizontal line $\alpha^c - S_0 + K$ (see panel (a) of Figure 8.6).

If we combine a short position in one unit of the underlying asset with a long position in a call option, then the profit function will be the negative of the function $\psi_{CLW}(\alpha^c, S_0, S_T, K)$ in (8.7) and the corresponding figure will be the transpose of the figure for $\psi_{CLW}(\alpha^c, S_0, S_T, K)$ around the horizontal axis (see panel (b) of Figure 8.6).

Figure 8.6　Profit Function of a Portfolio consisting of

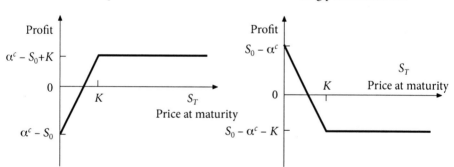

(a) Long position in a stock and short position in a call

(b) Short position in a stock and long position in a call

A protective put is a portfolio designed for achieving hedging effect and is composed of a long position in a European put option and in one unit of the underlying asset. The long position in the stock protects the trader from any necessary payoff on the long put that arises because of a sharp reduction in the stock price. The premium paid for acquiring the put option is α^p. Then it can be derived that the associated profit function is given by

$$\psi_{PP}(\alpha^p, S_0, S_T, K) = S_T - S_0 + \max(K - S_T, 0) - \alpha^p$$
$$= \begin{cases} -\alpha^p - S_0 + S_T \ if \ S_T \geq K, \\ -\alpha^p - S_0 + K \ if \ S_T < K. \end{cases} \tag{8.8}$$

Figure 8.7   Profit Function of a Portfolio consisting of

(a) Long position in a stock and long position in a put

(b) Short position in a stock and short position in a put

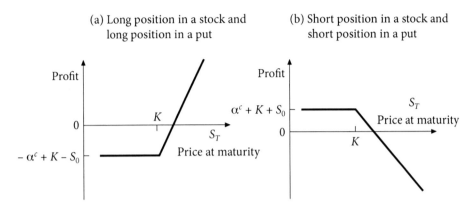

This function is shown graphically in panel (a) of Figure 8.7. Panel (b) of the figure shows graphically a combination of a short position in a put option and in one unit of the underlying asset. This is the opposite of a protective put.

8.5 BOUNDARIES FOR OPTION VALUES

In this section we derive some boundaries for prices of all types of options. The price paid for an option is called the premium. Some of the standard questions that arise in this context are: (i) How are the prices of European and American options related? (ii) How is the price of the underlying asset related to an option price? (iii) What can be an unambiguous lower bound of an option price? (iv) How are put and call options prices related? We try to answer these types of questions sequentially. Parts of the discussion in this section are based on Lyuu (2002), Capinski and Zastawniak (2003), Kwok (2008) and Hull and Basu (2010).

Let $B(\tau)$ be the discounted present value of a zero coupon risk-free bond with a face value of 1 dollar, where τ is the time to maturity. If the continuously compounded risk-free interest rate is given by λ, then $B(\tau) = exp(-\lambda\tau)$, where "exp" represents the exponential transformation (see Section 7.4). This value of $B(\tau)$ is the discount factor over τ time period.

The price of an option depends on the price of the underlying asset, strike price, time remaining for the option to be exercised, the volatility of the stock price, risk-free interest rate on the stock, and expected dividends during the lifespan of the option. Since the underlying asset is risky, its price is a random variable. Consequently, the price of any option derived from it will also be a random variable. But once the price of the underlying asset is set, the price of the derived option is also determined. Let O_{AC} and O_{AP} respectively be the prices of an American call option and a put option. The corresponding prices for their European counterparts are given respectively by O_{EC} and O_{EP}. Let S_t and S_T respectively be the price of the underlying asset at time t and at the time of expiry T. Let $\tau = T - t$ denote the time to expiry.

We divide our discussion into several subsections.

8.5.1 Non-negativity of Option Prices

Since all option prices are non-negative, it must be the case that

$$O_{AC} \geq 0,\ O_{AP} \geq 0,\ O_{EC} \geq 0,\ O_{EP} \geq 0. \tag{8.9}$$

If an option price were negative, then the buyer receives a positive amount of money in exchange for the purchase and is also guaranteed of a non-negative profit at the time of expiration. This is a case of riskless arbitrage, which is ruled out by assumption. Thus, option prices are bounded from below by zero.

8.5.2 Degrees of Freedom in Exercise Time and Some Boundary Conditions

Let $O_{AC}(S_t, \tau, K)$ be the price function of an American call option with asset price S_t at time t, time to expiry τ and the strike price K. We write $O_{AP}(S_t, \tau, K)$ for the price of an American put option based on the vector (S_t, τ, K). The corresponding prices for European call and put options are denoted respectively by $O_{EC}(S_t, \tau, K)$ and $O_{EP}(S_t, \tau, K)$.

The holder of an American option can exercise the right at any date of trading during the time frame. Thus, the degrees of freedom in this case are the number of trading dates available during the time frame, whereas for a European option the degree of freedom is one since the privilege of early exercise does not exist in this case. The two options are identical in all other aspects. Consequently, the degrees of freedom for the American option is much higher than that associated with the European option and given that higher degrees of freedom should have a positive value, we must have

$$O_{AC}(S_t, \tau, K) \geq O_{EC}(S_t, \tau, K). \tag{8.10}$$

The discussion concerning the derivation of inequality (8.10) enables us to conclude that an American option with a higher degree of freedom should not have a lower value. That is, given $\tau_2 > \tau_1$, it follows that

$$O_{AC}(S_t, \tau_2, K) \geq O_{AC}(S_t, \tau_1, K) \geq 0,$$
$$O_{AP}(S_t, \tau_2, K) \geq O_{AP}(S_t, \tau_1, K) \geq 0. \tag{8.11}$$

As we have noted in Chapter 7, for perpetuity the date of maturity is infinity, that is, $T \to \infty$. Now, the holder of perpetuity enjoys some additional advantages such as receipt of dividends. If we regard the asset as a perpetuity with zero strike price, then for a given t, $S_t \geq O_{AC}(S_t, \infty, 0)$ For a given t, if we set $\tau_2 = \infty$ and $K = 0$ in the first term of the first inequality in (8.11), we get $O_{AC}(S_t, \infty, 0) \geq O_{AC}(S_t, \tau_1, K)$ ≥ 0. Hence $S_t \geq O_{AC}(S_t, \infty, K) \geq O_{AC}(S_t, \tau_1, K) \geq 0$. Combining this inequality for τ_1 $= \tau$ with (8.10) we get

$$S_t \geq O_{AC}(S_t, \infty, 0) \geq O_{AC}(S_t, \tau, K) \geq O_{EC}(S_t, \tau, K) \geq 0. \qquad (8.12)$$

This shows that European and American call options are bounded above by the asset value. The purchase price of an option can never be higher than the price of the underlying asset because this is the maximum value that the buyer can assign to the value of an option.

Inequality (8.12) is true for all $S_t \geq 0$. Putting $S_t = 0$ in (8.12), we get $0 \geq O_{AC}(0, \tau, K) \geq O_{EC}(0, \tau, K) \geq 0$, which gives

$$O_{EC}(0, \tau, K) = O_{AC}(0, \tau, K). \qquad (8.13)$$

That is, at the zero asset value the values of call options become zero.

For put options we have the following inequality

$$K \geq O_{AP}(S_t, \tau, K) \geq O_{EP}(S_t, \tau, K). \qquad (8.14)$$

The holder of a put option has the right to sell one share of a stock. The value of the option can never exceed the strike price—the price in the contract at which the option can be traded. The price of an American put option equals its strike price if the value of the underlying asset is zero.

If the time to expiry $\tau = 0$ ($t = T$), then

$$O_{AC}(S_T, 0, K) = O_{EC}(S_T, 0, K) = max(S_T - K, 0),$$

$$O_{AP}(S_T, 0, K) = O_{EP}(S_T, 0, K) = max(K - S_T, 0). \qquad (8.15)$$

The quantity $max(S_T - K, 0)$ the price of call option at expiry is known as its intrinsic value. Likewise, the intrinsic value of a put option is given by $max(K - S_T, 0)$. Given that in the earlier sections, we have denoted the premiums corresponding to a European call option and a European put option by α^c and α^p respectively and the stock's price at the initial date $t = 0$ is S_0, it is also true that $O_{EC}(S_0, T, K) = \alpha^c$ and $O_{EP}(S_0, T, K) = \alpha^p$. Similar equalities must hold for American options as well.

Thus, we want to know how much to pay as the premium. This shows that the problem of option pricing is a backward problem. We discuss this issue in the next section.

The difference between the option value before and at expiry is called the time value of the option. The time value of an American option is a reflection of the probability of whether it will gain in intrinsic value or be profitable to exercise before the date of expiration. From inequality (8.11) it follows that the time value of an American option is always non-negative. This is intuitively reasonable since the option value is at least as large as its intrinsic value.

Since higher degrees of freedom provide an additional advantage to the holder of an American option, it is clear that

$$O_{AC}(S_t, \tau, K) \geq max(S_T - K, 0), O_{AP}(S_t, T, K) \geq max(K - S_T, 0). \quad (8.16)$$

8.5.3 Variability of Strike Price and Its Implications

We wish to look at the monotonic behavior of the price of an option with respect to the strike price under *ceteris paribus* assumptions. A call option whose strike price is higher has less opportunity to provide positive payoff. At the time of expiry, its cash inflow is lower. Thus, this is certainly true for European call options because such options can be exercised only at the date of expiry and the strike price is negatively related with the payoff (see (8.15)). To see its validity for American call options, given $K_1 < K_2$ suppose $O_{AC}(S_t, \tau, K_1) < O_{AC}(S_t, \tau, K_2)$. One can have a long position in $O_{AC}(S_t, \tau, K_1)$ and short position in $O_{AC}(S_t, \tau, K_2)$ to derive a positive cash inflow. If the holder of $O_{AC}(S_t, \tau, K_2)$ exercises it before the date of expiration, the long option can be exercised immediately to generate an arbitrage cash inflow of $(K_2 - K_1)$ which is positive by assumption. Hence $O_{AC}(S_t, \tau, K_2) \leq O_{AC}(S_t, \tau, K_1)$. Thus, for $K_1 < K_2$,

$$O_{AC}(S_t, \tau, K_2) \leq O_{AC}(S_t, \tau, K_1), O_{EC}(S_t, \tau, K_2) \leq O_{EC}(S_t, \tau, K_1). \quad (8.17)$$

Thus, given other things, the price of a call option with a higher strike price cannot be higher than that with a lower strike price.

An argument from the opposite direction enables us to derive the following

$$O_{AP}(S_t, \tau, K_2) \geq O_{AP}(S_t, \tau, K_1), O_{EP}(S_t, \tau, K_2) \geq O_{EP}(S_t, \tau, K_1). \quad (8.18)$$

Given $K_1 < K_2$, we now investigate how the difference $O_{AC}(S_t, \tau, K_1) - O_{AC}(S_t, \tau, K_2)$ is related to $K_2 - K_1$. Suppose $O_{AC}(S_t, \tau, K_1) - O_{AC}(S_t, \tau, K_2) \geq K_2 - K_1$. A trader can write and sell an American call option with strike price K_1, buy an American call option with strike price K_2, and invest the balance $O_{AC}(S_t, \tau, K_1) - O_{AC}(S_t, \tau, K_2)$ in a risk-free asset. If the holder of the written option exercises it at time $t \leq T$, then the trader has to pay $max(0, S_t - K_1)$. Immediate exercise of the other option will give the trader a payoff of $max(0, S_t - K_2)$. Now, $max(0, S_t - K_2) - max(0, S_t - K_1)$ $\geq -(K_2 - K_1)$, with strict inequality if $S_t < K_2$. Together with the risk-free investment amounting to at least $K_2 - K_1$ the trader's final payoff will be a non-negative amount of money. Therefore, the trader can make an arbitrage profit if $O_{AC}(S_t, \tau, K_1) - O_{AC}(S_t, \tau, K_2) \geq K_2 - K_1$ holds (see Capinski and Zastawniak 2003). Hence

$$O_{AC}(S_t, \tau, K_1) - O_{AC}(S_t, \tau, K_2) < K_2 - K_1. \tag{8.19a}$$

By a similar argument

$$O_{AP}(S_t, \tau, K_2) - O_{AP}(S_t, \tau, K_1) < K_2 - K_1. \tag{8.19b}$$

We now demonstrate convexity property of option prices in strike prices under *ceteris paribus* assumptions. We first prove the property for European call options. Let K_1, K_3, where $K_1 < K_3$, be two strike prices. Define the strike price $K_2 = (1 - c) K_1 + cK_3$, where $0 < c < 1$ is arbitrary. Convexity of prices of European call options demands that $cO_{EC}(S_t, \tau, K_3) + (1 - c)O_{EC}(S_t, \tau, K_1) \geq O_{EC}(S_t, \tau, K_2)$. Now, consider two portfolios Ω^* and Π^*, where the former consists of c units of call with strike price K_3 and $(1 - c)$ units of call with strike price K_1. The latter portfolio consists of one call with strike price K_2. The payoffs of these two portfolios at expiry are given in Table 8.1.

From the table, we note that $\vartheta_{\Omega^*} \geq \vartheta_{\Pi^*}$ for all values of S_T. Thus, portfolio Ω^* Pareto dominates portfolio Π^*. Hence the discounted present value of the former is at least as large as that of the latter. This demonstrates the convexity property of European call options in strike prices. Since this demonstration does not involve time to expiry τ, it is independent of τ. Hence American call prices are also convex in strike prices. If we substitute the call options in the portfolios Ω^* and Π^* by put options, then it follows that European and American put options are as well convex in strike prices.

Table 8.1 Payoffs at Expiry for Portfolios Ω^* and Π^*

Payoff at expiry	$S_T \leq K$	$K_1 \leq S_T \leq K_2$	$K_2 \leq S_T \leq K_3$	$K_3 \leq S_T$
Portfolio Ω^*	0	$(1 - c)(S_T - K_1)$	$(1 - c)(S_T - K_1)$	$c(S_T - K_3)$ $+ (1 - c)(S_T - K_1)$
Portfolio Π^*	0	0	$(S_T - K_2)$	$(S_T - K_2)$
Comparison of payoffs	$\vartheta_{\Omega^*} = \vartheta_{\Pi^*}$	$\vartheta_{\Omega^*} \geq \vartheta_{\Pi^*}$	$\vartheta_{\Omega^*} \geq \vartheta_{\Pi^*}$	$\vartheta_{\Omega^*} \geq \vartheta_{\Pi^*}$

8.5.4 Variability of Asset Price and Its Consequences

If the current asset price increases, the chance for exercise of a call (put) option increases (decreases) and on exercise the induced cash inflow will be higher (lower). Thus, if S_t', S_t'', where $S_t' < S_t''$, are two different prices of the underlying asset prices at time t, then we have

$$O_{AC}\left(S'_t,\tau,K\right)<O_{AC}\left(S''_t,\tau,K\right),O_{EC}\left(S'_t,\tau,K\right)<O_{EC}\left(S''_t,\tau,K\right),$$

$$O_{AP}\left(S'_t,T,K\right)>O_{AP}\left(S''_t,T,K_1\right),O_{EP}\left(S'_t,T,K\right)>O_{EP}\left(S''_t,T,K\right). \quad (8.20)$$

To see this for American call options, suppose $O_{AC}\left(S'_t,\tau,K\right)\geq O_{AC}\left(S''_t,\tau,K\right)$, where $S'_t=c'S_0$ and $S''_t=c''S_0$. A trader can write and sell an American call option on a portfolio with c' shares and buy an American call option on a portfolio with c'' shares where both the options have same strike price and time to expiry. The balance $O_{AC}\left(S'_t,\tau,K\right)-O_{AC}\left(S''_t,\tau,K\right)$ of these two transactions can be invested in a risk-free asset. If the owner of the written option exercises it at time $t\leq T$, then the other option can be exercised immediately to meet the liability. Since $c'<c''$, the payoffs satisfy $\max(0,c'S_t-K)\leq\max(0,c''S_t-K)$ with $<$ if $K<c''S_t$. This trading strategy, therefore, provides an opportunity for earning a non-negative arbitrage profit. If in the above demonstration the time of exercise $t=T$, then we immediately have a proof for European call options. The remaining two inequalities can be proved analogously.

European and American option call and put prices are convex functions of asset prices. To state this formally, let $S'_t<S''_t$ and $c\in(0,1)$. Then

$$cO_{EC}\left(S'_t,\tau,K\right)+\left(1-c\right)O_{EC}\left(S''_t,\tau,K\right)\geq O_{EC}\left(cS'_t+\left(1-c\right)S''_t,\tau,K\right),$$

$$cO_{EP}\left(S'_t,\tau,K\right)+\left(1-c\right)O_{EP}\left(S''_t,\tau,K\right)\geq O_{EP}\left(cS'_t+\left(1-c\right)S''_t,\tau,K\right),$$

$$cO_{AC}\left(S'_t,\tau,K\right)+\left(1-c\right)O_{AC}\left(S''_t,\tau,K\right)\geq O_{AC}\left(cS'_t+\left(1-c\right)S''_t,\tau,K\right),$$

$$cO_{AP}\left(S'_t,\tau,K\right)+\left(1-c\right)O_{AP}\left(S''_t,\tau,K\right)\geq O_{AP}\left(cS'_t+\left(1-c\right)S''_t,\tau,K\right). \quad (8.21)$$

We prove this assertion for American call options. Define $S_t=cS'_t+\left(1-c\right)S''_t$ and let $S'_t=x'S_0,S''_t=x''S_0$, and $S_t=xS_0$. Clearly, the positive real numbers x', x'' and x exist. Suppose

$$cO_{AC}\left(S'_t,\tau,K\right)+\left(1-c\right)O_{AC}\left(S''_t,\tau,K\right)<O_{AC}\left(cS'_t+\left(1-c\right)S''_t,\tau,K\right). \quad (8.22)$$

Then a trader can sell a call option on a portfolio with x shares, purchase c call options on a portfolio with x' shares $(1-c)$ call options on a portfolio with x'' shares, where the strike price K and time to expiry for all the options are the same. The positive balance $O_{AC}\left(cS'_t+\left(1-c\right)S''_t,\tau,K\right)-cO_{AC}\left(S'_t,\tau,K\right)-\left(1-c\right)O_{AC}\left(S''_t,\tau,K\right)$ of these transactions can be invested in a risk-free asset. If the holder of the written option exercises at time $t\leq T$, then the trader has to pay $\max(xS_t-K,0)$ where by construction $x=cx'+(1-c)x''$. The other two options can be exercised immediately to cover the liability and since $\max(xS_t-K,0)\leq c\max(x'S_t-K,0)+(1-c)\max(x''S_t-K,0)$, the trader has a chance of earning a non-negative arbitrage profit. This is a contradiction. The proof for European call options follows immediately by setting $t=T$ in this proof. Analogous proofs hold for put options.

8.5.5 Put–Call Parity and Early Exercise: Non-dividend-paying Stocks

Consider a portfolio Ω consisting of one European call option on a non-dividend-paying stock and a discount bond with a face value of K whose maturity date coincides with the date of expiration of the call. Consider also a second portfolio Π that contains one unit of the underlying asset. If the price of the underlying asset S_T at the time of expiration of the option is less than K, then the option becomes worthless and the value of portfolio Ω is simply K, the face value of the bond. If $S_T \geq K$, then the value of portfolio Ω is $(S_T - K) + K = S_T$, the sum of payoffs from the option and the face value of the bond. The value of portfolio Π is S_T. Thus, the value of portfolio Ω is at least as large as that of portfolio Π. That is, portfolio Ω Pareto dominates portfolio Π. Therefore, the discounted present value of portfolio Ω is at least as large as that of portfolio Π. Otherwise, by arbitrage opportunities one can buy portfolio Ω and sell portfolio Π to make a positive profit. Thus, $O_{EC}(S_0, T, K) + KB(T) \geq S_0$. Since $B(T) = exp(-\lambda T)$, we have

$$O_{EC}(S_0, T, K) \geq S_0 - K\, exp(-\lambda T). \tag{8.23}$$

In view of non-negativity of the option value, we have

$$O_{EC}(S_0, T, K) \geq max(S_0 - K\, exp(-\lambda T), 0). \tag{8.24}$$

This combined with the inequality $S_0 \geq O_{EC}(S_0, T, K)$, which is obtained from (8.12) by setting $t = 0$, shows that

$$S_0 \geq O_{EC}(S_0, T, K) \geq max(S_0 - K\, exp(-\lambda T), 0). \tag{8.25}$$

Inequality (8.25) shows that the value of a European call option on a non-dividend-paying stock is bounded between $max(S_0 - K\, exp(-\lambda T), 0)$ and S_0.

Next, consider a third portfolio $\hat{\Omega}$ consisting of one European put option on a non-dividend-paying stock and one unit of the underlying asset. A fourth portfolio $\hat{\Pi}$ contains a discount bond with a face value of K whose maturity date coincides with the date of expiration of the put. If $S_T \geq K$ then the put option becomes worthless at the date of expiry and the value of the portfolio $\hat{\Omega}$ is S_T, the value of one unit of the underlying asset at the expiration date. If $S_T < K$, then the value of the portfolio is $(K - S_T) + S_T = K$. On the other hand, the value of $\hat{\Pi}$ at the date of expiration is S_T. Thus, portfolio $\hat{\Omega}$ Pareto dominates portfolio $\hat{\Pi}$. In the absence of arbitrage opportunities, $O_{EP}(S_0, T, K) + S_0 \geq K\, exp(-\lambda T)$. This along with non-negativity of the option price gives $O_{EP}(S_0, T, K) \geq max(K\, exp(-\lambda T) - S_0, 0)$. Thus; the price of a European put option on a non-dividend-paying stock is bounded below by $max(K\, exp(-\lambda T) - S_0, 0)$.

We now discuss the put–call parity, a relationship that exists between prices of European call and put options. For this, consider the portfolios Ω and $\hat{\Omega}$ defined above. As we have noted, the values of both the portfolios are $max(S_T, K)$. Since the two options considered in the portfolios are Ω and $\hat{\Omega}$ are European, they cannot be exercised prior to the date of expiry. Hence the discounted present values of the two portfolios are the same. That is,

$$O_{EC} + K \, exp(-\lambda T) = O_{EP} + S_0. \tag{8.26}$$

This relation is referred to as the put–call parity. It shows how one can derive the value of a European call option with a given strike price and the date of expiry from the value of a European put option with the same strike price and the date of expiry. The process can be reversed, that is, the relation (8.26) can be used to determine the price of a European put option from that of European call option under *ceteris paribus* assumptions.

We now look at a simple implication of the variability of the strike price using the put–call parity. For this, consider two European call and put options with strike prices K_1 and K_2, where $K_1 < K_2$. Then by the put call parity we have $O_{EC}(K_1) - O_{EP}(K_1) = S_0 - K_1 \, exp(-\lambda T)$ and $O_{EC}(K_2) - O_{EP}(K_2) = S_0 - K_2 \, exp(-\lambda T)$. Subtracting the second equation from the first equation we get $O_{EC}(K_1) - O_{EC}(K_2)) + O_{EP}(K_2) - O_{EP}(K_1)) = (K_2 - K_1) exp(-\lambda T)$. In view of (8.19) and (8.17) each first bracketed term on the left-hand of side of this equation is non-negative. Hence we have

$$(O_{EC}(K_1) - O_{EC}(K_2)) \leq (K_2 - K_1) exp(-\lambda T),$$

$$(O_{EP}(K_2) - O_{EP}(K_1)) \leq (K_2 - K_1) exp(-\lambda T). \tag{8.27}$$

We can also use the put–call parity to study a simple implication of the variability of the asset price. Suppose $S_0' < S_0''$. Then it follows that $O_{EC}(S_0') - O_{EP}(S_0') = S_0' - K \exp(-\lambda T)$ and $O_{EC}(S_0'') - O_{EP}(S_0'') = S_0'' - K \exp(-\lambda T)$. Subtracting the first equation from the second equation we get $(O_{EC}(S_0'') - O_{EC}(S_0')) + (O_{EP}(S_0') - O_{EP}(S_0'')) = S_0'' - S_0'$. Both the first bracketed terms on the left-hand side of this equation are non-negative. See (8.20). Hence we have

$$(O_{EC}(S_0'') - O_{EC}(S_0')) \leq S_0'' - S_0', (O_{EP}(S_0') - O_{EP}(S_0'')) \leq S_0'' - S_0'. \tag{8.28}$$

The put–call parity holds for the European options only. However, it is possible to derive upper and lower bounds on the difference between prices of American call and put options. To see this, recall that $O_{AC} \geq O_{EC}$ and $O_{AP} \geq O_{EP}$. Since the option is non-dividend paying, $O_{AC} = O_{EC}$ Plugging this information into (8.26) and using the fact that $O_{AP} \geq O_{EP}$, we have $O_{AC} - O_{AP} \leq S_0 - K \, exp(-\lambda T)$. Thus, $S_0 - K \, exp(-\lambda T)$ is an upper bound on $O_{AC} - O_{AP}$. It can also be demonstrated that $S_0 - K \leq O_{AC} - O_{AP}$ (see Kwok 2008). Therefore,

$$S_0 - K \le O_{AC} - O_{AP} \le S_0 - K\, exp(-\lambda T). \qquad (8.29)$$

We now wish to examine the effect of early exercise of American call and put options on a non-dividend-paying stock. Early exercise means exercise of the option at a date $t < T(\tau > 0)$. By positivity of λ, for any $t < T$, $exp(-\lambda T) < exp(-\lambda t)$. So $K\, exp(-\lambda T) < K\, exp(-\lambda t)$ and hence $S_0 - K\, exp(-\lambda T) > S_0 - K\, exp(-\lambda t)$. Since $O_{AC} \ge O_{EC}$ from (8.23) it follows that

$$O_{AC} \ge S_0 - K\, exp(-\lambda T) > S_0 - K\, exp(-\lambda t). \qquad (8.30)$$

Since we allow the possibility $O_{AC} = S_0 - K\, exp(-\lambda T)$ in (8.30), with early exercise the value of the option goes down. So, early exercise of an American call option on a non-dividend-paying stock is not optimal. Intuitively, by early exercise, the holder of the option loses the time value of money on the strike price. This follows from the inequality that for any $t < T$, $-K\, exp(-\lambda T) > -K\, exp(-\lambda t)$. The later payment of the strike price is better for the option holder. Also by early exercise, the holder loses the right to exercise the option at a later date.

The inequalities $O_{EP}(S_0, T, K) \ge max(K\, exp(-\lambda T) - S_0, 0)$ and $O_{AP} \ge O_{EP}$ derived earlier in the section enable us to state that $O_{AP} \ge K\, exp(-\lambda T) - S_0$. Note that given K and S_0, $K\, exp(-\lambda T) - S_0$ achieves its maximum value for $T = 0$ (immediate exercise). That is, $K - S_0 > K\, exp(-\lambda T) - S_0$ for any positive T. Now, in the inequality $O_{AP} \ge K\, exp(-\lambda T) - S_0$ we also allow the possibility that $O_{AP} = K\, exp(-\lambda T) - S_0$. For $T = 0$, $O_{AP} \ge K - S_0 > K\, exp(-\lambda t) - S_0$ for any $t > 0$. This means that under immediate exercise the price of the American put option is higher than that if exercised at a later date. Thus, immediate exercise of an American put option on a non-dividend-paying stock is optimal. Intuitively, by immediate exercise it is possible to avoid any depreciation in the strike price ($K > K\, exp(-\lambda t)$ for any positive $t \le T$). Delay in exercise time also includes the future possibility of the right not to exercise.

8.5.6 Put–Call Parity: Dividend-Paying Stocks

The objective of this subsection is to look at implications of dividend-paying stocks on the put–call parity. The discounted present value of the dividends is denoted by DI. Let us reconsider the portfolios Ω and Π, of which the first consists of a long position in a dividend-paying European call option and a discount bond with a face value of K whose maturity date coincides with the date of expiration of the call. The second portfolio consists of one unit of the asset. These portfolios can be redefined respectively as: (i) a non-dividend-paying European call option plus a cash amount of $DI + K\, exp(-\lambda T)$ and (ii) one unit of the asset. Likewise, we can redefine portfolios $\hat{\Omega}$ and $\hat{\Pi}$ respectively as: (i) a non-dividend-paying European put option and one unit of the asset and (ii) a cash amount of $DI + K\, exp(-\lambda T)$.

Then comparing the values of the redefined portfolios Ω and $\hat{\Omega}$ at the maturity period we can show that

$$O_{EC} + K \exp(-\lambda T) + DI = O_{EP} + S_0. \tag{8.31}$$

This is the put–call relation for dividend-paying stocks. When the underlying asset is non-dividend-paying, $DI = 0$ and the put–call relation in (8.31) coincides with its non-dividend-paying counterpart in (8.26).

Using arguments similar to that employed to derive the inequalities $O_{EC}(S_0, T, K) \geq max(S_0 - K \exp(-\lambda T), 0)$ and $O_{EP}(S_0, T, K) \geq max(K \exp(-\lambda T) - S_0, 0)$ we can also derive the inequalities: $O_{EC} \geq S_0 - DI - K \exp(-\lambda T)$ and $O_{EP} \geq DI - S_0 + K \exp(-\lambda T)$. For American options the following inequality is true: $S_0 - DI - K \leq O_{AC} - O_{AP} \leq S_0 - K \exp(-\lambda T)$.

8.6 FORWARD AND FUTURES CONTRACTS

A forward contract is an agreement between two parties to buy or sell an asset at a future date (the delivery date) for a predetermined price (the delivery price). While in the case of an option the buyer has to pay a premium to the seller in exchange of writing the option, no premium payment is involved in the transaction of a forward contract. The delivery price of the contract satisfies the condition that the value of contract is zero to both the parties at the time of initiation of the contract. In contrast to a forward contract, there may be an agreement to buy and sell an asset today. Such a contract is referred to as a spot contract. One major reason for getting involved into a forward contract is to become independent of the fluctuations in the unknown future price of an underlying risky asset. For instance, a trader may be interested in buying foreign currency at a fixed rate in the future; a farmer desires to finalize the sale price of his crops in advance and so on.

A forward contract is an obligatory contract. It is an over-the-counter contract. There is no question of not exercising the right at the delivery date. Consequently, the buyer's payoff at maturity T from one unit of the asset is simply the difference between the maturity price (price at the delivery date) S_T of the underlying asset and the delivery price K. Since K is treated as a parameter here, the function $S_T - K$ (the buyer's payoff function) that is, the payoff function from a long position in one unit of the asset is linearly increasing in S_T. Its graph intersects the horizontal axis at $S_T = K$. The seller's payoff function or the payoff function from a short position in an asset is $K - S_T$, the negative of the payoff function of the buyer. The graph of this function is obtained by taking the transpose of the graph of $S_T - K$ around the point K.

The forward price is defined as the delivery price at which the initial value of the contract is zero. Recall that in the context of options, we have used the terms "value" and "price" synonymously. However, here the terms "value" and "price" have different meanings. Let $V_{FOC}(t, T)$ be the value of a forward contract, where $t \leq T$ denotes the period of initiation of the contract. We write S_t for the price of the underlying asset at time t and $\tau = (T - t)$ is the time to maturity. Since the contract is settled today, this value must be its discounted value of the value at the period T. When t is the period of initiation of the contract, we write $\eta_{FOC}(t, T)$ for the price of the contract. As before, let λ be the risk-free interest rate.

Suppose the period of initiation of the contract is 0 so that $\tau = T$. Consider a portfolio with a long position in a forward contract and a zero coupon bond with a face value K whose maturity date is T. The other portfolio consists of one unit of the underlying asset. The bond price is $K \, exp(- \lambda T)$. The forward contract can be obliged by paying the price of the bond to buy one unit of the asset. Consequently, assuming that the asset is non-dividend-paying, in the absence of arbitrage, both the portfolios have the same value and this value is given by

$$V_{FOC}(0, T) = S_0 - K \, exp(- \lambda T). \tag{8.32}$$

The price $\eta_{FOC}(0, T)$ of the forward contract is then given by the value of K for which $V_{FOC}(0, T) = 0$. Thus,

$$\eta_{FOC}(0, T) = S_0 \, exp(\lambda T). \tag{8.33}$$

If $\eta_{FOC}(0, T) > S_0 \, exp(\lambda T)$, then an arbitrageur (a person who gets involved in arbitrage) can buy one unit of the asset by borrowing the amount S_0 at the risk-free interest rate λ and take a short position in the forward contract. At time T, the arbitrageur receives $\eta_{FOC}(0, T)$ from the buyer of the contract by selling the asset and out of this fund $S_0 \, exp(\lambda T)$ can be used to pay back the loan. In the process, the arbitrageur makes a riskless profit of $\eta_{FOC}(0, T) - S_0 \, exp(\lambda T)$. Conversely, if $\eta_{FOC}(0, T) < S_0 \, exp(\lambda T)$, the arbitrageur can take a short position in the asset, deposit the amount S_0 with a financial institution (say, a bank) at the risk-free interest rate λ for a period of T and take a long position in the forward contract. At the maturity period, the arbitrageur receives the asset by paying $\eta_{FOC}(0, T)$ to the seller of the contract and the asset can now be returned to close the short selling position. Note that since the asset is non-dividend paying, closing of short selling only requires the return of the asset. The riskless profit now turns out to be $S_0 \, exp(\lambda T) - \eta_{FOC}(0, T)$. Absence of arbitrage opportunity will ultimately lead to the equality $\eta_{FOC}(0, T) = S_0 \, exp(\lambda T)$. In general, $\eta_{FOC}(t, T) = S_t \, exp(\lambda t)$ (see Capinski and Zastawniak 2003, and Kwok 2008).

Futures contracts are also legally binding agreements to buy or sell specified quantities of assets (for example, gold, silver, copper, timber, grains, fruits, livestock etc.) with standardized qualities at a specified price and at a specified date. While forwards contracts are traded over the counter, futures contracts are traded in a standard manner in an exchange—they are exchange-traded contracts. Futures contracts allow the traders to observe gains and losses on each day of transactions in exchange, whereas forward contracts are cash settled contracts at the time of delivery. In essence, in a futures contract the payment of the delivery price takes place through a sequence of installments during the lifespan of the contract. At the time of initiation of the contract, these installments are unknown and treated as random. Such contracts do not involve assets like bonds, stocks etc. As in the case of a forward contract, there is no cost to initiate a futures contract. We write $\eta_{FUC}(t, T)$ to denote the price of a futures contract when the period of initiation is t. We retain the assumption that the interest rate λ is risk-free.

Since trading is organized in exchanges in such a way that defaults are minimized, a trader with a long (or short) position in futures is requested to maintain a deposit of certain amount of money in a margin account (with the broker) as a precautionary measure against any possible default. At the end of a trading day t_2 the futures holder will receive the amount of change in the price $\eta_{FUC}(t_2, T) - \eta_{FUC}(t_1, T)$ from the previous trading date t_1 through the margin account. If the difference $\eta_{FUC}(t_2, T) - \eta_{FUC}(t_1, T)$ is positive, then it is a receipt for the futures holder, otherwise it is a payment from his side (the opposite happens for a trader with a short futures position). This process is known as marking to market. An implication of this process is that the payment required at the date of maturity for buying the underlying asset is simply the spot price at that time. Since a forward contract is an over-the-counter traded contract, there are no interim payments of this type during the life time of the contract; cash transactions for such a contract take place only at the date of maturity.

An interesting relationship between the two contracts is that if the interest rate is risk-free, then the prices of a futures contract and a forward contract coincide. To demonstrate this analytically, following Capinski and Zastawniak (2003), assume that marking to market takes place at two intermediate time points t_1 and t_2 between 0 and T, that is, $0 < t_1 < t_2 < T$. Now, consider a trader with a long forward position, where the forward price is $\eta_{FOC}(0, T)$. He also invests the amount $exp(-\lambda T)\eta_{FOC}(0, T)$ at time 0 at the risk-free rate and receives $\eta_{FOC}(0, T)$ at time T. In view of the forward contract, he can purchase one share of the underlying asset using the amount $\eta_{FOC}(0, T)$ and sell the share at the market price S_T. Thus, the investor's final wealth from this trading business is S_T.

We will now replicate this trading strategy involving a forward contract by a strategy using futures contract. That is, the strategy that relies on futures contract will duplicate the payoff of the strategy formulated in terms of forward contract. The former strategy here is called a replicating trading strategy. Instead of holding one unit of futures throughout the period of transactions, the trader can change the amount of futures to be held in each intermediate period. At time 0, the investor opens a fraction $exp(-\lambda(T - t_1))$ of a long futures position. He also invests the amount $exp(-\lambda T)\eta_{FUC}(0, T)$ at time 0 at the risk-free rate and receives $v_0 = \eta_{FUC}(0, T)$ at time T.

By the marking to market process, at time t_1, the trader receives or pays $(\eta_{FUC}(t_1, T) - \eta_{FUC}(0, T))exp(-\lambda(T - t_1))$. He invests or borrows this amount immediately at the risk-free rate, which grows into $v_1 = (\eta_{FUC}(t_1, T) - \eta_{FUC}(0, T))$ at time T. He also increases his long futures position to $exp(-\lambda(T - t_2))$ at time t_1.

A second application of marking to market process shows that at time t_2, the trader receives or pays $(\eta_{FUC}(t_2, T) - \eta_{FUC}(t_1, T)) exp(-\lambda(T - t_2))$, which is invested or borrowed immediately at the risk-free rate. The amount grows into $v_2 = (\eta_{FUC}(t_2, T) - \eta_{FUC}(t_1, T))$ at time T. The long futures position at time t_2 is increased to 1.

At time T the amount received from risk-free investment is $v_0 + v_1 + v_2 = \eta_{FUC}(t_2, T)$. The amount received from closing the futures position at time T is $S_T - \eta_{FUC}(t_2, T)$. Thus, the final wealth from this futures trading strategy is S_T. Consequently, in the absence of arbitrage, the initial investments initiating the two strategies have to be identical, that is, $e^{-\lambda T}\eta_{FOC}(0, T) = e^{-\lambda T}\eta_{FUC}(0, T)$, which demonstrates the assertion that under risk-free interest rates the prices of a futures contract and a forward contract are the same. In this demonstration we have assumed only two intermediate time instants, t_1 and t_2. Evidently, the argument extends easily to more frequent marking to market situations. However, this equality relationship between the forward price and the futures price does not hold if the interest rate is stochastic. In Chapter 13, we indicate how the two prices differ when the interest rate is stochastic.

Because of the nature of the assets in the futures contracts there may be additional costs like storage costs, insurance etc. These additional costs can be regarded as negative income. Let C_s stand for the present value of all additional costs that will be spent during the life of the contract. Then the forward price of the asset is

$$\eta_{FUC}(0, T; C_s) = (C_s + S_0)exp(\lambda T). \tag{8.34}$$

To see how (8.34) can be derived using non-arbitrage conditions, suppose $\eta_{FUC}(0, T; C_s) > (C_s + S_0)exp(\lambda T)$. Then an arbitrageur can borrow $(C_s + S_0)$ at the risk-free rate of return λ for T periods to buy one unit of the asset and pay the storage cost. The arbitrageur also takes a short position in the forward contract. At the maturity period T, the arbitrageur receives $\eta_{FUC}(0, T; C_s)$ from the buyer as per the contract and the loan can be paid back using the amount $(C_s + S_0) exp(\lambda T)$. Hence the arbitrageur will derive a riskless profit of $\eta_{FUC}(0, T; C_s) - (C_s + S_0)exp(\lambda T)$. Likewise, if $\eta_{FUC}(0, T; C_s) < (C_s + S_0)exp(\lambda T)$, the arbitrageur's strategy will be to sell the asset which will save the additional cost. The next step of the strategy is to invest the proceeds S_0 with a bank at the risk-free rate of return λ for T periods and take a long position in the forward contract. It can be shown that this will enable the arbitrageur to generate a riskless profit of $(C_s + S_0)exp(\lambda T) - \eta_{FUC}(0, T; C_s)$. In the absence of arbitrage opportunity, we must have $\eta_{FUC}(0, T; C_s) = (C_s + S_0)exp(\lambda T)$.

Often additional cost incurred at any time is proportional to the initial price of the asset. For instance, fixed insurance premium may be proportional to the initial price. If c_s denotes the per period cost as a proportion of the spot price of the asset then the forward price becomes

$$\eta_{FUC}(0,\ T;\ c_s) = S_0\ exp((\lambda + c_s)T). \tag{8.35}$$

The factor $(\lambda + c_s)$ is referred to as the carrying cost or cost of carry. The first component of this cost is the interest cost for borrowing and the second component is the maintenance or holding cost (storage, insurance etc.).

Often the holder of the asset may have some advantage for holding a commodity (asset). For instance, suppose the holder has a forward contract to supply some commodity at a pre-specified time T. Often ownership of physical commodity provides some benefits that cannot be derived from holding of a futures contract. Ownership becomes helpful in running the production process and probably in generating profits from temporary local shortages (see Hull and Basu 2010). The benefit from holding the asset is known as the convenience yield, which we denote by y_c. Thus, the convenience yield can be treated as a negative holding cost. Therefore, if a holder enjoys convenience yield it must be the case that $\eta_{FUC}(0,\ T;\ c_s) \leq S_0\ exp((\lambda + c_s)T)$.

Convenience yield can be implicitly defined by the relation

$$\eta_{FUC}(0,\ T;\ c_s)\ exp(Ty_c) = S_0\ exp((\lambda + c_s)T), \tag{8.36}$$

which then gives

$$\eta_{FUC}(0,\ T;\ c_s) = S_0\ exp((\lambda + c_s - y_c)T). \tag{8.37}$$

Clearly, the convenience yield underlying the futures contract of a commodity is directly related to its possibility of shortage. If users of the commodity do not have a chance of shortage in the upcoming days, then the convenience yield is likely to be small. A necessary condition for a high value of the convenience yield is the existence of low inventories with users of the underlying commodity.

While a futures contract is obligatory, there can be a non-obligatory contract for entering into a futures contract by a specific date at a certain price of the futures. Such a contract is referred to as a futures option.

Example 8.1: Consider a European call option on a non-dividend-paying stock with a strike price of 43 dollars when the stock price is 43.5 dollars. The maturity period is six months and the annual risk-free interest rate is 10 percent. That is, and $S_0 = 43.5$, $K = 43$, $T = 0.5$ and $\lambda = 10$ percent. Then $S_0 = K\ exp(-\lambda T) = 43.5 - 43\ exp(0.5 \times 0.1) = 43.5 - 40.9 = 2.6$. Therefore, from (8.21) it follows that a lower bound on the price of the European call option under consideration is 2.6.

Applied Example 8.1: Broadie et al. (1996) proposed nonparametric estimation techniques to deal with computational complications involved in American options. Their method uses market data, both on exercise decisions and option prices. The data used by them are the end-of-the-trading-day daily data on S&P 100 Index American put and call options that are traded on the Chicago Board Options Exchange. The S&P 100 Index is a US stock market index maintained by Standard and Poor's. It is based on 100 leading US stocks with options enlisted in the exchange. The period of data coverage is January 3, 1884 to March 30, 1995. It turned out that the most of the exercises took place during the last week prior to the expiration period. Exercise decisions were taken, except for one or two days before maturity, when the ratio between the stock price and the strike price was close to one. In the last days before maturity, the dispersion of the observed ratios increased toward one (see Kim 1990 for a theoretical argument along this line). They estimated a boundary by a curve fitting method and a made a comparison between parametric and non-parametric boundaries. Parametric and non-parametric analysis of call prices was also reported.

BIBLIOGRAPHICAL NOTES

For an easy exposition of different types of options, the reader is encouraged to look at Hull and Basu (2010). A treatment of payoff and profit functions for options is available in Lyuu (2002), Kwok (2008) and Hull and Basu (2010). These three books along with the book by Capinski and Zastawniak (2003) provide detailed coverage of the boundaries of option values, which we subdivide into several subsections for the sake of convenience. The presentation of forward and futures contracts relies mostly on Capinski and Zastawniak (2003) and Kwok (2008).

EXERCISES

1. Each of the following statements is either true or false. If the statement is true prove it. If it is false, give a counter-example or justify your answer by logical reasoning.
   (a) The profit function of a straddle with a long position in a European call and a European put option achieves its minimum at the strike price.
   (b) A portfolio consisting of a long position in a European put option and a short position in the underlying asset has no hedging effect.
   (c) The constant portion of the profit function of a strangle, consisting of one European put and one European call option, always lies between the two strike prices.
   (d) The value of a European call option is at least as large as its American counterpart.
   (e) The graphs of the profit functions of (i) a strip with a long positions

in one European call option and two European put options, and (ii) a strap with a long position in two European call options and short position in one European put option are symmetric around the strike price, where symmetry of a graph means that its points of intersection with the line representing price at maturity are equidistant from the strike price.

2. Explain how both bullish and bearish spread strategies can limit trader's upside and downside risks.

3. Determine analytically the payoff functions for the following strategies: (a) a bearish strategy with two European put options, (b) a strangle strategy.

4. Give graphical expositions of the profit functions of (a) a bullish price-spread strategy composed of two European call options, (b) a bullish price-spread strategy composed of two European put options.

5. Explain how a strangle can be created and determine its payoff function analytically.

6. When do you say that a call option is: (a) in-the-money, (b) out-of-the-money? Illustrate your answer by an example.

7. Clearly explain the formation and usefulness of a butterfly price-spread strategy with two European call options. Represent the profit function of this strategy graphically.

8. Discuss the characteristics of a box-spread strategy.

9. Show that the early exercise of an American call option on a non-dividend-paying stock is sub-optimal.

10. Does the lower bound on the European call option on a non-dividend-paying stock considered in Example 8.1 get modified if the strike price is 42 dollars?

12. Graphically represent the profit functions of (a) a bearish price-spread strategy consisting of two European call options, (b) a bearish price-spread strategy consisting of two European put options.

13. Explain the usefulness of a foreign currency put option by giving an example.

14. Establish analytically the relationship between prices of two forward contracts if their maturity periods are different, given that the interest rate is constant.

15. Derive analytically the put–call parity relation for European options with dividend-paying stocks. Does your argument apply to American options as well?

16. Use the non-arbitrage condition to determine the price of a forward contract when the underlying asset is dividend paying.

17. Formulate the portfolio of a butterfly price-spread strategy consisting of European put options on the same non-dividend-paying underlying asset when strike prices are different but the dates of expirations are the same. Sketch the corresponding function.

18. Clearly distinguish between (a) the price and value of a forward contract, (b) a futures contract and a futures option, (c) cost of carry and holding cost, (d) writing a put option and buying a call option, (e) a strangle and a straddle.

19. A trader holds a portfolio in which he has a short position in a European put option on the non-dividend-paying underlying asset and a long position in a call option on the same asset, when the strike prices and dates of expirations are the same. Derive the payoff and profit functions. Represent these functions graphically.

20. Explain the usefulness of options by giving examples.

21. Consider a forward contract on a non-dividend-paying stock, where the current value of the stock is 300 dollars, the risk-free interest rate is 5 percent and the maturity period is six months. Determine the value and the price of the forward contract.

22. If the strike price grows at the risk-free interest rate, then the prices of an American and European put options on the same non-dividend-paying underlying asset coincide. Justify the validity/invalidity of this statement.

23. Consider American call and put options on a non-dividend-paying stock whose current price is 60 dollars and the strike price is 55 dollars. If the maturity period is six months and the risk-free interest rate is 5 percent, then determine an interval in which the difference between the prices of the call and put options lies.

24. Suppose the current price of a dividend-paying stock is 40 dollars and the strike price is 48 dollars. The maturity period is six months, the risk-free interest rate is 5 percent and the present value of the dividends is 2 dollars. Determine the relation between prices of a European call and put options.

25. Use the put–call parity to derive an upper bound on the price of a European put option on a non-dividend-paying stock.

26. Clearly distinguish between a forward contract and a futures contract.

CHAPTER 9

Arbitrage and Binomial Model

9.1 INTRODUCTION

An arbitrage opportunity refers to the possibility of deriving instantaneous profit without any risk. For instance, suppose gold is being sold at 400 dollars per ounce in city I but 399.90 dollars in a different city II. Then a trader can buy gold from city II and sell it in city I to make a riskless profit of 10 cents per ounce. This is arbitrage. That is, an arbitrage opportunity represents the production of something out of nothing. The non-arbitrage principle means the rule of a single price. The key principle behind the idea of asset pricing in financial economics is the principle of non-arbitrage. In fact, even if there are scopes for arbitrage opportunities, price adjustment will eliminate them eventually. Essential to the non-existence of arbitrage opportunities in our set up is risk-neutral valuation. According to risk-neutral valuation, the current price of a financial asset equals the expected future price of the asset discounted at the risk-free rate of interest. The central idea underlying risk-neutral valuation parallels the idea implicit in the certainty equivalent. In the certainty equivalent method a risky variable is replaced by one that can be obtained with certainty. The time periods considered in the framework for risk-neutral valuation are discrete.

In a binomial model, asset prices do not change continuously over time, but instead jump at discrete intervals to one of two new values. The two common features between the binomial model and non-arbitrage principle are discrete time periods and risk neutral valuation. As we have noted in Chapter 8, early exercise of an option often may be desirable. A useful application of the binomial model is that its structure enables us to deal with the possibility of the early exercise of an option very easily.

In Section 2 of this chapter we present a very simple model for non-arbitrage. A more general structure for non-arbitrage is considered in Section 9.3. In this section we also analyze a condition for completeness of the asset market. Finally, Section 9.4 discusses the Cox–Ross–Rubinstein (1979) binomial model.

9.2 CONDITIONS FOR NON-ARBITRAGE: A SIMPLE MODEL

In this section we consider a very simple model to identify a unique condition for existence of non-arbitrage. We assume at the outset that there are no transaction costs, there is a risk-free rate of interest at which borrowing and lending can be made, there are no restrictions on the buying– and selling—quantities, and also there are no restrictions on short selling. We will maintain these assumptions for our presentations throughout this section and the next section.

Let us consider a two-period world, $t = 0$ (today, the current period) and $t = 1$ (the future period). Suppose there are only two assets in this world, a bond which is trading currently at a price of 1, and a stock whose current period and future prices are denoted respectively by S_0 and S_1. Assume also that S_0 is known but S_1 is stochastic. The risk-free rate of interest is λ. Then the price of the bond in the future period is given by $(1 + \lambda)$. The stochastic nature of the stock price in the future period is described by the specification that S_1 takes on the values $S_0 u$ with probability p_u and $S_0 d$ with probability p_d, where $0 < d < 1 < u$. Evidently, $0 \leq p_u, p_d$, ≤ 1 and $p_u + p_d = 1$(see Sundaram 1997 and Bjork 2004).

This model is a one-step binomial model. The assumption that the stock price can move only to one of two possible values at the end of the current period is referred to as a one-step binomial formulation. Another simplifying assumption of this simple model is discrete compounding structure. A more general binomial model with many periods, in which continuous compounding is allowed in a particular way, was suggested by Cox, Ross and Rubinstein (1979) (see Section 9.4).

Let us define a stochastic variable Z which takes on the values u with probability p_u and d with probability p_d. Then S_1 can be written in a more compact form as $S_1 = S_0 Z$. Assume that u, d and p_u are known (hence p_d is also known).

Consider now a portfolio $\Omega = \left(n_b^\Omega, n_s^\Omega\right)$, where $n_b^\Omega\left(n_s^\Omega\right)$ the number of bonds (shares of the stock) in the portfolio. A negative value of $n_b^\Omega\left(n_s^\Omega\right)$ means that the trader has sold bonds (shares of the stock) in the current period, whereas a positive value of $n_b^\Omega\left(n_s^\Omega\right)$ indicates the number of bonds (shares of stocks) held by the trader in the current period. We say that a trader has a long position in bond (stock) if $n_b^\Omega\left(n_s^\Omega\right)$ is positive, whereas a negative value of $n_b^\Omega\left(n_s^\Omega\right)$ indicates that he has a short position in the bond (stock). We assume that fractional holdings of the numbers of bonds and stocks in a portfolio are permissible. This along with short position possibility indicates that a portfolio is an element of the 2-dimensional Euclidean space.

Clearly, the value of the portfolio in the current period is $V_0^\Omega = n_b^\Omega + n_s^\Omega S_0$. Since 1 dollar in the current period grows into $(1 + \lambda)$ dollars, the value of the portfolio in the future period is $V_1^\Omega = n_b^\Omega(1+\lambda) + n_s^\Omega S_0 Z$. One simple way of thinking about arbitrage in this model is that the value of the trader's portfolio in the current period is zero but in the future period its value is positive. This means that the trader is making money in the future period without making any investment in the current period. Formally,

Definition 9.1: The portfolio $\Omega = \left(n_b^\Omega, n_s^\Omega\right)$ provides an opportunity for arbitrage if $V_0^\Omega = 0$ but $V_1^\Omega > 0$ with probability 1.

Arbitrage opportunities are very rare in practice. If they exist, the gains are extremely small in comparison with the volume of transactions. This in turn implies that they are beyond the reach of small investors. Actually, the situations with a scope of arbitrage are short lived and difficult to identify. The arbitrageurs' preference for more to less profit effectively makes the market free from opportunity for arbitrage.

We can now state the non-arbitrage principle or the principle of non-arbitrage in the current context as follows.

Non-arbitrage Principle: There does not exist any portfolio $\Omega = \left(n_b^\Omega, n_s^\Omega\right)$ such that $V_0^\Omega = 0$ but $V_1^\Omega > 0$ with probability 1.

Equivalently, according to the non-arbitrage principle if the initial value of the portfolio is zero, $V_0^\Omega = 0$, then the value of the portfolio in period 1 is zero, $V_1^\Omega = 0$, with probability 1. This means that no investor can derive a profit without any initial investment.

The following theorem specifies a necessary and sufficient condition for non-existence of arbitrage opportunities.

Theorem 9.1: In the model considered above, the following conditions are equivalent:

(*i*) $d \le (1+\lambda) \le u$.

(*ii*) There is no opportunity for arbitrage.

Proof: See Appendix.

What this theorem says is the following: there is no scope for arbitrage if and only if the return on the bond lies in the interval $[d, u]$. That is, return on the stock cannot exceed the return on the bond and vice versa. This means that the absence of arbitrage is the requirement that neither asset dominates the other.

One specification for which condition (*i*) in Theorem 9.1 is satisfied is $(1 + \lambda) = q_d d + q_u u$, where $0 \le q_u, q_d \le 1$ and $q_u + q_d = 1$. The weights q_u and q_d can be interpreted as probabilities under a probability measure K, where $K(Z = u) = q_u$ and $K(Z = d) = q_d$. Then

$$\frac{1}{1+\lambda}\Xi^K\left(S_1\right) = \frac{1}{1+\lambda}\Xi^K\left(q_u S_0 u + q_d S_0 d\right) = \frac{1}{1+\lambda}S_0\left(1+\lambda\right) = S_0, \quad (9.1)$$

where Ξ stands for the expectation operator. Thus, $\Xi^K(S_1)$ is the expected value of the stock price in the future period under the probability measure K. Hence

$\frac{1}{1+\lambda}\Xi^{K}(S_1)$ is the discounted present value of the expected value of the stock price in the future period, where the discounting is done with the risk-free rate of interest. Equation (9.1), therefore, shows that the current period stock price is the discounted value of the expected value of future period stock price. This is a risk-neutral valuation. The probabilities q_u and q_d are risk-neutral probabilities and they constitute the risk-neutral measure K. The pricing principle in (9.1) is called risk-neutral pricing. It says that every asset can be priced by taking an appropriate expectation. In risk-neutral valuation all assets under consideration have the same expected rate of return; the risk-free rate. This does not imply that the traders are risk neutral.

Let us look at the similarity of (9.1) with the certainty equivalent. In the case of the certainty equivalent, the expected utility equals the utility value of a certain outcome. In this case also S_0 is known with certainty and it equals the discounted expected value $\frac{1}{1+\lambda}\Xi^{K}(S_1)$.

The above discussion enables us to state the following theorem.

Theorem 9.2: In the model considered above, the following conditions are equivalent:

(*i*) There exists a risk neutral measure K.

(*ii*) There is no opportunity for arbitrage.

The theorem says that the model under consideration does not permit arbitrage opportunities if and only if it admits at least one risk-neutral probability measure. This is equivalent to the condition that a risk-neutral probability fails to exist if and only if there is opportunity for arbitrage.

Observation 9.1: For the model considered above, the following unique risk-neutral probabilities are obtained by solving the equations $(1 + \lambda) = q_d d + q_u u$ and $q_u + q_d = 1$:

$$q_u = \frac{(1+\lambda)-d}{u-d}, q_d = \frac{u-(1+\lambda)}{u-d}. \tag{9.2}$$

Thus, q_u and q_d are unique risk-neutral probabilities ($0 \le q_u, q_d \le 1$ and $q_u + q_d = 1$) if and only if $d \le (1 + \lambda) \le u$.

Example 9.1: The current price S_0 of a stock is 80 dollars. The stock price S_1 in the period 1 takes on the values 96 dollars and 64 dollars with probabilities 0.6 and 0.4 respectively. We wish to determine the risk-free rate of return for which risk-neutral valuation holds.

We know that $S_1 = S_0 u$ with probability p_u and $S_1 = S_0 d$ with probability p_d. Thus, $u = 96/80 = 1.2$, $d = 64/80 = 0.8$, $p_u = 0.6$ and $p_d = 0.4$. Risk neutral valuation then needs that $80 = \frac{1}{1+\lambda}[0.6 \times 96 + 0.4 \times 64]$, which gives $(1+\lambda) = \frac{83.2}{80}$, from which it follows that the risk-free rate of return is $\lambda = .04$.

An extension of the above binomial model is the trinomial model in which instead of two probabilities p_u and $(1 - p_u)$, there will be three probabilities. This means that from the current period the asset price S_0 moves to three possible values with these probabilities to the next period. Formally,

$$S_1 = \begin{cases} S_0u \text{ with probability } p_u, \\ S_0d \text{ with probability } p_d, \\ S_0v \text{ with probability } p_v, \end{cases} \tag{9.3}$$

where $0 < d < 1 < u$, $v \in [d, u]$, $0 \le p_u, p_v, p_d, \le 1$ and $p_u + p_v + p_d = 1$. Assume also that there is a 1 dollar current-period bond which provides a return of $(1 + \lambda)$ in the next period. For the vector (p_u, p_v, p_d) to constitutes a risk-neutral probability vector in this model it must be the case that

$$p_u u + p_v v + p_d d = (1 + \lambda) \text{ and } p_u + p_v + p_d = 1. \tag{9.4}$$

In (9.4) we have two equations in three unknowns. There are infinitely many solutions that satisfy these two equations. Thus, there are infinitely many risk-neutral probability vectors in this trinomial model.

9.3 CONDITIONS FOR NON-ARBITRAGE: A MORE GENERAL MODEL

In this section also we consider a two-period world, $t = 0$ (today, the current period) and $t = 1$ (the future period) (see Bjork 2004). However in the financial market l assets are traded, where l is an arbitrary positive integer. These assets can be stocks, bonds, options or any other financial asset. Let S_0^i be the known price of asset i in the current period. The column vector

$$\begin{pmatrix} S_0^1 \\ S_0^2 \\ \cdot \\ \cdot \\ \cdot \\ S_0^l \end{pmatrix} \tag{9.5}$$

of prices of l assets in the current period is denoted by S_0.

The future period is characterized by k states of nature, where the positive integer k is arbitrary. The set of the states of nature is denoted by $\{\omega_1, \omega_2, ..., \omega_k\}$. By a state of nature we mean a description of the economic environment. This description contains all relevant information like the tastes of the traders, their endowments, firms' profits, dividends paid by each asset and so on. Let $S_1^i(\omega_j)$ be the price of asset i in the future period if state j materializes. The prices $S_1^i(\omega_j)$'s are referred to as state-contingent prices. We write $(S)_{l \times k}$ for the $l \times k$ matrix showing $S_1^i(\omega_j)$ values. Thus, the ith row of the matrix, which is a row vector with k columns, gives the prices of asset i in k different states of the world in period 1. Likewise, the jth column of the matrix, which is a column vector with l rows, shows the prices of l assets in the jth state of the world in period 1. We write $\underline{S_1}(\omega_j)$ to denote the jth column of the matrix. The matrix $(S)_{l \times k}$ can be written explicitly as

$$(S)_{l \times k} = \begin{bmatrix} S_1^1(\omega_1) & S_1^1(\omega_2) & \cdots & S_1^1(\omega_k) \\ S_1^2(\omega_1) & S_1^2(\omega_2) & \cdots & S_1^2(\omega_k) \\ \vdots & \vdots & \vdots & \vdots \\ S_1^l(\omega_1) & S_1^l(\omega_2) & \cdots & S_1^l(\omega_k) \end{bmatrix}. \tag{9.6}$$

A portfolio in this general model is a l-dimensional row vector $\Omega = \left(n_1^\Omega, n_2^\Omega, \ldots, n_l^\Omega \right)$. It is an element of the l-dimensional Euclidean space and its ith entry shows the number of units of asset i purchased by the trader in period 0 and held until period 1. That is, once the portfolio has been set, there is no exogenous cash inflow into, or cash outflow from, it until the date of maturity. Equivalently, we say that the portfolio is self-financed. By assumption for any i, n_i^Ω can be negative (short position), zero (non-possession) and positive (long position).

The value of the portfolio $\Omega = \left(n_1^\Omega, n_2^\Omega, \ldots, n_l^\Omega \right)$ in period 0 is $V_0^\Omega = \sum_{i=1}^{l} n_i^\Omega S_0^i = \Omega.\underline{S_0}$. However, the values of the portfolios in period 1 depend on the states of nature in period 1. More precisely; the values are components of a state-dependent vector. Thus, if state j materializes then the value of the portfolio in period 1 is $V_1^\Omega(\omega_j) = \sum_{i=1}^{l} n_i^\Omega S_1^i(\omega_j) = \Omega.\underline{S_1}(\omega_j)$. Scope for arbitrage in this model can be defined as a situation where the value of a trader's portfolio in period 0 is negative, but value in each state of nature in period 1 is non-negative. Such a situation can arise if a trader has short positions in all the assets in period 0 but still may have long positions in or more of the assets in period 1. Formally,

Definition 9.2: The portfolio $\Omega = \left(n_1^\Omega, n_2^\Omega, \ldots, n_l^\Omega \right)$ provides an opportunity for arbitrage if $V_0^\Omega < 0$ and $V_1^\Omega(\omega_j) \geq 0$ for all $j = 1, 2, \ldots, k$.

Here the non-arbitrage principle demands that there does not exist any portfolio $\Omega = \left(n_1^\Omega, n_2^\Omega, \ldots, n_l^\Omega \right)$ such that $V_0^\Omega < 0$ but $V_1^\Omega(\omega_j) \geq 0$ for all $j = 1, 2, \ldots, k$.

The following theorem identifies a condition for non-existence of scope for arbitrage in this general model.

Theorem 9.3: In the general model considered above, the following conditions are equivalent:

(i) There exist non-negative numbers $y_1, y_2, \ldots, y_k$ such that $S_0^i = \sum_{j=1}^{k} y_j S_1^i(\omega_j)$, $i = 1, 2, \ldots, l$, that is $\underline{S_0} = \sum_{j=1}^{k} y_j \underline{S_1}(\omega_j)$.

(*ii*) There is no opportunity for arbitrage.

Proof: See Appendix.

This theorem says that opportunity for arbitrage is absent if and only if the certain price of asset *i* in period 0 is a linear combination of the prices of asset *i* in different states of nature in period 1.

Let us now define $q_j = y_j/\kappa$, where $\kappa = \sum_{j=1}^{k} y_j > 0$. We may then regard the non-negative numbers $q_1, q_2, \ldots, q_k$ as probabilities by setting $K(\omega_j) = q_j$, $1 \le i \le k$. Thus,

K is a probability measure whose sample space is the set of states of nature $\{\omega_1, \omega_2, \ldots, \omega_k\}$. That is, $K(\omega_j)$ is the probability that state ω_j will materialize. Then condition (*i*) in Theorem 9.3 can be stated as

$$\underline{S_0} = \sum_{j=1}^{k} y_j \underline{S_1}(\omega_j) = \kappa \sum_{\backslash j=1}^{k} q_j \underline{S_1}(\omega_j) = \kappa \, \Xi^K(\underline{S_1}). \tag{9.7}$$

Here $\Xi^K(\underline{S_1})$ represents the column vector of the expected values of prices of *l* different assets in a future period under the probability measure K. We can, therefore, state the following theorem.

Theorem 9.4: In the general model considered above, the following conditions are equivalent:

(*i*) There exists a probability distribution K on the set of states of nature $\{\omega_1, \omega_2, \ldots, \omega_k\}$ and a positive constant κ such that $\underline{S_0} = \kappa \, \Xi^K(\underline{S_1})$.

(*ii*) There is no opportunity for arbitrage.

Assume now that asset 1 is a zero-coupon bond such that $S_1^1(\omega_j) = 1$ for all $j = 1, 2, \ldots, k$, which means that each entry in the first row of the matrix $(S)_{l \times k}$ in (9.6) is 1. In other words, the known price of asset 1 in period 1 is 1. Then the first component of the equality $\underline{S_0} = \kappa \, \Xi^K(\underline{S_1})$ is $S_0^1 = \kappa.1 = \kappa$

We know that 1 dollar in the current period grows into $(1 + \lambda)$ dollars in the future period. Therefore, the discounted present value of 1 dollar is simply $1/(1 + \lambda)$ dollars. But $S_0^1 = \kappa.1$ is as well the discounted present value of 1 dollar. Hence $\kappa = 1/(1 + \lambda)$. We can therefore state the following theorem, which is known as the first fundamental theorem of mathematical finance.

Theorem 9.5 (First Fundamental Theorem of Mathematical Finance): Assume that in the general model considered above, there is a risk-free asset. Then the following conditions are equivalent:

(*i*) There exists a probability distribution K on the set of states of nature $\{\omega_1, \omega_2, \ldots, \omega_k\}$ such that $\underline{S_0} = \dfrac{1}{1 + \lambda} \Xi^K(\underline{S_1})$.

(*ii*) There is no opportunity for arbitrage.

This theorem says that the current period asset prices are discounted values of the expected values of the future period prices, where expectation is taken with respect to the probability measure K and discounting is done with the risk-free interest rate. This is a risk-neutral pricing formula, where K a risk-neutral measure and $(q_1, q_2,..., q_k)$ are risk-neutral probabilities. Further discussion on risk-neutral evaluation is relegated to Chapter 13 because it is based on a martingale measure, which we introduce there.

To look at further implications of the principle of non-arbitrage, let us consider two portfolios Ω and Π. Suppose $V_1^\Omega \left(\omega_j \right) = V_1^\Pi \left(\omega_j \right)$ for all $j = 1, 2,..., l$. Then the principle of non-arbitrage demands that $V_0^\Omega = V_0^\Pi$. In other words, if irrespective of the state of nature it is known that the values of the two portfolios in the future period are equal, then their current period prices are equal as well. To demonstrate this, suppose $V_0^\Omega < V_0^\Pi$. Since there are no restrictions on borrowing or lending, a trader borrows money that can enable him exactly to buy the portfolio Π. To close the borrowing in the future period he has to payback $V_1^\Pi \left(j \right)$ if state j materializes. The trader actually buys the portfolio Ω. Since $V_1^\Omega \left(\omega_j \right) = V_1^\Pi \left(\omega_j \right)$ for all j, the borrowing can be closed by paying $V_1^\Omega \left(j \right)$ as well. Therefore, the trader can pocket the difference $V_0^\Pi - V_0^\Omega$, which is a riskless profit, at the initial period. This is arbitrage. A similar conclusion holds if $V_0^\Omega > V_0^\Pi$. Therefore, the non-arbitrage principle will lead to the equality $V_0^\Omega = V_0^\Pi$. Thus, to determine the initial value of a portfolio $\hat{\Omega}$ by the principle of non-arbitrage, we need to find another portfolio $\hat{\Pi}$ whose initial value is known and whose future prices in different states coincide with those of $\hat{\Omega}$. Then the initial price of $\hat{\Omega}$ must be equal to that of $\hat{\Pi}$. We have seen and will see many other applications of the non-arbitrage principle in the book.

An additional issue of investigation in terms of state-wise prices of different assets, more precisely, column vectors of $(S)_{l \times k}$, is completeness. For this, we first consider a state-contingent claim, a random variable X defined on the set of states of nature. We may interpret X as a stochastic return at the period $t = 1$. That is, $X(\omega_j)$ is the level of payment received when state j materializes. The vector $(X(\omega_1), X(\omega_2),..., X(\omega_k))$ of state-wise contingent claims is denoted by $\underline{X}$.

To illustrate this, consider a model with one risk-free asset; say a zero-coupon bond and one risky asset, a stock. There are three states of nature. Assume that $S_1^1 \left(\omega_j \right) = 1.1$ for all $j = 1, 2, 3$. That is, irrespective of the state of nature, the risk-free return on the zero-coupon bond in period 1 is 1.1. In vector notation, $\left(S_1^1 \left(\omega_1 \right), S_1^1 \left(\omega_2 \right), S_1^1 \left(\omega_3 \right) \right) = (1.1, 1.1, 1.1)$. Now, let $\left(S_1^2 \left(\omega_1 \right), S_1^2 \left(\omega_2 \right), S_1^2 \left(\omega_3 \right) \right) = (4.4, 3.3, 2.2)$. Suppose the contingent claim is given by $(X(\omega_1), X(\omega_2), X(\omega_3)) = (5.5, 4.4, 3.3)$. Then this contingent claim can be generated by the trading strategy or portfolio $(n_b, n_s) = (1, 1)$. That is,

$X\left(\omega_1\right) = 5.5 = \left(1,1\right)\begin{pmatrix} 1.1 \\ 4.4 \end{pmatrix} = 1 \times 1.1 + 1 \times 4.4$. Likewise, $X(\omega_2) = 4.4 = 1 \times 1.1 + 1 \times$ 3.3 and $X(\omega_3) = 3.3 = 1 \times 1.1 + 1 \times 2.2$. Equivalently, we say that the contingent claim (5.5, 4.4, 3.3) is reachable or attainable. But there does not exist any trading strategy associated with the given security market that can generate the contingent claim $(X(\omega_1), X(\omega_2), X(\omega_3)) = (5.5, 4.0, 3.3)$. That is, this contingent claim is not reachable.

Formally, a vector of contingent claims $\underline{X}$ is called reachable or attainable if there exists a self-financed portfolio $\Omega = \left(n_1^\Omega, n_2^\Omega, \ldots, n_l^\Omega\right)$ such that $V_1^\Omega\left(\omega_j\right) = X\left(\omega_j\right)$ for all $j = 1, 2,\ldots, k$. We also say that X is replicated by Ω. Such a portfolio Ω is called a replicating portfolio. Thus, for replication the portfolio should be self-financed and its value at maturity is identical to the value of the contingent claim in all states. That is, we are constructing a portfolio of original securities whose values exactly match the payoffs at maturity. The example we have considered above shows that a contingent claim may not be reachable.

Completeness of the asset market demands attainability of any given contingent claim.

Definition 9.3: Given the set of states of nature and prices of the assets in different states, an asset market is complete if for every contingent claim vector $\underline{X}$ there exists a portfolio $\Omega = \left(n_1^\Omega, n_2^\Omega, \ldots, n_l^\Omega\right)$ such that

$$X\left(\omega_j\right) = \Omega . \underline{S_1}\left(\omega_j\right) = \sum_{i=1}^{l} n_i^\Omega S_1^i\left(\omega_j\right) \text{ for all } j = 1, 2,\ldots, k.$$

Thus, completeness of the asset market means that given the states of nature and the prices of the assets in different states, there will be a portfolio by which any vector of contingent claims can be materialized. That is, completeness is a way of ensuring the stochastic payment vector $(X(\omega_1), X(\omega_2),\ldots, X(\omega_k))$ using a portfolio. For completeness, the number of assets should be at least as large as the number of states of nature, that is, $l \geq k$. The market is clearly complete if there is one asset contingent on each state of nature. The following theorem gives us a necessary and sufficient condition for completeness of the asset market.

Theorem 9.6: The asset market is complete if and only if the rank of the matrix $(S)_{l \times k}$ is k.

Proof: See Appendix.

Example 9.2: We now illustrate Theorem 9.6 using an example. Assume that there are three assets and two states of nature. Further, asset 1 is a zero coupon bond with a principal value of 1, so that $S_1^1\left(\omega_1\right) = S_1^1\left(\omega_2\right) = 1$. Then the corresponding $(S)_{l \times k}$ matrix becomes

$$(S)_{3 \times 2} = \begin{bmatrix} 1 & 1 \\ S_1^2\left(\omega_1\right) & S_1^2\left(\omega_2\right) \\ S_1^3\left(\omega_1\right) & S_1^3\left(\omega_2\right) \end{bmatrix}.$$

The rank of a matrix is the highest order of any non-zero minor in it. A minor of a matrix is the determinant of a square sub-matrix of the matrix and its order is the order of the square sub-matrix. In this case the highest order of a sub-matrix is 2. Let us consider the sub-matrix

$$\begin{bmatrix} 1 & 1 \\ S_1^2(\omega_1) & S_1^2(\omega_2) \end{bmatrix}.$$

The determinant of this sub-matrix is non-zero if $S_1^2(\omega_1) \ne S_1^2(\omega_2)$. That is, a sufficient condition for rank of the matrix $(S)_{3\times 2}$ to be 2 is that $S_1^2(\omega_1) \ne S_1^2(\omega_2)$. This in turn implies that a sufficient condition for completeness of the security market, considered in the example, is $S_1^2(\omega_1) \ne S_1^2(\omega_2)$. In other words, completeness demands that the price of asset 2 in period 1 should be different across the states.

9.4 THE BINOMIAL MODEL

The binomial model, due to Cox, Ross and Rubinstein (1979), is a general numerical method for the determination of asset prices. It is a discrete-time model. The model is easily tractable because of its identical simple structure at each node of the tree of the asset prices. An interesting application of the model is its use in determining the value of an American option at any date before the date of expiration. We subdivide our presentation into several subsections. It will be maintained throughout the presentation that the principle of non-arbitrage holds.

9.4.1 Assumptions and Implications

There are two major assumptions underlying the binomial model. The first assumption is that the model can be formulated by a discrete random walk with the following properties. (i) It has a finite number of time steps, $t_0 < t_1 < ... < t_T$. The time intervals are equidistant, that is, $t_i - t_{i-1} = \Delta t > 0$ for $i = 1, 2, ..., T$. We assume that Δt is small but non-infinitesimal. The lifespan of the model is $T\Delta t = t_T - t_0$. (ii) The asset price S_i at any time step t_i either evolves up to $S_i u$ or down to $S_i d$ at time step t_{i+1}, where $0 < d < 1 < u$. The direction of change in S_i is independent of past changes. This is same as the requirement that there are two rates of returns $(S_{i+1} - S_i)/S_i$ at each time step, $(u - 1) > 0$ and $(d - 1) < 0$. These rates are the same across time steps. (iii) The probability of S_i moving up to $S_i u$ at time step t_{i+1} is p_u and the probability that S_i moves down to $S_i d$ at time step t_{i+1} is $p_d = 1 - p_u$. These probabilities remain constant over time periods.

A consequence of parts (ii) and (iii) of this assumption is that

$$\Xi(S_{i+1}) = p_u S_i u + (1 - p_u)S_i d, \tag{9.8}$$

where, as before, Ξ stands for the expectation operator.

Starting with a given initial value S_0 of the asset price, a tree of all possible asset prices for the remaining T periods can be created. By assumption, these remaining T periods are subdivided into T equal time steps, each of size $\Delta t = (t_T - t_0)/T$. The construction of the tree proceeds as follows. Given S_0, at the first time step two possible values $S_0 u$ and $S_0 d$ of the asset price are generated. At the second step the starting point can be $S_0 u$ or $S_0 d$. If the starting point is $S_0 u$ then the prices can move upward to $S_0 u^2$ with probability p_u and downward to $S_0 ud$ with probability $1 - p_u$. Similarly, if the starting point is $S_0 d$, then the prices associated with the corresponding upward and downward movements are $S_0 du$ and $S_0 d^2$. Since $S_0 ud = S_0 du$, at the second time step there are three possible asset values: $S_0 u^2$, $S_0 ud$ and $S_0 d^2$. This process continues until the expiry period of the asset prices arrives (see Figure 9.1). Since an upward jump followed by a downward jump generates the same value of the asset price as that produced when a downward jump is followed by an upward jump, at the end of i time steps there will be $(i + 1)$ possible asset prices instead of $2i$ prices (check that this holds for $i = 2$).

Figure 9.1   Binomial Tree

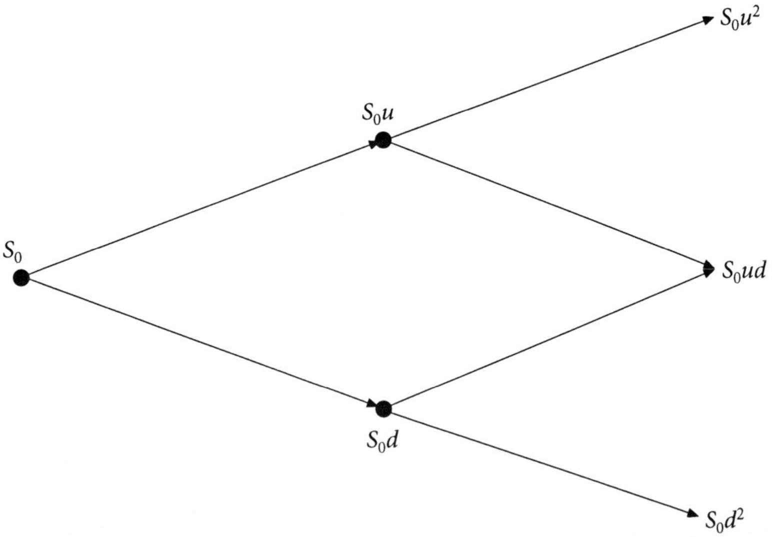

The second assumption is that of risk neutrality. According to this assumption, the asset price at time step t_i is the expected value of its price at time step t_{i+1} discounted by the risk-free interest rate λ. That is, $S_i = exp(-\lambda\Delta t)\Xi(S_{i+1})$, where "exp" stands for the exponential transformation. This gives

$$\Xi(S_{i+1}) = S_i exp(\lambda\Delta t). \tag{9.9}$$

The probability p_u, considered above, does not reflect the expectations of a trader in the market. It is a risk-neutral probability that matches (9.9).

In a binomial model, given the initial asset price, we first construct a tree of possible values of asset prices and their probabilities. The tree is then used to determine the possible asset prices at the expiration period and probabilities of realization of these prices. We can then climb down the tree using (9.9) to determine the asset price at any time step. For the time being we assume that there are no dividend payments.

Equating (9.8) and (9.9) we get

$$exp(\lambda \Delta t) = p_u u + (1 - p_u)d. \tag{9.10}$$

We solve this equation to get

$$p_u = \frac{exp(\lambda \Delta t) - d}{u - d}. \tag{9.11}$$

The requirement $0 \le p_u \le 1$ implies that

$$d \le exp(\lambda \Delta t) \le u. \tag{9.12}$$

This inequality relates the upward and downward movements of the asset prices to the risk-free rate of interest. It does not contradict the assumption that $0 < d < 1 < u$.

The next step is to equate variances of the discrete and the continuous random walks. The stochastic differential equation usually assumed for the price of a non-dividend-paying asset is $dS_t = \mu S_t \, dt + \sigma S_t \, dW$. The parameter μ is the expected growth rate of the price of the underlying asset, σ represents the volatility of the stock price S, dt and dW_t are respectively the increments in time and the underlying Weiner process (see Chapter 10). If we replace μ in this equation by the risk-free rate λ, then it follows that

$$\frac{dS_t}{S_t} = \lambda \, dt + \sigma \, dW_t. \tag{9.13}$$

This form of the stochastic differential equation satisfies the risk neutrality condition given by (9.9) (see Chapter 10). This in turn implies that the probability p_u of an upward jump and jump sizes u and d are chosen such that the discrete random walk underlying the tree and the continuous random walk represented by (9.13) have the same mean and variance.

We assume that an asset's price S_{i+1} at time step t_{i+1}, given S_i, follows a lognormal distribution with parameters λ and σ^2. (See Chapter 10.) Therefore

$$\Xi \left(S_{i+1}^2 \right) = S_i^2 \exp \left[\left(2\lambda + \sigma^2 \right) \Delta t \right]. \tag{9.14}$$

Then under the continuous random walk the variance of S_{i+1}, given S_i, becomes

$$\text{Var}\left(S_{i+1}\right) = \Xi\left(S_{i+1}^2\right) - \left(\Xi\left(S_{i+1}\right)\right)^2 = S_i^2 \exp\left[\left(2\lambda + \sigma^2\right)\Delta t\right] - S_i^2 \exp\left(2\Delta t\right)$$
$$= S_i^2 \exp\left(2\lambda\Delta t\right)\left[\exp\left(\sigma^2\Delta t\right) - 1\right]. \quad (9.15)$$

For the discrete binomial process it follows that

$$\text{Var}\left(S_{i+1}\right) = \Xi\left(S_{i+1}^2\right) - \left(\Xi\left(S_{i+1}\right)\right)^2 = \left(p_u\left(S_i u\right)^2 + \left(1 - p_u\right)\left(S_i d\right)^2\right)$$
$$- S_i^2 \left(p_u u + \left(1 - p_u\right)d\right)^2. \quad (9.16)$$

Equating the two variances and using (9.10) we get

$$\exp\left(2\lambda\Delta t\right)\left[\exp\left(\sigma^2\Delta t\right) - 1\right] = P_u u^2 + \left(1 - p_u\right)d^2 - \left(\exp\left(\lambda\Delta t\right)\right)^2, \quad (9.17)$$

which on simplification gives

$$\exp\left[\left(2\lambda\Delta t + \sigma^2\right)\Delta t\right] = p_u u^2 + \left(1 - p_u\right)d^2. \quad (9.18)$$

This gives

$$p_u = \frac{\exp\left[\left(2\lambda + \sigma^2\right)\Delta t\right] - d^2}{u^2 - d^2}. \quad (9.19)$$

Equating (9.11) and (9.19) we get

$$\frac{\exp\left(\lambda\Delta t\right) - d}{u - d} = \frac{\exp\left[\left(2\lambda + \sigma^2\right)\Delta t\right] - d^2}{u^2 - d^2}. \quad (9.20)$$

from which it follows that

$$u + d = \frac{\exp\left[\left(2\lambda + \sigma^2\right)\Delta t\right] - d^2}{\exp\left(\lambda\Delta t\right) - d}. \quad (9.21)$$

From equation (9.21), we cannot determine u and d, which in turn implies that p_u cannot be determined using (9.10) or (9.19). The reason is that equations (9.10) and (9.18) involve three unknowns p_u, u and d. In order to determine these three unknowns uniquely from the equations (9.10) and (9.18), we need a third equation. Two popular choices in this context are

$$ud = 1, \quad (9.22)$$

and

$$p_u = \frac{1}{2}. \quad (9.23)$$

The first choice reflects symmetry between upward jump and downward jump of the asset price at any time step. The second choice is a symmetric probability assumption—at any time step t_i the chance of the asset price moving up to $S_i u$ or moving down to $S_i d$ is the same.

Under (9.22) we obtain a binomial model where p_u, u and d are determined by (9.10) and (9.18). In view of (9.22) we can write $d = 1/u$ in (9.21) and get the following quadratic equation

$$u^2 - 2Bu + 1 = 0, \tag{9.24}$$

where

$$B = \frac{1}{2}\left[\exp(-\lambda\Delta t) + \exp\left[(\lambda + \sigma^2)\Delta t\right]\right]. \tag{9.25}$$

We solve the equation (9.24) for u, then invoke (9.20) to determine the value of d and finally use (9.11) to find p_u. These values are given by

$$u = B + \sqrt{B^2 - 1}, d = B - \sqrt{B^2 - 1} \text{ and } p_u = \frac{\exp(\lambda\Delta t) - d}{u - d}. \tag{9.26}$$

In order to avoid negative values of p_u, Δt should not be too large. With negative values of p_u, the binomial method becomes inappropriate.

Under the assumption $p_u = \frac{1}{2}$, equations (9.10) and (9.18) reduce respectively to

$$u + d = 2\exp(\lambda\Delta t); u^2 + d^2 = 2\exp\left[(2\lambda + \sigma^2)\Delta t\right]. \tag{9.27}$$

Since these equations are invariant under reordering of u and d, we can choose $u = B_1 + B_2$ and $d = B_1 - B_2$. Note that under these choices of u and d, $u + d = d + u$ and $u^2 + d^2 = d^2 + u^2$. Then

$$u = \exp(\lambda\Delta t)\left[1 + \sqrt{\exp(\sigma^2\Delta t) - 1}\right], d = \exp(\lambda\Delta t)\left[1 - \sqrt{\exp(\sigma^2\Delta t) - 1}\right] \text{ and}$$

$$p_u = \frac{1}{2}. \tag{9.28}$$

We find that in this case $ud > 1$. This does not contradict the assumption $0 < d < 1 < u$. Once again in order to avoid failure of the binomial method the choice of Δt should not be too large. With a large Δt, d may become negative, which is an unrealistic feature.

9.4.2 The Binomial Tree

It is possible to construct a tree of all possible asset prices over the lifespan $t_T - t_0$ using either (9.26) or (9.28). We start at $t_0 = 0$ with the known asset price S_0. At time step t_1 there are two possible prices: $S_1^0 = S_0 d, S_1^1 = S_0 u$. At time step t_2 the three possible prices are $S_2^0 = S_0 d^2$, $S_2^1 = S_0 u d$, and $S_2^2 = S_0 u^2$. Note that the tree is recombining. It does not matter which of the two paths is used to reach $S_0 u d$. This property applies to any arbitrary time step t_i. Thus, the binomial method is path independent. A path-dependent option, in general, cannot be evaluated using a binomial tree. The proportionality condition given by (ii) in the first assumption, between S_i and S_{i+1}, reflects exponential growth or decay of the asset price over time.

In general, the sequence of j prices at time step t_i is given by

$$S_i^j = S_0 d^{i-j} u^j, \tag{9.29}$$

where $j = 0, 1, 2, ..., i$; $i = 1, 2, ..., T$. More precisely, in time step t_i each path with exactly j upward, and $(i - j)$ downward, price movements produces the same asset price $S_0 d^{i-j} u^j$. There are $^i c_j$ such paths and the probability of each is $p_d^{i-j} p_u^j$. Consequently $S_0 d^{i-j} u^j$ occurs with probability $^i c_j\, p_d^{i-j} p_u^j$. Thus, the stock price at time step t_i is a discrete random variable with $(i + 1)$ different values. The number j of upward movements of the price at time step t_i is a discrete random variable which follows a binomial distribution. This is true as well for $(i - j)$ downward movements. That is why this price process is referred to as a binomial tree. Under the symmetry assumption given by (9.22), $S_i^j = S_0 d^{i-2j} = u^{2j-i} S_0$. So if j is even, $S_i^{i/2} = S_0$.

9.4.3 Valuation of Options

The objective of this subsection is to evaluate European and American call and put options using the binomial process. Given that the payoff function of an option depends on the strike price and the price of the underlying asset at the expiry period, we can evaluate it at the date of expiry T. Let us first consider European call and put options with strike price K. The payoff functions are given respectively by

$$\vartheta_{ECT}^j = \max\left(S_T^j - K, 0\right),$$
$$\vartheta_{EPT}^j = \max\left(K - S_T^j, 0\right), \tag{9.30}$$

where $j = 0, 1, 2, ..., T$ (see Chapter 8).

The probability of S_i^j moving to S_{i+1}^{j+1} is p_u and the probability of it moving to S_{i+1}^j is $(1 - p_u)$. This follows from the sequence given by (9.29). Increasing i to $i + 1$ and changing j to $j + 1$ in the sequence simply increases the power of u by 1, keeping the power of d unchanged. More precisely, $\left(S_{i+1}^{j+1}/S_i^j\right) = u$. Hence the probability of price S_i^j moving to S_{i+1}^{j+1} is p_u. Likewise, $\left(S_{i+1}^j/S_i^j\right) = d$ and the probability S_i^j moving to S_{i+1}^j is $(1 - p_u)$. This holds for all $j = 0, 1, 2, ..., i; i = 1, 2, ...,$ T. This gives $p_u S_i^j u + (1 - p_u) S_i^j d = p_u S_{i+1}^{j+1} + (1 - p_u) S_{i+1}^j$. An application of (9.10) with double index gives $p_u S_i^j u + (1 - p_u) S_i^j d = S_i^j \exp(\lambda \Delta t)$. Hence we have

$$S_i^j \exp(\lambda \Delta t) = p_u S_i^j u + (1 - p_u) S_i^j d, \tag{9.31}$$

$$S_i^j \exp(\lambda \Delta t) = p_u S_{i+1}^{j+1} + (1 - p_u) S_{i+1}^j. \tag{9.32}$$

We now invoke the risk neutrality assumption (9.9) in the evaluation of option. The risk neutrality assumption for an arbitrary option payoff function ϑ will be of the type $\Xi(\vartheta_{i+1}) = \vartheta_i \exp(\lambda \Delta t)$, where the subscript refers to the time. Therefore, with our double index notation we have

$$\vartheta_i^j = \exp(-\lambda \Delta t)\left[p_u \vartheta_{i+1}^{j+1} + (1 - p_u) \vartheta_{i+1}^j \right]. \tag{9.33}$$

This equation applies to both call and put options. Since we know the value of ϑ_T^j for $j = 0, 1, 2, ..., T$ from the payoff function, we can determine the values of ϑ_m^j recursively for each $j = 0, 1, 2, ..., m; m < T$, to get the current value of the option ϑ_0^0.

Note that we only need S_T^j to determine ϑ_T^j, knowledge of S_i^j other than S_T^j is not necessary. At each time step we can discard old S_i^j values once S_{i+1}^j values have been calculated. In fact, we can discard S_T^j's also as soon as ϑ_T^j's have been found.

For American options the recurrence relations developed for European options have to be modified by adding the constraint that the early exercise of the options is permissible. It will, therefore, be necessary to investigate whether early exercise is profitable. The structure of the binomial tree we have considered remains the same. The only extra thing to consider is that the American option counterpart to the value of (9.33) needs to be compared with the value of the payoff at each time step. The two equations in (9.30) will now be modified as follows:

$$\vartheta_{ACi}^j = \max\left\{ (S_i^j - K, 0), \exp(-\lambda \Delta t)\left[p_u \vartheta_{i+1}^{j+1} + (1 - p_u) \vartheta_{i+1}^j \right] \right\},$$

$$\vartheta_{APi}^j = \max\left\{ (K - S_i^j, 0), \exp(-\lambda \Delta t)\left[p_u \vartheta_{i+1}^{j+1} + (1 - p_u) \vartheta_{i+1}^j \right] \right\}. \tag{9.34}$$

Observe that provision for early exercise enables us to replace T by i. Here also a tree of S_i^j values is built first. We can evaluate the payoff function ϑ_T^j and climb down the tree to determine the value of the option. It will be necessary for us to check whether early exercise or retaining the option is better. For checking this efficiently it will be necessary for us to store the S_i^j values.

So far we have assumed that the underlying asset is non-dividend paying. Let us now investigate the impact of a constant dividend yield paid on the asset. Consequently, the effective growth rate of the asset becomes $(\lambda - DI_0)$ instead of λ, where DI_0 is the constant dividend amount. If we assume that $ud = 1$, then solutions for u and d in (9.26) will be modified

as: $\quad B = \dfrac{1}{2}\left[\exp\left[-\left(\lambda - DI_0\right)\Delta t\right] + \exp\left[\left(\lambda - DI_0 + \sigma^2\right)\Delta t\right]\right], u = B + \sqrt{B^2 - 1},$

$d = B - \sqrt{B^2 - 1},$ and $\quad p_u = \dfrac{\exp\left[\left(\lambda - DI_0\right)\Delta t\right] - d}{u - d}$. If $\;p_u = 1/2$, then the

modified solutions are $\quad u = \exp\left[\left(\lambda - DI_0\right)\Delta t\right]\left[1 + \sqrt{\exp\left(\sigma^2\Delta t\right) - 1}\right]\quad$ and

$d = \exp\left[\left(\lambda - DI_0\right)\Delta t\right]\left[1 - \sqrt{\exp\left(\sigma^2\Delta t\right) - 1}\right]$. However, the discounted present value

of the asset is calculated using the risk-free rate of return λ so that equations (9.33) and (9.34) remain valid. Thus, with these data in the dividend payment case we can now proceed to evaluate options using the same procedure adopted earlier (for further discussion along this line, see Wilmott et al. 1995 and Seydel 2004).

Example 9.4: Consider a one-step binomial model under risk neutrality in which the current asset price is 30 dollars. This price evolves up to 32 dollars after three months with probability 0.6. The annual risk-free interest rate is 9 percent. We wish to determine the asset price to which the current price evolves down with probability 0.4.

The formula we employ here is $S_0 \exp(\lambda\Delta t) = S_0(p_u u + (1 - p_u)d)$, where $S_0 = 30$, $S_0 u = 32$, $p_u = 0.6$, $\Delta t = 3$ months and $\lambda = 0.1$. The value of $S_0 d$ is to be determined. From the given information $30 \exp(1 \times 1/4) = 32 \times 0.6 + S_0 d \times 0.4$, which gives $S_0 d = 28.9$.

Applied Example 9.1: Bakstein and Howison (2003) developed a model to investigate liquidity effects resulting from the trading of an asset. Liquidity is defined in terms of the average transaction per unit of asset traded and the degree of market slippage due to individual transactions. This definition enables liquidity to be observable in a centralized order book of the asset. The discrete-time version of the model considered in the paper is based on the Cox–Ross–Rubinstein binomial process. An empirical illustration of the model using German data has also been provided. Their model proved to fit the real-world data very accurately and it allowed ranking the liquidity of an asset systematically.

APPENDIX

Proof of Theorem 9.1: $(i) \Rightarrow (ii)$ Consider an arbitrary portfolio $\Omega = \left(n_b^{\Omega}, n_s^{\Omega}\right)$ such that $V_0^{\Omega} = 0$. This implies that $n_b^{\Omega} = -n_s^{\Omega} S_0$, which in turn implies that V_1^{Ω} can be written as

$$V_1^{\Omega} = \begin{cases} n_s^{\Omega} S_0 \left[u - \left(1 + \lambda\right)\right] & \text{if } Z = u, \\ n_s^{\Omega} S_0 \left[d - \left(1 + \lambda\right)\right] & \text{if } Z = d. \end{cases}$$

Assume that $n_s^\Omega < 0$. Given that $S_0 > 0$, for $V_1^\Omega > 0$ to hold we need $u < (1 + \lambda)$ and $d < (1 + \lambda)$. But this means a violation of condition (i). Thus, given condition (i) there is no opportunity for arbitrage. We can deal with the case $n_s^\Omega > 0$ analogously.

(ii)$\Rightarrow$(i) The proof is by contradiction. It is shown that if condition (i) does not hold then there exists a portfolio that provides an opportunity for arbitrage. Assume the inequality $(1 + \lambda) > u$, which implies that $S_0(1 + \lambda) > S_0 u$. Since $u > d$, it also true that $S_0(1 + \lambda) > S_0 d$. Consider the portfolio $\hat{\Omega} = (S_0, -1)$. That is, there is a short position in the stock and all the money is invested in bonds. Then $V_0^{\hat{\Omega}} = 0$ and $V_1^\Omega = S_0(1 + \lambda) - S_0 Z$, which is positive by assumption. That is, violation of condition (i) implies violation of condition (ii). Hence condition (ii) implies condition (i).

The proof of Theorem 9.3 relies on the following Lemma.

Farkas' Lemma: Let d^0, d^1, d^2,..., d^k, be $k + 1$ column vectors in the l-dimensional Euclidean space. Then exactly one of the following conditions holds.

(a) There exist non-negative numbers $y_1, y_2,..., y_k$ such that $d^0 = \sum_{j=1}^{k} y_j d^j$.

(b) There exists a row vector $\Omega = (n_1^\Omega, n_2^\Omega,......, n_l^\Omega)$ of dimension l such that $\Omega d^0 < 0$ and $\Omega d^j \geq 0$ for $j = 1, 2,..., k$.

Proof of Theorem 9.3: (i)$\Rightarrow$(ii) By assumption there exist non-negative numbers $y_1, y_2,..., y_k$ such that $\underline{S_0} = \sum_{j=1}^{k} y_j \underline{S_1}(\omega_j)$. We can choose $\underline{S_0} = d^0$ and $\underline{S_1}(\omega_j) = d^j$. Then condition ($a$) of Farkas' Lemma holds. Thus, condition (b) of the lemma is violated. But violation of condition (b) means that there is no opportunity for arbitrage (see the statement of the non-arbitrage principle given after Definition 9.2).

(ii)$\Rightarrow$(i)By assumption there does not exist any portfolio $\Omega = (n_1^\Omega, n_2^\Omega,......, n_l)$ such that if $V_0^\Omega < 0$ and $V_1^\Omega(j) \geq 0$ for all $j = 1, 2,..., k$. Choose $\underline{S_0} = d^0, \underline{S_1}(\omega_j) = d^j$, in the Farkas' Lemma. Then satisfaction of condition (ii) of the theorem means that condition (b) of the lemma is violated. Hence condition (a) of the lemma holds. This means that condition (i) of the theorem holds.

Proof of Theorem 9.6: By definition, completeness requires that for every $\underline{X}$, there exists a row vector $\Omega = (n_1^\Omega, n_2^\Omega,......, n_l^\Omega)$ such that $\underline{X} = \Omega.(S)_{l \times k}$. In other words, given the row vector $\underline{X}$, which can be regarded as row vector in the k-dimensional Euclidean space, and the matrix $(S)_{l \times k}$, the market is complete if and only if the system $\underline{X} = \Omega.(S)_{l \times k}$ has a solution. The system $\underline{X} = \Omega.(S)_{l \times k}$ has a solution if and only if the row vector $\underline{X}$ is a linear combination of the rows of the matrix $(S)_{l \times k}$, that is, it belongs to the row space of $(S)_{l \times k}$. But $\Omega.(S)_{l \times k}$ is a linear combination of the rows of $(S)_{l \times k}$ with the components of Ω as coefficients, that is, the rows of the matrix $(S)_{l \times k}$ span the k-dimensional Euclidean space. This is same as the condition that the rank of the matrix $(S)_{l \times k}$ is k.

BIBLIOGRAPHICAL NOTES

Arbitrage theory was pioneered by Ross (1976a, 1976b, 1978a). Our presentation of conditions for non-arbitrage resembles that of Bjork (2004). The binomial model, which has been advanced by Cox, Ross and Rubinstein (1979), is a discrete approach to option valuation. Wilmott et al. (1995) and Seydel (2004) present the model quite lucidly.

EXERCISES

1. Each of the following statements is either true or false. If the statement is true prove it. If it is false, give a counter-example or justify your answer by logical reasoning.
   (a) Completeness of the asset market implies that every contingent claim is attainable.
   (b) In a trinomial model the asset price at time step two takes on 6 values.
   (c) If in a complete asset market the number of assets is same as the number of states of the nature, then every contingent claim is uniquely attainable.
   (d) In a binomial model the direction of change in S_i, the price at time step t_i, is independent of past changes.
   (e) In the binomial model the condition $d \leq e^{\lambda \Delta t} \leq u$ implies and is implied by the requirement that $0 \leq p_u \leq 1$.

2. Consider a one-step binomial model in which the current asset price is 30 dollars. This price will be 32 dollars or 29 dollars after four months. The annual risk-free interest rate is 9 percent. Determine the risk-neutral probability with which the current price evolves up to 32 dollars.

3. Provide intuitive explanation for the non-arbitrage principle stated in Section 9.3.

4. Give a graphical exposition of the two-step trinomial tree.

5. Develop an alternative sufficient condition for the asset market to be complete in the scenario presented in Example 9.2.

6. In a binomial model, let S_i be the asset price at time step t_i. How many different values do the random variables S_2 and S_3 take? Determine these values and the corresponding probabilities. Demonstrate your arguments rigorously.

7. An asset is currently traded at 150 dollars. At the end of 3 months the price will be either 5 percent higher or 4 percent lower than the current price. The annual risk-free interest rate is 9 percent. Determine the value of a 3-month European call option with a strike price of 140 dollars.

8. Clearly explain how the binomial method becomes helpful in checking whether early exercise of an American option is profitable.

9. Given $d = 0.8$ and risk-free interest rate is 9 percent, investigate the behavior of the risk-neutral probability with respect to u.

10. In exercise 7, suppose the price will go up either by 5 percent or down by 4 percent over each of the next three months. If the annual risk-free interest rate is 9 percent, determine the value of a 6-month European call option. What will be the value of a European put option?

11. Explain in the context of the general model in Section 9.3 why existence of a risk-neutral probability is sufficient to ensure that there is no opportunity for arbitrage.

12. In a binomial model the possible values of the asset price at time step two are 20 dollars, 30 dollars and y dollars. Determine the value of y when the initial price of the asset is 25 dollars. Can you complete the tree? Is your presentation of the tree, if it can be completed, unique?

CHAPTER 10

Brownian Motion and Itō's Lemma

10.1 INTRODUCTION

Financial models rarely rely on functions that depend on a single variable. Generally, functions which themselves are functions of two or more variables are used. Itō's Lemma, which is regarded as the fundamental instrument in stochastic calculus, allows functions of this type to be differentiated. Stochastic calculus is the type of calculus that operates on stochastic processes. A stochastic process is a random variable that evolves over time.

We begin this chapter with a discussion on the stochastic process. Our starting point is an extremely simple discrete-time process and then we give an introduction to the Brownian motion (or Weiner process), which is a fundamental instrument to model the building of stock prices. These issues are discussed in Sections 10.2 and 10.3, respectively. We then indicate in Section 10.4 how the Weiner process can be generalized to a broader class of continuous-time processes, known as the Itō process. In Section 10.4 we also show how Itō's Lemma can be employed to differentiate functions of stochastic processes. A derivation of Itō's Lemma is presented in the Appendix and two illustrations of the lemma are provided in Section 10.5.

10.2 RANDOM WALK

Suppose a trader is interested in the movement of the price of a stock over a finite sequence of times $t_0 < t_1 < \ldots < t_T$. Let us denote the stock price at time t_i by S_i. Since there is uncertainty about these prices initially, they can be regarded as random variables. The stock price is then said to follow a discrete-time stochastic process. Formally, a stochastic process is a sequence of random variables $\{Y_t\}$, which are defined for a set of parameters $\{t\}$. If we consider a discrete-time situation $\{t\}$, then $\{Y_t\}$ is a discrete-time stochastic process. If the parameter t varies continuously in time interval, then we have a continuous-time stochastic process $\{Y_t\}$. A stochastic process $\{Y_t\}$ is called a Markovian process if given the value of Y_s, the value of Y_u, $u > s$, depends only on Y_s but not on values taken by Y_v, $v < s$. Stock prices are generally assumed to follow a Markovian process; only the current asset price is useful for forecasting its future values. Actually, this is a weak form of a market efficiency condition, which says that the present value of an asset price incorporates all information contained in its past prices. The assumption that the stock price process follows a Markovian process makes sure that the probability distribution of the asset price in the future does not depend on the past pattern of the prices. The path followed by the price in the past has no future prediction value.

In order to illustrate the idea, let us suppose that the stochastic process is a discrete-time, discrete-state random walk. This is a discrete Markovian process. Here Y_t is the position of a particle moving on a line at time $t = 1, 2, 3,...$ with $Y_0 = 0$. At time $t = 1, 2, 3,...,$ Y_t takes a jump of size 1 or -1, each with probability $\frac{1}{2}$. Thus, the possible values of Y_1 are -1 and 1. Then $\Xi(Y_1) = 0$ and $Var(Y_1) = 1$, where Ξ stands for the expectation operator and "Var" represents the variance.

Given $Y_1 = -1$, the two possible values that Y_2 can take are -2 and 0, each with probability $\frac{1}{4}$. Similarly, given $Y_1 = 1$, the two possible values of Y_2 are 2 and 0, each with probability $\frac{1}{4}$, which shows that Y_2 takes on the value 0 with probability $\frac{1}{2}$. Thus, the possible values of Y_2 are then $(-2, 0, 2)$. It takes on the values -2 and 2, with probability $\frac{1}{4}$ each. Consequently, $\Xi(Y_2) = 0$ and $Var(Y_2) = 2$.

It is easy to verify that possible values of Y_3 are $(-3, -1, 1, 3)$ and the respective probabilities are $\frac{1}{8}, \frac{3}{8}, \frac{3}{8}$, and $\frac{1}{8}$. Hence $\Xi(Y_3) = 0$ and $Var(Y_3) = 3$. In general, for any odd value of t, the possible values of Y_t are $(-t, -t+2,..., -1, 1,..., t)$ and for any even value of t, the possible values of Y_t are $(-t, -t+2,..., -2, 0, 2,..., t)$. Then one can check that for any value of t, $\Xi(Y_t) = 0$ and $Var(Y_t) = t$.

It is possible to generalize the above example using a different probability structure. The random variable Y_t now takes a jump of size 1, either up or down, with probabilities p and $(1-p)$ respectively. (We may also assume that the jump is of any arbitrary positive size.) This gives $\Xi(Y_1) = (2p - 1)$ and $Var(Y_1) = 4p(1-p)$. In general, $\Xi(Y_t) = t(2p - 1)$ and $Var(Y_t) = 4tp(1-p)$. The standard deviation of Y_t, the positive square root of the variance of Y_t, equals $SD(Y_t) = 2\sqrt{tp(1-p)}$.

If we define $\mu = (2p - 1)$, then $\Xi(Y_t) = t\mu$. The variable μ is referred to as the drift of the random walk. The process $\{Y_t\}$ is said to follow the discrete-time discrete-state random walk with drift μ if $p \neq (1-p)$. It becomes a driftless random walk if $p = (1-p)$. We note that the expected value of the random walk is directly proportional to time and hence increases with time, but the standard deviation, although increasing with time, is directly proportional to square root of time.

An alternative way to generalize this process is to assume that the size of the jump at each step is a continuous-type random variable. For instance, the size of each jump can be assumed to be normally distributed with a mean of zero and standard deviation σ. This is an example of a discrete-time continuous-state stochastic process.

10.3 WEINER PROCESS (BROWNIAN MOTION)

In 1827 Robert Brown, an English botanist, examined the movements of small pollen grains immersed in a liquid medium. He concluded that, when observed under microscope, pollen grains followed a "swarming motion generated in a continuous manner." This phenomenon is now known as Brownian motion in the scientific literature. In 1905 Albert Einstein, who is regarded as the father of modern physics, showed how the movement of molecules in a liquid can give rise to Brownian motion. Louis Bachelier, a French mathematician, was the first to use Brownian motion to model the movement of stock prices in his doctoral dissertation in 1900. A rigorous mathematical treatment of Brownian motion was provided by Norbert Weiner, a great mathematician, in 1918. The terms "Weiner process" and "Brownian motion" are now used interchangeably in the literature.

A Weiner process $\{W_t\}$ is a continuous-time stochastic process possessing four important characteristics. Here the time variable t, which indexes the stochastic process $\{W_t\}$, varies over the interval $[0, \infty]$ in a continuous manner.

Definition 10.1: A Weiner process (or Brownian motion) $\left\{ W_t \middle| t \in [0, \infty) \right\}$ is a continuous-time stochastic process satisfying the following conditions:

(i) $W_0 = 0$.

(ii) For all $t \geq 0$, W_t is normally distributed with mean $\Xi(W_t) = 0$ and variance $Var\left(W_t\right) = \Xi\left(W_t^2\right) = t$.

(iii) For any $0 \leq t_1 < t_2, W_{t_2} - W_{t_1}$ depends only on the value of $(t_2 - t_1)$, that is, the process $\{W_t\}$ possesses stationary increments.

(iv) All increments on non-overlapping time intervals are independent, that is, for any $0 \leq t_1 \leq t_2 \leq t_3 \ldots \ldots \leq t_n$, the non-overlapping increments $W_{t_2} - W_{t_1}, W_{t_3} - W_{t_2}, \ldots \ldots, W_{t_n} - W_{t_{n-1}}$, are independent.

An implication of conditions (i), (ii) and (iii) is that $W_{t_2} - W_{t_1}$, which has the same distribution as $W_{t_2 - t_1} - W_0 = W_{t_2 - t_1}$, has mean 0 and variance $(t_2 - t_1)$. That is, the change in the process over any finite time interval $[t_1, t_2]$ follows normal distribution with mean 0 and variance $(t_2 - t_1)$.

If in the above definition, condition (ii) is replaced by the more general condition that for all $t \geq 0$, W_t is normally distributed with mean $\Xi(W_t) = \mu t$ and variance $Var(W_t) = \sigma^2 t$, where $\mu \neq 0$, $\sigma > 0$ is a constant, and conditions (i), (iii) and (iv) remain unchanged, then $\{W_t | t \in [0, \infty)\}$ is called a generalized Weiner process (or Brownian motion) with volatility σ and drift μ. If $\mu = 0$ and $\sigma = 1$, then $\{W_t | t \in [0, \infty)\}$ we get the Weiner process (or Brownian motion) considered in the above definition. If $\{W_t\}$ is a generalized Weiner process with volatility σ and drift μ, then it can be expressed as

$$W_t = \mu t + \sigma Z_t, \tag{10.1}$$

where $\{Z_t | t \in [0, \infty)\}$ is a Weiner process.

Let us now look at the role of a Weiner processes in explaining the movement of the price of a stock. It is probably reasonable to assume that stock prices have independent increments. Since a Weiner process can be negative and the price of a stock can never be negative, the behavior of stock price as a Weiner process does not look appropriate in this context. For a Weiner process with drift μ it follows that the expected price change over an interval is given by the product of the drift and the length of the interval, so that dependence of the expected change on the initial stock price is ignored. A more reasonable assumption is that the rate of return of the stock price can be modeled as a Weiner process.

The rate of return of the stock price over the short time interval $[t, t + \Delta t]$ is defined as

$$\frac{\Delta S_t}{S_t} = \frac{S_{t+\Delta t} - S_t}{S_t}, \tag{10.2}$$

where $\Delta t > 0$ is small. If $\Delta t \to 0$, then the rate of return defined above becomes the instantaneous rate of return and is denoted by $\frac{dS_t}{S_t}$. We now assume that the instantaneous rate of return of the stock price can be modeled as a generalized Weiner process. More precisely,

$$\frac{dS_t}{S_t} = \mu\, dt + \sigma\, dW_t, \tag{10.3}$$

where dW_t is normally distributed with mean zero and variance dt and, μ and σ are constants. Here μ represents the expected rate of return on the stock price. The number σ, the positive square root of σ^2, is called the volatility of the stock price. Loosely speaking, volatility of a stock price is a measure of the extent to which uncertainty exists in the future movements of the stock price. It indicates uncertainty on stock return. For rapid up and down movements of stock price over a short time period, volatility is high, whereas for minor changes volatility is low. The condition of independence assumption means that the probability distribution for the change in the process over any time interval is independent of that over any other non-overlapping time interval.

We can rewrite the formula (10.3) as

$$dS_t = \mu S_t dt + \sigma S_t dW_t. \tag{10.4}$$

This is a stochastic differential equation and the term dW_t in this equation is referred to as the Weiner increment. If in a differential equation at least one term is a stochastic process, then it is called a stochastic differential equation. A stock price process satisfying equation (10.4) is said to follow a (μ, σ)-geometric Brownian motion. The definitions of the drift and volatility μ and σ are based on percentage changes or returns on the security prices from time to time. It assumes that the relative change $\dfrac{dS_t}{S_t}$ in the stock price during the time interval of length dt consists of a deterministic drift component μ and stochastic fluctuation term of the form $\sigma\, dW_t$. Here $\dfrac{dS_t}{S_t}$ has a normal distribution with mean μdt and variance $\sigma^2 dt$. Therefore, the probability density function will shift and flatten as time progresses. Note that equation (10.4) does not refer to the past history of the asset price. The future period price $(S_t + dS_t)$ depends only on today's price S_t. This independence of the asset price from the past values is the Markovian process property.

In order to estimate drift and volatility from real life data, we first choose a small value for Δt. For instance, Δt may be one day. The estimation of drift and volatility rely on logarithmic growth factors defined as the logarithm of stock price at the end of the period minus the logarithm of stock price at the beginning of the period. Given a $(T + 1)$ time series $S_0, S_1,..., S_T$, we look at the logarithmic growth factors, that is, the ratios $\ln\left(\dfrac{S_i}{S_{i-1}}\right), 1 \le i \le T$, where "$ln$" represents natural logarithm. The average $\dfrac{1}{T}\sum\limits_{i=1}^{T}\ln\left(\dfrac{S_i}{S_{i-1}}\right)$ of these values is an estimate of $\mu\Delta t$. The sample variance $\dfrac{1}{T-1}\sum\limits_{i=1}^{T}\left(\ln\dfrac{S_i}{S_{i-1}} - \dfrac{1}{T}\sum\limits_{i=1}^{T}\ln\left(\dfrac{S_i}{S_{i-1}}\right)\right)^2$ of the sample values $\ln\left(\dfrac{S_i}{S_{i-1}}\right)$ is an estimate of $\sigma^2\Delta t$. This enables us to estimate the drift and volatility of the underlying geometric Brownian motion. These estimated values are referred to as historical estimates.

10.4 ITŌ'S LEMMA

Itō's Lemma is a fundamental tool in stochastic process. Before we proceed for a formal statement of the lemma, we observe that the equation given by (10.4) is a special case of the formula

$$dS_t = a(S_t, t)dt + b(S_t, t)dW_t, \tag{10.5}$$

where dW_t is normally distributed with mean zero and variance dt, $a(S_t, t) = \mu S_t$ and $b(S_t, t) = \sigma S_t$. A process $\{S_t\}$ satisfying equation (10.5) is called an Itō's process, where $a(S_t, t)$ is the drift function and $b(S_t, t)$ is the volatility for an increment in S_t (see Oksendal 2003). It is also known as the Itō stochastic differential equation.

If we have a two-coordinated function of the type $f(S_t, t)$, then we are interested in an expression for $df(S_t, t)$. Itō's Lemma gives us precisely this.

Itō's Lemma: Assume that $\{S_t\}$ follow an Itō process, that is, $dS_t = a(S_t, t)dt + b(S_t, t)dW_t$, where dW_t is normally distributed with a mean zero and the variance dt, $a(S_t, t)$ and $b(S_t, t)$ are two-coordinated functions. Let $f(x, t)$ be a twice continuously differentiable two-coordinated function. Then $f(S_t, t)$ follows an Itō process and

$$df\left(S_t, t\right) = \left[\frac{\partial f}{\partial x}a + \frac{\partial f}{\partial t} + \frac{1}{2}\frac{\partial^2 f}{\partial x^2}b^2\right]dt + \frac{\partial f}{\partial x}b\,dW_t, \tag{10.6}$$

where the derivatives of f as well as the coefficient functions a and b depend on (S_t, t), and it is assumed that $dt.dt = dt.dW_t = dW_t.dt = 0$, $dW_t.dW_t = dt$.

Proof: See Appendix.

Thus, loosely speaking, this lemma says that smooth functions of an Itō process are themselves Itō processes.

10.5 APPLICATIONS

We have already observed situations where stochastic differential equations arise in finance. In this section we see how Itō's Lemma can be used to solve them. As the first illustrative example, consider $f(S_t, t) = ln(S_t)$. Then

$$\frac{\partial f\left(S_t, t\right)}{\partial S_t} = \frac{1}{S_t}, \quad \frac{\partial^2 f\left(S_t, t\right)}{\partial S_t^2} = -\frac{1}{S_t^2}, \quad \frac{\partial f\left(S_t, t\right)}{\partial t} = 0. \tag{10.7}$$

By Itō's Lemma we have

$$d\left(\ln S_t\right) = \left[\frac{1}{S_t}\mu S_t - \frac{1}{2}\cdot\frac{1}{S_t^2}\sigma S_t^2\right]dt + \frac{1}{S_t}\sigma S_t dW_t$$

$$= \left(\mu - \frac{\sigma^2}{2}\right)dt + \sigma\,dW_t. \tag{10.8}$$

This says that $d(lnS_t)$ is normally distributed with mean $\left(\mu - \dfrac{\sigma^2}{2}\right)dt$ and variance $\sigma^2 dt$.

We are now in a position to derive an explicit formula for the evolution of stock price. Integrating the expression $\left(\mu - \dfrac{\sigma^2}{2}\right)d\tau + \sigma\,dW_\tau$ between 0 and t we get

$$\int_0^t d\big(\ln(S_\tau)\big) = \left(\mu - \frac{\sigma^2}{2}\right)\int_0^t d\tau + \int_0^t \sigma\, dW_\tau. \tag{10.9}$$

The expression in (10.9) can be written more explicitly as

$$\ln(S_t) - \ln(S_0) = \left(\mu - \frac{\sigma^2}{2}\right)t + \sigma\,(W_t - W_0). \tag{10.10}$$

Since $W_0 = 0$, we can rewrite (10.10) as

$$\ln(S_t) = \ln(S_0) + \left(\mu - \frac{\sigma^2}{2}\right)t + \sigma W_t. \tag{10.11}$$

From the properties of the Weiner process $\{W_t\}$ we conclude that, given the price S_0 at the initial period, $ln(S_t)$ is normally distributed with mean $\ln(S_0) + \left(\mu - \frac{\sigma^2}{2}\right)t$

and variance $\sigma^2 t$. That is, the expectation of the Itō process $\big\{\ln(S_t)\big\}$ is $\ln(S_0) + \left(\mu - \frac{\sigma^2}{2}\right)t$ and its variance is $\sigma^2 t$. Since $\dfrac{d\ln(S_t)}{dS_t} = \dfrac{1}{S_t}$, the density of $ln(S_t)$ is given by

$$g\big(S_t, t, S_0, \mu, \sigma\big) = \frac{1}{S_t\sqrt{2\pi\sigma^2 t}}\exp\left[-\frac{\left[\ln S_t - \ln S_0 - \left(\mu - \frac{\sigma^2}{2}\right)t\right]^2}{2\sigma^2 t}\right], \tag{10.12}$$

where "exp" represents the exponential function. This is the density function of the lognormal distribution. A non-negative random variable X is said to follow a lognormal distribution if its logarithm $ln(X)$ follows a normal distribution. Thus, the stock price S_t follows a lognormal distribution under the assumption of geometric Brownian motion.

An alternative to interest arises from the specification, $f(S_t, t) = S_t \exp(\lambda(T - t))$, where λ is the risk-free rate of interest. As we have noted in Chapter 8, this is the price of a forward contract when the period of initiation of the contract is t, S_t is the price of the underlying asset at t and T is the period of maturity. Then

$$\frac{\partial f(S_t, t)}{\partial S_t} = \exp\left[\lambda(T - t)\right], \frac{\partial^2 f(S_t, t)}{\partial S_t^2} = 0 \text{ and}$$

$$\frac{\partial f(S_t, t)}{\partial t} = -\lambda S_t \exp\left[\lambda(T - t)\right]. \tag{10.13}$$

Then an application of Itō's Lemma shows that

$$d(S_t \exp[\lambda(T-t)]) = [\mu S_t \exp[\lambda(T-t)] - \lambda S_t \exp[\lambda(T-t)]]dt + \sigma S_t \exp[\lambda(T-t)]\, dW_t, \quad (10.14)$$

which when rewritten in terms of the forward price $\eta_{FOC}(t, T) = S_t \exp[\lambda(T-t)]$ becomes

$$d(\eta_{FOC}(t, T)) = [\mu - \lambda]\eta_{FOC}(t, T)dt + \sigma\,\eta_{FOC}(t, T)dW_t. \quad (10.15)$$

This shows that the forward price process is a geometric Brownian motion with an expected growth rate $(\mu - \lambda)$.

Example 10.1: Consider a coin-tossing game between two individuals, I and II. If it is heads then person I pays 1 dollar to person II and the opposite happens if it is tails. The game is repeated T times and the outcome of each trial is independent of that of the previous trial. In any trial the probability of heads appearing is same as that of tails appearing. This repeated game is a discrete-time discrete-state random walk.

Example 10.2: Let $(gr)_{t-1,t}$ be the gross return on a stock between periods $(t-1)$ and t. Then the total gross return on the stock between the periods 0 and T is given by $(gr)_{0,T} = \sum_{j=1}^{T}(gr)_{j-1,j}$. Gross returns over the successive non-overlapping time intervals $(t-1)$ and t, and t and $(t+1)$ are independent and have the same probability distribution. For each j, $(gr)_{j-1,j}$ has a constant variance σ^2 so that the variance of the total return is $\sigma^2 T$. This example shows that stock returns can be modeled as random walks.

Example 10.3: The initial price of a stock is 50 dollars. Over a 5-day period, the price at the end of the ith day is given by 49.82 dollars, 50.02 dollars, 49.69 dollars, 49.34 dollars and 50.10 dollars, where $i = 1, 2,...5$. Assume that Δt is 1 day so that $\Delta t = \dfrac{1}{365}$. We wish to estimate the instantaneous drift and volatility (see Roman 2004).

The average of logarithmic ratios $\ln\left(\dfrac{49.82}{50}\right), \ln\left(\dfrac{50.02}{49.82}\right), \ln\left(\dfrac{49.69}{50.02}\right), \ln\left(\dfrac{49.34}{49.69}\right)$ and $\ln\left(\dfrac{50.10}{49.34}\right)$ is 0.0003996. This is an estimate of $\mu_0\Delta t$. In order to get the drift term μ_0 we need to multiply the average by $\dfrac{1}{\Delta t} = 365$. Thus, the instantaneous drift is given by $0.0003996 \times 365 \approx 0.15$. By a similar calculation the instantaneous volatility becomes 0.03 (approximately).

APPENDIX

Proof of Itô's Lemma: By Taylor's formula for two variables, for small Δt we have
$f(S_{t+\Delta t} - S_t, t + \Delta t) - f(S_t, t)$

$$= \left(S_{t+\Delta t} - S_t\right)\frac{\partial f}{\partial x} + \Delta t\,\frac{\partial f}{\partial t} + \frac{1}{2}\frac{\partial^2 f}{\partial x^2}\left(S_{t+\Delta t} - S_t\right)^2 + \frac{\partial^2 f}{\partial t\partial x}\left(\Delta t\left(S_{t+\Delta t} - S_t\right)\right)$$

$$+ \frac{1}{2}(\Delta t)^2 \frac{\partial^2 f}{\partial t^2} + \text{ higher order terms.} \qquad (10.16)$$

Ignoring higher order terms and using the fact $(S_{t+\Delta t} - S_t) = a(S_t, t)\Delta t + b(S_t, t)dW_t$, we note that the right-hand side of (10.16) equals

$$\left[a\left(S_t,t\right)\Delta t + b\left(S_t,t\right)dW_t\right]\frac{\partial f}{\partial x} + \Delta t\,\frac{\partial f}{\partial t} + \left[\Delta t\left(a\left(S_t,t\right)\Delta t + b\left(S_t,t\right)dW_t\right)\right]\frac{\partial^2 f}{\partial t\partial x} + $$
$$\left[\left(a\left(S_t,t\right)\Delta t\right)^2 + \left(b\left(S_t,t\right)\right)^2\left(dW_t\right)^2 + 2a\left(S_t,t\right)\Delta t b\left(S_t,t\right)dW_t\right]$$
$$\frac{1}{2}\frac{\partial^2 f}{\partial x^2} + \frac{1}{2}(\Delta t)^2\frac{\partial^2 f}{\partial t^2}. \qquad (10.17)$$

Now, we write dt for Δt, approximate $(dW_t)^2$ by dt, ignore all terms involving $(dt)^2$ and $(dW_t\, dt)$. Then we have

$$df\left(S_t,t\right) = a\left(S_t,t\right)\frac{\partial f}{\partial x}dt + b\left(S_t,t\right)\frac{\partial f}{\partial x}dW_t + \frac{\partial f}{\partial t}dt + \frac{1}{2}\left(b\left(S_t,t\right)\right)^2\frac{\partial^2 f}{\partial x^2}dt$$

$$= \left[a\left(S_t,t\right)\frac{\partial f}{\partial x} + \frac{\partial f}{\partial t} + \frac{1}{2}\left(b\left(S_t,t\right)\right)^2\frac{\partial^2 f}{\partial x^2}\right]dt + b\left(S_t,t\right)\frac{\partial f}{\partial x}dW_t. \qquad (10.18)$$

Replacing x by S_t in (10.18) we get the desired result.

BIBLIOGRAPHICAL NOTES

For a rigorous exposition of Brownian motion the interested reader is referred to Seydel (2004). Itô's Lemma is stated rigorously in Oksendal (2003). Applications of the lemma can be found in many books, including Seydel (2004), Baz and Chacko (2008) and Hull and Basu (2010).

EXERCISES

1. Suppose $\{S_t\}$ follows a (μ, σ)-arithmetic Brownian motion, that is, $dS_t = \mu dt + \sigma dW_t$, where μ and σ are constants, and dW_t is normally distributed with

mean zero and variance dt. Then provide an analytical form for the Brownian motion process $\{exp(S_t)\}$.

2. Consider the Itō process $dY_t = \mu(t)dt + \sigma(t)dW_t$, dW_t is normally distributed with mean zero and variance dt and, $\mu(t)$ and $\sigma(t)$ are assumed to be dependent on time. Determine the distribution of Y_t.

3. Suppose $\{X_t\}$ follows a (μ, σ)-geometric Brownian motion. Determine the Brownian motion for process $\ln\left(X_t\right) + \dfrac{\sigma^2 t}{2}$.

4. Let $\{W_t\}$ and $\{\hat{W}_t\}$ be two uncorrelated Weiner processes, where the drift-volatility vectors for the two processes are respectively (μ, σ) and $\left(\hat{\mu}, \hat{\sigma}\right)$. Then determine the processes for $\{W_t + \hat{W}_t\}$ and $\{W_t - \hat{W}_t\}$.

5. Show that if $\{W_t\}$ is a Weiner process with volatility σ and drift μ, then $W_t = \mu t + \sigma Z_t$, where $\left\{Z_t \middle| t \in [0, \infty)\right\}$ is a Weiner process.

6. Suppose a random variable X follows lognormal distribution, that is, $ln(X)$ follows normal distribution with mean μ and variance σ^2. Find the mean and variance of X.

7. Let Δt be the equally spaced time interval between S_{t-1} and S_t. Determine the distribution of $\ln\left(\dfrac{S_t}{S_{t-1}}\right)$ under the assumption of geometric Brownian motion.

CHAPTER 11

The Black–Scholes–Merton Model

11.1 INTRODUCTION

In Chapter 9 we examined the binomial model for the pricing of derivatives where the stock price takes on only two values in a period and trading takes place at discrete time points. In a realistic stock price evolution process, the number of trading intervals is large and the time between trades is small. As the number of trading intervals increases, the stock price is likely to vary over a larger number of values and trading takes place almost continuously. In the limit as the length of the trading period becomes infinitesimally small, the trading process becomes continuous. The analytical formulation of the majority of option theory is based on continuous-time set-up.

In this chapter we study the most well-known continuous-time model, the Black–Scholes–Merton model. This model, developed by Fischer Black and Myron Scholes, with help from Robert C. Merton, is a breakthrough in the theory of option pricing (see Black and Scholes 1973 and Merton 1973). This model describes the formulae for European call and put options on an asset. The next section of the chapter presents the Black–Scholes–Merton partial differential equation. The Black–Scholes pricing formulae for European options are discussed in Section 11.3. Section 11.4 is concerned with comparative static analysis of these formulae. Finally, a discussion on volatility is presented in Section 11.5.

11.2 THE BLACK–SCHOLES–MERTON PARTIAL DIFFERENTIAL EQUATION

The reduction of risk in a portfolio is known as hedging. More precisely, hedging means reduction of the sensitivity of a portfolio to the movements in the value of an underlying asset by choosing opposite positions in different financial instruments. To understand this, consider a trader with a short position on a risky asset. If the asset price is above the strike price, the trader faces the possibility of a loss. To avoid this loss, the trader can buy a certain amount of the asset so that the loss resulting from the short position can be compensated by the gain obtained from the long position. The central idea underlying the Black–Scholes–Merton model is hedging to eliminate risk. Under continuous adjustment of the proportion of the underlying asset with option in a portfolio, Black, Scholes and Merton showed that it is possible to create a riskless hedging portfolio, where risk associated with stochastic asset price can be eliminated. In the absence of risk-free arbitrage opportunities, the expected rate of return on a portfolio with zero risk will be the risk-free interest rate. Clearly, this approach provides a strong intuition about the economics underlying the valuation of a risky asset.

Before presenting the Black–Scholes–Merton partial differential equation, we state the underlying assumptions.

(i) The stock price follows the geometric Brownian motion (10.3) with μ and σ constant.

(ii) The risk-free interest rate λ is constant.

We look at implications of relaxation of this assumption in Chapter 13.

(iii) There are no transaction costs or taxes.

(iv) The underlying asset does not pay any dividend during the life of the option.

(v) Trading of the underlying asset takes place in a continuous process.

(vi) There are no opportunities for riskless arbitrage.

As we have argued in Chapter 9, under absence of non-arbitrage opportunities, there is no scope for riskless profit without any investment.

(vii) Short selling is permitted and the assets are perfectly divisible.

Thus, it is possible to buy and sell any quantity (not necessarily an integer) of the underlying asset and because of the short selling assumption a trader can buy and sell assets that are not owned by him.

Now, suppose we have an option whose value or price $f(S_t, t)$ depends on the current stock price S_t and time t of initiation of the contract (since we are going to apply Itô's Lemma here, in order to maintain consistency in notation use, we write f to denote the value of an option in this chapter). Given that the stock price follows the geometric Brownian motion (10.4), in Itô's Lemma we put $a(S_t, t) = \mu S_t$, $b(S_t, t) = \sigma S_t$ and $x = S_t$. Then (10.6) becomes

$$df\left(S_t,t\right) = \left[\frac{\partial f}{\partial S_t}\mu S_t + \frac{\partial f}{\partial t} + \frac{1}{2}\frac{\partial^2 f}{\partial S_t^2}\sigma^2 S_t^2\right]dt + \frac{\partial f}{\partial S_t}\sigma S_t dW_t. \qquad (11.1)$$

This gives the process followed by f.

We now construct a portfolio Π which is short in one derivative f and long in the amount $\dfrac{\partial f}{\partial S_t}$ of the underlying asset. At time t the value of the portfolio is

$$\Pi_t = -f + \frac{\partial f}{\partial S_t} S_t. \qquad (11.2)$$

These portfolio weights are chosen such that the market risk is completely eliminated. The portfolio is called dynamic since its composition is allowed to vary over time. It is assumed to be closed for $0 < t < T$. In other words, no money can be injected into or taken out of the portfolio during the period under consideration. Consequently, the jump in the value of the portfolio Π in one time-step is given by

$$d\Pi_t = -df + \frac{\partial f}{\partial S_t} dS_t. \qquad (11.3)$$

The amount $\dfrac{\partial f}{\partial S_t}$ is assumed to be unchanged during the time-step. Thus, the change in the value of Π_t can only be due to a change in f and/or S. This property of a portfolio is known as the self-financing property.

Putting (10.4), (11.1) and (11.3) together we get

$$d\Pi_t = \left[-\frac{\partial f}{\partial t} - \frac{1}{2} \frac{\partial^2 f}{\partial S_t^2} \sigma^2 S_t^2 \right] dt. \qquad (11.4)$$

Thus, we note that the random component in dW_t the process has been completely eliminated. Therefore, we now have a portfolio whose increment is completely deterministic. As we will see later, the quantity $\dfrac{\partial f}{\partial S_t}$ is referred to as the delta of option f and it is shown that the sensitivity of the portfolio to changes in the asset price is reduced to zero by delta-hedging, a dynamic hedging strategy.

We now invoke the assumptions (*ii*), (*iii*) and (*vi*). The return on an amount Π_t invested in a risk-free asset would generate a growth of $\lambda \Pi_t \, dt$ in the time length dt, where λ is constant by assumption (*ii*). To demonstrate this, suppose the right-hand side of (11.4) is greater than $\lambda \Pi_t \, dt$. An arbitrageur can borrow the amount Π_t to invest in the portfolio. Because of assumption (*iii*) there is no transaction cost. The return on this risk-free trading strategy will be greater than the cost of borrowing. This is a case of the existence of an opportunity for riskless arbitrage. Conversely, if the right-hand side of (11.4) is less than $\lambda \Pi_t \, dt$, then the arbitrageur can have a short position in the portfolio Π_t and invest the amount in the bank to earn a risk-free profit. Thus, either way the arbitrageur can instantaneously generate a risk-free, no cost profit. Hence in view of assumption (*vi*) it must be the case that

$$\lambda \Pi_t dt = \left[-\frac{\partial f}{\partial t} - \frac{1}{2} \frac{\partial^2 f}{\partial S_t^2} \sigma^2 S_t^2 \right] dt . \tag{11.5}$$

Substituting Π_t given by (11.2) into (11.5) and cancelling dt from both sides we get

$$\lambda S_t \frac{\partial f}{\partial S_t} - \lambda f = -\frac{\partial f}{\partial t} - \frac{1}{2} \sigma^2 S_t^2 \frac{\partial^2 f}{\partial S_t^2}, \tag{11.6}$$

which is satisfied by any asset price S_t if f satisfies the equation

$$\frac{\partial f}{\partial t} + \frac{1}{2} \sigma^2 S_t^2 \frac{\partial^2 f}{\partial S_t^2} + \lambda S_t \frac{\partial f}{\partial S_t} - \lambda f = 0. \tag{11.7}$$

The above parabolic partial differential equation is known as the Black–Scholes–Merton partial differential equation.

A partial differential equation generally has many solutions. The value of an option should be unique; otherwise scope for arbitrage possibilities will arise. To derive the solution uniquely, we need to impose some auxiliary conditions. The differential equation can be solved directly for European options subject to appropriate auxiliary conditions. These conditions specify the values of the derivative for possible values of S_t and t. For a European call option with strike price K, the condition is

$$f(S_t, t) = max(S_T, - K, 0) \text{ when } t = T \tag{11.8}$$

and for a European put option with strike price K, the condition is

$$f(S_t, t) = max(K - S_T, 0) \text{ when } t = T. \tag{11.9}$$

Thus, using our notation in Subsection 8.5.2, we have $O_{EC}(S_t, \tau, K) = f(S_t, t) = max(S_T - K, 0)$ when $t = T$, and $O_{EP}(S_t, \tau, K) = f(S_t, t) = max(K - S_T, 0)$ when $t = T$, where $\tau = T - t$ is the time to expiry. The differential equation (11.7) is the necessary tool to derive the Black–Scholes option pricing formula for a European option. To show that a unique solution for the call (respectively put) option value on a non-dividend-paying stock exists it will be necessary to impose the condition (11.8) (respectively 11.9)) on the equation (11.7).

It is important to note that the portfolio used in the derivation of equation (11.7) is riskless for an infinitesimally small period of time. In other words, in this dynamic strategy the delta-hedge is only instantaneously risk-free. If $\frac{\partial f}{\partial S_t}$ changes when S_t and t change, the portfolio needs continuous adjustments to ensure that it remains riskless. This is called re-hedging. Thus, the delta-hedge position must be monitored continuously and continuous rebalancing is necessary to maintain this position.

Note that the equation in (11.7) does not depend on the drift parameter μ. Thus, the value of an option does not depend on how slowly or quickly an asset price changes. The only parameter of the stochastic differential equation (10.4) on which (11.7) depends is the volatility, σ. Thus, the Black–Scholes–Merton partial differential equation indicates that two traders may differ with respect to their estimates of the drift parameter but still may agree on the value of an option.

All the parameters that appear in the equation, namely, the current stock price, time, volatility and the risk-free interest rate are independent of risk preferences. The expected growth rate that depends on such preferences does not appear in the equation. It may be noted that except for volatility, all other parameters are directly observable. Now, any risk preference, including the risk-neutral valuation, can be employed for pricing options. In a risk-neutral world the expected rate of return on all assets is the risk-free rate $λ$. Thus, under the risk neutrality assumption, an investor does not demand any extra return above the risk-free rate. The present value of any cash flow stream can then be obtained by discounting the expected value at the risk-free rate. The risk neutrality assumption makes the analysis of derivatives quite simple and the instantaneous rate of return on a stock under this assumption is simply the risk-free rate $λ$.

We can also derive the Black–Scholes–Merton partial differential equation using the argument that the payoff of the derivative security can be exactly replicated using a dynamic portfolio of the underlying asset and a risk-free bond. The bond is risk-free so that $dB_t = λB_t dt$, where B_t represents the value of the bond at time t. We will now construct dynamic trading strategy that replicates the instantaneous change of the derivative security. Let X_t be the amount of investment in the derivative security at time t. With this amount it is possible to buy $\dfrac{X_t}{f(S_t,t)}$ units of the derivative security. It is assumed that $\dfrac{X_t}{f(S_t,t)}$ remains fixed. Then the instantaneous change in this investment is $dX_t = \dfrac{X_t}{f(S_t,t)} df(S_t,t)$

$$= \frac{X_t}{f(S_t,t)}\left[\frac{\partial f}{\partial S_t}\mu S_t + \frac{\partial f}{\partial t} + \frac{1}{2}\frac{\partial^2 f}{\partial S_t^2}\sigma^2 S_t^2\right]dt + \frac{X_t}{f(S_t,t)}\frac{\partial f}{\partial S_t}\sigma S_t dW_t. \qquad (11.10)$$

An alternative trading strategy is to invest the fractional amount $\dfrac{S_t}{f(S_t,t)}\dfrac{\partial f(S_t,t)}{\partial S_t}$ in the stock and remaining fraction $1 - \dfrac{S_t}{f(S_t,t)}\dfrac{\partial f(S_t,t)}{\partial S_t}$ in the risk-free bond. Since the stock price follows the geometric Brownian motion and $dB_t = λB_t dt$, the dynamics of the investment strategy in this case is

$$dX_t = \frac{\dfrac{S_t}{f(S_t,t)} \dfrac{\partial f(S_t,t)}{\partial S_t}}{S_t} X_t\, dS_t + \frac{\left(1 - \dfrac{S_t}{f(S_t,t)} \dfrac{\partial f(S_t,t)}{\partial S_t}\right) X_t}{B_t}\, dB_t$$

$$= \frac{S_t}{f(S_t,t)} \frac{\partial f(S_t,t)}{\partial S_t} X_t \mu\, dt + \frac{S_t}{f(S_t,t)} \frac{\partial f(S_t,t)}{\partial S_t} X_t \sigma\, dW_t$$

$$+ \left(1 - \frac{S_t}{f(S_t,t)} \frac{\partial f(S_t,t)}{\partial S_t}\right) X_t \lambda dt$$

$$= \left[\frac{S_t}{f(S_t,t)} \frac{\partial f(S_t,t)}{\partial S_t} X_t \mu + \left(1 - \frac{S_t}{f(S_t,t)} \frac{\partial f(S_t,t)}{\partial S_t}\right) X_t \lambda \right] dt$$

$$+ \frac{S_t}{f(S_t,t)} \frac{\partial f(S_t,t)}{\partial S_t} X_t \sigma\, dW_t. \tag{11.11}$$

In (11.10) and (11.11) the Weiner processes are the same and the volatility levels of the two investments are equal as well. Thus, the risks associated with the two investments are the same. In view of the non-arbitrage principle the expected returns on the two equal-risk investments will be equal. Then the drift components of (11.10) and (11.11) must be equal. Thus,

$$\frac{X_t}{f(S_t,t)} \left[\frac{\partial f}{\partial S_t} \mu S_t + \frac{\partial f}{\partial t} + \frac{1}{2} \frac{\partial^2 f}{\partial S_t^2} \sigma^2 S_t^2 \right]$$

$$= \left[\frac{S_t}{f(S_t,t)} \frac{\partial f(S_t,t)}{\partial S_t} X_t \mu + \left(1 - \frac{S_t}{f(S_t,t)} \frac{\partial f(S_t,t)}{\partial S_t}\right) X_t \lambda \right], \tag{11.12}$$

from which we get

$$\frac{\partial f}{\partial S_t} \mu S_t + \frac{\partial f}{\partial t} + \frac{1}{2} \frac{\partial^2 f}{\partial S_t^2} \sigma^2 S_t^2 = \frac{\partial f}{\partial S_t} \mu S_t + \lambda f - \lambda S_t \frac{\partial f(S_t,t)}{\partial S_t}. \tag{11.13}$$

Equation (11.13), on simplification, becomes

$$\frac{\partial f}{\partial t} + \frac{1}{2} \sigma^2 S_t^2 \frac{\partial^2 f}{\partial S_t^2} + \lambda S_t \frac{\partial f}{\partial S_t} - \lambda f = 0, \tag{11.14}$$

which is the Black–Scholes–Merton partial differential equation. Thus, we have made use of replication of the derivative security exactly by a dynamic portfolio involving the underlying asset and the risk-free bond.

11.3 THE BLACK–SCHOLES PRICING FORMULAE

It is clear that we can apply the risk-neutral valuation approach to determine the price of a European call option by computing the expectation of the discounted payoff at the terminal period. For a European call option on a non-dividend-paying stock the expected value of the option at the period of maturity is $\hat{\Xi}\left[\max\left(K - S_T, 0\right)\right]$, where $\hat{\Xi}$ stands for the expected value of the option at the period of maturity T in a risk-neutral world. In view of risk neutrality, the value of the option at period 0 is this expected value discounted at the risk-free rate of interest. That is,

$$O_{EC} = \exp\left(-\lambda T\right)\hat{\Xi}\left[\max\left(K - S_T, 0\right)\right]. \tag{11.15}$$

We show in the Appendix that this value is given by

$$O_{EC} = S_0\Phi(d_1) - K\,exp(-\lambda T)\Phi(d_2), \tag{11.16}$$

where "exp" represents the exponential transformation,

$$d_1 = \frac{\ln\left(\dfrac{S_0}{K}\right) + \left(\lambda + \dfrac{\sigma^2}{2}\right)T}{\sigma\sqrt{T}}, \tag{11.17}$$

and

$$d_2 = \frac{\ln\left(\dfrac{S_0}{K}\right) + \left(\lambda - \dfrac{\sigma^2}{2}\right)T}{\sigma\sqrt{T}}. \tag{11.18}$$

Here Φ is the distribution function of standard normal random variable, a random variable which is normally distributed with mean zero and variance one. More precisely,

$$\Phi(x) = \int_{-\infty}^{x} \frac{1}{\sqrt{2\pi}}\exp\left[-\frac{z^2}{2}\right]dz. \tag{11.19}$$

The integral kernel or integrand $\dfrac{1}{\sqrt{2\pi}}\exp\left[-\dfrac{z^2}{2}\right]$ in (11.19) is the density function of the standard normal random variable. From (11.16) it follows that a European call option can be replicated by $\Phi(d_1)$ units of the risky asset plus a negative amount $- K\,exp(-\lambda T)\Phi(d_2)$.

Using arguments similar to that employed for determining the price of a European call option, it can be shown that the price of a European put option is given by

$$O_{EP} = K\,exp(-\lambda T)\Phi(-d_2) - S_0\Phi(-d_1). \tag{11.20}$$

Note that as S_0 becomes very large O_{EC} tends to $S_0 - K\,exp(-\lambda T)$ and O_{EP} tends to zero, since for sufficiently large S_0, both $\Phi(d_1)$ and $\Phi(d_2)$ can be approximated by one. By a parallel argument, as S_0 becomes very small O_{EP} tends to $K\,exp(-\lambda T) - S_0$ and O_{EC} tends to zero. As σ approaches zero, the stock, being virtually riskless, will have a price $S_T = S_0\,exp(\lambda T)$ in the terminal period. The payoff from a call option is then given by $[max(S_0\,exp(\lambda T) - K, 0)]$. This value, discounted at the risk-free rate of interest, that is, $exp(-\lambda T)\,[max(S_0\,exp(\lambda T) - K, 0)] = [max(S_0 - K\,exp(-\lambda T),0)]$ is the price of a European call option in this almost risk-free case. Likewise, the value of a European put option in this case is given by $[max(K\,exp(-\lambda T) - S_0, 0)]$.

One of the assumptions on which the derivation of the Black–Scholes–Merton partial differential equation relies is that the underlying asset does not pay any dividend during the life of the option. However, we can drop this assumption if dividends are known at the outset. In order to see how dividends can be incorporated into the Black–Scholes pricing formulae, let DI be the discounted present value of the dividend payments. Let the initial value of the risky asset be revised as $S - DI$. Then the Black–Scholes formulae can be applied directly to a risky asset whose current price is $S - DI$.

11.4 COMPARATIVE STATICS: THE GREEK LETTERS

To understand a model in detail, it is necessary to look at the implications in terms of changes in the value of the model when the input parameters change. The option price formulae are price functions of five parameters: the stock price, the time to maturity, the strike price, the risk-free interest rate and the volatility. To understand the pricing behavior of European vanilla options in greater detail, we now consider a comparative statics analysis. In other words, we look at sensitivity of the option value with respect to changes in each of these parameters. These rates of changes are referred to as Greeks of an option price since generally Greek letters are used to denote different types of rates of change.

First, the delta, of a derivative security indicates the change in the value of a derivative security for a unit change in the value of the underlying asset. From (11.10) it follows the delta of the price of a European call option is given by

$$Delta_C = \frac{\partial O_{EC}}{\partial S_0} = \Phi(d_1) + S_0 \frac{1}{\sqrt{2\pi}} exp\left[-\frac{d_1^2}{2}\right]\frac{\partial d_1}{\partial S_0}$$

$$- K\,exp(-\lambda T)\frac{1}{\sqrt{2\pi}} exp\left[-\frac{d_2^2}{2}\right]\frac{\partial d_2}{\partial S_0}$$

$$= \Phi(d_1) + \frac{1}{\sigma\sqrt{2\pi T}}\left[exp\left(-\frac{d_1^2}{2}\right) - exp\left(-\lambda T - ln\left(\frac{S_0}{K}\right)exp\left(-\frac{d_2^2}{2}\right)\right)\right]$$

$$= \Phi(d_1) > 0. \tag{11.21}$$

From the put-call parity relation, it follows that the delta of the price of a European put option becomes

$$Delta_P = \frac{\partial O_{EP}}{\partial S_0} = Delta_C - 1 = \Phi(d_1) - 1 = \Phi(-d_1) < 0. \qquad (11.22)$$

Thus, while $Delta_C$ is bounded between zero and one, $Delta_P$ is bounded between minus one and zero. An increase in the current value of the underlying asset increases the probability of a positive payoff at the maturity period resulting in a higher price of the call option. That is, O_{EC} is an increasing function of the asset price. This is confirmed by the positive value of $Delta_C$. With an increase in asset price, the call is more likely to end up in-the-money. A parallel argument from the opposite direction can be used to justify the negative value of $Delta_P$. As asset price increases, the put is less likely to end up in-the-money. Since $\Phi(d_1)$ is an increasing function of asset price, $Delta_C$ is also increasing in asset price. As the time to expiry approaches infinity, for all values of the asset price the value of $Delta_C$ tends to unity.

The delta of a portfolio can be calculated from the deltas of the options in the portfolios. In a portfolio consisting of n options, if w_i and $Delta_i$ represent respectively the weight and the delta of option i in the portfolio, then the delta of the portfolio is given by $\sum_{i=1}^{n} w_i Delta_i$. A position/portfolio with a total delta equal to zero is called a delta-neutral position/portfolio. For instance, a portfolio consisting of a call option and minus delta share of a stock is delta-neutral. Thus, a trader can short delta shares of stock to hedge a long call.

When we are hedging an option, it is natural to investigate how sensitive the hedge is to changes in the asset price. The sensitivity of the delta with respect to change in the asset price is called the gamma. Since $Delta_C$ and $Delta_P$ differ by a constant, the gammas of the European call and put options coincide. Formally,

$$Gamma_C = Gamma_P = \frac{\partial(Delta_C)}{\partial S_0} = \frac{\partial(Delta_P)}{\partial S_0} = \frac{\partial^2 O_{EC}}{\partial S_0^2} = \frac{\partial^2 O_{EP}}{\partial S_0^2}$$

$$= \frac{1}{S_0 \sigma \sqrt{2\pi T}} \exp\left[-\frac{d_1^2}{2}\right] > 0. \qquad (11.23)$$

The gamma indicates how fast the delta will change relative to a one-unit change in the price of the underlying asset. It shows how stable the delta is. A small value of the gamma means that the delta changes slowly. However, if the value of the gamma is large, then the sensitivity of the delta to change in the price of the underlying asset is quite high. The knowledge of the gamma of a portfolio becomes helpful for hedging away the effects due to the curvature of the portfolio value with respect to the underlying asset.

The theta of a derivative security is the change in the value of security with respect to a unit decrease in the time to expiry. Thus, the theta of a European call option is defined as

$$Theta_C = -\frac{\partial O_{EC}}{\partial T}$$

$$= -\left[S_0 \frac{1}{\sqrt{2\pi}} \exp\left(-\frac{d_1^2}{2}\right) \frac{\partial d_1}{\partial T} + \lambda K \exp(-\lambda T) \Phi(d_2) - K \frac{1}{\sqrt{2\pi}} \exp\left[-\left(\frac{d_2^2}{2}\right)\right] \frac{\partial d_2}{\partial T} \right]$$

$$= -\left[S_0 \sigma \frac{1}{2\sqrt{2\pi T}} \exp\left(-\frac{d_1^2}{2}\right) + \lambda K \exp(-\lambda T) \Phi(d_2) \right] < 0. \qquad (11.24)$$

Similarly, the theta of a European put option is

$$Theta_P = -\frac{\partial O_{EP}}{\partial T} = -\frac{\partial O_{EC}}{\partial T} + \lambda K \exp(-\lambda T) \quad \text{(by the put-call parity relation)}$$

$$= -\left[S_0 \sigma \frac{1}{2\sqrt{2\pi T}} \exp\left(-\frac{d_1^2}{2}\right) - \lambda K \exp(-\lambda T) \Phi(-d_2) \right]. \qquad (11.25)$$

Thus, the theta of an option represents the time decay or the decay of the time value of the option. The theta of a European call option is negative. That is, the value of the option increases as the time to maturity T increases. The reasoning behind this is that with an increase in the value of T, the variance $\sigma^2 T$ of the stock's return increases, which in turn makes the call more valuable. The discounted present value $K \exp(-\lambda T)$ of the strike price, that is, the cost of exercising the option, decreases as T increases and this as well makes the option more valuable. The sign of the theta of a European put option may be positive or negative depending on the relative strength of the two terms appearing in (11.25). For instance, if S_0 is small so that the put is deeply in-the-money, then $\Phi(-d_2)$ approaches 1. In this case $Theta_p$ is positive. The increased value of the variance $\sigma^2 T$ for an increase in T makes the put more valuable. But the discounted present value of payment for exercise decreases, reducing the put's value. This makes the net effect ambiguous.

In the Black–Scholes–Merton model it has been assumed that the volatility of the asset price process is a constant, but in practice volatility is likely to vary. The response of the option price to changes in the volatility value is known as the vega of the option. Formally, the vega of a European call option is defined as

$$Vega_C = \frac{\partial O_{EC}}{\partial \sigma} = S_0 \Phi'(d_1) \frac{\partial d_1}{\partial \sigma} - K \exp(-\lambda T) \Phi'(d_2) \frac{\partial d_2}{\partial \sigma}$$

$$= S_0 \frac{\sqrt{T}}{\sqrt{2\pi}} \exp\left[-\frac{d_1^2}{2}\right] > 0, \qquad (11.26)$$

where Φ' is the first order derivative of the distribution function Φ. On the other hand, the vega of a European put option is

$$Vega_P = \frac{\partial O_{EP}}{\partial \sigma} = \frac{\partial O_{EC}}{\partial \sigma} + \frac{\partial \left(K \exp(-\lambda T) - S_0 \right)}{\partial \sigma} = Vega_C. \qquad (11.27)$$

With an increase in the volatility, the distribution of the stock price at the period of expiration spreads out. Consequently, there is a higher probability that the option expires either deeper in-the-money or deeper out-of-the-money. Assets moving deeper in-the-money will lead to a greater payoff, but assets moving deeper out-of-the money will have no effect on the option price (the payoff remains zero). Because of this asymmetric treatment, increasing volatility has a net positive effect, that is, the vega of either option is positive.

The sensitivity of the value of a derivative security with respect to variation in the rate of interest is known as the rho of the security. The rho of a European call option price is given by

$$Rho_C = \frac{\partial O_{EC}}{\partial \lambda} = S_0 \Phi'(d_1) \frac{\partial d_1}{\partial \lambda} + TK \exp(-\lambda T) \Phi(d_2) - K \exp(-\lambda T) \Phi'(d_2) \frac{\partial d_2}{\partial \lambda}$$

$$= TK \exp(-\lambda T) \Phi(d_2) > 0. \qquad (11.28)$$

Similarly, the rho of a European put option price is

$$Rho_P = \frac{\partial O_{EP}}{\partial \lambda} = \frac{\partial O_{EC}}{\partial \lambda} - TK \exp(-\lambda T) \text{ (from the put-call parity relation)}$$

$$= -TK \exp(-\lambda T) \Phi(-d_2) < 0. \qquad (11.29)$$

With an increase in the risk-free interest rate, the discounted present value of the strike price goes down. Loosely speaking, this is same as reducing the strike price of the call option. Hence the price of the call option increases. The opposite happens for the price of a put option.

Hedging against any of the dependences of a portfolio on asset price, time, volatility and rate of interest requires information on the asset and another option. With suitable balance of the underlying asset and other derivatives, hedgers can eliminate risk associated with movements of such dependent factors of the portfolio.

We can also consider the elasticities of the European call and put option prices with respect to the asset price in order to look at the percentage change in the option price for a one percent change in the asset price. For a European call option, the elasticity is defined as

$$e_C = \left(\frac{\partial O_{EC}}{\partial S_0} \right) \left(\frac{S_0}{O_{EC}} \right)$$

$$= \frac{S_0 \Phi(d_1)}{S_0 \Phi(d_1) - K \exp(-\lambda T) \Phi(d_2)} > 1. \qquad (11.30)$$

Thus, a 10 percent increase in the price of the underlying asset will increase the call option price by a higher percentage. Likewise, we can define the elasticity of a European put option as $e_P = \left(\dfrac{\partial O_{EP}}{\partial S_0}\right)\left(\dfrac{S_0}{O_{OP}}\right)$, which can be shown to be negative.

11.5 IMPLIED VOLATILITY

In the Black–Scholes pricing formulae, the risk-free interest rate, the time to expiry, the price of the underlying asset and the strike price are either defined as the part of the contract or quoted continuously. However, the assumption that volatility is constant in the formulae is highly unrealistic. Since the vega of a call (or put) price is positive, there exists a one-to-one correspondence between the volatility and the option price. A trader can therefore use the option price quoted in the market and deduce the market's opinion of the underlying volatility value for the remaining period of option's lifespan. This is known as implied volatility. Formally, let O be the market price of a European option. The implied volatility of this option is the level of volatility that, when substituted into the Black–Scholes pricing formula, generates the value of the option price equal to O.

Clearly, the implied volatility can be calculated from the Black–Scholes pricing formula. One feature of the implied volatility is that it is not constant across the strike prices. If the value of the underlying asset, the risk-free interest rate and time

Figure 11.1   Volatility Smile

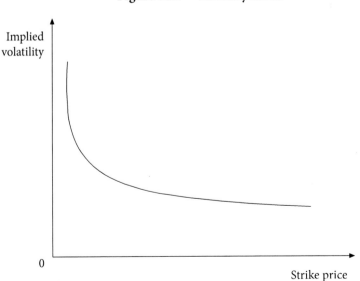

to expiry remain unchanged, then for different strike prices we get different values of the implied volatility. We can use some kind of weighted average of different implied volatility values for a single value. Evidently, the options that are most sensitive to volatility get higher weights in the aggregation. The plot of implied volatility against the strike price gives a graph, which is convex to the origin. Because of its shape, the graph is called a volatility smile.

In the financial markets it is a common practice for traders to quote the option price in terms of its implied volatility. An extensive market view of implied volatility can be provided by viewing several implied volatility values for different options under alternative strike prices for the same underlying asset with the same maturity date. This may be helpful in order for a trader to have an idea about the volatility value of an option. One trading strategy can be to have a long position in the option with the lowest volatility and short position in the one with the highest volatility. The expectation is that the prices move so that the implied volatilities become comparable and the portfolio will make a profit.

Now, let σ_H be a historical estimate of the volatility for a stock. Then for only one strike price, say K_H, the Black–Scholes pricing formula corresponds to an option price that will fit with the market price. For lower strike prices associated with in-the-money calls and out-of-the money puts, the market price will correspond to a volatility level that is much larger than σ_H. Since volatility is increasingly related with option price, this implies that the market price will be greater than the Black–Scholes historical price. By a similar argument, for larger strike prices associated with out-of-the-money calls and in-the-money puts, the market price is lower than the Black–Scholes historical price (see Roman 2004).

Example 11.1: Consider a European call option on a risky asset that is currently trading at 40 dollars. The option expires in six months at a strike price of 40 dollars. The annual risk-free interest rate is 10 percent and the volatility is 0.20 per year. We wish to determine the value of the option in terms of standard normal distribution function. Here

$$d_1 = \frac{\ln\left(\dfrac{40}{40}\right) + \left(0.1 + \dfrac{0.2^2}{2}\right)0.5}{0.2\sqrt{0.5}} = \frac{0.6}{0.14} = 0.43,$$

$$d_2 = \frac{\ln\left(\dfrac{40}{40}\right) + \left(0.1 - \dfrac{0.2^2}{2}\right)0.5}{0.2\sqrt{0.5}} = \frac{0.04}{0.14} = 0.29 \text{ and } K\exp(-\lambda T) = 40 \times \exp(-0.1 \times 0.5)$$

$= 40\exp(0.05) = 38.049.$ Then the value of the option is $40 \times \Phi(0.43) - 38.049 \times (0.29).$

Applied Example 11.1: Macbeth and Merville (1979) made a comparison of market prices of call options with the Black–Scholes option pricing model using data on "daily closing prices of all call options traded on the Chicago Board of Trade Options for American Telephone and Telegraph, Avon Products, Eastman Kodak, Exxon, International Business Machines, and Xerox from December 31, 1975 to December 31, 1976" (Macbeth and Merville 1979, 1174). The source of option prices and prices of the underlying stock was the *Wall Street Journal*. While dividend information came from Standard and Poor's Stock Records, the risk-free return has been imputed from the bid and asks yields shown in the *Wall Street Journal* for US Treasury Bills and was updated weekly. The time to expiry and risk-free return were measured on a daily basis. It was found that on any given day, alternative market prices of options written on the same underlying asset produced different values of the implied volatility and for the same option they changed through time. However, it was found that the differences between implied volatalities were related to differences between stock price, time to expiry and strike price systematically. Under certain assumptions, these systematic implied volatility differences were translated into systematic differences between observed market prices for call options and prices predicted by the Black–Scholes formula.

APPENDIX

In this appendix we explicitly derive the pricing formulae for a European call option and a European put option under the risk neutrality assumption. We follow the assumption that S_T follows geometric Brownian motion so that $ln(S_T)$ is normally distributed with mean $\ln(S_0) + \left(\lambda - \dfrac{\sigma^2}{2}\right)T$ and variance $\sigma^2 T$. Since we follow the risk neutrality assumption, in the geometric Brownian motion we replace μ by the risk-free rate λ. The proof relies on the following lemma.

Lemma 11.1: Let X be a non-negative random variable which follows lognormal distribution with parameters α and υ, that is, $ln\ X$ follows normal distribution with mean α and standard deviation υ. Then

$$\Xi\big[\max(X-K,0)\big] = \big[\Xi(X)\big]\Phi\left(\frac{\ln\left(\dfrac{\Xi(X)}{K}\right) + \dfrac{\upsilon^2}{2}}{\upsilon}\right) - K\Phi\left(\frac{\ln\left(\dfrac{\Xi(X)}{K}\right) - \dfrac{v^2}{2}}{\upsilon}\right),$$

(11.31)

where Ξ denotes expectation, K is a constant and Φ is the distribution function of a standard normal random variable.

Proof: Let g be the density function of X. It is known that $\Xi(X) = \exp\left(\alpha + \dfrac{\upsilon^2}{2}\right)$, which implies that $\alpha = \ln\big[\Xi(X)\big] - \dfrac{\upsilon^2}{2}$ (see Aitchison and Brown 1957).

Now, define the transformation $Z = \dfrac{\ln X - \alpha}{\upsilon}$. From the distribution of $ln\ X$, it follows that Z is normally distributed with a mean of zero and a variance of one. The density function of Z is $h(Z) = \dfrac{1}{\sqrt{2\pi}} \exp\left[-\dfrac{Z^2}{2}\right]$, where "exp" stands for the exponential function.

Next, we note that

$$\Xi\left[\max(X-K,0)\right] = \int_K^\infty (X-K)g(X)dX. \tag{11.32}$$

This integral can be rewritten as in terms of the density of Z as

$$\Xi\left[\max(X-K,0)\right] = \int_c^\infty \left[\exp(Z\upsilon+\alpha)-K\right]h(Z)dZ$$
$$= \int_c^\infty \exp(Z\upsilon+\alpha)h(Z)dZ - \int_c^\infty Kh(Z)dZ, \tag{11.33}$$

where $c = \dfrac{\ln K - \alpha}{\upsilon}$. Now, $exp(Z\upsilon+\alpha)h(Z)$ equals $\dfrac{1}{\sqrt{2\pi}}\exp\left[-\dfrac{Z^2}{2}\right]\exp(Z\upsilon+\alpha)$

$$= \exp\left(\alpha+\dfrac{\upsilon^2}{2}\right)\dfrac{1}{\sqrt{2\pi}}\exp\left[-\dfrac{(Z-\upsilon)^2}{2}\right]. \text{ It may be noted that } \dfrac{1}{\sqrt{2\pi}}\exp\left[-\dfrac{(Z-\upsilon)^2}{2}\right]$$

can be treated as the density function of the normally distributed random variable $(Z - \upsilon)$ whose mean is zero and variance is one. Hence, $\exp(Z\upsilon+\alpha)h(Z) = \exp\left(\alpha+\dfrac{\upsilon^2}{2}\right)h(Z-\upsilon)$. Thus,

$$\Xi\left[\max(X-K,0)\right] = \exp\left(\alpha+\dfrac{\upsilon^2}{2}\right)\int_c^\infty h(Z-\upsilon)dZ - \int_c^\infty Kh(Z)dZ. \tag{11.34}$$

We can write (11.34) in terms of the distribution function of the standard normal distribution as

$$\Xi\left[\max(X-K,0)\right] = \exp\left(\alpha+\dfrac{\upsilon^2}{2}\right)\left[1-\Phi\left(\dfrac{\ln K-\alpha}{\upsilon}-\upsilon\right)\right]-K\left[1-\Phi\left(\dfrac{\ln K-\alpha}{\upsilon}\right)\right], \tag{11.35}$$

which in view of the fact that $1 - \Phi(x) = \Phi(-x)$, becomes

$$\Xi\left[\max(X-K,0)\right] = \exp\left(\alpha+\dfrac{\upsilon^2}{2}\right)\Phi\left(\upsilon+\dfrac{(\alpha-\ln K)}{\upsilon}\right)-K\Phi\left(\dfrac{\alpha-\ln K}{\upsilon}\right). \tag{11.36}$$

Substituting $\alpha = \ln\left[\Xi(X)\right]-\dfrac{\upsilon^2}{2}$ in (11.36) we get

$$\Xi\left[\max(X-K,0)\right] = \left[\Xi(X)\right]\Phi\left(\dfrac{\ln\left(\dfrac{\Xi(X)}{K}\right)+\dfrac{\upsilon^2}{2}}{\upsilon}\right)-K\Phi\left(\dfrac{\ln\left(\dfrac{\Xi(X)}{K}\right)-\dfrac{\upsilon^2}{2}}{\upsilon}\right),$$

which completes the proof of the lemma.

Now, in order to determine the price of a European call option, we assume in the lemma that X is the asset price at the maturity period, that is, $X = S_T$ and that K is the strike price. Then $\hat{\Xi}(S_T) = \exp\left[\ln S_0 + \left(\lambda - \dfrac{\sigma^2}{2}\right)T + \dfrac{\sigma^2}{2}T\right] = S_0 \exp(\lambda T)$

(under risk neutrality) and $\upsilon = \sigma\sqrt{T}$. It then follows that $\hat{\Xi}\left[\max\left(S_T - K, 0\right)\right] =$

$$\Xi(S_T) = S_0 \exp(\lambda T)\Phi\left(\frac{\ln\left(\dfrac{S_0}{K}\right) + \left(\lambda + \dfrac{\sigma^2}{2}\right)T}{\sigma\sqrt{T}}\right) - K\Phi\left(\frac{\ln\left(\dfrac{S_0}{K}\right) + \left(\lambda - \dfrac{\sigma^2}{2}\right)T}{\sigma\sqrt{T}}\right), \quad \text{from}$$

which the desired result follows.

BIBLIOGRAPHICAL NOTES

There has been a culmination of continuous-time derivative pricing formula with the publication of path breaking Black–Scholes–Merton option pricing model. Good references for derivation of the Black–Scholes–Merton partial differential equation and associated hedging issues are Wilmott et al. (1995), Baz and Chacko (2008) and Hull and Basu (2010). Our analysis of Greek Letters follows mostly Kwok (2008). A good discussion on implied volatility is available in Roman (2004).

EXERCISES

1. Each of the following statements is either true or false. If the statement is true prove it. If it is false, give a counter-example or justify your answer by logical reasoning.
    (a) The vega of a European option is uni-modal (a function is called uni-modal if it has a single peak).
    (b) Implied volatility is always lower than historical volatility.
    (c) At-the-money options have the maximum time value.
    (d) The absolute values of the rho of a call European option and a put European option are the same.
    (e) The elasticity of a European call option with respect to asset price is always bounded above by one.
2. Use the put-call-parity relation to determine the price of a European put option from that of a European call option.
3. Consider a portfolio containing at time t, α_t^1 shares of the underlying asset with value S_t and α_t^2 shares of a risk-free bond which satisfies the condition $dB_t = \lambda B_t dt$, where B_t represents the value of the bond at time t. This portfolio

is supposed to hedge an option with value $f(S_t, t)$ and payoff $f(S_T, T)$. Show how Itō's Lemma, in conjunction with replication and self-financing property, can be employed to derive the Black–Scholes–Merton partial differential equation.

4. How does the Black–Scholes formula for a European put option get modified if the dividend amount is known at the outset?

5. Clearly explain the concept "delta-hedging" and explain its usefulness.

6. Consider a stock with an initial price of 80 dollars. The annual expected return is 10 percent and the volatility is 0.20 per year. Determine the probability distribution of S_T, the stock price at the period of expiry.

7. Determine the probability distribution of the continuously compounded rate of return earned on an asset between periods 0 and T under that assumption that the stock price follows the geometric Brownian motion.

8. Let the derivative $f(S_t, t)$ be a forward contract on a non-dividend-paying stock, that is, $f(S_t, t) = S_t - K \exp(- \lambda(T - t))$. Verify fulfillment of the Black–Scholes–Merton partial differential equation in this case.

9. Express the Black–Scholes–Merton partial differential equation for the derivative $f(S_t, t)$ using its gamma, delta and theta.

10. Determine the price of a European put option on a risky asset that is currently trading at 40 dollars. The option expires in six months at a strike price of 40 dollars. The annual risk-free interest rate is 10 percent and the volatility is 0.20 per year.

CHAPTER 12

Exotic Options

12.1 INTRODUCTION

So far we have discussed only European and American options, which are standard put and call exchange-traded options. Exotic options, which are over-the-counter derivatives, are nonstandard options. The term "exotic" is used to denote something not ordinary. They often have more flexibility. Such options have been designed by financial institutions to meet the needs of clients. For instance, an option that allows the holder to lock in gains in the underlying asset over the period of contract may be of interest to some traders. An exotic option of this variety is called a ladder option. A farmer or owner of a ski resort, who is affected by weather conditions, may be interested in insurance against risk associated with unexpected weather conditions. An exotic option of this type is called a weather option. A basket option, which enables the holder to receive two or more foreign currencies for a base currency at a designated price, is a hedging policy for foreign exchange risk. It is also an exotic option. A trader may be interested in an option that pays according to the average value of the underlying asset over the period of contract. This kind of exotic option is known as an Asian option.

One of the major differences between standard and exotic options lies in payoff structure. Pricing of exotic options is harder than that of standard options. In this chapter we describe some exotic options and discuss their valuations. A very simple exotic option is a binary or digital option. The term "binary" or "digital" describes an option which is a straight bet on whether the price of the underlying asset would be at least as high as, or below, the strike price. The payment for a call option is a cash amount or nothing according as the price of underlying asset is at least as high as or below the strike price. Similarly, for a put option the payment is a cash amount or nothing according as the price of underlying asset is below or at least as high as the strike price. In Section 12.2 we present the derivation of the price of a digital option. Section 12.3 is concerned with Asian options. In Section 12.4 we discuss barrier options. An analysis of gap options is presented in Section 12.5. Finally, Section 12.6 is concerned with some alternative exotic options.

12.2 DIGITAL OPTIONS

A digital or binary option is a cash-or-nothing exotic option. A digital or a cash-or-nothing call option differs from an European call option in the sense that the payoff at the date of expiry is

$$\vartheta_{DC}\left(S_T, K\right) = \begin{cases} 1 \, if \, S_T \geq K, \\ 0 \, if \, S_T < K. \end{cases} \tag{12.1}$$

Holding this option amounts to making a bet that the European call option will be in-the-money at the terminal period—that is, the asset price at the period of expiration will not be less than the strike price. If the bet is won, the holder gets the amount 1, otherwise his payoff is zero. This contrasts with the payoff associated with a European call option, which is the excess of the asset price over the strike price. Note that the payment is independent of how high or low the asset price over the strike price is and this makes the payoff function discontinuous (see Figure 12.1).

Figure 12.1   Payoff Function of a Digital Call Option

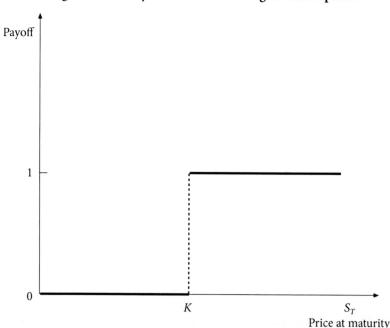

A cash-or-nothing put option has the discontinuous payoff function

$$\vartheta_{DP}\left(S_T, K\right) = \begin{cases} 1 \ if \ S_T < K, \\ 0 \ if \ S_T \geq K. \end{cases} \tag{12.2}$$

Holding this option amounts to making a bet that the asset price at the period of expiration will be less than the strike price, that is, the European put option will be in-the-money at the terminal period. A digital or cash-or-nothing put option is used quite often because it enables the holder to receive fixed coupons, subject to the condition that the price of the underlying asset at maturity is below a predetermined level.

To see an application of digital options, suppose an Italian firm has made a commitment to buy some machine parts from a US firm. The payment has to be made in four weeks' time from today in US dollars. The firm has a concern that the euro-cost of buying machine parts may increase because the US dollar may appreciate against the euro. To insure against this risk, the firm could purchase a foreign currency digital call option. The option, on maturity, pays 1 euro if it is in-the-money at the terminal period and pays nothing otherwise.

Let O_{CD} be the price of a digital call option. Recall that the risk-neutral logarithmic price process is given by

$$d\ln\left(S_t\right) = \left(\lambda - \frac{\sigma^2}{2}\right) dt + \sigma \, dW_t, \tag{12.3}$$

where, as before, S_t represents the stock price at time t, "ln" represents natural logarithm, λ is the instantaneous rate of return on the stock, σ stands for volatility of the stock's return and dW_t is normally distributed with mean zero and variance dt, λ and σ are assumed to be constants. Then

$$O_{CD} = \exp\left(-\lambda T\right)\hat{\Xi}\left[\max\left(0,1|S_T \geq K\right)\right] = \exp\left(-\lambda T\right)\Pr\left(S_T \geq K\right),$$
$$= \exp\left(-\lambda T\right)\Pr\left(\ln\left(S_T\right) \geq \ln\left(K\right)\right), \tag{12.4}$$

where $\hat{\Xi}$ stands for expected value in a risk-neutral world, "exp" is the exponential function and "Pr" denotes probability (see equation 11.15). We know that for geometric Brownian motion $\ln(S_T)$ follows normal distribution with mean $\ln\left(S_0\right) + \left(\lambda - \frac{\sigma^2}{2}\right) T$ and variance $\sigma^2 T$. Thus,

$$O_{CD} = \exp\left(-\lambda T\right) \int_{\ln(K)}^{\infty} \frac{1}{\sqrt{2\pi\sigma^2 T}} \exp\left[-\frac{\left[\ln\left(S_T\right) - \ln\left(S_0\right) - \left(\lambda - \frac{\sigma^2}{2}\right) T\right]}{2\sigma^2 T}\right] d\ln\left(S_T\right). \tag{12.5}$$

Making the transformation, $Z_T = \dfrac{\left[\ln(S_T) - \ln(S_0) - \left(\lambda - \dfrac{\sigma^2}{2}\right)T\right]}{\sigma\sqrt{T}}$, we rewrite O_{CD} in (12.5) as

$$O_{CD} = \exp(-\lambda T) \int_{\frac{\ln(K) - \ln(S_0) - \left(\lambda - \frac{\sigma^2}{2}\right)T}{\sigma\sqrt{T}}}^{\infty} \frac{1}{\sqrt{2\pi}} \exp\left(-\frac{Z_T^2}{2}\right) dZ_T. \qquad (12.6)$$

The integral kernel, that is, the integrand in (12.6) is a standard normal density function. Consequently,

$$O_{CD} = \exp(-\lambda T)\left(1 - \Phi\left(\frac{\ln\left(\dfrac{K}{S_0}\right) - \left(\lambda - \dfrac{\sigma^2}{2}\right)T}{\sigma\sqrt{T}}\right)\right) = \exp(-\lambda T)\Phi\left(\frac{\ln\left(\dfrac{K}{S_0}\right) + \left(\lambda - \dfrac{\sigma^2}{2}\right)T}{\sigma\sqrt{T}}\right),$$

$$(12.7)$$

where Φ is the standard normal distribution function. Equation (12.7) gives the price of a digital call option.

12.3 ASIAN OPTIONS

An Asian option can be of either European or American type. The payoff from an option is determined by the average price of the underlying asset. There are several ways how we can average asset prices across time periods. Let S_t denote the stock price at time t. Assume that there are a finite number of time steps, $t_1 < ... < t_n$. The time intervals are equidistant, that is, $t_i - t_{i-1} = \Delta t > 0$ for $i = 2,...,n$. Thus, we obtain a finite time series $S_{t_1}, S_{t_2}, \cdots, S_{t_n}$. One choice of average is the arithmetic mean:

$$\frac{1}{n}\sum_{i=1}^{n} S_{t_i} = \frac{1}{T}\Delta t \sum_{i=1}^{n} S_{t_i}. \qquad (12.8)$$

Alternatively, we can use the geometric mean as the average:

$$\left(\prod_{i=1}^{n} S_{t_i}\right)^{1/n} = \exp\left(\frac{1}{n}\ln\left(\prod_{i=1}^{n} S_{t_i}\right)\right) = \exp\left(\frac{1}{n}\sum_{i=1}^{n}\ln\left(S_{t_i}\right)\right), \qquad (12.9)$$

where "exp" stands for the exponential function.

If we assume that the observations of asset price are sampled continuously over the period $[0, T]$, then the arithmetic and geometric means correspond respectively to:

$$\overline{S}_a = \frac{1}{T} \int_0^T S_t \, dt, \tag{12.10}$$

and

$$\overline{S}_g = \exp\left(\frac{1}{T} \int_0^T \ln(S_t) dt\right). \tag{12.11}$$

The averages formulated in (12.10) and (12.11) are for the time period $[0, T]$, which is associated with a European option. If we allow early exercise at time $t < T$, then $\overline{S}_g$ in (12.11) will be modified as

$$\overline{S}_g = \exp\left(\frac{1}{t} \int_0^t \ln(S_\tau) d\tau\right). \tag{12.12}$$

A similar modification holds for $\overline{S}_a$.

Definition 12.1: With an average $\overline{S}_a$ of the price evolution S_t, strike price K, Asian options have the following payoff functions at the date of expiry T:

(*i*) $\max(\overline{S}_a - K, 0)$: average price call

(*ii*) $\max(K - \overline{S}_a, 0)$: average price put

(*iii*) $\max(S_T - \overline{S}_a, 0)$: average strike call

(*iv*) $\max(\overline{S}_a - S_T, 0)$: average strike put

In (i) and (ii), we replace the final asset price S_T in a European option by the average asset price S_a over the period $[0, T]$. In (iii) and (iv), we replace the strike price K in a European option by the average asset price $\overline{S}_a$. Since the payoff of an Asian option is based on an average, the uncertainty about the fluctuations of the price of the underlying asset at the date of expiration goes down.

To illustrate the usefulness of Asian options, consider a French firm that manufactures and supplies equipment to a British firm. It receives fortnightly inflows of British pounds. Since the manufacturing costs of equipment are in euros, the French firm's profits will decrease if British pounds depreciate. In order to avoid the risk of a reduction in profits the French firm can purchase a number of fortnightly average put options on the British pound. Such a strategy may not be able to eliminate the firm's exposure to risk arising from depreciation in the British pound, but it can reduce the risk.

The price of the Asian option is a function of the average and hence of the history of S_t. The dependence of payoff is on the range of asset prices, not simply on the extreme values. This path dependence of the Asian options is more complicated than that for barrier options, which we discuss in the next section.

12.4 BARRIER OPTIONS

A barrier option is an option whose payoff is contingent on whether the path of the underlying asset has crossed a second strike price, known as the barrier or trigger. A barrier option is thus a path-dependent option in the sense that its payoff depends on the entire path followed by the underlying asset, not simply its final value. There are two types of barrier options; knock-out or extinguishable and knock-in or lightable. The knock-out options are those path-dependent options which expire when the underlying asset price crosses the barrier. The observation of the barrier can be at any time during the life of the option (American option type) or at maturity (European option type). A barrier can be regarded as a feature of the option contract. Thus, introduction of a barrier makes the option path dependent. The time the asset price takes from the period of inception for the barrier to be crossed is called the stopping time. A stopping time is random since we do not know when the barrier will be breached. Knock-in options are those path-dependent options that become alive if the underlying asset price crosses the barrier during the life of the option. (The presentation of this section is based, mostly, on Jarrow and Turnbull 2000, Seydel 2002, Baz and Chacko 2004, Higham 2004 and Bouzoubaa and Osseiran 2010.)

Barriers can be set above or below the value of the stock price at time t, when the option is written. A barrier is called upper or lower accordingly, if it is above or below the asset price at time t. With a lower barrier, an option is called a down-and-out option if it ceases to exist when this barrier is crossed. For such options sometimes a rebate is provided if the barrier is breached. The rebate, which is specified at the time of initiation of the contract, might make the contract more attractive to potential users. Given the strike price and the date of expiration, the price of a down-and-out call option can never be larger than that of an ordinary call option. The reason behind this is that the value of the former depends on the probability of the asset price crossing the barrier and this probability is usually positive. The price of the down-and-out call option is decreasingly related to this probability. The price of an ordinary call option is independent of this probability.

Consider a British firm that has to make a payment to a French firm in euros in two months. The British firm has an apprehension that euros may appreciate against British pounds during this period. To hedge this risk it can purchase a foreign currency down-and-out call option instead of an ordinary call option at a cheaper price. This will enable the firm to purchase euro at a fixed price. If the spot exchange rate never falls below the lower barrier set during the lifetime of the option, then the firm holds a plain vanilla call option and the price paid for it was lower.

The payoff function associated with a down-and –out call option is defined as

$$\vartheta_{DOC}\left(S_T, K, b\right) = \max\left(S_T - K, 0\right) \times I\left\{\min_{t \in [0,T]} S_t > b\right\},$$

where b is the barrier and $I\left\{\min_{t\in[0,T]} S_t > b\right\}$ is an indicator function defined as

$$I\left\{\min_{t\in[0,T]} S_t > b\right\} = \begin{cases} 1 \; if \; \min_{t\in[0,T]} S_t > b \\ 0 \; otherwise. \end{cases} \tag{12.13}$$

That is, the indicator function takes on the value 1 if the minimum value of the stock price S_t over the period $[0, T]$ is greater than the barrier b. It takes on the value zero, otherwise. Likewise, the payoff function of a down-and –out put option is defined as

$$\vartheta_{DOP}\left(S_T, K, b\right) = \max\left(K - S_T, 0\right) \times I\left\{\min_{t\in[0,T]} S_t > b\right\}. \tag{12.14}$$

With a lower barrier, if the option becomes activated when the spot asset price goes below barrier during the life time of the option, then it is called a down-and-in-option. Given the strike price and the date of expiration, the price of a down-and-in option can never be greater than that of an ordinary option. This is because the probability that the barrier will be crossed is generally less than one and there will be a match between the two values only if there is a cross.

The payoff from a down-and-in call option is represented by the function

$$\vartheta_{DIC}\left(S_T, K, b\right) = \max\left(S_T - K, 0\right) \times I\left\{\min_{t\in[0,T]} S_t \leq b\right\}, \tag{12.15}$$

where $I\left\{\min_{t\in[0,T]} S_t \leq b\right\}$ is an indicator function that takes on the value 1 if the stock price S_t crosses the barrier by the date of expiration T. Similarly, the payoff from a down-and-in put option is given by

$$\vartheta_{DIP}\left(S_T, K, b\right) = \max\left(K - S_T, 0\right) \times I\left\{\min_{t\in[0,T]} S_t \leq b\right\}. \tag{12.16}$$

Consider again the British firm that expects to receive a payment from an Italian firm in euros in two months. This time it apprehends that the euro may depreciate against the pound and as a hedging policy it can purchase a down-in-put option. If the euro starts depreciating the put option comes into existence as soon as the lower barrier set is crossed. This will protect the British firm with required insurance.

An option is called an up-and-out option if the option has an upper barrier and ceases to exist when the spot price exceeds that barrier during the lifespan of the option. If the asset price never hits the barrier during its lifespan, then it runs in the same way as a plain vanilla option. Such options are not costlier than plain vanilla options because they involve an additional restriction of being knocked-out. This often makes an option of this type more attractive than its plain vanilla counterpart to some traders. The position of the barrier determines how much cheaper such an option is than a vanilla option. If for an up-and-out call option the asset price is near the barrier level, then an increase in volatility is likely to increase the probability that the asset price will cross the barrier. This in turn implies that the option price will go down.

With an upper barrier, if the option gets activated when the spot price of the asset exceeds this barrier during the lifetime of the option, then it is called up-and-in option. If the barrier is never breached during the lifespan of the option, we can say that the option holder paid a premium for an option whose existence was never recognized. This indicates that the closer the initial spot price is to the barrier, the higher should be the price of the option. Clearly, a higher volatility in this case increases the probability of breaching the barrier and getting alive. Consequently, under ceteris paribus assumptions, the vega of such an option is larger than the vega of a vanilla option. The price of such an option can never exceed that of its plain vanilla counterpart.

In the case of an up-and-out option the barrier b is set above the current stock price S_t and the strike price K. If $b > K$ does not hold, then the option cannot end up in-the-money without crossing the barrier. But once the barrier is crossed, the life of the option expires. If the barrier is not crossed during the lifetime of the option, then the option's payoff is given by $\max(S_T - K, 0)$. Formally, the payoff function associated with an up-and-out call option is defined as

$$\vartheta_{UOC}\left(S_T, K, b\right) = \max\left(S_T - K, 0\right) \times I\left\{\max_{t \in [0,T]} S_t < b\right\}, \quad (12.17)$$

where $I\left\{\max_{t \in [0,T]} S_t < b\right\}$ is an indicator function defined as

$$I\left\{\max_{t \in [0,T]} S_t < b\right\} = \begin{cases} 1 \ if \ \max_{t \in [0,T]} S_t < b \\ 0 \ otherwise. \end{cases} \quad (12.18)$$

That is, the indicator function takes on the value 1 if the maximum value of the stock price S_t over the period [0, T] is less than the barrier b. It takes on the value 0 otherwise.

The payoff from an up-and-out put option is given by

$$\vartheta_{UOP}\left(S_T, K, b\right) = \max\left(K - S_T, 0\right) \times I\left\{\max_{t \in [0,T]} S_t < b\right\}. \quad (12.19)$$

Consider a French firm that will receive a payment from a British firm in four weeks' time. The current exchange rate is €1.23699 per pound. There has been an appreciation in the value of pound against euro. However, the French firm has an apprehension that there may be depreciation in the value of the pound in the near future. It decides to buy an up-and-out put option, where €1.23737 is the upper barrier. The firm thinks that if the spot exchange rate reaches this level, its exposure to risk will be negligible. If the exchange rate never crosses this barrier the put option covers any risk that may arise from apprehended depreciation.

With an upper barrier if the option gets activated when the barrier is crossed, then it is called an up-and-in option. The payoff associated with an up-and-in call option is given by

$$\vartheta_{UIC}\left(S_T,K,b\right) = \max\left(S_T - K,0\right) \times I\left\{\max_{t \in [0,T]} S_t \geq b\right\}, \quad (12.20)$$

where the indictor function $I\left\{\max_{t \in [0,T]} S_t \geq b\right\}$ takes on the value 1 if the maximum value of the stock price S_t over the period [0, T] crosses the barrier b. Its value is 0, otherwise. The payoff function of an up-and-in put option is defined as

$$\vartheta_{UIP}\left(S_T,K,b\right) = \max\left(K - S_T,0\right) \times I\left\{\max_{t \in [0,T]} S_t \geq b\right\}. \quad (12.21)$$

Suppose an Italian firm has to pay the principal on a bond in euros to a US party in 60 days. Suppose the firm decides to purchase an up-and-in call option. If the euro appreciates and the barrier set is crossed, then the call option will be alive and will guard any risk that arises from appreciation.

We now determine the price of an up-and-out call option. For this we make the usual assumption that the stock price process is a geometric Brownian motion and the rate of interest is a constant. Then the risk-neutral log price process is given by equation (12.3). In this case $ln(S_T)$ is normally distributed with mean

$$ln\left(S_t\right) + \left(\lambda - \frac{\sigma^2}{2}\right)\tau \text{ and variance } \sigma^2\tau, \text{ where } \tau = (T - t).$$

Recall that under risk neutrality we determined the price of a digital call option assuming that the geometric Brownian motion $ln(S_T)$ follows normal distribution

with mean $ln\left(S_0\right) + \left(\lambda - \frac{\sigma^2}{2}\right)T$ and variance $\sigma^2 T$. This corresponds to an expected

value of the payoff in a risk-neutral world.

More generally, under risk neutrality, we can regard the price of an up-and-out call option on the asset price S_t at time t as the suitably discounted expectation of

the payoff, where $ln(S_T)$ follows normal distribution with mean $ln\left(S_t\right) + \left(\lambda - \frac{\sigma^2}{2}\right)\tau$

and variance $\sigma^2\tau$. Letting O_{UOC}^t denote this value, we have

$$O_{UOC}^t = \exp(-\lambda\tau)\hat{\Xi}\left(\vartheta_{UOC}\right) = \exp(-\lambda\tau)\hat{\Xi}\left[\max\left(S_T - K,0\right) \times I\left\{\max_{t \in [0,T]} S_t < b\right\}\right],$$

$$= \exp(-\lambda\tau)\hat{\Xi}\left[\max\left\{\exp\left(ln\left(S_T\right)\right) - K,0\right\} \times I\left\{\max_{t \in [0,T]} S_t < b\right\}\right]. \quad (12.22)$$

where $\tau = (T - t)$, $\hat{\Xi}$ denotes expectation in a risk-neutral world and "exp" stands for exponential function. The explicit derivation of the formula for O_{UOC}^t is quite complicated and hence is relegated to the appendix.

The parity relation between payoffs of up-and-out and up-and-in call options is given by

$$\vartheta_{UOC}(S_T, K, b) + \vartheta_{UIC}(S_T, K, b) = max(S_T - K, 0). \tag{12.23}$$

Thus, a European call option is equivalent to a portfolio consisting of an up-and-out and up-and-in call options. Hence the price of an up-and-in call option can be determined by subtracting the price of an up-and-out call option from that of a European call option.

The payoff parity relation between down-and-out and down-and-in put options is given by

$$\vartheta_{UOP}(S_T, K, b) + \vartheta_{DIP}(S_T, K, b) = max(K - S_T, 0). \tag{12.24}$$

This relationship can be used to determine the price of a down-and-in (down-and-out) put option from the price of a European put option and that of a down-and-out (down-and-in) put option.

12.5 GAP OPTIONS

A gap option (or a gap risk swap) is an exotic equity derivative that offers protection against a rapid drop in the value of the underlying asset. That is, a gap option is designed to capture gap risk—the risk that arises from the possibility that an investor will lose on an investment resulting from a significant drop in the stock price.

The payoff function of a European gap call option is given by

$$\vartheta_{GC}\left((S_T, K_1, K_2)\right) = \begin{cases} S_T - K_1 \ if \ S_T > K_2, \\ 0 \ if \ S_T \le K_2, \end{cases} \tag{12.25}$$

where K_2 is a constant, known as the trigger price and is generally different from the strike price K_1. Thus, while the trigger price determines whether the option has a non-zero payoff, the strike price determines the magnitude of payoff. The trigger price may be less or greater than the strike price. If the trigger price is greater than the strike price, then payoff is unambiguously non-negative. However, if trigger price is less than the strike price, then negative payoffs are possible (see Figure 12.2). There is a gap at $S_T = K_2$. Observe that for a barrier option, which never has a negative payoff, the barrier can be crossed anytime before the date of expiration.

Figure 12.2   Payoff Function of a Gap Call Option

(a) When $K_2 > K_1$ (b) When $K_2 < K_1$

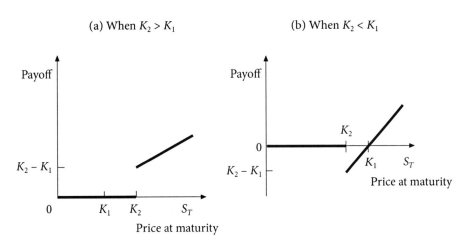

Price at maturity

For a gap option we compare the stock price at the date of expiration with the trigger price.

We can rewrite the payoff function as

$$\vartheta_{GC}\left(S_T, K_1, K_2\right) = \begin{cases} S_T - K_2 & \text{if } S_T > K_2, \\ 0 & \text{if } S_T \le K_2, \end{cases} + \left(K_2 - K_1\right)\begin{cases} 1 & \text{if } S_T > K_2, \\ 0 & \text{if } S_T \le K_2. \end{cases} \quad (12.26)$$

The first term on the right-hand side of (12.26) is the payoff from a European call option whose strike price is the trigger price K_2 and the second term is the payoff from $(K_2 - K_1)$ digital call options with the same strike price K_2. Thus, a gap option with trigger price K_2 and strike price K_1 is essentially a portfolio consisting of a European call option with strike price K_2 and a $(K_2 - K_1)$ digital call option with strike price K_2. The price of a European gap call option can, therefore, be determined using the pricing formulae of a European call option and a digital call option.

The payoff from a European gap put option is given by

$$\vartheta_{GP}\left((S_T, K_1, K_2\right) = \begin{cases} K_1 - S_T & \text{if } S_T < K_2, \\ 0 & \text{if } S \ge K_2. \end{cases} \quad (12.27)$$

If the trigger price is less than the strike price then payoffs are positive. However, if the trigger price is greater than the strike price, there are possibilities of negative payoffs (see Figure 12.3). A gap exists at $S_T = K_2$. As with a European gap call option, we can express the payoff from a European gap put option with trigger price K_2 and strike price K_1 as the sum of a European put option with strike

Figure 12.3   Payoff Function of a Gap Put Option

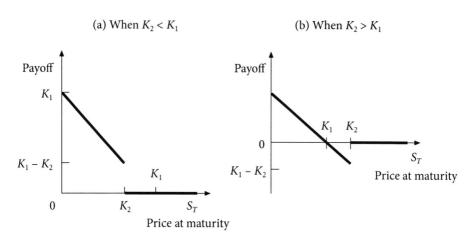

(a) When $K_2 < K_1$ (b) When $K_2 > K_1$

price K_2 and $(K_2 - K_1)$ digital put options with strike price K_2. We can, therefore, apply the price formulae for a European put option and a digital put option for pricing a European gap put option.

12.6 DISCUSSION

In this section we briefly discuss some additional exotic options without going into technical details. A chooser, also known as preference or as-you-like option is a path-dependent option that will enable the holder to choose a call or a put option. The holder has a fixed period of time to make the choice. The price of the option increases as the length of the choice period increases. The holder of such an option enjoys some degrees of freedom to take an action. In a pay-later option, also known as contingent premium option, the premium is paid on maturity of the option and only when the option is in-the-money. Thus, it is essentially a standard option in which the seller lends the buyer the premium. The premium is chosen such that the value of the option at period zero is zero. A pay-later call option with strike price K and period of maturity T is equivalent to a portfolio consisting of a European call option and $- \alpha^l$ digital call options, where the strike price maturity period combination for both these later options is (K, T) and α^l is the premium of the pay-later option. The benefit of a pay-later option is that the premium is not paid if the option expires out-of-the-money.

A Bermudan option possesses the property that it can be exercised on pre-determined dates before expiration or on the date of expiration. Thus, a Bermudan option is an intermediate option between a European option and an American option. A shout call option enables its holder to shout at most once during the lifetime of the option. Thus, it is a path-dependent option and clearly at the time of shout the price of the underlying asset should be at least as large as the strike price. A shout generally takes place if the holder has a feeling that the asset price has attained its maximum value and then it is likely to come down rapidly.

Suppose a French computer-producing firm is participating in an auction to sell laptops to a British university. The firm will be able to know the outcome of the auction after two weeks and, if successful, it has to supply the laptops immediately. Payments will be received in British pounds after three weeks from the date of supply. There is a chance that the British pound will depreciate in the three weeks from the date of supply, which implies that the French firm has an exposure to risk resulting from fluctuation in foreign exchange rate. In order to avoid this risk the firm can buy a call option on foreign exchange today with a maturity of two weeks that will confer the right of it to buy a put option on foreign exchange with a maturity of three weeks. This is an example of a call option on a put option. An option of this type is called a compound option. In general, a compound option is an option written on another option. As we have explained, such options are used by organizations to hedge foreign exchange risk associated with a business deal. Variants of options of this type can be calls on calls, calls on puts, puts on calls and puts on puts.

The payoff of a look-back option relies on the maximum or the minimum value of the underlying asset during the lifespan of the option. The strike prices can be fixed or floating. The fixed-strike price look-back options differ from European options in the sense that the price of the underlying asset in the terminal period is replaced by the maximum value for a call option and minimum value for a put option. A floating strike price look-back call option is obtained from a European call option by replacing the strike price by the minimum value of the underlying asset. A floating strike price look-back put option replaces the strike price by the maximum asset price in a European put option. Evidently, the look-back options are more valuable than the corresponding European options. Note that in the floating case it is always worthwhile to exercise the right to buy or sell the option.

Example 12.1: Consider 40 digital call options on a stock where the stock price is 42 dollars, strike price is 40 dollars, the annual risk-free interest rate is 10 percent, volatility is 0.2 and the time to maturity is 6 months. We wish to determine the value of the options. We are given that $S_0 = 42$, $K = 40$, $\lambda = 0.1$, $\sigma = 0.2$, $T = 0.5$. Then

$$= 40e^{-\lambda T}\Phi\left(\frac{\ln\left(\dfrac{S_0}{K}\right)+\left(\lambda-\dfrac{\sigma^2}{2}\right)T}{\sigma\sqrt{T}}\right) 40\times e^{-0.05}\Phi\left(\frac{\ln\left(\dfrac{42}{40}\right)+\left(0.1-\dfrac{0.2^2}{2}\right)\times 0.5}{0.2\sqrt{0.5}}\right).$$

When simplified, this expression becomes $40O_{CD} = 38.05 \times \Phi(0.6278)$. It is known that $\Phi(0.6278) = 0.74$ (Such values are available in any standard statistics book.) Hence $400_{CD} = 38.05 \times 0.74 = 28.16$. This is the price of the digital call options with the given data.

Applied Example 12.1: An and Suo (2009) examined the performance of several option pricing models in hedging exotic options, like barrier and compound options. The data used for the analysis include euro/US dollar currency option volatility index and euro/US dollar LIBOR rates for the period from January 2, 2002 to June 29, 2007. The data source is the British Bankers' Association website. Their results indicated several interesting features. For instance, the performance of different models depends on the exotic nature of the hedged option. It turns out that, for any given model, as the exotic feature in the option is assigned more importance the hedging performance goes down. It was found that in order to hedge up-and-out call options, the impact of the barrier level as well as the maturity on the hedging effectiveness was quite high. Hedging of up-and-out call options with a very low barrier level was found highly risky.

APPENDIX

Determination of the Price of an Up-and-Out Call Option

We first solve the problem for zero drift in the logarithmic stock price process and then extend the result to the case with the drift $\left(\lambda - \dfrac{\sigma^2}{2}\right)$ (see also Baz and Chacko 2004). That is, for the time being we assume that given risk neutrality the logarithmic stock price follows the Brownian motion

$$d\,ln(S_t) = \sigma\,dW_t, \tag{12.28}$$

and the current value of $ln(S_t)$ is 0. Then $ln(S_T)$ follows normal distribution with mean 0 and variance $\sigma^2\tau$, where $\tau = T - t$. We denote the corresponding distribution function by $\hat{F}$, while F will stand for the true distribution function with mean $\left(\lambda - \dfrac{\sigma^2}{2}\right)$.

Then the price of the option at time t is given by

$$O_{UOC}^t = \exp(-\lambda\tau) \int_{\ln(K)}^{\infty} \max\left\{\exp(\ln(S_T)) - K, 0\right\} d\hat{F}\left[\ln(S_T), m_T \le b\right]$$

$$= \exp(-\lambda\tau) \int_{\ln(K)}^{\infty} \exp(\ln(S_T)) d\hat{F}\left[\ln(S_T), m_T \le b\right]$$

$$-K\exp(-\lambda\tau) \int_{\ln(K)}^{\infty} d\hat{F}\left[\ln(S_T), m_T \le b\right], \tag{12.29}$$

where m_T is the maximum price that the stock price can assume between time t and T. In (12.29) we take suitably discounted expectation of $[\max(\exp(\ln(S_T)) - K, 0)]$ in a risk-neutral world in conjunction with the condition that the maximum of the stock price between time t and T does not cross the barrier.

It is now necessary to calculate the cumulative probability distribution of the stock price along with the condition that the stock price does not breach the barrier, that is, $\hat{F}\left[\ln\left(S_T\right), m_T \leq b\right]$. Now,

$$\hat{F}\left[\ln\left(S_T\right), m_T \leq b\right] = \Pr\left(\ln\left(S_T\right) \leq y, m_T \leq b\right), \qquad (12.30)$$

where "Pr" stands for probability. It is known that

$$Pr(\ln(S_T) \leq y) = Pr[\ln(S_T) \leq y, m_T \leq b] + Pr(\ln(S_T) \leq y, m_T > b). \quad (12.31)$$

Hence

$$Pr(\ln(S_T) \leq y, m_T \leq b] = Pr(\ln(S_T) \leq y) - Pr[\ln(S_T) \leq y, m_T > b). \quad (12.32)$$

Now, by the reflection principle (Karlin and Taylor 1975, 350) $Pr(\ln(S_T) \leq y, m_T > b) = Pr(\ln(S_T) \geq 2b - y)$. Hence

$$Pr[\ln(S_T) \leq y, m_T \leq b] = Pr(\ln(S_T) \leq y) - Pr[\ln(S_T) \geq 2b - y] \quad (12.33)$$

$$= \Phi\left(\frac{y}{\sigma\sqrt{\tau}}\right) - \left[1 - \Phi\left(\frac{2b - y}{\sigma\sqrt{\tau}}\right)\right],$$

$$= \Phi\left(\frac{y}{\sigma\sqrt{\tau}}\right) - \Phi\left(\frac{y - 2b}{\sigma\sqrt{\tau}}\right), \qquad (12.34)$$

where Φ is the distribution function of the standard normal distribution. Therefore, the derivative of (12.34) gives us the density function $d\hat{F}\left[\ln\left(S_T\right), m_T \leq b\right]$. Thus, $d\hat{F}\left[\ln\left(S_T\right), m_T \leq b\right]$

$$\frac{1}{\sqrt{2\pi\sigma^2\tau}}\exp\left[\frac{-\left(\ln\left(S_T\right)\right)^2}{2\sigma^2\tau}\right]d\ln\left(S_T\right) - \frac{1}{\sqrt{2\pi\sigma^2\tau}}\exp\left[\frac{-\left(\ln\left(S_T\right) - 2b\right)^2}{2\sigma^2\tau}\right]d\ln\left(S_T\right).$$

$$(12.35)$$

The density function in (12.35) was derived under the assumption that the logarithmic stock price has a zero drift and $\ln(S_t) = 0$. But in the general case, the risk-neutral distribution of log stock price has a drift of $\left(\lambda - \frac{\sigma^2}{2}\right)$ and $\ln(S_t) \neq 0$.

For this, note that if we multiply the density function $\dfrac{1}{\sqrt{2\pi\sigma^2}}\exp\left[-\dfrac{Z^2}{2\sigma^2}\right]$ of

normal variable Z with mean 0 and variance σ^2 by $\exp\left(\dfrac{\lambda}{\sigma^2}Z - \dfrac{\lambda^2}{2\sigma^2}\right)$, then we

get the expression $\dfrac{1}{\sqrt{2\pi\sigma^2}}\exp\left[-\dfrac{(Z-\lambda)^2}{2\sigma^2}\right]$, which is the density function of the

normal distribution with mean λ and variance σ^2. Likewise, in order to get the

density of the risk-neutral log stock price distribution with drift $\left(\lambda - \dfrac{\sigma^2}{2}\right)$, we

multiply the zero drift density function in (12.35) by the factor

$$\exp\left[\frac{\left[\left(\lambda - \dfrac{\sigma^2}{2}\right)\tau + \ln(S_t)\right]}{\sigma^2\tau}\ln(S_T) - \frac{1}{2}\frac{\left[\left(\lambda - \dfrac{\sigma^2}{2}\right)\tau + \ln(S_t)\right]^2}{\sigma^2\tau}\right]. \qquad (12.36)$$

The resulting non-zero drift density function is then given by

$$dF\left[\ln(S_T), M_T \le b\right] = \frac{1}{\sqrt{2\pi\sigma^2\tau}}\exp\left(-\frac{\left[\ln(S_T) - \left(\left(\lambda - \dfrac{\sigma^2}{2}\right)\tau + \ln(S_t)\right)\right]^2}{2\sigma^2\tau}\right)$$

$$\frac{1}{\sqrt{2\pi\sigma^2\tau}}\exp\left(-\frac{\left[\left(\ln(S_T)-2b\right)^2 - 2\left(\left(\lambda - \dfrac{\sigma^2}{2}\right)\tau + \ln(S_t)\right)\right]\ln(S_T)}{2\sigma^2\tau} - \frac{\left(\left(\lambda - \dfrac{\sigma^2}{2}\right)\tau + \ln(S_t)\right)^2}{2\sigma^2\tau}\right) \times d\ln(S_T).$$

$$(12.37)$$

Using the density function in (12.37) we can write the option price in (12.29) as

$$O_{UOC}^t = \frac{\exp(-\lambda\tau)}{\sqrt{2\pi\sigma^2\tau}} \int\limits_{\ln(K)}^{\ln(b)} \exp(\ln(S_T))\exp\left(-\frac{\left[\ln(S_T)-\left(\left(\lambda-\frac{\sigma^2}{2}\right)\tau+\ln(S_t)\right)\right]^2}{2\sigma^2\tau}\right)$$

$$d\ln(S_T)-\frac{\exp(-\lambda\tau)}{\sqrt{2\pi\sigma^2\tau}} \int\limits_{\ln(K)}^{\ln(b)} \exp(\ln(S_T))\times$$

$$\exp\left(-\frac{\left[(\ln(S_T)-2b)^2 -2\left(\left(\lambda-\frac{\sigma^2}{2}\right)\tau+\ln(S_t)\right)\ln(S_T)+\left(\left(\lambda-\frac{\sigma^2}{2}\right)\tau+\ln(S_t)\right)^2\right]}{2\sigma^2\tau}\right)$$

$$d\ln(S_T)-\frac{K\exp(-\lambda\tau)}{2\sqrt{\pi\sigma^2\tau}} \int\limits_{\ln(K)}^{\ln(b)} \exp\left(-\frac{\left[\ln(S_T)-\left(\left(\lambda-\frac{\sigma^2}{2}\right)\tau+\ln(S_t)\right)\right]^2}{2\sigma^2\tau}\right)$$

$$d\ln(S_T)+\frac{K\exp(-\lambda\tau)}{\sqrt{2\pi\sigma^2\tau}} \int\limits_{\ln(K)}^{\ln(b)}$$

$$\exp\left(-\frac{\left[(\ln(S_T)-2b)^2 -2\left(\left(\lambda-\frac{\sigma^2}{2}\right)\tau+\ln(S_t)\right)\ln(S_T)+\left(\left(\lambda-\frac{\sigma^2}{2}\right)\tau+\ln(S_t)\right)\right]}{2\sigma^2\tau}\right)$$

$$d\ln(S_T). \qquad (12.38)$$

Determination of the option price requires evaluation of the four integrals in (12.38). The first integral in (12.38) can be rewritten as

$$\int\limits_{\ln(K)}^{\ln(b)} \exp(\ln(S_T))$$

$$\exp\left(-\frac{\left[\ln(S_T)^2 -2\left(\left(\lambda-\frac{\sigma^2}{2}\right)\tau+\ln(S_t)\right)\ln(S_T)+\left(\left(\lambda-\frac{\sigma^2}{2}\right)\tau+\ln(S_t)\right)^2\right]}{2\sigma^2\tau}\right)\times d\ln(S_T).$$

$$(12.39)$$

We can express this integral more explicitly as

$$\int_{\ln(K)}^{\ln(b)} \exp\left(-\frac{\left[\left(\ln(S_T)\right)^2 - 2\left(\left(\lambda - \frac{\sigma^2}{2}\right)\tau + \ln(S_t) + \sigma^2\tau\right)\ln(S_T) + \left(\left(\lambda - \frac{\sigma^2}{2}\right)\tau + \ln(S_t)\right)^2\right]}{2\sigma^2\tau}\right)$$

$$\times dn(S_T). \tag{12.40}$$

This expression can alternatively be written as

$$\exp\left(\lambda\tau + \ln(S_t)\right) \int_{\ln(K)}^{\ln(b)} \exp\left(-\frac{\left[\ln(S_T) - \left(\left(\lambda + \frac{\sigma^2}{2}\right)\tau + \ln(S_t)\right)\right]^2}{2\sigma^2\tau}\right) dln(S_T). \tag{12.41}$$

Define the transformation $Z = \dfrac{\ln(S_T) - \left[\left(\lambda + \frac{\sigma^2}{2}\right)\tau + \ln(S_t)\right]}{\sigma\sqrt{\tau}}$. Then the integral in (12.41) can be written as

$$\sigma\sqrt{\tau}\exp\left(\lambda\tau + \ln(S_t)\right)\int_{c''}^{c'}\exp\left(-\frac{Z^2}{2}\right)dZ, \tag{12.42}$$

where

$$c' = \frac{\ln(b) - \left[\left(\lambda + \frac{\sigma^2}{2}\right)\tau + \ln(S_t)\right]}{\sigma\sqrt{\tau}}, \tag{12.43}$$

and

$$c'' = \frac{\ln(K) - \left[\left(\lambda + \frac{\sigma^2}{2}\right)\tau + \ln(S_t)\right]}{\sigma\sqrt{\tau}}. \tag{12.44}$$

We rewrite (12.42) as

$$\sigma\sqrt{2\pi\tau}\exp\left(\lambda\tau + \ln(S_t)\right)\int_{c''}^{c'}\frac{1}{\sqrt{2\pi}}\exp\left(-\frac{Z^2}{2}\right)dZ. \tag{12.45}$$

The integral kernel in (12.45) is simply the density of the normal distribution with mean 0 and variance 1. Consequently, (12.45) becomes

$$\sigma\sqrt{2\pi\tau}\,\exp\left(\lambda\tau+\ln(S_t)\right)$$

$$\left[\Phi\left(\frac{\ln\left(\frac{b}{S_t}\right)-\left(\lambda+\frac{\sigma^2}{2}\right)\tau}{\sigma\sqrt{\tau}}\right)-\Phi\left(\frac{\ln\left(\frac{K}{S_t}\right)-\left(\lambda+\frac{\sigma^2}{2}\right)\tau}{\sigma\sqrt{\tau}}\right)\right]$$

$$=\sigma\sqrt{2\pi\tau}\,\exp\left(\lambda\tau+\ln(S_t)\right)\times$$

$$\left[1-\Phi\left(-\frac{\ln\left(\frac{b}{S_t}\right)-\left(\lambda+\frac{\sigma^2}{2}\right)\tau}{\sigma\sqrt{\tau}}\right)-\left[1-\Phi\left(-\frac{\ln\left(\frac{K}{S_t}\right)-\left(\lambda+\frac{\sigma^2}{2}\right)\tau}{\sigma\sqrt{\tau}}\right)\right]\right]$$

$$=\sigma\sqrt{2\pi\tau}\,\exp\left(\lambda\tau+\ln(S_t)\right)\times$$

$$\left[\Phi\left(\frac{\ln\left(\frac{S_t}{K}\right)+\left(\lambda+\frac{\sigma^2}{2}\right)\tau}{\sigma\sqrt{\tau}}\right)-\Phi\left(\frac{\ln\left(\frac{S_t}{b}\right)+\left(\lambda+\frac{\sigma^2}{2}\right)\tau}{\sigma\sqrt{\tau}}\right)\right]. \tag{12.46}$$

Since this is the value of the first integral in (12.38), the first term of the option price in (12.38) becomes

$$\frac{\exp(-\lambda\tau)}{\sqrt{2\pi\sigma^2\tau}}\times\sigma\sqrt{2\pi\tau}\,\exp\left(\lambda\tau+\ln(S_t)\right)\times$$

$$\left[\Phi\left(\frac{\ln\left(\frac{S_t}{K}\right)+\left(\lambda+\frac{\sigma^2}{2}\right)\tau}{\sigma\sqrt{\tau}}\right)-\Phi\left(\frac{\ln\left(\frac{S_t}{b}\right)+\left(\lambda+\frac{\sigma^2}{2}\right)\tau}{\sigma\sqrt{\tau}}\right)\right]$$

$$=S_t\left[\Phi\left(\frac{\ln\left(\frac{S_t}{K}\right)+\left(\lambda+\frac{\sigma^2}{2}\right)\tau}{\sigma\sqrt{\tau}}\right)-\Phi\left(\frac{\ln\left(\frac{S_t}{b}\right)+\left(\lambda+\frac{\sigma^2}{2}\right)\tau}{\sigma\sqrt{\tau}}\right)\right]. \tag{12.47}$$

Next, we evaluate the second integral in (12.38). Proceeding in a way similar to that we followed for evaluation of the first integral it can be shown that the second integral can be written as

$$
\exp\left(\lambda\tau + \frac{\left(\lambda - \frac{\sigma^2}{2}\right)}{\sigma^2} + \frac{b}{\sigma\tau}\ln(S_t) - S_t - b \right) \times
$$

$$
\int_{\ln(K)}^{\ln(b)} \exp\left(-\frac{\left[\ln(S_T) - \left(\left(\lambda + \frac{\sigma^2}{2}\right)\tau + \ln(S_t) + b\right)\right]^2}{2\sigma^2\tau} \right) d\ln(S_T). \tag{12.48}
$$

We can now define

$$
Z = \frac{\ln(S_T) - \left[\left(\lambda + \frac{\sigma^2}{2}\right)\tau + \ln(S_t) + b\right]}{\sigma\sqrt{\tau}}, \tag{12.49}
$$

and write the expression under integration in (12.48) in terms of Z as

$$
\int_{\hat{c}}^{\bar{c}} \exp\left(-\frac{Z^2}{2}\right) dZ, \tag{12.50}
$$

where

$$
\bar{c} = \frac{\ln(b) - \left[\left(\lambda + \frac{\sigma^2}{2}\right)\tau + \ln(S_t) + b\right]}{\sigma\sqrt{\tau}}, \tag{12.51}
$$

and

$$
\hat{c} = \frac{\ln(K) - \left[\left(\lambda + \frac{\sigma^2}{2}\right)\tau + \ln(S_t) + b\right]}{\sigma\sqrt{\tau}}. \tag{12.52}
$$

Therefore, the second term of the option price will be

$$
-S_t^{(b/\sigma^2\tau)-1} \exp\left(\frac{2\lambda - \sigma^2}{2\sigma^2} - b\right)
$$

$$
\left[\Phi\left(\frac{\ln\left(\frac{S_t}{K}\right) + \left(\lambda + \frac{\sigma^2}{2}\right)\tau + b}{\sigma\sqrt{\tau}} \right) - \Phi\left(\frac{\ln\left(\frac{S_t}{b}\right) + \left(\lambda + \frac{\sigma^2}{2}\right)\tau + b}{\sigma\sqrt{\tau}} \right) \right]. \tag{12.53}
$$

By a similar argument it can be shown that the third integral in (12.38) can be written as

$$\int_{\ln(K)}^{\ln(b)} \exp\left(-\frac{\left[\ln(S_T)-\left(\left(\lambda-\frac{\sigma^2}{2}\right)\tau+\log S_t\right)\right]^2}{2\sigma^2\tau}\right) d\ln(S_T). \qquad (12.54)$$

Here we employ the transformation

$$Z = \frac{\ln(S_T)-\left[\left(\lambda-\frac{\sigma^2}{2}\right)\tau+\ln(S_t)\right]}{\sigma\sqrt{\tau}} \qquad (12.55)$$

and observe that the third term in the option price can be written as

$$-K\exp(-\lambda\tau)\left[\Phi\left(\frac{\ln\left(\frac{S_t}{K}\right)+\left(\lambda-\frac{\sigma^2}{2}\right)\tau}{\sigma\sqrt{\tau}}\right)-\Phi\left(\frac{\ln\left(\frac{b}{K}\right)+\left(\lambda-\frac{\sigma^2}{2}\right)\tau}{\sigma\sqrt{\tau}}\right)\right]. \qquad (12.56)$$

Finally, the fourth integral in the option price turns out to be

$$\exp\left(\frac{2\left(\lambda-\frac{\sigma^2}{2}\right)\tau+\ln(S_t)}{\sigma^2\tau}\right)$$

$$\int_{\ln(K)}^{\infty} \exp\left(-\frac{\left[\ln(S_T)-\left(\left(\lambda-\frac{\sigma^2}{2}\right)\tau+2b+\ln(S_t)\right)\right]^2}{2\sigma^2\tau}\right) d\ln(S_T). \qquad (12.57)$$

Using the transformation

$$Z = \frac{\ln(S_T)-\left[\left(\lambda-\frac{\sigma^2}{2}\right)\tau+2b+\ln(S_t)\right]}{\sigma\sqrt{\tau}} \qquad (12.58)$$

we can express the fourth component of the option price as

$$K \exp(-\lambda\tau)\exp\left(\dfrac{2\left(\lambda - \dfrac{\sigma^2}{2}\right)\tau + \ln(S_t)}{\sigma^2\tau}\right) \times$$

$$\left[\Phi\left(\dfrac{\ln\left(\dfrac{S_t}{K}\right) + \left(\lambda - \dfrac{\sigma^2}{2}\right)\tau + 2b}{\sigma\sqrt{\tau}}\right) - \Phi\left(\dfrac{\ln\left(\dfrac{b}{K}\right) + \left(\lambda - \dfrac{\sigma^2}{2}\right)\tau + 2b}{\sigma\sqrt{\tau}}\right)\right]. \qquad (12.59)$$

Therefore, the price of an up-and-out call option can now be found using (12.47), (12.53), (12.56) and (12.59).

BIBLIOGRAPHICAL NOTES

Exotic options are not exchange-traded—they are nonstandard options. Financial institutions create them to satisfy the needs of customers under particular circumstances. Jarrow and Turnbull (2000) provide an excellent overview of exotic options. Wilmott et al. (1995) and Hull and Basu (2010) are also good references.

EXERCISES

1. Each of the following statements is either true or false. If the statement is true prove it. If it is false, give a counter-example or justify your answer by logical reasoning.
   (a) The payoff function for a digital call option has exactly one point of discontinuity.
   (b) There are exotic options that are not path dependent.
   (c) All path-dependent options are exotic.
   (d) A European binary option is not path dependent but exotic.
   (e) An up-and-out put option is worth a positive value if the barrier is less than the strike price.
2. Represent analytically the payoff functions of a look-back call option and a put option graphically.
3. Determine the price of a digital put option.
4. Consider a European gap call option on a stock with a strike price of 48 and a trigger price of 50. The annual risk-free interest rate is 10 percent, the volatility is 0.2 and the time to maturity is 6 months. Determine the price of the option if the price of the stock at the date of expiry is 49.

5. Graphically explain the concept of stopping time for a down-and-out call option.
6. Determine the pricing formula for a European gap call option directly from its definition.
7. Explain the features of a barrier option that make it path dependent.
8. Give an analytical expression for a payoff function of a shout call option at the date of expiry.
9. Explain the usefulness of exotic options by giving examples.
10. Determine the price of a European gap put option.

CHAPTER 13

Risk-Neutral Valuation and Martingales

13.1 INTRODUCTION

We noted in Chapter 9 that under constancy of the interest rate, risk-neutral valuation does not provide scope for arbitrage. A risk-neutral probability measure is also known as an equivalent martingale measure. A martingale is a process whose expected future value is given by its current value. Section 13.2 provides a motivation for considering a martingale in Financial Economics using Arrow–Debreu securities. Section 13.3 explains the reasoning behind calling a risk-neutral measure an equivalent martingale measure. The models we use in this section are discrete-time models. In Section 13.4 we consider a continuous-time model and identify the corresponding equivalent martingale measure.

In our discussion of Sections 13.2–13.4 we assume that interest rates are constant. However, in reality interest rate may be floating. Because of short lifespans, the impact of interest rate changes on option prices is rather negligible. There are many other securities with longer duration that are influenced by interest rate changes. Analysis of such securities under the variability of interest rate is of high importance. In the analysis of immunization of interest rate risk presented in Chapter 7, the variation in the rate of interest was assumed to be rather minor. But in practice, variation may be more general. Variable interest rates may be realized in many ways. A coupon bond maturing at a fixed date with random coupons implies variability of the underlying interest rate. The objective of Section 13.5 of this chapter is to look at implications of stochastic interest rates in terms of equivalent martingale measure. In particular, we discuss how forward and futures prices can be determined using equivalent martingale measures.

13.2 MARTINGALE: BACKGROUND AND INTERPRETATION

We consider an individual who allocates his wealth between two securities whose current (period t) prices are known, but prices at time $t + 1$ (the future period) are uncertain. There are k states of nature in the future period, where the positive integer k is arbitrary. The set of the states of nature is denoted by $\omega = \{\omega_1, \omega_2, ..., \omega_k\}$. The probability of occurrence of state ω_i is given by p_i. Clearly, $0 \leq p_i \leq 1$ and $\sum_{i=1}^{k} p_i = 1$. In this economy there can be at most k Arrow–Debreu securities. An Arrow–Debreu security is a state-contingent security. It is a promise to deliver one unit of purchasing power (say, 1 dollar) if the specified state realizes. It is a title or a piece of paper that says anyone possessing this piece of paper is entitled to one unit of purchasing power in the specified state. It is therefore related to the likelihood of the state. Arrow–Debreu securities are the most general type of contingent claims that can be considered in any economic model. It is possible to express all other contingent claims and derivative securities in terms of Arrow–Debreu securities and to evaluate accordingly. For instance, if a contingent claim pays an amount $L(\omega_i)$ when state ω_i materializes, the payoff can be duplicated by purchasing $L(\omega_i)$ units of the Arrow–Debreu securities associated with the state ω_i. This quantity of duplicated purchasing power is then used to purchase quantities of the commodities on spot markets, once the state of the world materializes. This way any vector of contingent claims can be recreated using Arrow–Debreu securities. For the time being, for simplicity of exposition, we assume that there are only two possible states of nature and the prices of the corresponding Arrow–Debreu securities are $AD(1)$ and $AD(2)$.

The investor's problem is to maximize his utility by consuming his wealth at periods t and $t + 1$, and investing his wealth appropriately in the Arrow–Debreu securities between periods t and $t + 1$. The investor's intertemporal separable utility function is given by

$$U = h(c_t) + \Xi\left[h(c_{t+1})\right], \tag{13.1}$$

where c_i refers to an individual's composite consumption (in terms of money) in period $i = t, t + 1$, the function h is increasing, strictly concave and differentiable, and Ξ stands for expectation taken at time t. Since there is uncertainty about the future, c_{t+1} will depend on the materialization of state ω_1 or state ω_2. Hence we use the expected value of c_{t+1} in the optimization problem (see Baz and Chacko 2008).

The individual starts with an initial wealth and consumes a part of it. The remaining amount is invested in the Arrow–Debreu securities. Let $\Omega = \left(n_1^\Omega, n_2^\Omega\right)$ be a typical portfolio, where n_i^Ω shows the number of shares bought of the security $AD(i)$, $i = 1, 2$. At period $t + 1$ the state of the economy materializes and some of the securities pay 1 dollar each. The resulting payoffs are used for consumption.

The investor's optimization problem is then given by

$$\max_{c_t, c_{t+1}, n_1^\Omega, n_2^\Omega} h(c_t) + \Xi\big(h(c_{t+1})\big), \tag{13.2}$$

subject to the budget constraint

$$M_t = c_t + AD(1)n_1^\Omega + AD(2)n_2^\Omega, \tag{13.3}$$

where M_t is the investor's initial endowment. Now, observe that $c_{t+1}(\omega_i) = n_i^\Omega$. To understand this, suppose state ω_2 materializes. Then $n_1^\Omega = 0$, since state ω_1 does not materialize and hence no share of $AD(1)$ will be purchased. Given that $AD(2)$ promises a purchasing power of 1 dollar and n_2^Ω shares of $AD(2)$ are purchased, these shares are worth of exactly n_2^Ω dollars. Since $c_{t+1}(\omega_i)$ is the investor's composite consumption in terms of money in period $t + 1$ when state (ω_2) materializes, it must be the case that $c_{t+1}(\omega_2) = n_2^\Omega$. Likewise, $c_{t+1}(\omega_1) = n_1^\Omega$.

Consequently, the investor's optimization now becomes

$$\max_{c_t, c_{t+1}, n_1^\Omega, n_2^\Omega} h(c_t) + \Xi\big(h(n^\Omega)\big), \tag{13.4}$$

subject to the budget constraint

$$c_t = M_t - AD(1)n_1^\Omega - AD(2)n_2^\Omega. \tag{13.5}$$

Plugging the value of c_t given by (13.5) into (13.4) we can redefine the optimization problem in (13.4) as

$$\max_{n_1^\Omega, n_2^\Omega} h\big(M_t - AD(1)n_1^\Omega - AD(2)n_2^\Omega\big) + \Xi\big(h(n^\Omega)\big). \tag{13.6}$$

Now, $\Xi\big(h(n^\Omega)\big) = p_1 h(n_1^\Omega) + p_2 h(n_2^\Omega)$, where p_1 and p_2 are the probabilities of moving into states 1 and 2 respectively. Plugging this information into (13.6), we can redefine the optimization problem in (13.6) as

$$\max_{n_1^\Omega, n_2^\Omega} h\big(M_t - AD(1)n_1^\Omega - AD(2)n_2^\Omega\big) + p_1 h(n_1^\Omega) + p_2 h(n_2^\Omega). \tag{13.7}$$

The first order conditions for the investor's utility maximization are then given by

$$AD(1)h'\big(M_t - AD(1)n_1^\Omega - AD(2)n_2^\Omega\big) = p_1 h'(n_1^\Omega),$$
$$AD(2)h'\big(M_t - AD(1)n_1^\Omega - AD(2)n_2^\Omega\big) = p_2 h'(n_2^\Omega), \tag{13.8}$$

where h' stands for the derivative of h.

We can rewrite these two equations as

$$AD(1)h'(c_t) = p_1 h'(c_{t+1}(\omega_1)), \tag{13.9}$$

$$AD(2)h'(c_t) = p_2 h'(c_{t+1}(\omega_2)). \tag{13.10}$$

From the two equations in (13.9) and (13.10) it follows that

$$AD(1) = p_1 \frac{h'(c_{t+1}(\omega_1))}{h'(c_t)},$$

$$AD(2) = p_2 \frac{h'(c_{t+1}(\omega_2))}{h'(c_t)}. \tag{13.11}$$

The two equations in (13.11) give us the prices of the two Arrow–Debreu securities in the current period. What they say is the following. The intertemporal marginal rate of substitution between the current period consumption and the future period state-contingent consumption multiplied by the probability of the realization of the state is the price of the Arrow–Debreu state-contingent security. The intertemporal marginal rates of substitutions $\dfrac{h'(c_{t+1}(\omega_i))}{h'(c_t)}$ are also referred to as pricing kernel or state-price density. Under certainty, in equation (2.3), the ratio between the two prices equals the marginal rate of time preference. In this case the difference arises because the probability of the realization of a state in the uncertain future plays an important role.

Let us now assume that there are k possible states and k Arrow–Debreu securities. This implies that the market of Arrow–Debreu securities is complete. That is, given a vector of state-contingent securities, there exists a portfolio that can generate the vector of securities (see Chapter 9). Under the assumption that there are k possible states and Arrow–Debreu securities, (13.11) becomes

$$AD(i) = p_i \frac{h'(c_{t+1}(\omega_i))}{h'(c_t)}, \tag{13.12}$$

where $i = 1, 2,..., k$. One question that arises in this context is: how does this result relate to the pricing of securities we have identified in Chapter 9? Does risk-neutral valuation work in this case also?

To answer these questions, consider a portfolio with two Arrow–Debreu securities containing one share of $AD(1)$ and one share of $AD(2)$. This portfolio pays 1 dollar regardless of which state realizes. By the non-arbitrage principle, its payoff can be matched by the payoff of a risk-free bond whose current price is 1 dollar. In other words, the portfolio can be replicated by a risk-free bond currently trading at 1 dollar. The current price of the portfolio

$$AD(1) + AD(2) = p_1 \frac{h'\big(c_{t+1}(\omega_1)\big)}{h'(c_t)} + p_2 \frac{h'\big(c_{t+1}(\omega_2)\big)}{h'(c_t)}. \qquad (13.13)$$

The right-hand side of this equality is simply the expected value of the intertemporal marginal rate of substitution in the current period. Since the bond grows into $(1 + \lambda)$ dollars in the future period, its discounted present value is $1/(1 + \lambda)$ dollar, where λ is the risk-free interest rate. Consequently,

$$\frac{1}{1+\lambda} = p_1 \frac{h'\big(c_{t+1}(\omega_1)\big)}{h'(c_t)} + p_2 \frac{h'\big(c_{t+1}(\omega_2)\big)}{h'(c_t)} = \Xi\left(\frac{h'(c_{t+1})}{h'(c_t)}\right). \qquad (13.14)$$

That is, the price of a risk-free bond is the expected value of the intertemporal marginal rate of substitution.

In the general case consider a security with state-contingent future payoff function or a price function $Y_{t+1}(\omega_i)$, where $i = 1, 2,..., k$. To see how this security can be replicated by Arrow–Debreu securities, consider the portfolio that contains $n_i(\omega_i) = Y_{t+1}(\omega_i)$ Arrow–Debreu securities, where $i = 1, 2,..., k$. That is, the portfolio consists of holding $n_i(\omega_i)$ Arrow–Debreu securities given that state of nature that materializes at time $t + 1$ is ω_i. Here $AD_{t+1}(\omega_i)$ represents the Arrow–Debreu security if the state of nature realized at time $t + 1$ is ω_i. Now, for a portfolio with one share of $AD(1)$ and one share of $AD(2)$, the price of the portfolio at time t is given by (13.13). Consequently, in the general case with $Y_{t+1}(\omega_i)$ shares, when state of nature materialized is ω_i, $1 \le i \le k$, the price of the portfolio of the Arrow–Debreu securities at time t is given by

$$Y_t = \sum_{i=1}^{k} p_i \frac{h'\big(c_{t+1}(\omega_i)\big)}{h'(c_t)} Y_{t+1}(\omega_i) = \Xi\left[\frac{h'\big(c_{t+1}(\omega)\big)}{h'(c_t)} Y_{t+1}(\omega)\right], \qquad (13.15)$$

where p_i values represent probabilities of moving into different states. This formula is a generalized version of (13.14) and it says that the price of any security today can be calculated using the payoff structure in a future period.

Clearly, we can rewrite (13.15) as

$$h'(c_t)Y_t = \Xi\big[h'\big(c_{t+1}(\omega)\big)Y_{t+1}(\omega)\big]. \qquad (13.16)$$

Any sequence of discrete-time random variables $\{Y_t\}$, that is, a discrete-time stochastic process $\{Y_t\}$, satisfying the relation $Y_t = \Xi\big[Y_{t+1}\,|\,Y_t, Y_{t-1}, \cdots, Y_0\big]$ is called a discrete-time martingale. In words, a stochastic process in which the conditional expected value of the next observation, given all the previous observations, is the current observation. If $Y_t \ge \Xi\big[Y_{t+1}\,|\,Y_t, Y_{t-1}, \cdots, Y_0\big]$ holds, then the process is called a super-martingale. This means that the current value is always greater than or equal to the future expected value. On the other hand, when $Y_t \le \Xi\left[Y_{t+1} \middle| Y_t, Y_{t-1}, \cdots, Y_0\right]$ holds, we say that the process is a sub-martingale. In this case, the current value is always less than or equal to the future expected value. Note that in our case there are only two periods, t and $t+1$, and Y_t and $h'(c_t)$ are known. We can, thus, rewrite (13.16) as $h'(c_t)Y_t = \Xi\left[h'(c_{t+1}(\omega))Y_{t+1} \middle| h'(c_t)Y_t\right]$. This shows that the stochastic process $\left\{h'(c_t)Y_t\right\}$ is a martingale. In words, the price of any security multiplied by marginal utility is a martingale.

Given positivity of the marginal utility function, that is, $h' > 0$, and $0 \le p_i \le 1$,

$\sum_{i=1}^{k} p_i = 1$, it must be true that $\sum_{i=1}^{k} p_i \dfrac{h'\left(c_{t+1}(\omega_i)\right)}{h'(c_t)} > 0$. Hence

$$q_i = \frac{p_i \dfrac{h'\left(c_{t+1}(\omega_i)\right)}{h'(c_t)}}{\sum_{i=1}^{k} p_i \dfrac{h'\left(c_{t+1}(\omega_i)\right)}{h'(c_t)}} \tag{13.17}$$

is well defined and, $0 \le q_i \le 1$ and $\sum_{i=1}^{k} q_i = 1$. Thus, q_i values can be interpreted as probabilities on the possible future states of the world $\{\omega_1, \omega_2, ..., \omega_k\}$ under a probability measure K, that is, $K(\omega_i) = q_i$. We can refer to q_i values as pseudo-probabilities. Note that $p_i = 0$ if and only if $q_i = 0$. Two probability measures satisfying this relationship are called "equivalent probability measures." This is same as the requirement that equivalent probability measures have the same null set. Thus, the probability measures $(p_1, p_2, ..., p_k)$ and $(q_1, q_2, ..., q_k)$ are equivalent.

Equation (13.14), when expressed in terms of k states of nature, becomes

$$\frac{1}{1+\lambda} = \sum_{i=1}^{k} p_i \frac{h'\left(c_{t+1}(\omega_i)\right)}{h'(c_t)}. \tag{13.18}$$

Substituting $\sum_{i=1}^{k} p_i \dfrac{h'\left(c_{t+1}(\omega_i)\right)}{h'(c_t)} = \dfrac{1}{1+\lambda}$ from (13.18) into (13.17) and simplifying the resulting expression we get

$$q_i = p_i \frac{h'\left(c_{t+1}(\omega_i)\right)}{h'(c_t)}(1+\lambda). \tag{13.19}$$

From (13.19) we plug $p_i \dfrac{h'\big(c_{t+1}(\omega_i)\big)}{h'(c_t)} = \dfrac{q_i}{1+\lambda}$ into the second term of (13.15) and get

$$Y_t = \sum_{i=1}^{k} \frac{q_i}{1+\lambda} Y_{t+1}(\omega_i) = \frac{1}{1+\lambda} \Xi\big(Y_{t+1}(\omega)\big). \qquad (13.20)$$

That is, the price of a security in the current period is the discounted expected value of its future prices, where the discounting is done using the risk-free interest rate. Since the left-hand sides of (13.15) and (13.20) are the same, it follows that the expectation of products of state-contingent prices and intertemporal marginal rate of substitution with respect to the state-contingent probabilities is equivalent to expectation of prices under the equivalent pseudo-probability measure, discounted to the present at the riskless rate of interest. The coefficient $\dfrac{h'\big(c_{t+1}(\omega_i)\big)}{h'(c_t)}(1+\lambda)$ that establishes a relationship between p_i and q_i is called the Radon–Nikodym derivative.

Equation (13.20) is a risk-neutral valuation formula with risk-neutral probabilities $(q_1, q_2,..., q_k)$. Note that the prices with zero probability under risk-neutral valuation should also occur with zero probability in the original model. We can also say that the same set of prices should have positive probability in the two models.

13.3 EQUIVALENT MARTINGALE MEASURE: DISCRETE-TIME MODELS

The risk-neutral probability measure is also referred to as an "equivalent martingale measure." To understand the reasoning behind this term in discrete-time models, we divide our discussion into several subsections.

13.3.1 The Simple Binomial Model

Let us recall the simple binomial model analyzed in Section 9.2, where it was assumed that the interest rate is fixed. As before, there are only two assets, a bond which is trading currently at a price of 1, and a stock whose current period and future prices are denoted respectively by S_0 and S_1. Consider the discounted asset prices, where at each time point the discounting is done by the price of the zero-coupon bond at that point. Thus, the discounted or relative prices of the stock at period 0 and 1 are given respectively $\left(\dfrac{S_0}{1}\right) = S_0$ and $\dfrac{S_1}{(1+\lambda)}$. That is, we take zero-coupon bond as a numéraire in this illustration. Now, under risk-neutral valuation S_1 takes on the values $S_0 u$ and $S_0 d$ with probabilities

$$q_u = \frac{(1+\lambda)-d}{u-d}, q_d = \frac{u-(1+\lambda)}{u-d}$$ respectively (see Theorem 9.2 and Observation 9.1). Then the expected value of $\dfrac{S_1}{(1+\lambda)}$ under the risk-neutral measure K is

$$\Xi^K\left(\frac{S_1}{1+\lambda}\right) = S_0 u \cdot \frac{(1+\lambda)-d}{(u-d)(1+\lambda)} + S_0 d \frac{u-(1+\lambda)}{(u-d)(1+\lambda)} = S_0, \qquad (13.21)$$

the value of the discounted stock price in the current period. Thus, the expected rate of growth in discounted prices under risk-neutral probability is zero. In other words, given the discounted stock price in the current period, under risk-neutral probabilities the expected value of the discounted stock price in the future period is its given value in the current period. Thus, the discounted stock price can be regarded as a martingale under risk-neutral probability. That is, the discounted stock price fulfills the martingale requirement on the risk-neutral probabilities.

13.3.2 The More General Model

In the more general model considered in Section 9.4, there are k states of nature $\{\omega_1, \omega_2, ..., \omega_k\}$. But we maintain the assumption of Subsection 13.3.1 that there are only two assets, a bond which is trading currently at a price of 1 and a stock whose current period and future prices are denoted respectively by S_0 and S_1. The risk-neutral probabilities are $(q_1, q_2, ..., q_k)$. The discounted price of the stock at period 0 is $\left(\dfrac{S_0}{1}\right) = S_0$. If state ω_j materializes, then the discounted price of the stock in the future period is $\dfrac{S_1(\omega_j)}{(1+\lambda)}$. In view of the discussion following Theorem 9.5, it follows that

$$S_0 = \sum_{j=1}^{k} q_j \left(\frac{S_1(\omega_j)}{(1+\lambda)}\right). \qquad (13.22)$$

Thus, in the general model the discounted stock price in the current period is also the expected value of the discounted state-contingent stock prices in the future period under risk-neutral probabilities. This means that the discounted stock price in the general model is a martingale with risk-neutral probabilities.

13.4 EQUIVALENT MARTINGALE MEASURE: CONTINUOUS-TIME MODELS

In this section we preset a brief discussion on continuous-time risk neutrality models of asset price evolution. The presentation is based on Duffe (1996), Sundaram (1997) and Jarrow and Turbull (2000). Most of such models rely on Weiner process. For simplicity of exposition, we assume that there are only two assets. The first asset is a risk-free one, a bond. The rate of interest λ, expressed in continuously compounded terms, is constant. Consequently, the bond price P_t at time t changes from its initial period value $P_0 = 1$ according to the following differential equation

$$dP_t = \lambda P_t dt. \tag{13.23}$$

The second asset, a stock, is a risky security. Its price S_t at time t changes from its initial value S_0 according to the following stochastic differential equation

$$dS_t = \mu S_t dt + \sigma S_t dW_t, \tag{13.24}$$

where t denotes time, μ represents the instantaneous drift of the process underlying stock price change, σ is its volatility, and dW_t has a normal distribution with mean zero and variance dt.

The relative value of S_t with respect to P_t is given by normalized price $H_t = \dfrac{S_t}{P_t}$.

This is the discounted stock price process, where the discounting is done by the bond price. Thus, P_t is taken as a numéraire here. Now, we wish to determine the instantaneous drift and variance of the process H_t. For this, note first that the change in normalized stock price is given by

$$dH_t = \frac{dS_t}{P_t} - \frac{S_t}{\left(P_t\right)^2} dP_t. \tag{13.25}$$

From (13.23) and (13.24) it follows immediately that

$$dH_t = H_t[(\mu - \lambda)dt + \sigma dW_t]. \tag{13.26}$$

Under risk-neutral probability the discounted price process H_t must be a martingale. Therefore, it must be true that under risk-neutral probability structure, H_t must have zero drift. Furthermore, the risk-neutral probability must be equivalent to the original probability. For this we use the Girsonav Theorem. According to the Girsanov Theorem there is a probability distribution K equivalent to the original distribution such that $d\hat{W}_t$ is normally distributed with mean zero and variance dt, where

$$d\hat{W}_t = c\,dt + dW_t, \tag{13.27}$$

with c being the drift. Substituting the value of dW_t from (13.27) into (13.26) we get

$$dH_t = H_t\Big[\big(\mu - \lambda - c\sigma\big)dt + \sigma\,d\hat{W}_t\Big]. \tag{13.28}$$

Under the equivalent martingale distribution K, we know that H_t is a martingale so that

$$\Xi^K[H_{t+dt}] = H_t, \tag{13.29}$$

where Ξ^K in (13.29) indicates that the expectation is taken under K. Hence

$$\Xi^K(dH_t) = \Xi^K[H_{t+dt}] - H_t = 0. \tag{13.30}$$

Thus,

$$H_t(\mu - \lambda - c)dt = 0, \tag{13.31}$$

which implies that

$$(\mu - \lambda - c\sigma) = 0. \tag{13.32}$$

This gives $c = \dfrac{(\mu - \lambda)}{\sigma}$. This is the market price of risk.

The change in the stock price process under K becomes

$$\begin{aligned}
dS_t &= \mu S_t\,dt + \sigma S_t\Big[\,d\hat{W}_t - c\,dt\Big]\\
&= \big(\mu - c\sigma\big)S_t\,dt + \sigma\,S_t\,d\hat{W}_t\\
&= \lambda S_t\,dt + \sigma\,S_t\,d\hat{W}_t.
\end{aligned} \tag{13.33}$$

Thus, under the probability distribution Q, the expected rate of return on the stock is the risk-free rate.

13.5 EQUIVALENT MARTINGALE MEASURE: CONTINUOUS-TIME PATH AND STOCHASTIC INTEREST RATE

We begin this section by defining a bank account or money-market account. In a money-market account, profit of risk-free investment is accrued continuously at the risk-free rate prevailing in the market at each instant.

Definition 13.1: The money account process B_t, where $t \geq 0$ denotes time and $B_0 = 1$, evolves according to the following differential equation

$$dB_t = \lambda_t B_t dt, \; B_0 = 1, \tag{13.34}$$

where λ_t is a positive function of time. Consequently,

$$B_t = \exp\left\{ \int_0^t \lambda_\tau \, d\tau \right\}. \tag{13.35}$$

where "exp" is the exponential function. According to this definition, one unit of money invested at time 0 yields at time t the amount given by (13.35), and λ_t is the instantaneous interest rate at which accrual takes place. We may think of the process as that taking place in a bank with a stochastic interest rate λ_t. This instantaneous rate is also referred to as instantaneous spot rate or as short rate.

Since the interest rate λ_t is instantaneous, the discount factor in the current context will be stochastic.

Definition 13.2: The stochastic discount factor $DF(t, T)$ between two instantaneous times t and T is given by the amount at time t, which is equivalent to one unit of currency payable at time T:

$$DF(t,T) = \frac{B_t}{B_T} = \exp\left\{ -\int_t^T \lambda_\tau \, d\tau \right\}. \tag{13.36}$$

That is, $DF(t, T)$ gives the value of one unit of money payable at time T, as seen from the time t, where $t \le T$. We can also interpret $DF(t, T)$ as the price at time t of a zero-coupon bond that promises to pay 1 dollar at maturity T. A zero-coupon bond is also known as a pure prospect bond (see Brigo and Mercurio 2006).

Now, following Bjork (2004), we consider a financial market with X_t defined on $[0, T]$ being the underlying process. For instance, if the interest rate is stochastic, we include it in X_t. Let J be a simple T-claim, that is, a claim of the form $J = \psi(X_T)$, where the function ψ is referred to as a contract function.

Definition 13.3: Let J be a simple T-claim. Then a forward contract on J, contracted at t, with a time of delivery T, and with the forward price $\eta_{FOC}(t, T, J)$, is defined as a contract satisfying the following conditions:

(*i*) The holder of the contract receives the stochastic amount J at time T from the writer of the contract.

(*ii*) The forward price $\eta_{FOC}(t, T, J)$ is determined at time t when the contract is made.

(*iii*) The forward price $\eta_{FOC}(t, T, J)$ is determined in such a way that the value of the forward contract equals zero at time t when the contract is made.

(*iv*) The holder of the contract pays the amount $\eta_{FOC}(t, T, J)$ at time T to the writer.

The mathematical definition of the forward price process can now be presented.

Definition 13.4: Let J be a simple T-claim. By the forward price process we mean a process $\eta_{FOC}(t, T, J) = \eta_{FOC}(t, X_t; T, J)$ where η is some deterministic, that is, non-random, function satisfying the condition

$$E(t, J - \eta_{FOC}(t, X_t; T, J)) = 0, \tag{13.37}$$

with

$$E(t, J) = G(t, X_t; T, J), \tag{13.38}$$

$$G(t, X_t; T, J) = \Xi_{t,x}^K \left(J . \exp\left\{ -\int_t^T \lambda_\tau \, d\tau \right\} \right), \tag{13.39}$$

where $X_t = x, \Xi_{t,x}^K$, denotes expectation under some fixed equivalent martingale measure K, and the subscript t is used to indicate that the interest rate is stochastic.

The value of $G(t, X_t; T, J)$ given by (13.39) is the expected discounted value of the contingent T-claim J, as seen from when the contract is made, using the stochastic discount factor $DF(t, T)$. Here expectation is taken with respect to some fixed equivalent martingale (risk-neutral) measure K. In (13.37) we subtract the process $\eta_{FOC}(t, X_t; T, J)$ from the contingent T-claim J, take expectation of the resulting expression using the equivalent martingale measure K and set the expected value equal to zero. The process $\eta_{FOC}(t, X_t; T, J)$ using the deterministic function η, for which this expected value becomes zero, gives the forward price process. We can look at similarities and dissimilarities of this definition with the definition of the forward price in a discrete-time path presented in Chapter 8. In the discrete framework the contract is made today (period 0) and obligates the holder of the contract to buy or sell an asset at a future date T for a predetermined price. The forward price is that level of price for which the value of the contract at the period of initiation of the contract (today) is zero. We essentially use the same idea here, with the exceptions that the time path is continuous and the interest rate is stochastic. Because the interest rate is stochastic, we use the expected value using an equivalent martingale to determine the forward price process.

The following proposition, which is based on Bjork (2004) and stated without proof, gives us the fundamental formula for forward price process.

Proposition 13.1: The forward price process is given by any one of the following expressions:

$$\eta_{FOC}(t, T, J) = \frac{E(t, J)}{DF(t, T)}, \tag{13.40}$$

$$\eta_{FOC}(t, T, J) = \eta_{FOC}(t, X_t; T, J), \tag{13.41}$$

where

$$\eta_{FOC}\left(t,x;T,J\right)=\frac{1}{DF\left(t,T\right)}\,\Xi_{t,x}^{K}\left(J.\exp\left\{-\int_{t}^{T}\lambda_{\tau}\,d\tau\right\}\right),\qquad(13.42)$$

$$\eta_{FOC}\left(t,x;T,J\right)=\Xi_{t,x}^{T}\left[J\right],\qquad(13.43)$$

where $\Xi_{t,x}^{K}$ denotes expectation with respect to the forward neutral measure K, the martingale measure for the numéraire process $DF(t, T)$.

Next, we present a discussion on futures contracts in the present framework (see Bjork 2004).

Definition 13.5: Let J be a simple T-claim. A futures contract on J, with time of delivery T, is a system that fulfills the following conditions:

(*i*) At every time point t, $0 \le t \le T$, there exists a market quoted price $\eta_{FUC}(t, T, J)$, which is known as futures price at t for delivery of J at time T.

(*ii*) At the time of delivery, the holder of the contract pays $\eta_{FUC}(T, T, J)$ and receives J.

(*iii*) During any time interval (t_1, t_2) the holder of the contract receives the difference $\eta_{FUC}(t_2, T, J) - \eta_{FUC}(t_1, T, J)$.

(*iv*) At any time t prior to the date of delivery, the spot price of obtaining a futures contract is zero.

The futures contract defined above describes the delivery of J at time T. Condition (*iv*) of the definition shows that a trader does not gain or lose from entering, or closing, a futures contract. If a trader signs a futures contract at any arbitrary time $t < T$ with a corresponding price $\eta_{FUC}(t, T, J)$, then he is not obliged to deliver J at T at the price $\eta_{FUC}(t, T, J)$. Likewise, if a person has a long position in futures at $t < T$ at the price $\eta_{FUC}(t, T, J)$, then he is not obliged to pay $\eta_{FUC}(t, T, J)$ in exchange of J at T. In view of condition (*iii*), we can loosely say that in a futures contract payments are made in a continuous manner with respect to time, instead of the entire payment being made at T. As stated in Chapter 8, the difference $\eta_{FUC}(t_2, T, J) - \eta_{FUC}(t_1, T, J)$ is known as marking to market. Marking to market is a process to record price changes in the futures market. The payment schedule is organized in a manner such that in order to avoid any default, the holder of the futures position, whether in long or in short position, maintains a deposit of certain amount of money with the broker. If a trader has a long position in futures, and if the difference $\eta_{FUC}(t_2, T, J) - \eta_{FUC}(t_1, T, J)$ is negative, then it is a payment from the trader's side. If the difference is positive, then it is a receipt for the trader. We can explain the difference similarly if a trader has a short position (see also Chapter 8).

The following mathematical definition of the futures process can now be presented.

Definition 13.6: The futures contract on an underlying simple T-claim J with price process $E(t)$ and a dividend process $DI(t)$ is a system satisfying the following conditions:

$$DI(t) = \eta_{FUC}(t, T, J),\tag{13.44}$$

$$J = \eta_{FUC}(T, T, J),\tag{13.45}$$

$$E(t) = 0 \text{ for all } t \le T.\tag{13.46}$$

Equation (13.46) of Definition 13.6 is condition (iv) in Definition 13.5. Conditions (ii) and (iv) of Definition 13.5 ensure that $J = \eta_{FUC}(T, T, J)$, which is shown in Equation (13.45). Condition (iii) of Definition 13.5 is represented by Equation (13.44).

The following proposition can now be stated (see Bjork 2004):

Proposition 13.2: Let J be a simple T-claim. Assume that market prices are obtained from the fixed-risk neutral martingale measure K. Then the following statements hold:

(i) The futures price process is given by

$$\eta_{FUC}(t,T,J) = \Xi^K_{t,X_t}(J).\tag{13.47}$$

(ii) If the short rate is deterministic, then the forward and futures price processes become identical and the common process is given by

$$\eta_{FOC}(t,T,J) = \eta_{FUC}(t,T,J) = \Xi^K_{t,X_t}(J).\tag{13.48}$$

This proposition indicates that risk-neutral valuation can be used to determine the arbitrage-free futures price process when the interest rate is stochastic.

Example 13.1: Consider a sequential gambling. Let the initial stake be Y_0. After the first round of gambling the stake becomes Y_1. Since the outcome of gambling is uncertain, Y_1 is a random variable. If the expected value of Y_1 equals Y_0, that is, $\Xi(Y_1) = Y_0$, then the gamble is called fair. In general, let Y_t denotes the bet at the tth round. If complete information of all the bets Y_1, Y_2,..., Y_n before the $(n + 1)^{th}$ round of the play is available, and the expectation of Y_{n+1} equals Y_n (that is, $\Xi(Y_{n+1}|Y_1,Y_2,\cdots,Y_n) = Y_n$), then the gamble is called fair (see Jiang 2003 and Williams 2010). The fair gamble defined here is a discrete-time martingale.

Applied Example 13.1: Since in the absence of arbitrage, the price of a derivative contract can be expressed as a discounted expected value of its random payoffs; the Monte Carlo simulation is a standard tool for approximation of this expected value. In this context the Monte Carlo simulation can be briefly described as follows. First, sample paths for the underlying asset price are simulated. Then the corresponding option payoff for each sample path is computed. Finally, the simulated payoffs are averaged and the discounted value of this average yields the Monte Carlo price of the option. However, this procedure is numerically intensive if a high degree of accuracy is required. Simulated sample paths for underlying asset price often fail to possess the martingale property (see, for example, Duan and Simonato 1998). The reason for this is that asset price dynamics are typically modeled as exponential semi-martingale. Duan and Simonato (1998) suggested a procedure which ensures that the simulated sample paths constitute a martingale in an empirical sense. They referred to this as "empirical martingale simulation." It is demonstrated that apart from yielding more accurate price estimates, this procedure can reduce the Monte Carlo errors substantially. The error reduction does not depend on the number of sample paths and is obtained for the plain-vanilla European options and path-dependent ones like Asian options. The results also hold for the Black–Scholes–Merton option-pricing framework.

BIBLIOGRAPHICAL NOTES

Baz and Chacko (2008) provide a preliminary discussion on Arrow–Debreu securities and martingale. Sundaram (1997) and Jarrow and Turnbull (2000) constitute a useful reading list for continuous-time equivalent martingale measure. Money account process is analyzed in detail in Brigo and Mercurio (2006). Bjork (2004) is a good reference for forward and futures processes.

EXERCISES

1. Each of the following statements is either true or false. If the statement is true prove it. If it is false, give a counter-example or justify your answer by logical reasoning.
   (a) A martingale is a super-martingale as well as a sub-martingale.
   (b) In the simple one period binomial model considered in Subsection 13.3.1, the equivalent martingale measure is unique.
   (c) A concave transformation of a martingale is a super-martingale.
   (d) A stochastic process, which is a super-martingale and a sub-martingale, is a martingale.
   (e) A convex transformation of a martingale is a sub-martingale.
2. Formulate analytically an equivalent martingale measure associated with a trinomial model. Is your measure unique?
3. Consider the general discrete model considered in Subsection 13.3.2. What are the martingale implications if the discounted stock price in the current period is less (greater) than its expected future value?
4. The relative price of a stock in the current period is 100 dollars. In the next period the corresponding price may be 110 dollars or 90 dollars. Determine the underlying risk-neutral probability.
5. An individual has invested A dollars in a gamble. How do you interpret the situation in terms of martingale if there is a (i) 50:50, (ii) 60:40, (iii) 40:60 chance of losing or winning B dollars, where $B<A$?

PART IV

Portfolio Management Theory

Portfolio Management: The Mean-Variance Approach

14.1 INTRODUCTION

An investment in a risky security always includes the possibility of a loss or bad performance. An investor, therefore, would like to explore the issue of risk management in a portfolio, a list of financial assets held by the investor. The major issue here is to maintain a balance of the portfolio, that is, how to choose a combination of the assets so that for a given expected return the overall risk is minimized.

Since the pioneering contribution of Markowitz (1952) the mean-variance model of asset choice has been used extensively in finance. In Chapter 3 we examined the implications of the quadratic utility function that shows a preference for higher expected return and an aversion for variance in the portfolio choice problem with two prospects. But for arbitrary distributions and utility functions it is not possible to define expected utility over expected returns and variances of the prospects. However, the mean-variance model of portfolio choice is immensely popular because of its extensive empirical applications and analytical tractability. It will be shown that the risks of individual assets (variances) in the portfolio are not sufficient to understand the risks of the portfolio itself. The interaction (covariance) between any two assets plays an important role in this context. This chapter, therefore, develops analytical relations between the means and the variances of feasible portfolios.

After presenting the preliminaries in Section 14.2, we identify the risk-minimizing weights in a portfolio that contains only two risky assets in Section 14.3. The issue of Section 14.3 is analyzed for general portfolios with many risky assets in Section 14.4. The concern of Section 14.5 is the relationship between risk-minimizing portfolios. Finally, Section 14.6 presents the capital asset pricing model (CAPM), which looks at risks and returns of individual assets/portfolios and compares them with the overall market risk–return characteristics.

14.2 PRELIMINARIES

One of the basic assumptions of the mean-variance portfolio theory is that the portfolio contains both risky and risk-free assets. It is also assumed that all investors are rational with homogeneous expectations, the number of assets is fixed, no individual can affect security prices, there are no transaction costs, all assets are tradable and infinitely divisible, there are no market imperfections such as taxes, and decisions are made solely on the basis of expected returns and variances. Let us consider a two-period world, $t = 0$ (the initial period) and $t = 1$ (the final period). Each asset i, held by an investor, has a value $V_0^i = n_i(0)S_0^i$ in the initial period, where $n_i(0)$ and S_0^i are respectively the number of units of asset i held by the investor and its price in the initial period. The value of asset i in the final period is V_1^i.

A portfolio consists of a combination of assets in a given proportion. Formally, we define a portfolio Ω as $\Omega = (n_1, n_2,..., n_l)$, where n_i is the number of units of asset i in the portfolio. If n_i is negative then the portfolio is said to have a short position in asset i and a positive value of n_i means the investor has a long position on the asset in the portfolio. The number of assets l is assumed to be arbitrary in the portfolio.

A portfolio can, thus, be regarded as an investment strategy. The number $\sum_{j=1}^{l} V_0^j$ can be interpreted as the initial wealth of the investor invested in the portfolio or value of the strategy. Let $w_i = \dfrac{V_0^i}{\sum_{j=1}^{l} V_0^j}$ be the share of wealth invested in asset i at time 0, $\sum_{i=1}^{l} w_i = 1$. If w_i is negative then the portfolio is said to have a short position in asset i and a positive value of w_i means the investor has a long position in the asset. We write $\underline{w}$ for $(w_1, w_2,...,w_l)$, which is a one-row matrix with l columns. The transpose of $\underline{w}$ is denoted by $\underline{w}'$. More precisely $\underline{w}'$, the one-column matrix with l rows, is given by

$$\underline{w}' = \begin{pmatrix} w_1 \\ w_2 \\ \cdot \\ \cdot \\ \cdot \\ w_l \end{pmatrix}. \tag{14.1}$$

Given S_0^i's we can as well represent the portfolio by the vector $\underline{w}$.

The rate of return, or return for short, on asset i, $1 \le i \le l$, over the single time step $[0, 1]$ is defined as

$$r_i = \frac{S_1^i - S_0^i}{S_0^i},$$ (14.2)

which implies that $S_0^i(1+r_i) = S_1^i$. Since the value of an asset at time 1 in the future is a random variable, each r_i is a random variable. For ease of exposition, we assume that r_i takes values in a non-degenerate bounded interval in the real line $\mathfrak{R}$. The expected return on asset i is denoted by

$$\mu_i = \Xi(r_i),$$ (14.3)

where Ξ stands for the expectation operator, that is, μ_i is the expected value of r_i. Let $\underline{\mu}$ stand for the row vector $(\mu_1, \mu_2,..., \mu_l)$ and its transpose is denoted by $\underline{\mu}'$. The l–coordinated vector of ones $(1, 1,..., 1)$ is denoted by 1^l and $\left(1^l\right)'$ represents its transpose.

The variance of the return on the ith asset

$$\sigma_i^2 = \Xi\left(r_i - \mu_i\right)^2 = \Xi\left(r_i^2\right) - \left(\mu_i\right)^2$$ (14.4)

is called the risk of asset i. Often the standard deviation $\sigma_i = \sqrt{\sigma_i^2}$, the positive square root of the variance, is used as an indicator of risk associated with asset i.

The return r_Ω on the portfolio is given by $r_\Omega = \sum_{i=1}^{l} w_i r_i$ and the expected return μ_Ω on the portfolio as a whole is

$$\mu_\Omega = \sum_{i=1}^{l} w_i \Xi(r_i) = \sum_{i=1}^{l} w_i \mu_i = \underline{w}\,\underline{\mu}',$$ (14.5)

where $\mu_i = \Xi(r_i)$ and $\underline{w}\,\underline{\mu}'$ denotes the product of the matrices $\underline{w}$ and $\underline{\mu}'$.

The risk of the portfolio is the variance of the return on the portfolio as a whole. Since the individual returns are not generally independent, the variance of the portfolio, $Var\left(\sum_{i=1}^{l} w_i r_i\right)$, is defined as

$$\sigma_\Omega^2 = \sum_{i=1}^{l}\sum_{j=1}^{l} w_i w_j Cov\left(r_i, r_j\right) = \sum_{i=1}^{l}\sum_{j=1}^{l} w_i w_j \sigma_{ij} = \sum_{i=1}^{l}\sum_{j=1}^{l} w_i w_j \Xi\left[\left(r_i - \mu_i\right)\left(r_j - \mu_j\right)\right]$$

$$= \sum_{i=1}^{l}\sum_{j=1}^{l} w_i w_j\left[\Xi\left(r_i r_j\right) - \mu_i \mu_j\right] = \sum_{i=1}^{l}\sum_{j=1}^{l} w_i w_j \rho_{ij}\sigma_i\sigma_j,$$ (14.6)

where $Cov(r_i, r_j) = \sigma_{ij} = \Xi\left[(r_i - \mu_i)(r_j - \mu_j)\right] = \left[\Xi(r_i r_j) - \mu_i \mu_j\right]$ is the covariance

between r_i and r_j, and $\rho_{ij} = \dfrac{\sigma_{ij}}{\sigma_i \sigma_j}$ is the correlation coefficient between r_i and r_j.

Note that $\sigma_{ii} = \sigma_i^2$, the variance of r_i and $\sigma_{ij} = \sigma_{ji}$ for all $i, j = 1, 2,..., l$. If asset i is risky then $\sigma_i > 0$ and if it is risk-free then $\sigma_i = 0$. The maximum value that σ_{ij} (ρ_{ij}) can take is $\sigma_i \sigma_j (1)$ and its minimum value is $-\sigma_i \sigma_j (-1)$. In the former case the two assets i and j move together in the sense that they are perfectly positively correlated and in the latter case they move in the opposite direction—that is, they are perfectly negatively correlated. If assets i and j are independent, then $\rho_{ij} = 0$. It is well known that the converse is not true.

14.3 CONSTRUCTION OF A PORTFOLIO: THE TWO-ASSET CASE AND A DIAGRAMMATIC EXPOSITION

In the construction of a portfolio some of the important questions that arise are as follows (i) What is the basic principle in a portfolio management problem? (ii) How can investors structure their choices of assets in the portfolios? (iii) In what proportions should different assets be held in a portfolio? (iv) What makes one portfolio better than another? (v) How are the compositions of portfolios chosen?

As we argued at the outset, the central idea underlying the Markowitz model is to spread investment among assets for minimizing risks. To understand this, suppose all the l assets considered above are independent so that $\rho_{ij} = 0$ and $w_i = \dfrac{1}{l}$.

Then σ_Ω^2 in (14.6) becomes $\displaystyle\sum_{i=1}^{l} \dfrac{\sigma_i^2}{l^2}$. This expression, being a decreasing function

of l, indicates that risk associated with the portfolio decreases when investment is spread among a larger number of assets. However, this conclusion is based on an extremely simple structure that does not recognize interdependence among the assets, and it also assumes that they are combined in equal proportions.

If not all pairs of the assets are uncorrelated so that $\rho_{ij} \neq 0$ for some pairs (i, j) and $w_i = \dfrac{1}{l}$ for all i, then

$$\sigma_\Omega^2 = \sum_{i=1}^{l}\sum_{j=1}^{l}\frac{1}{l^2}\sigma_{ij} = \sum_{i=1}^{l}\frac{1}{l}\sigma_{ii} + \sum_{i=1}^{l}\sum_{j\neq i=1}^{l}\frac{1}{l^2}\sigma_{ij} = \frac{1}{l}\left(\frac{1}{l}\sum_{i=1}^{l}\sigma_i^2\right) + \frac{(l-1)}{l}\left[\frac{1}{l(l-1)}\sum_{i=1}^{l}\sum_{j\neq i=1}^{l}\sigma_{ij}\right].$$

$$(14.7)$$

Given that there are l assets, there are $l(l - 1)$ distinct pairs of assets. Therefore,

$\left[\dfrac{1}{l(l-1)}\displaystyle\sum_{i=1}^{l}\sum_{j\neq i=1}^{l}\sigma_{ij}\right]$ is the average of covariances between $l(l - 1)$ possible pairs of assets. On the other hand, $\left(\dfrac{1}{l}\sum_{i=1}^{l}\sigma_i^2\right)$ is simply the average of variances of individual

assets. Thus, σ_Ω^2 in (14.7) can be rewritten as

$$\sigma_\Omega^2 = \frac{1}{l}(average\ var iance) + \frac{(l-1)}{l}(average\ cov ariance). \qquad (14.8)$$

For a sufficiently large l the first term on the right-hand side of (14.8) tends to zero and the second term tends to the average covariance. Thus, by spreading the investment among a large number of assets, we can eliminate the risk of individual assets, but the risk arising from interaction between assets (covariance) cannot be eliminated. In this case, although we take into account the interdependence among the assets, the assumption of combining them in equal proportion is retained. In the general case we have to recognize interdependence and there is no *a priori* reason to make the equal proportion assumption.

The type of risk we are considering here is diversifiable or unsystematic risk. This notion of risk is associated with an individual asset uniquely. For instance, if an investor has decided to invest in an ice cream company, then a reduction in the demand for ice cream produced by the company might make the investment quite vulnerable. The other notion of risk generally considered in the theory of finance is non-diversifiable—also known as systemic or market—risk. A change in the interest rate affects the market as a whole and hence it is a contributor to systematic risk. A macroeconomic shock is also a contributor to systematic risk. The major difference between the two notions of risk is that while the unsystematic risk is diversifiable, the systematic risk is not. An investor can reduce the risk associated with a high level of uncertainty in demand for specific ice cream by diversifying investment in all ice cream producing companies. More generally, diversifiable risk can be reduced or eliminated by investing in many projects or by holding shares of many companies.

To keep the analysis simple, we assume, for the time being, that the portfolio Ω contains only two risky assets. Then

$$\sigma_\Omega^2 = w_1^2\sigma_1^2 + w_2^2\sigma_2^2 + 2w_1w_2\sigma_1\sigma_2\rho_{12}. \qquad (14.9)$$

Assuming without loss of generality that $\sigma_1^2 \le \sigma_2^2$, we have $w_1\sigma_1 + w_2\sigma_2 \le (w_1 + w_2)\sigma_2 = \sigma_2$. Since $-1 \le \rho_{ij} \le 1$, from (14.9) it follows that $\sigma_\Omega^2 \le w_1^2\sigma_1^2 + w_2^2\sigma_2^2 + 2w_1w_2\sigma_1\sigma_2 = (w_1\sigma_1 + w_2\sigma_2)^2 \le (w_1\sigma_2 + w_2\sigma_2)^2 = \sigma_2^2$ If $\sigma_1^2 \ge \sigma_2^2$, using a similar argument we can show that $\sigma_\Omega^2 \le \sigma_1^2$. This demonstrates that

$$\sigma_\Omega^2 \le \max(\sigma_1^2, \sigma_2^2). \qquad (14.10)$$

We may summarize the observation made in (14.10) in the following proposition.

Proposition 14.1: In a two-asset portfolio with only risky assets, the maximum of the variances of the components of the portfolio is at least as large as the variance of the portfolio.

We now look at some implications of the situation where ρ_{12} equals 1 or -1. For $\rho_{12} = 1$, that is, when the two assets are perfectly positively correlated, we have $\sigma_\Omega^2 = \left(w_1\sigma_1 + w_2\sigma_2\right)^2$ which implies that $\sigma_\Omega = (w_1\sigma_1 + w_2\sigma_2)$. Now, let $w_2 = q$ so that $w_1 = (1 - q)$. Then $\sigma_\Omega = ((1 - q)\sigma_1 + q\sigma_2)$ and $\mu_\Omega = (1 - q)\mu_1 + q\mu_2$. Consequently, for $\rho_{12} = 1$, risk is minimized, that is, $\sigma_\Omega = 0$ if and only if $((1 - q)\sigma_1 + q\sigma_2) = 0$. In such a case for $\sigma_1 \neq \sigma_2$,

$$w_2 = q = \frac{-\sigma_1}{\left(\sigma_2 - \sigma_1\right)}, w_1 = (1 - q) = \frac{\sigma_2}{\left(\sigma_2 - \sigma_1\right)}. \tag{14.11}$$

Given that $\sigma_2 > \sigma_1$, we have $q < 0$, which is a case of short selling in asset 2, and $(1 - q) > 0$. The opposite happens if $\sigma_1 > \sigma_2$. If $\sigma_1 = \sigma_2$, then all weights give the same (minimum) risk, which is $\sigma_1 = \sigma_2$.

If $\rho_{12} = -1$, then $\sigma_\Omega^2 = \left((1 - q)\sigma_1 - q\sigma_2\right)^2$, from which we get $\sigma_\Omega = \left|(1 - q)\sigma_1 - q\sigma_2\right|$, which equals 0, that is, risk is minimum if and only if $\left|(1 - q)\sigma_1 - q\sigma_2\right| = 0$. In this case

$$w_1 = (1 - q) = \frac{\sigma_2}{\left(\sigma_1 + \sigma_2\right)}, w_2 = q = \frac{\sigma_1}{\left(\sigma_1 + \sigma_2\right)}, \tag{14.12}$$

which are positive.

The following proposition summarizes the observations made in (14.11) and (14.12).

Proposition 14.2: (i) For a two-asset portfolio with only risky assets, if the assets in the portfolio are perfectly positively correlated, then for $\sigma_2 > \sigma_1$ the risk-minimizing weights of the assets in the portfolio are: $w_2 = q = \frac{-\sigma_1}{\left(\sigma_2 - \sigma_1\right)} < 0, w_1 = (1 - q) = \frac{\sigma_2}{\left(\sigma_2 - \sigma_1\right)} > 0$. The signs of the weights are reversed if $\sigma_2 < \sigma_1$. For $\sigma_1 = \sigma_2$, all weights generate the same (minimum) risk, which is, $\sigma_1 = \sigma_2$.

(ii) For a two-asset portfolio with only risky assets, if the assets in the portfolio are perfectly negatively correlated, then the risk-minimizing weights of the assets in the portfolio are: $w_1 = (1 - q) = \frac{\sigma_2}{\left(\sigma_1 + \sigma_2\right)}, w_2 = q = \frac{\sigma_1}{\left(\sigma_1 + \sigma_2\right)}$.

In order to see how this risk compares to the risks associated with the individual assets, we first consider the case $\rho_{12} = 1$ and assume that $\sigma_1 < \sigma_2$. Then $\sigma_\Omega = ((1 - q)\sigma_1 + q\sigma_2)$ and $\mu_\Omega = (1 - q)\mu_1 + q\mu_2$. Multiplying σ_Ω by $(\mu_2 - \mu_1)$ and then adding $\sigma_2\mu_1 - q_1\mu_2$ to the resulting expression we get $\sigma_\Omega(\mu_2 - \mu_1) + (\sigma_2\mu_1 - \sigma_1\mu_2) = \mu_\Omega(\sigma_2 - \sigma_1)$, from which it follows that

$$\mu_\Omega = \frac{\sigma_\Omega\left(\mu_2 - \mu_1\right) + \left(\sigma_2\mu_1 - \sigma_1\mu_2\right)}{\sigma_2 - \sigma_1}. \tag{14.13}$$

This gives us a linear risk (σ_Ω)–reward (μ_Ω) relationship on the $(\sigma - \mu)$ plane and the slope of the straight line given by (14.13) is $\dfrac{\left(\mu_2 - \mu_1\right)}{\left(\sigma_2 - \sigma_1\right)}$.

Panel (a) of Figure 14.1 shows the risk–return diagram in the case when the two assets are perfectly positively correlated. Portfolio risk and return are respectively weighted averages of asset-wise risks and returns. Consequently, nothing is achieved from diversification in this case. Higher reward needs to be accompanied by higher risk. The parts of the figure with broken lines represent short selling.

Since $\mu_\Omega = (1 - q)\,\mu_1 + q\mu_2$, for $\rho_{12} = -1$ the corresponding reward is $\dfrac{\sigma_2\mu_1 + \sigma_1\mu_2}{\left(\sigma_1 + \sigma_2\right)}$.

This means that with two perfectly negatively correlated assets we can construct a risk-free portfolio that yields a positive reward. This is a case of perfect hedging—a positive reward with zero risk. Thus, in this case the risk can be reduced to zero without short selling. It may be noted that in many situations short selling may not be possible. It may also involve additional costs. We can express the portfolio reward in terms of the portfolio risk in the case when $\rho_{12} = -1$ as

$$\mu_\Omega = \begin{cases} \dfrac{\sigma_\Omega\left(\mu_1 - \mu_2\right) + \left(\sigma_2\mu_1 + \sigma_1\mu_2\right)}{\sigma_1 + \sigma_2}, & \text{if } q < \dfrac{\sigma_1}{\sigma_1 + \sigma_2}, \\[3mm] \dfrac{\sigma_\Omega\left(\mu_2 - \mu_1\right) + \left(\sigma_2\mu_1 + \sigma_1\mu_2\right)}{\sigma_1 + \sigma_2}, & \text{if } q > \dfrac{\sigma_1}{\sigma_1 + \sigma_2}. \end{cases} \tag{14.14}$$

The corresponding risk–reward curve is shown in panel (b) of Figure 14.1. Again, the parts of the figure with broken lines represent short selling.

Figure 14.1   Risk–Reward Diagram for Two Perfectly Correlated Assets

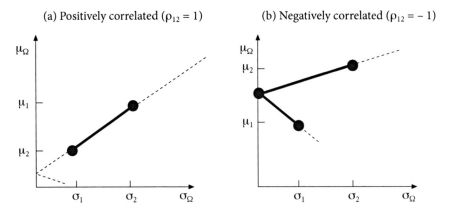

(a) Positively correlated $(\rho_{12} = 1)$ (b) Negatively correlated $(\rho_{12} = -1)$

Next, we need to find a portfolio with minimum risk when $-1 < \rho_{12} < 1$. We assume, for simplicity, that $\sigma_2 \geq \sigma_1 > 0$. In the intermediate situation where $-1 < \rho_{12} < 1$, the parametric equations in terms of q are:

$$\mu_\Omega = (1-q)\mu_1 + q\mu_2, \tag{14.15}$$

$$\sigma_\Omega^2 = (1-q)^2\sigma_1^2 + q^2\sigma_2^2 + 2q(1-q)\sigma_1\sigma_2\rho_{12} \tag{14.16}$$

$$= \left(\sigma_1^2 + \sigma_2^2 - 2\sigma_1\sigma_2\rho_{12}\right)q^2 - 2\sigma_1\left(\sigma_1 - \rho_{12}\sigma_2\right)q + \sigma_1^2. \tag{14.17}$$

Since $\rho_{12} < 1$, the coefficient of q^2 in (14.17) satisfies the inequality

$$\left(\sigma_1^2 + \sigma_2^2 - 2\sigma_1\sigma_2\rho_{12}\right) = \left(\sigma_1 - \sigma_2\right)^2 + 2\sigma_1\sigma_2\left(1 - \rho_{12}\right) > 0. \tag{14.18}$$

This shows that σ_Ω^2 is quadratic in q.

In order to find the minimum risk, we differentiate σ_Ω^2 in (14.17) with respect to q and set the derivative equal to 0 to get

$$\frac{d\sigma_\Omega^2}{dq} = 2\left(\sigma_1^2 + \sigma_2^2 - 2\sigma_1\sigma_2\rho_{12}\right)q - 2\sigma_1\left(\sigma_1 - \rho_{12}\sigma_2\right) = 0. \tag{14.19}$$

The second derivative is $2\left(\sigma_1^2 + \sigma_2^2 - 2\sigma_1\sigma_2\rho_{12}\right)$, which is positive. This shows that the value of q obtained by solving (14.19) is variance-minimizing. Now, solving (14.19) for q and denoting the solution by q_0 we have

$$q_0 = \frac{\sigma_1^2 - \rho_{12}\sigma_1\sigma_2}{\sigma_1^2 + \sigma_2^2 - 2\rho_{12}\sigma_1\sigma_2}. \tag{14.20}$$

Since σ_Ω^2 is quadratic in q, this minimum is a global minimum. The corresponding expected return is

$$\min \mu_\Omega = (1 - q_0)\mu_1 + q_0\mu_2. \tag{14.21}$$

Substituting the value of q_0 in (14.17) we find the minimum risk:

$$\min\sigma_\Omega^2 = \frac{\sigma_1^2\sigma_2^2 - \rho_{12}^2\sigma_1^2\sigma_2^2}{\sigma_1^2 + \sigma_2^2 - 2\rho_{12}\sigma_1\sigma_2}. \tag{14.22}$$

There will be no short position in the minimum risk portfolio if and only if $0 \leq q_0 \leq 1$.

From (14.20) it follows immediately that the inequality $0 < q_0 < 1$ holds if and only if $-1 \leq \rho_{12} < \frac{\sigma_1}{\sigma_2}$. Further, it is easy to verify from (14.22) that the inequality $\min\sigma_\Omega^2 < \sigma_1^2$ becomes equivalent to the condition that $(\sigma_1 - \sigma_2\rho_{12})^2 > 0$, which is true whenever $-1 \le \rho_{12} < \dfrac{\sigma_1}{\sigma_2}$ holds. This means that if $-1 \le \rho_{12} < \dfrac{\sigma_1}{\sigma_2}$, then there exists a portfolio without short selling such that $\min \sigma_\Omega^2 < \sigma_1^2 = \min\{\sigma_1^2, \sigma_2^2\}$. However, from (14.22) it also follows that $\min \sigma_\Omega^2 = 0$ if and only if $\rho_{12} = -1$.

Next, it emerges from (14.20) that $q_0 = 0$ is necessary and sufficient for the condition that $\rho_{12} = \dfrac{\sigma_1}{\sigma_2}$ (given that $\rho_{12} \ne 1$ and $\sigma_1 \ne \sigma_2$). From (14.22) it then follows that $\min \sigma_\Omega^2 = \sigma_1^2$.

Since the denominator of q_0 is positive, $q_0 < 0$ if and only if $\sigma_1^2 - \rho_{12}\sigma_1\sigma_2 < 0$, which is same as the condition that $\dfrac{\sigma_1}{\sigma_2} < \rho_{12} \le 1$. Recall that $\sigma_1^2 = \min\{\sigma_1^2, \sigma_2^2\}$. Then given that $1 > \rho_{12} > \dfrac{\sigma_1}{\sigma_2}$ the inequality $\min \sigma_\Omega^2 < \sigma_1^2$ reduces to the condition $\sigma_2^2 > \sigma_1^2$, which is true by assumption. Thus, for $q_0 < 0$, $\min \sigma_\Omega^2 < \min\{\sigma_1^2, \sigma_2^2\}$. For $\rho_{12} = 1$ to hold, the necessary and sufficient condition is $\min \sigma_\Omega^2 = 0$.

We can now summarize the above observations in the following proposition.

Proposition 14.3: For a two-asset portfolio with only risky assets, assume that $\sigma_2 \ge \sigma_1 > 0$. Let q_0 denote the risk-minimizing weight assigned to asset 2 of the portfolio, and $\min \mu_\Omega$ and $\min \sigma_\Omega^2$ stand respectively for the corresponding expected return and risk. Then

(i) $q_0 = \dfrac{\sigma_1^2 - \rho_{12}\sigma_1\sigma_2}{\sigma_1^2 + \sigma_2^2 - 2\rho_{12}\sigma_1\sigma_2}$,

(ii) $\min \mu_\Omega = (1 - q_0)\mu_1 + q_0\mu_2$,

(iii) $\min \sigma_\Omega^2 \dfrac{\sigma_1^2\sigma_2^2 - \rho_{12}^2\sigma_1^2\sigma_2^2}{\sigma_1^2 + \sigma_2^2 - 2\rho_{12}\sigma_1\sigma_2}$.

(iv) The inequality $0 < q_0 < 1$ (absence of short selling in the portfolio) is equivalent to the condition that $-1 \le \rho_{12} < \dfrac{\sigma_1}{\sigma_2}$. For $\rho_{12} > -1$, $\min \sigma_\Omega^2 < \min\{\sigma_1^2, \sigma_2^2\}$ and $\rho_{12} > -1$ implies and is implied by the condition that $\min \sigma_\Omega^2 = 0$.

(v) The condition $q_0 = 0$ (the portfolio contains only asset 1) is same as the requirement that $\rho_{12} = \dfrac{\sigma_1}{\sigma_2}$ (given that $\rho_{12} \ne 1$ and $\sigma_1 \ne \sigma_2$) and in this case $\min \sigma_\Omega^2 = \sigma_1^2$.

(vi) The inequality $q_0 < 0$ (there is short selling in asset 2) holds if and only if we have $\dfrac{\sigma_1}{\sigma_2} < \rho_{12} \le 1$. Furthermore, for $0 < \rho_{12} < 1$, $\min \sigma_\Omega^2 < \min\{\sigma_1^2, \sigma_2^2\}$ but $\rho_{12} = 1$ is necessary and sufficient for the condition that $\min \sigma_\Omega^2 = 0$.

The risk–reward curve traced out by the equations (14.15) and (14.16) on the $(\sigma^2 - \mu)$ plane represents all possible portfolio combinations for the general case $-1 \le \rho_{12} \le 1$. The graph of the points $(\sigma^2 - \mu)$ is a parabola lying on its side going through the points $\left(\sigma_1^2, \mu_1\right)$ and $\left(\sigma_2^2, \mu_2\right)$. As q increases from 0 to 1, the corresponding point on the curve moves in the direction from $\left(\sigma_1^2, \mu_1\right)$ to $\left(\sigma_2^2, \mu_2\right)$. In the case of short selling, q can take any real value. Figure 14.2 shows two typical examples of such curves. In the graph of panel (a) ρ_{12} is close to -1 but greater than -1, whereas for the graph of panel (b) ρ_{12} is close to 1 but less than 1. The broken parts of the curves represent portfolios with short selling.

Figure 14.2   Risk–Reward Diagram for Portfolios when $-1 < \rho_{12} < 1$

(a) ρ_{12} is close to but less than 1   (b) ρ_{12} is close to but greater than -1

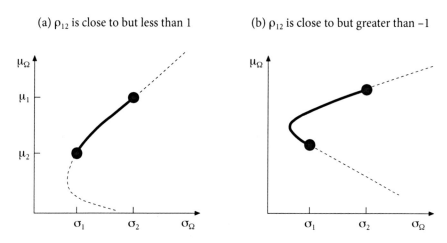

Figure 14.3   Risk–Reward Diagram for One Risky and One Risk-Free Asset

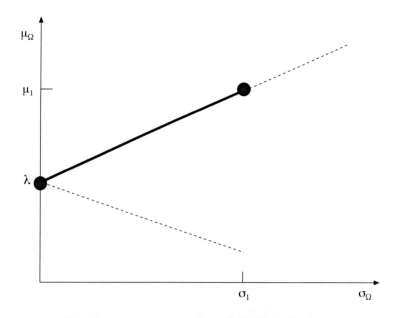

If the portfolio Ω consists of one risk-free asset (asset 1) and one risky asset (asset 2) then the expected return on the portfolio is given by $\mu_\Omega = (1 - q) \lambda + q\mu_2$, where λ is the risk-free rate of return. The investor controls risks through an allocation between a risky asset and a risk-free asset. The excess return μ_e is defined as the return net of the risk-free rate of return, that is, $\mu_e = \mu_2 - \lambda$. The variance associated with the portfolio is $\sigma_\Omega^2 = q^2\sigma_2^2$, since asset 1 is risk-free, $\sigma_1 = 0$. Hence $\sigma_\Omega = |q|\sigma_2$. This is the risk of this portfolio. The risk–reward curve representing portfolios that have one risk-free asset and one risky asset is shown in Figure 14.3. The part with the broken lines of the curve represents short selling.

14.4 CONSTRUCTION OF A PORTFOLIO: THE MULTI-ASSET CASE

In this section we consider portfolios with arbitrary $l \geq 2$ risky assets. The covariances between returns are entries of the following $l \times l$ covariance matrix

$$\Sigma = \begin{bmatrix} \sigma_{11} & \sigma_{12} & \cdots & \sigma_{1l} \\ \sigma_{21} & \sigma_{22} & \cdots & \sigma_{2l} \\ \vdots & \vdots & \vdots & \vdots \\ \sigma_{l1} & \sigma_{l2} & \cdots & \sigma_{ll} \end{bmatrix}. \tag{14.23}$$

Since $\sigma_{ij} = \sigma_{ji}$ for all $i, j = 1, 2,..., l$, the covariance matrix Σ is symmetric, so $\Sigma = \Sigma'$, the transpose of Σ. We assume that the return on any asset cannot be expressed as a linear combination of the returns on other assets. In other words, the returns are linearly independent. Their covariance matrix Σ has a unique inverse, which we denote by Σ^{-1}. The covariance matrix Σ is called positive definite if for any nonzero l-coordinated vector $\underline{x} = (x_1, x_2, \cdots, x_l), \underline{x}\Sigma\underline{x}' > 0$, where $\underline{x}'$ is the transpose of $\underline{x}$. The matrix Σ is positive definite since $\underline{x}\Sigma\underline{x}'$ is the (positive) portfolio variance when the x_i's are interpreted as the weights assigned to different assets even if the x_i's do not add up to one. The inverse of Σ is also symmetric and positive definite.

From the second expression for σ_Ω^2 in (14.6) it follows that we can write σ_Ω^2 as

$$\sigma_\Omega^2 = \underline{w}\Sigma\underline{w}'. \tag{14.24}$$

We can write $\underline{w}\Sigma\underline{w}'$ more explicitly as

$$\underline{w}\Sigma\underline{w}' = w_1^2\sigma_{11} + w_1w_2\sigma_{12} + \cdots + w_1w_l\sigma_{1l} + w_1w_2\sigma_{21} + w_2^2\sigma_{22} + \cdots + w_2w_l\sigma_{2l}$$
$$+ \cdots + w_1w_l\sigma_{l1} \cdots + w_{(l-1)}w_l\sigma_{l(l-1)} + w_l^2\sigma_{ll}. \tag{14.25}$$

Since $\sigma_{ij} = \sigma_{ji}$ for all $i, j = 1, 2,..., l$, $\underline{w}\Sigma\underline{w}'$ in (14.25) can be rewritten as

$$\underline{w}\Sigma\underline{w}' = w_1^2\sigma_{11} + 2w_1w_2\sigma_{12} + \cdots + 2w_1w_l\sigma_{1l} + w_2^2\sigma_{22} + 2w_2w_3\sigma_{23}\cdots\cdots + 2w_2w_l\sigma_{2l}$$
$$+\cdots\cdots+ w_l^2\sigma_{ll}. \tag{14.26}$$

Graphical representation of the risk–return points $\left(\sqrt{\underline{w}\,\Sigma\underline{w}'},\mu(\Omega)\right)$ in the (σ, μ) plane is known as the Markowitz curve. This curve is not a parabola.

In view of what we have investigated in the two-asset case, it is clear that our objective in this general case should be to find a minimum risk (variance) portfolio with a given μ_Ω. In other words, we need to minimize σ_Ω^2 subject to the condition that expected return on the portfolio is given, and that the sum of weights assigned to different assets in the portfolio is one.

The following theorem identifies the weight vector in a portfolio with minimum-variance.

Theorem 14.1: For a given expected return the vector of weights adding up to one, in a portfolio with minimum-variance, is given by:

$$\underline{w} = \frac{\begin{vmatrix} 1 & \left(1^l\right)\Sigma^{-1}\underline{\mu}' \\ \mu_\Omega & \underline{\mu}\Sigma^{-1}\underline{\mu}' \end{vmatrix}\left(1^l\right)\Sigma^{-1} + \begin{vmatrix} \left(1^l\right)\Sigma^{-1}\left(1^l\right)' & 1 \\ \underline{\mu}\Sigma^{-1}\left(1^l\right)' & \mu_\Omega \end{vmatrix}\underline{\mu}\Sigma^{-1}}{\begin{vmatrix} \left(1^l\right)\Sigma^{-1}\left(1^l\right)' & \left(1^l\right)\Sigma^{-1}\underline{\mu}' \\ \underline{\mu}\Sigma^{-1}\left(1^l\right)' & \underline{\mu}\Sigma^{-1}\underline{\mu}' \end{vmatrix}}. \tag{14.27}$$

Proof: See Appendix.

Throughout our discussion below we maintain the assumption that the portfolios are attainable, that is, $\sum_{i=1}^{l} w_i = 1$. The weights specified in (14.27) are associated with a risk-minimizing portfolio for which expected return is given. More precisely, given an expected return these weights are necessary and sufficient for the associated portfolio to be a risk-minimizing portfolio. Thus, Theorem 14.1 shows that a minimal-risk portfolio can be represented by the weight vector (14.27). We note from the formula (14.27) that the minimum-risk weight associated with a portfolio is a linear function of the expected return on the portfolio. Particularly, each weight w_i is linearly related to the given expected return on the portfolio. This weight line is known as the minimum-risk weight line. The minimum-risk weight line is given by a linear function of the expected return μ_Ω on the portfolio, that is, it the form, $\underline{w} = \underline{g} + \underline{h}\mu_\Omega$ where $\underline{g}$ and h are vectors of dimension l (see Appendix).

Given an expected return, a risk-minimizing portfolio is called mean-standard deviation frontier portfolio. The graphical exposition of all mean-standard deviation frontier portfolios on the (σ, μ) plane generates a curve, which we refer to as the Markowitz frontier. This curve is not a parabola. All points of the form

Figure 14.4   The Markowitz Bullet

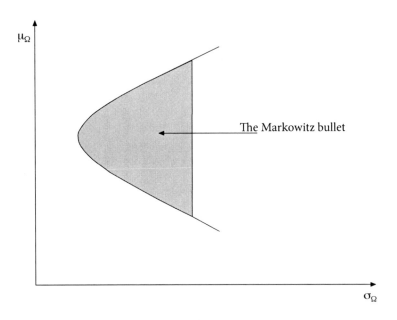

The Markowitz bullet

(σ, μ) must lie on this curve or to the right (showing higher risk) of some point on this curve. This region, including the curve itself, is known as Markowitz bullet (see Figure 14.4).

Given two assets, a rational investor will always choose, if possible, the one with higher expected return and lower risk. Given two assets with expected return and standard deviation, that is, reward–risk vectors (μ_1, σ_1) and (μ_2, σ_2), the former is said to dominate the latter if $\mu_1 \geq \mu_2$ and $\sigma_1 \leq \sigma_2$. This ordering involving any two assets is transitive. For any three assets with reward–risk vectors (μ_1, σ_1), (μ_2, σ_2) and (μ_3, σ_3) if $\mu_1 \geq \mu_2$, $\sigma_1 \leq \sigma_2$ and $\mu_2 \geq \mu_3$, $\sigma_2 \leq \sigma_3$, then $\mu_1 \geq \mu_3$ and $\sigma_1 \leq \sigma_3$. That is, of three assets if the first dominates the second and the second dominates the third, then the first dominates the third. However, if $\mu_1 \geq \mu_2$ and $\sigma_1 > \sigma_2$, then the two assets are not comparable by this relation. That is, the ordering is not complete in the sense that there may be a pair of assets that cannot be compared by this ordering. In Figure 14.5 we represent the dominance relation using two assets: (μ_1, σ_1) dominates (μ_2, σ_2).

Clearly, the above definition extends to portfolios. A portfolio is called mean-standard deviation efficient (or Markowitz efficient, efficient, or optimal) if there does not exist any portfolio other than itself that dominates it. The Markowitz efficient frontier is simply the collection of all efficient portfolios. In particular, an efficient portfolio has the maximum return for a given level of standard deviation and has the minimum standard deviation for a given level of expected return. In other words, for an efficient portfolio (i) there does not exist any portfolio

Figure 14.5 Dominated Security

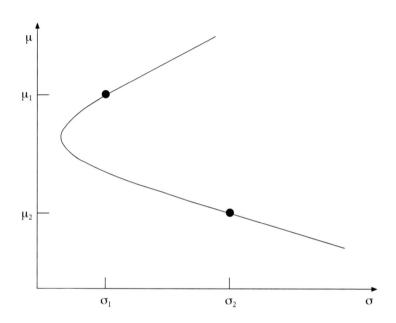

having the same standard deviation with a higher expected return, and (ii) there does not exist any portfolio possessing the same expected return with a lower standard deviation.

It is evident that any Markowitz efficient frontier portfolio is not dominated by a non-frontier portfolio in the Markowitz bullet. Since a portfolio on the lower part of the Markowitz frontier is dominated by one on the upper part at the same standard deviation and higher expected return, the lower part is excluded. The collection of Markowitz efficient portfolios is a subset of the set of Markowitz frontier portfolios. As we note from the shape of the Markowitz bullet, there is a minimum-variance portfolio with min μ_Q. The Markowitz efficient frontier is given by the part of the Markowitz frontier that lies above this portfolio.

The above discussion, therefore, indicates that an investor seeking to minimize risk for any expected return should concentrate on Markowitz efficient frontier portfolios. While a rational investor will always prefer a dominating portfolio to a dominated one, some investors may prefer a portfolio with higher return and higher risk to a one with lower return and lower risk, where higher return may be interpreted as a compensation for risk. Thus, an investor may be more satisfied with a non-frontier portfolio in the Markowitz bullet than a portfolio on the Markowitz efficient frontier. A graphical representation of the Markowitz efficient frontier is given in Figure 14.6.

Figure 14.6   The Markowitz Efficient Frontier

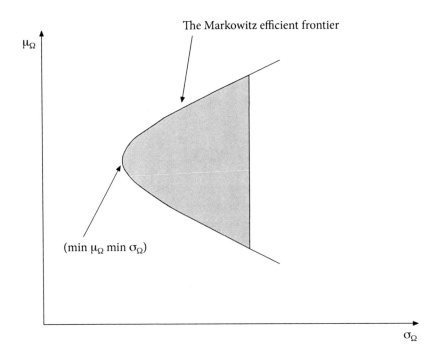

14.5 TWO-FUND SEPARATION THEOREM

We now present the two-fund separation theorem, which says that as long as the investors care about only mean and variance, the entire set of minimum-variance portfolios (hence the efficient portfolios) can be generated by forming linear combinations of any two distinct minimum-variance portfolios.

Theorem 14.2 (Two-Fund Separation): Let $\underline{w}\left(\hat{\Omega}\right)$ and $\underline{w}\left(\tilde{\Omega}\right)$ be the weight vectors associated with two distinct minimum-variance portfolios $\hat{\Omega}$ and $\tilde{\Omega}$ with mean returns $\mu\left(\underline{w}\left(\hat{\Omega}\right)\right)$ and $\mu\left(\underline{w}\left(\tilde{\Omega}\right)\right)$ respectively, where $\mu\left(\underline{w}\left(\hat{\Omega}\right)\right) \neq \mu\left(\underline{w}\left(\tilde{\Omega}\right)\right)$. Then the following statements are true.

(i) The weight vector $\underline{w}\left(\dot{\Omega}\right)$ of every minimum-variance portfolio is a linear combination of the weight vectors $\underline{w}\left(\hat{\Omega}\right)$ and $\underline{w}\left(\tilde{\Omega}\right)$.

(ii) Every portfolio whose weight vector is a linear combination of the weight vectors $\underline{w}\left(\hat{\Omega}\right)$ and $\underline{w}\left(\tilde{\Omega}\right)$ is a minimum-variance portfolio.

(iii) If $\hat{\Omega}$ and $\tilde{\Omega}$ are minimum-variance efficient portfolios with weight vectors

$\underline{w}\left(\hat{\Omega}\right)$ and $\underline{w}\left(\tilde{\Omega}\right)$, then the convex combination $\alpha\underline{w}\left(\hat{\Omega}\right)+(1-\alpha)\underline{w}\left(\tilde{\Omega}\right)$, where $0 \le \alpha \le 1$, is the weight vector of a minimum-variance efficient portfolio.

Proof: See Appendix.

The theorem thus says that if an investor desires to invest in a mean-variance efficient portfolio with a given expected return and variance, then he can achieve this objective by spreading his investment in an appropriate linear combination of two mean-variance efficient portfolios (see Constantinides and Malliaris 1995).

14.6 CAPITAL ASSET PRICING MODEL

The general idea of the capital asset pricing model is to improve risk–reward position of an investor by spreading investment in risky and risk-free assets (Sharpe 1964 and Lintner 1965). In fact, most real portfolios include risk-free assets. (Parts of our presentation in this section are based on Roaman 2004.)

We consider a portfolio Ω with a risk-free asset with weight w_f and l risky assets, with weights $w_1, w_2,..., w_l$. Write $\hat{w} = \sum_{i=1}^{l} w_i$, the total weight of all risky assets in the portfolio. Then the weight assigned to the risk-free asset is $w_f = 1 - \hat{w}$. The expected return on the portfolio is $\mu_\Omega = w_f\lambda + \sum_{i=1}^{l} w_i\mu_i$, which we can rewrite as

$\mu_\Omega = w_f\lambda + \hat{w}\sum_{i=1}^{l}\frac{w_i}{\hat{w}}\mu_i$. Thus, $\frac{w_i}{\hat{w}}, i = 1,2,\cdots,l$, can be interpreted as the weight associated with the ith risky asset, as a proportion of the total weight of all risky assets in the portfolio. Since $w_f + \hat{w} = 1$, it follows that $\mu_\Omega = \lambda + \hat{w}\left(\hat{\mu} - \lambda\right)$, where

$\hat{\mu} = \sum_{i=1}^{l}\frac{w_i}{\hat{w}}\mu_i$.

Now, the variance of the return for the risk-free asset is zero. Therefore, in view of (14.6), $\sigma_\Omega^2 = Var\left(\sum_{i=1}^{l} w_i r_i\right) = \sum_{i=1}^{l}\sum_{j=1}^{l} w_i w_j Cov\left(r_i, r_j\right)$. We can rewrite σ_Ω^2 as

$\sigma_\Omega^2 = \hat{w}^2 Var\left(\sum_{i=1}^{l}\frac{w_i}{\hat{w}} r_i\right) = \hat{w}^2\hat{\sigma}^2$, where $\hat{\sigma}^2 = Var\left(\sum_{i=1}^{l}\frac{w_i}{\hat{w}} r_i\right)$. This gives $\hat{w} = \frac{\sigma_\Omega}{\hat{\sigma}}$.

Substituting this value of $\hat{w}$ in $\mu_\Omega = w_f\lambda + \hat{w}\sum_{i=1}^{l}\frac{w_i}{\hat{w}}\mu_i$ we get

$$\mu_\Omega = \lambda + \frac{\sigma_\Omega}{\hat{\sigma}}\left(\hat{\mu} - \lambda\right). \tag{14.28}$$

The line given by (14.28) passes through the points $(\sigma, \mu) = (0, \lambda)$ and

$(\sigma,\mu)=(\hat{\sigma},\hat{\mu})$. These points correspond respectively to the weights $w_f = 1$ and $\hat{w} = 1$. That is, in the former case all investments are in the risk-free asset and in the latter case the entire investment is in risky assets only. However, if the investor splits his investment between the risk-free asset and risky assets, then his risk–reward point will lie somewhere on the line joining these two extreme points. This line is shown graphically in Figure 14.7. It is now evident from Figure 14.7 that among all lines passing through $(0, \lambda)$, and points of the type $(\hat{\sigma},\hat{\mu})$ in the Markowitz bullet, the line that will pass through points with highest expected return for a given risk will be tangent to Markowitz efficient frontier. The tangent line in Figure 14.7 is known as the capital market line and the point of tangency (σ_m, μ_m) is referred to as the capital market portfolio of only risky assets. This reasoning works as long as the risk-free return λ is not very high so that the upward sloping line through λ touches the Markowitz bullet. If λ is too high the upward sloping line through λ will not be tangent to the bullet.

Figure 14.7   The Capital Market Line

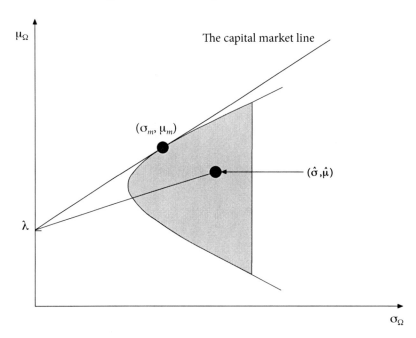

In order to derive the explicit form of the capital market line, let us rewrite the expected overall portfolio return $\mu_\Omega = w_f \lambda + \sum_{i=1}^{l} w_i \mu_i$ as

$$\mu_\Omega = \lambda + \sum_{i=1}^{l} w_i \left(\mu_i - \lambda\right) = \lambda + \left(\underline{\mu} - \lambda 1^l\right)\underline{w}'. \tag{14.29}$$

Note that we have already incorporated the constraint $w_f + \sum_{i=1}^{l} w_i = 1$ into (14.29). Therefore, the objective here is to minimize the variance $\sigma_\Omega^2 = \underline{w} \, \Sigma \, \underline{w}'$ of the portfolio return with respect to the weights assigned to different assets in the portfolio subject to the constraint (14.29).

We show in the Appendix that from the first order condition for this optimization problem for any Markowitz efficient frontier portfolio Ω and any arbitrary portfolio $\hat{\Omega}$ with l risky assets,

$$\mu_{\hat{\Omega}} = \lambda + \frac{\sigma_{\Omega\hat{\Omega}}}{\sigma_\Omega^2} \left(\mu_\Omega - \lambda \right). \tag{14.30}$$

This equation says that expected return on any portfolio $\hat{\Omega}$ with weight vector $\left(1 - \sum_{i=1}^{l} q_i, q_1, q_2, \ldots, q_l \right)$ is simply equal to the sum of the risk-free return and a risk sensitivity measure, which is defined as the ratio between its covariance with some efficient portfolio Ω and the variance of the efficient portfolio, multiplied by the expected excess return $(\mu_\Omega - \lambda)$ on the portfolio Ω over the risk-free return. It holds for any efficient portfolio of risky assets.

A natural question here is: what is the contribution of an asset to the risk of the portfolio Ω? To answer this question, let us assume that the portfolio Ω contains only two risky assets. Then $\sigma_\Omega^2 = w_1^2 \sigma_1^2 + w_2^2 \sigma_2^2 + 2w_1 w_2 \sigma_{12}$, from which it follows that $\dfrac{\partial \sigma_\Omega}{\partial w_1} = \dfrac{d\sigma_\Omega}{d\sigma_\Omega^2} \dfrac{\partial \sigma_\Omega^2}{\partial w_1} = \dfrac{w_1 \sigma_1^2 + w_2 \sigma_{12}}{\sigma_\Omega}$ and $\dfrac{\partial \sigma_\Omega}{\partial w_2} = \dfrac{d\sigma_\Omega}{d\sigma_\Omega^2} \dfrac{\partial \sigma_\Omega^2}{\partial w_2} = \dfrac{w_2 \sigma_2^2 + w_1 \sigma_{12}}{\sigma_\Omega}$.

Then $q_1 \dfrac{\partial \sigma_\Omega}{\sigma_\Omega \partial w_1} + q_2 \dfrac{\partial \sigma_\Omega}{\sigma_\Omega \partial w_2} = \dfrac{w_1 q_1 \sigma_1^2 + w_2 q_1 \sigma_{12}}{\sigma_\Omega^2} + \dfrac{w_2 q_2 \sigma_2^2 + w_1 q_2 \sigma_{12}}{\sigma_\Omega^2} = \dfrac{\sigma_{\Omega\hat{\Omega}}}{\sigma_\Omega^2}$. In the general case of l assets, we have $\sum_{i=1}^{l} q_i \dfrac{\partial \sigma_\Omega}{\sigma_\Omega \partial w_i} = \dfrac{\sigma_{\Omega\hat{\Omega}}}{\sigma_\Omega^2}$ (see Reisinger 2008). We interpret $\dfrac{\partial \sigma_\Omega}{\sigma_\Omega \partial w_i}$ as the contribution of the ith asset to the risk of the portfolio Ω.

Thus, the weighted sum of contributions of risky assets to the risk of portfolio Ω is the risk sensitivity measure $\dfrac{\sigma_{\Omega\hat{\Omega}}}{\sigma_\Omega^2}$, where the weights assigned in the sum are the weights of the risky assets in the portfolio $\hat{\Omega}$.

To understand this in greater detail, let us now discuss the market portfolio of risky assets. Let the number of units of risky asset i held by person j in the initial period be $n_i^j(0)$. Then the value of asset i in the portfolio of risky assets held by person j is $n_i^j(0) S_0^i$. Therefore, $M_0^j = \sum_{i=1}^{l} n_i^j(0) S_0^i$ is person j's initial wealth invested in the risky portfolio. Then $w_{ij} = \dfrac{n_i^j(0)S_0^i}{M_0^j}$ is the proportion of the initial

wealth invested by person j in risky asset i. The total wealth in the risky assets in

the economy consisting of u persons is $\sum_{j=1}^{u} M_0^j = M_{m0}$. Therefore, the total value of

risky assets is $\sum_{i=1}^{l}\sum_{j=1}^{u} n_i^j(0)S_0^i$. In equilibrium, the total wealth invested in risky assets

is the total value of risky assets, which means $\sum_{i=1}^{l}\sum_{j=1}^{u} n_i^j(0)S_0^i = M_{m0}$. We write w_{mi}

for the proportion of total wealth M_{m0} contributed by the total value $\sum_{j=1}^{u} n_i^j(0)S_0^i$
of asset i, that is,

$$w_{mi} = \dfrac{\displaystyle\sum_{j=1}^{u} n_i^j(0)S_0^i}{M_{mo}} = \sum_{j=1}^{u} w_{ij}\dfrac{M_0^j}{M_{m0}}. \tag{14.31}$$

The fractions, w_{mi}'s, are referred to as the market portfolio weights. This condition must be satisfied for clearance of the risky asset markets. It says that for any risky asset i the market portfolio weight is simply the weighted average of weights assigned by individuals to this asset in their portfolios, where the weighted average is calculated using the individuals' wealth invested in risky assets as a fraction of total wealth invested in the risky assets. We have demonstrated that a linear combination of frontier portfolios is on the frontier. Each individual holds a frontier portfolio. Since the market portfolio is a linear combination of frontier portfolios, it is definitely on the frontier.

Let us now determine the mean and the variance of the market portfolio. Note

that the market return is defined as $r_m = \sum_{i=1}^{l} w_{mi}r_i + \left(1 - \sum_{i=1}^{l} w_{mi}\right)\lambda$, which shows that,

$\mu_m = \Xi(r_m) = \sum_{i=1}^{l} w_{mi}\Xi(r_i) + \left(1 - \sum_{i=1}^{l} w_{mi}\right)\lambda = \sum_{i=1}^{l} w_{mi}\mu_i + \left(1 - \sum_{i=1}^{l} w_{mi}\right)\lambda$, where Ξ is the

expectation operator. The variance of the market portfolio is

$$Var(r_m) = \sigma_m^2 = Cov(r_m,r_m) = \Xi(r_m - \mu_m)(r_m - \mu_m) = \Xi\left(\sum_{i=1}^{l} w_{mi}(r_i - \mu_i)\right)(r_m - \mu_m)$$

$$= \sum_{i=1}^{l} w_{mi}Cov(r_i,r_m) = \sum_{i=1}^{l} M_{m0}w_{mi}\left(\dfrac{Cov(r_i,r_m)}{M_{m0}}\right). \tag{14.32}$$

Hence

$$\frac{\partial \sigma_m^2}{\partial \left(M_{m0} w_{mi} \right)} = \left(\frac{Cov\left(r_i, r_m \right)}{M_{m0}} \right). \tag{14.33}$$

This gives the change in the variance of the market when an additional unit of money is invested in asset i.

Since the market portfolio m of risky assets is one Markowitz efficient portfolio, we have

$$\mu_{\hat{\Omega}} = \lambda + \frac{\sigma_{m\hat{\Omega}}}{\sigma_m^2} \left(\mu_m - \lambda \right) = \lambda + \beta_{\hat{\Omega}} \left(\mu_m - \lambda \right). \tag{14.34}$$

This is the standard version of the capital asset pricing model (CAPM). Equation (14.34) is the explicit form of the capital market line. The value of the coefficient $\beta_{\hat{\Omega}} = \frac{\sigma_{m\hat{\Omega}}}{\sigma_m^2}$, which is a measure of the magnitude of market risk, is called the beta of portfolio $\hat{\Omega}$. It is an indicator of expected change in the return on a portfolio in response to a change in market conditions. The difference $(\mu_m - \lambda)$ is the excess return on the market portfolio. The beta multiplied by the excess return on the market portfolio is the risk premium. This is the additional return that an investor can expect for undertaking risk.

Every investor holds a portfolio on the capital market line and hence everyone will select a portfolio with the same relative proportions of risky assets. But this implies that the portfolio characterized by $\left(\mu_m, \sigma_m^2 \right)$ has to contain all risky assets with weights equal to corresponding relative shares in the whole market. Because of this, the portfolio characterized by $\left(\mu_m, \sigma_m^2 \right)$ is referred to as the market portfolio.

The model can be regarded as predicting a portfolio's behavior as a function of beta. That is, if one knows the asset's beta, then one knows the value of the return that an investor expects to have. (We discuss this issue in greater detail later in this section.) By definition the beta of the market portfolio is 1, that is, market portfolio makes 100 percent contribution to its own risk. Since a risk-free asset has no contribution to market risk, it has a beta of value zero. For a positive value of beta, the expected return on a portfolio increases as market return increases. On the other hand, for a negative value of the beta the portfolio return increases if the market return decreases. The only cause of change in the expected return on the portfolio, given the risk-free and market returns, is the beta of the portfolio. The variance of a portfolio whose beta is higher (lower) than one changes more (less) than proportionately in response to a change in market conditions.

The CAPM provides a description of state of equilibrium in the market. Each investor holds an efficient portfolio and the average portfolio of all investors is the market portfolio. It describes the relationship of the expected return on a portfolio and the risk when the market is at equilibrium. It says that the investors need higher levels of expected return to compensate for higher level of risk. Investors are compensated only for bearing the market risk, given by the magnitude of the beta. All unsystematic or diversifiable risks have been eliminated since all investors hold an equal share of market portfolio weights in equilibrium. The investment decisions of all the investors are based on the same values of expected returns, variances and covariances of all assets. The efficient frontier on which a portfolio is to be chosen will be the same for all investors. However, because of differences in attitudes towards risks, individual investors may choose different portfolios on the efficient frontier. Everybody holds a portfolio of risky assets with the same weights as the market portfolio. Any trade among investors will affect the distributions of funds between the risk-free and risky assets. The demand and supply of all assets will be balanced.

If the arbitrary portfolio $\hat{\Omega}$ with weight vector $\left(1 - \sum_{i=1}^{l} q_i, q_1, q_2, ..., q_l\right)$ is such that $q_i > 0$ for some risky asset i and $q_j = 0$ for all risky assets $j \neq i$, then the CAPM in (14.34) reduces to

$$\mu_i = \lambda + \frac{\sigma_{mi}}{\sigma_m^2}(\mu_m - \lambda) = \lambda + \beta_{im}(\mu_m - \lambda). \tag{14.35}$$

This equation is the asset counterpart to the portfolio CAPM. It says that the expected return on asset i is the sum of risk-free return and the asset's market beta (β_{im}) multiplied by $(\mu_m - \lambda)$, the premium per unit of beta risk.

Note that $\sigma_m^2 = \text{cov}(r_m, r_m) = \text{cov}\left(\sum_{i=1}^{l} w_{im} r_i, r_m\right) = \sum_{i=1}^{l} w_{im} \text{cov}(r_i, r_m)$. That is, the risk of the market portfolio is the weighted average of covariances of returns on different assets with the market return, where the averaging is done using the weights of the assets in the market portfolio. We can thus write β_{im} as

$$\beta_{im} = \frac{\text{cov}(r_i, r_m)}{\sigma_m^2} = \frac{\text{cov}(r_i, r_m)}{\sum_{i=1}^{l} w_{im} \text{cov}(r_i, r_m)}. \tag{14.36}$$

Therefore, β_{im} may be interpreted as the covariance risk of asset relative to the average covariance risk of all the assets. Computation of the beta of an asset can be done by running a regression of the return on the specific asset against the return on the market portfolio using monthly data for a few months (see Perold 2004). Consequently, betas have become a standard product in the literature on applied finance. They are available commercially and used in stock market analysis. Thus, an appealing feature of the CAPM is that it involves things that are empirically observable.

If an asset i is characterized by large variation in return, that is, σ_i is quite high, and if these variations are positively correlated with the variations in the market return ($\beta_{im} > 0$), then the asset will require a positive premium. If the asset is negatively correlated with the market return, then it can be used as a hedging instrument to control risk associated with other assets in the portfolio. The investor would like to hold it even with an expected return less than the risk-free return, since more and more investment in this asset will help reduce the overall risk of the market portfolio. This becomes evident from (14.33). If variations are uncorrelated with the market return, then the risk can be diversified away and equilibrium return will be equal to the risk-free return.

A plot of expected returns for portfolios/individual assets against their respective betas is known as the security market line. This is shown in panel (b) of Figure 14.8. For the purpose of comparison, we show the capital market line in panel (a) of the figure. The major difference between the two lines is that any portfolio lies on the security market line in the sense that its expected return—whether above, below or equal to risk-free return—along with the corresponding beta will be a point on the security market line. That is, the security market line graphically shows the expected returns on the portfolios with risky assets for different risks (betas). This line is useful for understanding whether a portfolio has reasonable expected return against risk. In contrast, no portfolio other than the market portfolio and the risk-free asset, and all points joining these two extreme points, will lie on the capital market line. Clearly, all portfolios whose expected returns correspond to negative values of beta have expected returns less than the risk-free return.

Figure 14.8   The Capital Market Line and the Security Market Line

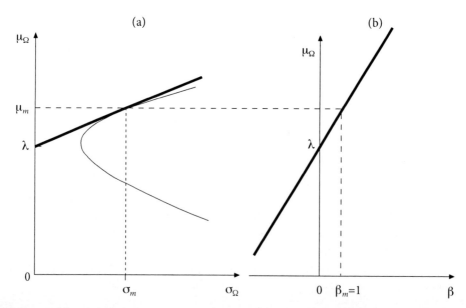

We can rewrite the CAPM in (14.34) as

$$\mu_{\hat{\Omega}} - \lambda = \left(\frac{\mu_m - \lambda}{\sigma_m}\right)\beta_{\hat{\Omega}}\sigma_m. \qquad (14.37)$$

The left-hand side of equation (14.37) is the expected excess return on the portfolio over the risk-free return. The first bracketed term $\left(\dfrac{\mu_m - \lambda}{\sigma_m}\right)$ on the right-hand side of equation (14.37) is known as the market Sharpe ratio. Under CAPM, the market portfolio is the Markowitz efficient portfolio that generates the highest Sharpe ratio. To demonstrate this rigorously, recall that $\beta_{\hat{\Omega}} = \dfrac{\text{cov}\left(r_{\hat{\Omega}}, r_m\right)}{\sigma_m^2} = \dfrac{\rho_{\hat{\Omega}m}\sigma_m\sigma_{\hat{\Omega}}}{\sigma_m^2}$, which gives $\rho_{\hat{\Omega}m}\sigma_{\hat{\Omega}} = \sigma_m\beta_{\hat{\Omega}}$, where $\rho_{\hat{\Omega}m}$ is the correlation coefficient between the returns on $\hat{\Omega}$ and the market portfolio. So $\dfrac{\left(\mu_{\hat{\Omega}} - \lambda\right)}{\sigma_{\hat{\Omega}}} = \rho_{\hat{\Omega}m}\dfrac{\left(\mu_{\hat{\Omega}} - \lambda\right)}{\sigma_m}$. Since $\rho_{\hat{\Omega}m} \leq 1, \dfrac{\left(\mu_{\hat{\Omega}} - \lambda\right)}{\sigma_{\hat{\Omega}}} \leq \dfrac{\left(\mu_{\hat{\Omega}} - \lambda\right)}{\sigma_m}$, Thus, $\dfrac{\left(\mu_{\hat{\Omega}} - \lambda\right)}{\sigma_m}$ is the highest Sharpe ratio.

In general, for any arbitrary portfolio Ω we define the Sharpe ratio as $\left(\dfrac{\mu_{\Omega} - \lambda}{\sigma_{\Omega}}\right)$. The numerator of this ratio is the return on the portfolio in excess of risk-free return. The denominator is a measure of risk. Thus, the Sharpe ratio is the return generated over the risk-free return per unit of risk. In other words, this ratio is a tool for comparing return with risk. It indicates how well the return on a portfolio compensates the investor for the risk taken. The higher the ratio, the better the individual's return is relative to the risk from the portfolio. Equation (14.37) says that given the risk, expected excess return $\left(\mu_{\hat{\Omega}} - \lambda\right)$ on a portfolio $\hat{\Omega}$ equals the product of the highest Sharpe ratio and the beta of the portfolio $\beta_{\hat{\Omega}}$ multiplied by the market risk σ_m.

We can derive equation (14.37) using the definition of beta and equilibrium condition. To see this, note that the amount of risk in a given asset i relative to the total risk in the market is given by β_{im}. In order to get the total amount of risk in asset i, we need to multiply β_{im} by the market risk σ_m. Thus, the total amount of risk in asset i is $\beta_{im}\sigma_m$. We know that the price of risk associated with an asset is given by the corresponding Sharpe ratio $\dfrac{\mu_m - \lambda}{\sigma_m}$. Therefore, cost of risk in asset i is

$$\beta_{im}\sigma_m \frac{\mu_m - \lambda}{\sigma_m} = \beta_{im}\left(\mu_m - \lambda\right).$$ We call this the risk-adjustment coefficient.

In equilibrium all assets should have the same risk-adjusted return. Otherwise, if one asset has higher risk-adjusted return than another, people would like to hold the one with higher risk-adjusted return. Thus, in equilibrium risk-adjusted returns must be equal across assets. That is, if i and j are two assets, then the following condition must be satisfied in equilibrium

$$\mu_i - \beta_{im}(\mu_m - \lambda) = \mu_j - \beta_{jm}(\mu_m - \lambda). \tag{14.38}$$

Since beta measures the risk of an asset and the risk-free asset has zero risk, for the risk free asset $\beta_{fm} = 0$. Thus, for any asset i,

$$\mu_i - \beta_{im}(\mu_m - \lambda) = \lambda - \beta_{fm}(\mu_m - \lambda) = \lambda, \tag{14.39}$$

which on readjustment gives us equation (14.35). This, therefore, shows how we can derive the capital asset pricing model using the definition of beta and equilibrium condition.

A vector $\underline{r} = (r_1, r_2,..., r_k)$ of asset returns is said to exhibit two-mutual-fund separation if there exist two mutual funds α and ρ of k assets such that for any given portfolio Ω there is a scalar c satisfying

$$\Xi(U(cr_\alpha + (1 - c))r_p) \geq \Xi(U(r_\Omega)), \tag{14.40}$$

where Ξ stands for the expectation operator, U is any increasing and concave utility function, r_α is the return on the mutual fund α and so on. Inequality (14.40) captures the idea that portfolios generated by two mutual funds are at least as good as any arbitrary portfolio Ω. It can be shown that α and ρ are minimum-variance portfolios (see Huang and Litzenberger 1988). Ross (1978b) showed that if asset returns satisfy two-mutual-fund separation and if asset variances are finite, then the CAPM holds. If there is only one-mutual fund α so that $c = 1$, then $\underline{r} = (r_1, r_2,..., r_k)$ exhibits one-mutual-fund separation. This is a degenerate case of two-mutual-fund separation.

There are several limitations of the CAPM. It assumes that the variance of returns is an adequate indicator of risk. But there are other measures of risks as well. Next, it is based on the assumption that for a given level of expected return, investors will prefer lower risk. But gamblers in casinos clearly pay for risk. Assumption of homogeneity of expectation is quite strong. The market portfolio is comprised of all assets in all markets. There is no preference for investors between markets; they choose assets simply on the basis of risk–return profile. The model also makes the strong assumption that the assets are infinitely divisible.

Example 14.1: Consider two risky assets with expected returns $\mu_1 = 2$ and $\mu_2 = 3$. The covariance matrix is $\Sigma = \begin{vmatrix} 1 & 1 \\ 1 & 2 \end{vmatrix}$. Let Ω be a portfolio consisting of these two assets. We wish to determine the risk-minimizing weights assigned to the two assets in this portfolio.

Note that in this case the correlation coefficient between the returns on the two assets is $\rho_{12} = \dfrac{\sigma_{12}}{\sigma_1 \sigma_2} = \dfrac{1}{1.\sqrt{2}} = \dfrac{1}{\sqrt{2}} = \dfrac{\sigma_1}{\sigma_2}$. We, thus, have $\rho_{12} \neq 1$ and $\sigma_1 \neq \sigma_2$.

Therefore, in view of the observations made after equation (14.22) it follows that $\min \sigma_\Omega^2 = \sigma_1^2 = 1$ and the risk-minimizing weight assigned to the second asset in the portfolio is 0, so that the portfolio consists of only the first asset.

Applied Example 14.1: Bower and Wentz (2005) considered the issue of portfolio optimization, where portfolios were created consisting of five stocks randomly selected from the S&P (Standard and Poor's) 500 and a six-month bond. The S&P 500 is a stock market index that includes 500 leading companies in leading US industries. The selected data were from July 1, 2004 to December 31, 2004. They used the Markowitz minimum-variance model as well as the mean absolute deviation model to determine allocation of funds to each asset in each portfolio. The mean absolute deviation model minimizes the average of the weighted absolute values of the deviations between daily returns minus the average return for each asset for each time, where the weights are the proportions of the total investment in the respective assets and the averaging is done using the time horizon. The constraints used in both the models are the same. No statistically significant difference between the returns in the two models was found at 5 percent. However, the mean absolute deviation model was found to involve a less complicated methodology.

APPENDIX

Proof of Theorem 14.1

We use the Lagrangian technique to prove this theorem. We have to minimize the expression (14.22) subject to the constraints

$$\left(1^l\right)\underline{w}' = w_1 + w_2 + \cdots + w_l = 1 \tag{14.41}$$

and

$$\underline{\mu}\,\underline{w}' = w_1 \mu_1 + w_2 \mu_2 + \cdots + w_l \mu_l = \mu_\Omega. \tag{14.42}$$

The Lagrangian method starts by setting up the expression

$$\Im = w_1^2 \sigma_{11} + 2w_1 w_2 \sigma_{12} + \cdots + 2w_1 w_l \sigma_{1l} + w_2^2 \sigma_{22} + 2w_2 w_3 \sigma_{23} \cdots \cdots + 2w_2 w_l \sigma_{2l}$$
$$+ \cdots \cdots + w_l^2 \sigma_{ll} - \varsigma_1 \left(w_1 + w_2 + \cdots + w_l - 1\right) - \varsigma_2 \left(w_1 \mu_1 + w_2 \mu_2 + \cdots + w_l \mu_l - \mu_\Omega\right), \tag{14.43}$$

where ς_1 and ς_2 are the Lagrange multipliers. We set the partial derivatives of the expression (14.43) with respect to w_i equal to zero and use the fact that $\sigma_{ij} = \sigma_{ji}$ to get the following system of l equations:

$$2(w_1 \sigma_{11} + w_2 \sigma_{12} +...+ w_1 \sigma_{1l}) - \varsigma_1 - \varsigma_2 \mu_1 = 0,$$

$$2(w_1 \sigma_{21} + w_2 \sigma_{22} +...+ w_1 \sigma_{2l}) - \varsigma_1 - \varsigma_2 \mu_2 = 0,$$

$$\cdots\cdots\cdots\cdots\cdots\cdots\cdots\cdots\cdots\cdots\cdots\cdots\cdots\cdots \tag{14.44}$$

$$\cdots\cdots\cdots\cdots\cdots\cdots\cdots\cdots\cdots\cdots\cdots\cdots\cdots$$

$$2(w_1 \sigma_{1l} + w_2 \sigma_{l2} +...+ w_l \sigma_{ll}) - \varsigma_1 - \varsigma_2 \mu_l = 0.$$

The system (14.44) gives us the first order conditions for minimum risk given the constraints (14.41) and (14.42). Since Σ is positive definite, the first order conditions are necessary and sufficient for a global minimum.

The system (14.44) can be written in a more compact form as

$$2\Sigma \underline{w}' = \varsigma_1 \left(1^l\right)' + \varsigma_2 \underline{\mu}'. \tag{14.45}$$

Note that $\Sigma \underline{w}'$ is symmetric in the sense that $\Sigma \underline{w}' = (\Sigma \underline{w}')'$. But $(\Sigma \underline{w}')' = \underline{w}\Sigma' = \underline{w}\Sigma$, since $\Sigma' = \Sigma$. We therefore take the transpose of the expression on the right-hand side of (14.45), which is $\varsigma_1 (1^l) + \varsigma_2 \underline{\mu}$. Hence

$$2\underline{w}\Sigma = \varsigma_1 \left(1^l\right) + \varsigma_2 \underline{\mu}, \tag{14.46}$$

from which we have

$$\underline{w} = \frac{1}{2}\left(\varsigma_1 \left(1^l\right) + \varsigma_2 \underline{\mu}\right)\Sigma^{-1}. \tag{14.47}$$

Substituting the form of $\underline{w}$ given by (14.47) in the matrix forms of the constraints (14.41) and (14. 42) we get

$$\left(1^l\right)\left(\frac{1}{2}\left(\varsigma_1\left(1^l\right) + \varsigma_2 \underline{\mu}\right)\Sigma^{-1}\right)' = 1 \tag{14.48}$$

and

$$\underline{\mu}\left(\frac{1}{2}\left(\varsigma_1\left(1^l\right) + \varsigma_2 \underline{\mu}\right)\Sigma^{-1}\right)' = \mu_\Omega, \tag{14.49}$$

which on simplification becomes

$$\varsigma_1\left(1^l\right)\Sigma^{-1}\left(1^l\right)' + \varsigma_2\left(1^l\right)\Sigma^{-1}\underline{\mu}' = 2 \tag{14.50}$$

and

$$\varsigma_1\left(\underline{\mu}\Sigma^{-1}\left(1^l\right)'\right) + \varsigma_2\left(\underline{\mu}\Sigma^{-1}\underline{\mu}'\right) = 2\mu_\Omega, \tag{14.51}$$

where we have used the fact that $\left(\Sigma^{-1}\right)' = \Sigma^{-1}$.

We can write the system displayed from (14.50) to (14.51) as

$$a_{11}\,\varsigma_1 + a_{12}\,\varsigma_2 = b_1, \tag{14.52}$$

$$a_{21}\,\varsigma_1 + a_{22}\,\varsigma_2 = b_2, \tag{14.53}$$

where $a_{11} = \left(1^l\right)\Sigma^{-1}\left(1^l\right)'$ and so on. Solving these two equations for ς_1 and ς_2, we get

$$\varsigma_1 = \frac{b_1 a_{22} - b_2 a_{12}}{a_{11}a_{22} - a_{21}a_{12}} = \frac{\begin{vmatrix} b_1 & a_{12} \\ b_2 & a_{22} \end{vmatrix}}{\begin{vmatrix} a_{11} & a_{12} \\ a_{21} & a_{22} \end{vmatrix}} = \frac{2\begin{vmatrix} 1 & \left(1^l\right)\Sigma^{-1}\underline{\mu}' \\ \mu_\Omega & \underline{\mu}\Sigma^{-1}\underline{\mu}' \end{vmatrix}}{\begin{vmatrix} \left(1^l\right)\Sigma^{-1}\left(1^l\right)' & \left(1^l\right)\Sigma^{-1}\underline{\mu}' \\ \underline{\mu}\Sigma^{-1}\left(1^l\right)' & \underline{\mu}\Sigma^{-1}\underline{\mu}' \end{vmatrix}}, \tag{14.54}$$

$$\varsigma_2 = \frac{b_2 a_{11} - b_1 a_{21}}{a_{11}a_{22} - a_{21}a_{12}} = \frac{\begin{vmatrix} a_{11} & b_1 \\ a_{21} & b_2 \end{vmatrix}}{\begin{vmatrix} a_{11} & a_{12} \\ a_{21} & a_{22} \end{vmatrix}} = \frac{2\begin{vmatrix} \left(1^l\right)\Sigma^{-1}\left(1^l\right)' & 1 \\ \underline{\mu}\Sigma^{-1}\left(1^l\right)' & \mu_\Omega \end{vmatrix}}{\begin{vmatrix} \left(1^l\right)\Sigma^{-1}\left(1^l\right)' & \left(1^l\right)\Sigma^{-1}\underline{\mu}' \\ \underline{\mu}\Sigma^{-1}\left(1^l\right)' & \underline{\mu}\Sigma^{-1}\underline{\mu}' \end{vmatrix}}. \tag{14.55}$$

Substituting these values of ς_1 and ς_2 into the expression for $\underline{w}$ given by (14.47) we get the desired form of $\underline{w}$. This completes the proof of the theorem.

Minimizing Portfolio Variance Subject to the Constraint (14.29)

The Lagrangian for this problem is

$$\Im = \underline{w}\Sigma\underline{w}' - \varsigma\left(\left(\underline{\mu} - \lambda 1^l\right)\underline{w}' - \mu_\Omega + \lambda\right)\underline{w}', \tag{14.56}$$

where ς is the Lagrange multiplier. From (14.45) it follows that the first order condition takes the form

$$2\Sigma\underline{w}' = \varsigma\left(\underline{\mu} - \lambda 1^l\right)'. \tag{14.57}$$

Pre-multiply this equation with $\underline{w}$ to get

$$2\sigma_\Omega^2 = 2\underline{w}\Sigma\underline{w}' = \varsigma\,\underline{w}\left(\underline{\mu} - \lambda 1^l\right)' = \varsigma\left(\underline{w}\underline{\mu}' - \lambda\right) = \varsigma\left(\mu_\Omega - \lambda\right). \tag{14.58}$$

We also pre-multiply equation (14.57) by the weight vector $\underline{q} = \left(q_1, q_2, \ldots, q_l\right)$ of an arbitrary portfolio $\dot{\Omega}$ with l risky assets to get

$$2\sigma_{\Omega\hat{\Omega}} = 2\underline{q}\Sigma\underline{w}' = \varsigma\,\underline{q}\left(\underline{\mu} - \lambda\underline{1}'\right)' = \varsigma\left(\underline{q}\underline{\mu}' - \lambda\right) = \varsigma\left(\mu_{\Omega} - \lambda\right). \qquad (14.59)$$

From (14.58) and (14.59) it follows that

$$\frac{\sigma_{\Omega}^2}{\sigma_{\Omega\hat{\Omega}}} = \frac{\left(\mu_{\Omega} - \lambda\right)}{\left(\mu_{\hat{\Omega}} - \lambda\right)}, \qquad (14.60)$$

which, on simplification, becomes

$$\mu_{\hat{\Omega}} = \lambda + \frac{\sigma_{\Omega\hat{\Omega}}}{\sigma_{\Omega}^2}\left(\mu_{\Omega} - \lambda\right). \qquad (14.61)$$

The Minimum-Risk Weight Line

The minimum-risk weight line is given by a linear function of the expected return μ_{Ω} on the portfolio, that is, it is of the form $\underline{w} = \underline{g} + \underline{h}\mu_{\Omega}$, where $\underline{g}$ and h are vectors of dimension l. To see this, note that we can write (14.27) more explicitly as

$$\underline{w} = \frac{\mu\Sigma^{-1}\underline{\mu}'\left((1^l)\Sigma^{-1}\right) - \mu_{\Omega}\left(1^l\right)\Sigma^{-1}\underline{\mu}'\left((1^l)\Sigma^{-1}\right) + \mu_{\Omega}\left(1^l\right)\Sigma^{-1}\left(1^l\right)'\left(\underline{\mu}\Sigma^{-1}\right) - \underline{\mu}\Sigma^{-1}\left(1^l\right)'\left(\underline{\mu}\Sigma^{-1}\right)}{\begin{vmatrix} \left(1^l\right)\Sigma^{-1}\left(1^l\right)' & \left(1^l\right)\Sigma^{-1}\underline{\mu}' \\ \underline{\mu}\Sigma^{-1}\left(1^l\right)' & \underline{\mu}\Sigma^{-1}\underline{\mu}' \end{vmatrix}}. \qquad (14.62)$$

That is,

$$\underline{w} = \frac{\mu\Sigma^{-1}\underline{\mu}'\left((1^l)\Sigma^{-1}\right) - \underline{\mu}\Sigma^{-1}\left(1^l\right)'\left(\underline{\mu}\Sigma^{-1}\right) + \mu_{\Omega}\left[\left(1^l\right)\Sigma^{-1}\left(1^l\right)'\left(\underline{\mu}\Sigma^{-1}\right) - \left((1^l)\Sigma^{-1}\right)\underline{\mu}'\left((1^l)\Sigma^{-1}\right)\right]}{\begin{vmatrix} \left(1^l\right)\Sigma^{-1}\left(1^l\right)' & \left(1^l\right)\Sigma^{-1}\underline{\mu}' \\ \underline{\mu}\Sigma^{-1}\left(1^l\right)' & \underline{\mu}\Sigma^{-1}\underline{\mu}' \end{vmatrix}}. \qquad (14.63)$$

Hence $\underline{w} = \underline{g} + \underline{h}\mu_{\Omega}$, where

$$\underline{g} = \frac{\mu\Sigma^{-1}\underline{\mu}'\left((1^l)\Sigma^{-1}\right) - \underline{\mu}\Sigma^{-1}\left(1^l\right)'\left(\underline{\mu}\Sigma^{-1}\right)}{\begin{vmatrix} \left(1^l\right)\Sigma^{-1}\left(1^l\right)' & \left(1^l\right)\Sigma^{-1}\underline{\mu}' \\ \underline{\mu}\Sigma^{-1}\left(1^l\right)' & \underline{\mu}\Sigma^{-1}\underline{\mu}' \end{vmatrix}}, \qquad (14.64)$$

$$\underline{h}=\frac{\left[\left(\left(1^{l}\right)\Sigma^{-1}\right)\left(1^{l}\right)'\left(\underline{\mu}\Sigma^{-1}\right)-\left(1^{l}\right)\Sigma^{-1}\underline{\mu}'\left(\left(1^{l}\right)\Sigma^{-1}\right)\right]}{\begin{vmatrix}\left(1^{l}\right)\Sigma^{-1}\left(1^{l}\right)' & \left(1^{l}\right)\Sigma^{-1}\underline{\mu}'\\ \underline{\mu}\Sigma^{-1}\left(1^{l}\right)' & \underline{\mu}\Sigma^{-1}\underline{\mu}'\end{vmatrix}}.$$

(14.65)

It follows from (14.64) and (14.65) that $\underline{g}$ and h are vectors of dimension l. This is true for all portfolios on the minimum-risk weight line.

Proof of the Two-Mutual-Fund Separation Theorem

(*i*) Let $\underline{w}\left(\hat{\Omega}\right)$ and $\underline{w}\left(\tilde{\Omega}\right)$ be the weight vectors associated with two distinct minimum-variance portfolios $\hat{\Omega}$ and $\tilde{\Omega}$, with mean returns $\mu\left(\underline{w}\left(\hat{\Omega}\right)\right)$ and $\mu\left(\underline{w}\left(\tilde{\Omega}\right)\right)$ respectively where $\mu\left(\underline{w}\left(\hat{\Omega}\right)\right)\neq\mu\left(\underline{w}\left(\tilde{\Omega}\right)\right)$. Let $\mu\left(\underline{w}\left(\dot{\Omega}\right)\right)$ be the mean return on a third minimum-variance portfolio $\dot{\Omega}$. Choose α satisfying the condition

$$\mu\left(\underline{w}\left(\dot{\Omega}\right)\right)=\alpha\mu\left(\underline{w}\left(\hat{\Omega}\right)\right)+\left(1-\alpha\right)\mu\left(\underline{w}\left(\tilde{\Omega}\right)\right),$$

(14.66)

that is, α is defined uniquely as

$$\alpha=\frac{\left(\mu\left(\underline{w}\left(\dot{\Omega}\right)\right)-\mu\left(\underline{w}\left(\tilde{\Omega}\right)\right)\right)}{\left(\mu\left(\underline{w}\left(\hat{\Omega}\right)\right)-\mu\left(\underline{w}\left(\tilde{\Omega}\right)\right)\right)}.$$

(14.67)

We now show that

$$\underline{w}\left(\dot{\Omega}\right)=\alpha\underline{w}\left(\hat{\Omega}\right)+\left(1-\alpha\right)\underline{w}\left(\tilde{\Omega}\right).$$

(14.68)

To demonstrate this, note from (14.27) that

$$\underline{w}\left(\dot{\Omega}\right)=\frac{\begin{vmatrix}\alpha+\left(1-\alpha\right) & \left(1^{l}\right)\Sigma^{-1}\underline{\mu}'\\ \alpha\mu_{\hat{\Omega}}+\left(1-\alpha\right)\mu_{\tilde{\Omega}} & \underline{\mu}\Sigma^{-1}\underline{\mu}'\end{vmatrix}\left(1^{l}\right)\Sigma^{-1}+\begin{vmatrix}\left(1^{l}\right)\Sigma^{-1}\left(1^{l}\right)' & \alpha+\left(1-\alpha\right)\\ \underline{\mu}\Sigma^{-1}\left(1^{l}\right)' & \alpha\mu_{\hat{\Omega}}+\left(1-\alpha\right)\mu_{\tilde{\Omega}}\end{vmatrix}\underline{\mu}\Sigma^{-1}}{\begin{vmatrix}\left(1^{l}\right)\Sigma^{-1}\left(1^{l}\right)' & \left(1^{l}\right)\Sigma^{-1}\underline{\mu}'\\ \underline{\mu}\Sigma^{-1}\left(1^{l}\right)' & \underline{\mu}\Sigma^{-1}\underline{\mu}'\end{vmatrix}}.$$

(14.69)

Using a property of determinants we can write the first term in the numerator of (14.69) as

$$\begin{vmatrix} \alpha & (1^l)\Sigma^{-1}\underline{\mu}' \\ \alpha\mu_{\hat{\Omega}} & \underline{\mu}\Sigma^{-1}\underline{\mu}' \end{vmatrix} (1^l)\Sigma^{-1} + \begin{vmatrix} (1-\alpha) & (1^l)\Sigma^{-1}\underline{\mu}' \\ (1-\alpha)\mu_{\tilde{\Omega}} & \underline{\mu}\Sigma^{-1}\underline{\mu}' \end{vmatrix} (1^l)\Sigma^{-1}$$

$$= \alpha \begin{vmatrix} 1 & (1^l)\Sigma^{-1}\underline{\mu}' \\ \mu_{\hat{\Omega}} & \underline{\mu}\Sigma^{-1}\underline{\mu}' \end{vmatrix} (1^l)\Sigma^{-1} + (1-\alpha) \begin{vmatrix} 1 & (1^l)\Sigma^{-1}\underline{\mu}' \\ \mu_{\tilde{\Omega}} & \underline{\mu}\Sigma^{-1}\underline{\mu}' \end{vmatrix} (1^l)\Sigma^{-1}. \quad (14.70)$$

Likewise, the second term of the numerator of (14.69) becomes

$$\alpha \begin{vmatrix} (1^l)\Sigma^{-1}(1^l)' & 1 \\ \underline{\mu}\Sigma^{-1}(1^l)' & \mu_{\hat{\Omega}} \end{vmatrix} \underline{\mu}\Sigma^{-1} + (1-\alpha) \begin{vmatrix} (1^l)\Sigma^{-1}(1^l)' & 1 \\ \underline{\mu}\Sigma^{-1}(1^l)' & \mu_{\tilde{\Omega}} \end{vmatrix} \underline{\mu}\Sigma^{-1}. \quad (14.71)$$

Substituting the expressions (14.70) and (14.71) for the respective terms in the numerator of (14.69) and simplifying the resulting expression we get

$$\underline{w}(\dot{\Omega}) = \alpha \frac{\begin{vmatrix} 1 & (1^l)\Sigma^{-1}\underline{\mu}' \\ \mu_{\hat{\Omega}} & \underline{\mu}\Sigma^{-1}\underline{\mu}' \end{vmatrix} (1^l)\Sigma^{-1} + \begin{vmatrix} (1^l)\Sigma^{-1}(1^l)' & 1 \\ \underline{\mu}\Sigma^{-1}(1^l)' & \mu_{\hat{\Omega}} \end{vmatrix} \underline{\mu}\Sigma^{-1}}{\begin{vmatrix} (1^l)\Sigma^{-1}(1^l)' & (1^l)\Sigma^{-1}\underline{\mu}' \\ \underline{\mu}\Sigma^{-1}(1^l)' & \underline{\mu}\Sigma^{-1}\underline{\mu}' \end{vmatrix}}$$

$$+ (1-\alpha) \frac{\begin{vmatrix} 1 & (1^l)\Sigma^{-1}\underline{\mu}' \\ \mu_{\tilde{\Omega}} & \underline{\mu}\Sigma^{-1}\underline{\mu}' \end{vmatrix} (1^l)\Sigma^{-1} + \begin{vmatrix} (1^l)\Sigma^{-1}(1^l)' & 1 \\ \underline{\mu}\Sigma^{-1}(1^l)' & \mu_{\tilde{\Omega}} \end{vmatrix} \underline{\mu}\Sigma^{-1}}{\begin{vmatrix} (1^l)\Sigma^{-1}(1^l)' & (1^l)\Sigma^{-1}\underline{\mu}' \\ \underline{\mu}\Sigma^{-1}(1^l)' & \underline{\mu}\Sigma^{-1}\underline{\mu}' \end{vmatrix}}, \quad (14.72)$$

which is $\alpha\underline{w}(\hat{\Omega}) + (1-\alpha)\underline{w}(\tilde{\Omega})$.

(ii) Conversely, suppose the weight vector $\underline{w}(\dot{\Omega})$ of the portfolio $\dot{\Omega}$ is a linear combination of the minimum-variance weight vectors $\underline{w}(\hat{\Omega})$ and $\underline{w}(\tilde{\Omega})$. Then
$$\underline{w}(\dot{\Omega}) = \alpha\underline{w}(\hat{\Omega}) + (1-\alpha)\underline{w}(\tilde{\Omega})$$

$$
= \alpha \frac{\begin{vmatrix} 1 & \dfrac{(1^l)\Sigma^{-1}\underline{\mu}'}{} \\ \mu_{\hat{\Omega}} & \underline{\mu}\Sigma^{-1}\underline{\mu}' \end{vmatrix}\left[(1^l)\Sigma^{-1} + \begin{vmatrix} (1^l)\Sigma^{-1}(1^l)' & 1 \\ \underline{\mu}\Sigma^{-1}(1^l)' & \mu_{\hat{\Omega}} \end{vmatrix}\underline{\mu}\Sigma^{-1}\right]}{\begin{vmatrix} (1^l)\Sigma^{-1}(1^l)' & (1^l)\Sigma^{-1}\underline{\mu}' \\ \underline{\mu}\Sigma^{-1}(1^l)' & \underline{\mu}\Sigma^{-1}\underline{\mu}' \end{vmatrix}}
$$

$$
+(1-\alpha)\frac{\begin{vmatrix} 1 & (1^l)\Sigma^{-1}\underline{\mu}' \\ \mu_{\tilde{\Omega}} & \underline{\mu}\Sigma^{-1}\underline{\mu}' \end{vmatrix}\left[(1^l)\Sigma^{-1} + \begin{vmatrix} (1^l)\Sigma^{-1}(1^l)' & 1 \\ \underline{\mu}\Sigma^{-1}(1^l)' & \mu_{\tilde{\Omega}} \end{vmatrix}\underline{\mu}\Sigma^{-1}\right]}{\begin{vmatrix} (1^l)\Sigma^{-1}(1^l)' & (1^l)\Sigma^{-1}\underline{\mu}' \\ \underline{\mu}\Sigma^{-1}(1^l)' & \underline{\mu}\Sigma^{-1}\underline{\mu}' \end{vmatrix}}
$$

$$
= \frac{\begin{vmatrix} \alpha+(1-\alpha) & (1^l)\Sigma^{-1}\underline{\mu}' \\ \alpha\mu_{\hat{\Omega}}+(1-\alpha)\mu_{\tilde{\Omega}} & \underline{\mu}\Sigma^{-1}\underline{\mu}' \end{vmatrix}\left[(1^l)\Sigma^{-1} + \begin{vmatrix} (1^l)\Sigma^{-1}(1^l)' & \alpha+(1-\alpha) \\ \underline{\mu}\Sigma^{-1}(1^l)' & \alpha\mu_{\hat{\Omega}}+(1-\alpha)\mu_{\tilde{\Omega}} \end{vmatrix}\underline{\mu}\Sigma^{-1}\right]}{\begin{vmatrix} (1^l)\Sigma^{-1}(1^l)' & (1^l)\Sigma^{-1}\underline{\mu}' \\ \underline{\mu}\Sigma^{-1}(1^l)' & \underline{\mu}\Sigma^{-1}\underline{\mu}' \end{vmatrix}}.
$$

$$(14.73)$$

By (14.27) we can claim that $\underline{w}(\dot{\Omega})$ is the weight vector of the minimum-variance portfolio with expected return $\alpha\mu\big(\underline{w}(\hat{\Omega})\big)+(1-\alpha)\mu\big(\underline{w}(\tilde{\Omega})\big)$.

(iii) This is proved as in (ii) noting that if $\mu\big(\underline{w}(\hat{\Omega})\big) \leq \mu\big(\underline{w}(\tilde{\Omega})\big)$, then for $0 \leq \alpha \leq 1$, $\mu\big(\underline{w}(\hat{\Omega})\big) \leq \alpha\mu\big(\underline{w}(\hat{\Omega})\big)+(1-\alpha)\mu\big(\underline{w}(\tilde{\Omega})\big) \leq \mu\big(\underline{w}(\tilde{\Omega})\big)$.

BIBLIOGRAPHICAL NOTES

Mean-variance analysis, an issue of risk management in a portfolio of assets where the variance is taken as an indicator of risk, was founded by Markowitz (1952). It is explored quite nicely in Huang and Litzenberger (1988), Capinski and Zastawniak (2003) and Roman (2004). We follow mostly Constantinides and Malliaris (1995) in presenting the two-fund separation theorem. The capital asset pricing model was developed by Sharpe (1964) and Linter (1965). Capinski and Zastawniak (2003) and Roman (2004) are two good references for this model.

EXERCISES

1. Each of the following statements is either true or false. If the statement is true prove it. If it is false, give a counter-example or justify your answer by logical reasoning.

   (a) An important characteristic of the CAPM is that the beta of an asset is always non-negative.

   (b) In a risk-minimizing portfolio with two risky assets, the inequality $\frac{\sigma_1}{\sigma_2} < \rho_{12} \leq 1$ is necessary and sufficient for the short selling of asset 2—where $\sigma_1 \leq \sigma_2$, with σ_i being the standard deviation of the return on asset i, and ρ_{12} is the correlation coefficient between the returns on the two assets.

   (c) The capital market line is upward sloping because the expected market return is assumed to be higher than the risk-free return.

   (d) The beta of a portfolio, consisting of k assets with weight shares w_1, w_2, ..., w_k, is given by $\sum_{i=1}^{k} w_i \beta_{im}$, where β_{im} is the beta of asset i.

   (e) In a risk-minimizing portfolio with two risky assets there is no short selling if the assets are perfectly negatively correlated.

2. Clearly distinguish between the following.

   (a) the security market line and the capital market line,

   (b) systemic risk and unsystematic risk.

3. Show the reward–risk diagram in the $(\sigma - \mu)$ plane when the two risky assets are uncorrelated.

4. Demonstrate analytically that the market portfolio is the unique point on the efficient frontier that maximizes the slope of the line joining risk-free return and risky portfolios in the Markowitz bullet.

5. Consider a portfolio with three risky assets a, b and c whose expected returns are respectively 2, 3 and 5. The three variances of the returns on the assets are respectively 1, 2 and 5. The correlation coefficients between the returns on pairs of assets (a, b) and (b, c) are respectively $\frac{1}{\sqrt{2}}$ and $\frac{1}{\sqrt{10}}$. Determine the expected return on the portfolio for which risk is minimized. Is short selling necessary in this case?

6. Determine the beta of a market portfolio analytically.

7. Clearly state the assumptions of the capital asset pricing model. Evaluate them critically.

8. Define the security market line. Explain its usefulness.

9. Suppose that a stock has an expected one-year return of 10. The market has an expected annual return of 15 and the risk-free return is 3. Calculate beta for this stock. Interpret your result.

10. How is the Sharpe ratio related to the CAPM? Discuss analytically.

CHAPTER 15

Stochastic Dominance

15.1 INTRODUCTION

In financial economics we are often confronted with the necessity of ordering distributions in terms of a decision-maker's preference, where the distributions considered are usually those of random returns on various financial assets. In other words, we need to make a prediction about a decision-maker's preference between given pairs of uncertain alternatives, without having any knowledge about the decision-maker's utility function. (All utility functions considered in this chapter are von Neumann–Morgenstern utility functions. See Chapter 3, for a full discussion.) Several approaches to this and related issues have appeared in the literature. One of the most important approaches of this type involves a comparison of means and variances of the distributions under consideration (see Tobin 1958, 1965; Markowitz 1959). If the expected utility function is of quadratic type—for instance, if it is of the type mean minus a positive multiple of variance—then a decision-maker, who is a risk-averter, will unambiguously prefer the risky asset that has lower variance, given that the assets under consideration have equal mean or prefer the one with higher mean when the variances of the assets are the same.

But a decision-maker's preferences need not be presented by a quadratic utility function. There are many other forms of utility functions that can be used for ranking risky assets. However, there is no guarantee that the ranking of two different assets by two different utility functions will be the same. Therefore, a natural question here is: how do you rank alternative risky assets when the utility function is unknown?

In this chapter, we show that the distributions of the rate of return on assets can be ordered using stochastic dominance relations for large classes of utility functions. In the next section, it is shown that in the absence of any restriction on the utility function (except for non-decreasingness), first order dominance implies preferences for higher expected utility and that the converse is also true. In Section 15.3, we show that a similar relationship holds between second order stochastic dominance and all non-decreasing and concave utility functions. Section 15.4 clearly demonstrates the role of the well-known Lorenz and generalized Lorenz orderings for ranking risky assets and their relationships with stochastic dominance. Finally, in Section 15.5, we show, how the results developed in the earlier sections, can be employed to rank portfolios under quite general assumptions. An Appendix presents the proofs of all the theorems presented in different sections of the chapter.

15.2 FIRST ORDER STOCHASTIC DOMINANCE

In order to examine whether a stochastic dominance relation holds between two distributions, it is necessary to characterize the distributions by their cumulative distribution functions (distribution functions, for short).

Let $F: [l, u] \to [0, 1]$ be the cumulative distribution function of the rate of return (return, for short) of the asset under consideration, where $[l, u]$ is a non-degenerate bounded interval in the set of real numbers $\Re$ (see Chapter 14). Unless specified, we will assume throughout the chapter that the returns on an asset are uncertain so that the assets involve some risk. Then $F(v)$ is the cumulative probability that the rate of return on the asset (or payoff from the asset) does not exceed the level v. F is non-decreasing, continuously differentiable, $F(l) = 0$ and $F(u) = 1$. Often F is referred to as the asset distribution function.

Let the assets A and B be represented respectively by the distribution functions F_A and F_B. We say that F_A first order stochastic dominates F_B, which is denoted by $F_A \geq_{FSD} F_B$, if and only if

$$F_A(z) \leq F_B(z) \tag{15.1}$$

for all $z \in [l, u]$. That is, the probability of asset A's return exceeding any given level is not lower than that of asset B's return exceeding the same level. Then our intuition suggests that any individual with a non-decreasing utility function will prefer asset A to asset B. It turns out the converse is true as well (see Hadar and Russell 1967). The above definition is of weak dominance. For strong dominance, it is necessary that the weak inequality $\leq$ should be a strict inequality $<$ for some values of the argument z. Since no statistical test can make a clear distinction between weak and strong inequalities, in empirical investigations the distinction is not of interest (Davidson 2008). (For further discussion, see Levy 2006; Shaked and Shanthikumar 2006; Chakravarty and Zoli 2012.) Throughout this chapter, we will restrict our attention to the weak form of dominance rules. We will not make

Figure 15.1 First Order Stochastic Dominance

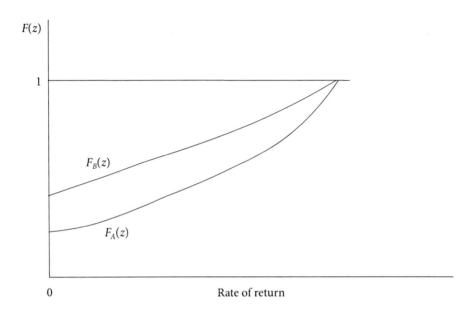

any distinction between the relations $F_A \geq_{FSD} F_B$ and $A \geq_{FSD} B$, and similar notation will be assumed for higher dominances as well.

Figure 15.1 gives a graphical representation of the relation (15.1). For simplicity, we assume in Figures 15.1 and 15.2 that $l = 0$. We observe that for any z, the cumulative probability that the return on asset A is less than or equal to z is not higher than that for asset B. Alternatively, the cumulative probability that the return on asset A is greater than z is at least as large as that for asset B. In order to relate stochastic dominances with utility ranking of assets, we assume that the real valued utility function U, defined on $[l, u]$, that is, $U : [l, u] \rightarrow \mathfrak{R}$, is thrice differentiable. The first, second and third order derivatives of U are denoted by U', U'' and U''' respectively.

The following theorem identifies the class of utility functions consistent with the ordering $\geq_{FSD}$.

Theorem 15.1: Let F_A, $F_B : [l, u] \rightarrow [0, 1]$, be the distribution functions of the assets A and B respectively. Then the following conditions are equivalent:

(i) $F_A \geq_{FSD} F_B$, that is, F_A first order stochastic dominates F_B.

(ii) $\int_l^u U(z)dF_A(z) \geq \int_l^u U(z)dF_B(z)$ for all utility functions $U : [l, u] \rightarrow \mathfrak{R}$ that are non-decreasing, that is, expected utility of A is not less than that of B for all non-decreasing utility functions.

Proof: See Appendix.

What this theorem says is the following. Of two assets A and B, with distribution F_A and F_B respectively, if F_A first order stochastic dominates F_B, then any decision-maker who has a non-decreasing utility function will prefer A to B. In other words, first order stochastic dominance of F_A over F_B implies the requirement that expected utility from A is at least as large as that from B for all utility functions with non-negative marginal utilities. This holds irrespective of the form of the utility function. Thus, in order to conclude that A is not worse than B, the decision-maker need not calculate the expected utilities of the distributions F_A and F_B. The converse is also true. That is, if asset A has at least as large as expected utility as asset B for all non-decreasing utility functions, then F_A first order stochastic dominates F_B. Condition (i) in Theorem 15.1 can be easily checked graphically. Since the class of non-decreasing utility functions is rather large, condition (ii) cannot be checked easily. However, because of its equivalence with condition (i), we can say that expected utility dominance of A over B holds for all utility functions with non-negative marginal utilities whenever (i) holds. An interesting example of a utility function of this type is $U(z) = z^\theta, \theta > 0$.

Example 15.1: Consider the following distribution functions of the assets I and II respectively:

$$F_I(v) = \begin{cases} 1 - e^{-v}, v \geq 0, \\ 0, v < 0. \end{cases}, F_{II}(v) = \begin{cases} 1 - e^{-2v}, v \geq 0, \\ 0, v < 0. \end{cases}$$

It is easy to see that $F_I(v) < F_{II}(v)$ for all finite positive values of v and $F_I(0) = F_{II}(0) = 0$. Hence F_I first order stochastic dominates F_{II}.

15.3 SECOND ORDER STOCHASTIC DOMINANCE

According to first order stochastic dominance, the main distinguishing characteristic between two uncertain assets is non-desirability for a lower expected utility. But this does not tell us anything about the decision-maker's attitude towards risks. The decision-maker may prefer more to less and at the same time can be a risk-averter, risk-lover or risk-neutral person (see Chapter 3). For instance, for two assets A and B if $F_A \geq_{FSD} F_B$ holds, then for the three utility functions $U_1(z) = \ln(z), z > 0, U_2(z) = z$ and $U_3(z) = z^2$, asset A does not generate lower expected utility than asset B, where "ln" represents natural logarithm. But while the first two utility functions represent preferences of two individuals who are risk averse and risk neutral respectively, the third shows that the concerned person is a risk-lover. Thus, first order stochastic dominance is unable to take care of this feature of an individual's preference.

This brings us to the concept of second order stochastic dominance. Let F_A and F_B be the distribution functions of the risky assets A and B respectively. We say that F_A second order stochastic dominates F_B, which is denoted by $F_A \geq_{SSD} F_B$, if and only if

$$\int_{l}^{z} F_A(v)\,dv \le \int_{l}^{z} F_B(v)\,dv \qquad (15.2)$$

for all $z\in[l, u]$. That is, for any $z\in[l, u]$ the area under the curve of F_A is not higher than that under the curve of F_B. In Figure 15.2 we note that up to any level of return z the area under the curve of F_B is higher than the corresponding area under the curve of F_A. Hence $F_A \ge_{SSD} F_B$ holds.

Figure 15.2   Second Order Stochastic Dominance

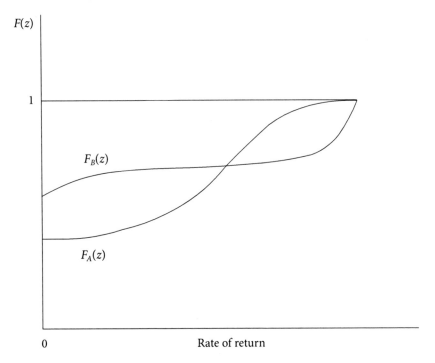

From Figure 15.1 it follows that $\ge_{FSD}$ implies $\ge_{SSD}$. But Figure 15.2 clearly indicates that $\ge_{SSD}$ does not imply $\ge_{FSD}$. That is, first order stochastic dominance is a sufficient but not a necessary condition for second order stochastic dominance. The reason behind this is that in the case of the latter, we need area-wise dominance starting from the initial value of the return and hence one or more intersections between the curves of the distribution functions are allowable. For the former to hold, we need point-wise dominance and as a result no intersection between the curves is permissible.

The following theorem shows that the ordering $\ge_{SSD}$ is consistent with expected utility dominance, where the utility functions have non-negative marginals and are weakly risk averse, that is, the utility functions are non-decreasing and concave.

Theorem 15.2: Let F_A, F_B : $[l, u] \rightarrow [0, 1]$ be the distribution functions of the assets A and B respectively. Then the following conditions are equivalent:

(i) $F_A \geq_{SSD} F_B$, that is, F_A second order stochastic dominates F_B.

(ii) $\int_l^u U(z) dF_A(z) \geq \int_l^u U(z) dF_B(z)$ for all utility functions $U : [l, u] \rightarrow \Re$ that are non-decreasing and concave; that is, expected utility of A is not less than that of B for all non-decreasing and concave utility functions.

Proof: See Appendix.

Theorem 15.2 says that if F_A second order stochastic dominates F_B, then F_A will be preferred to F_B by all individuals whose utility functions are non-decreasing and concave. Furthermore, the converse is also true. That is, if expected utility from A is not less than that from B for all non-decreasing, concave utility functions, then F_A second order stochastic dominates F_B. Thus, whenever $F_A \geq_{SSD} F_B$ holds, we can be sure that all weakly risk-averse individuals, who do not prefer less to more, will opt for the asset characterized by the distribution function F_A. An interesting example of a utility function of this type is $U(z) = z^\theta, 0 < \theta \leq 1$.

Example 15.2: Consider the following distribution functions of the assets III and IV respectively:

$$F_{III}(v) = \begin{cases} 0 & ,0 \leq v < 1, \\ (v-1), & 1 \leq v < 2, \\ 1 & ,2 \leq v \leq 3. \end{cases} \qquad F_{IV}(v) = \frac{v}{3}, 0 \leq v \leq 3.$$

It is easy to check that at any value of v area under the curve of F_{III} is not higher than that under the curve of F_{IV}. Hence F_{III} second order stochastic dominates F_{IV}.

We can also define higher orders of stochastic dominance. For this purpose we define the repeated integrals of the cumulative distribution functions:

$$F^j(z) = \int_l^z F^{j-1}(v) dv \qquad (15.3)$$

for all $z \in [l, u]$, where $j \leq 2$ is an integer and $F^1(z) = F(z)$.

Given two distribution functions F_A and F_B, defined on the same domain $[l, u]$ of the rate of return on the assets A and B respectively, we say that F_A dominates F_B by the jth degree/order stochastic dominance criterion if and only if

$$F_A^j(z) \leq F_B^j(z) \qquad (15.4)$$

for all $z \in [l, u]$, where $j \geq 1$ is an integer. Dominance of order j implies dominance of all orders higher than j. The particular cases $j = 1$ and 2 correspond respectively to the first and second order stochastic dominances. The third degree stochastic dominance is defined if we assume that $j = 3$ (see Whitmore 1970). Third order stochastic dominance of F_A over F_B requires at least as large expected utility value under F_A than that under F_B, where the marginal utility function is non-negative, non-decreasing and convex (that is, $U' \geq 0$, $U'' \leq 0$ and $U''' \geq 0$). Convexity of marginal utility function is a necessary requirement for the Arrow–Pratt absolute measure of risk aversion to be non-increasing (see Chapter 3). That is, the asset is not an inferior good. In other words, its demand does not decrease or remains invariant when the individual's wealth increases.

15.4 LORENZ ORDERING, GENERALIZED LORENZ ORDERING AND STOCHASTIC DOMINANCE

The Lorenz curve is a very useful tool for welfare comparisons of income distributions. For any given income distribution, its Lorenz curve represents the share of the total income enjoyed by the bottom $t(0 \leq t \leq 1)$ proportion of the population. On the other hand, the generalized Lorenz curve of an income distribution shows the total income, divided by the population size, possessed by the lowest $t(0 \leq t \leq 1)$ proportion of the population. If all the individuals in the society enjoy the same level of income, the Lorenz curve coincides with the "line of equality"; otherwise it falls below this line. Consequently, the area enclosed between the line of equality and the Lorenz curve can be taken as an indicator of inequality. However, in the present context we will employ the Lorenz and generalized Lorenz curves of assets for ranking purpose.

The inverse distribution function $F^{-1} : [0, 1] \rightarrow [l, u]$ corresponding to the distribution function $F : [l, u] \rightarrow [0, 1]$ of the asset under consideration is defined as

$$F^{-1}(q) = \inf \{v : F(v) \geq q\} \text{ for all } q \in [0, 1]. \tag{15.5}$$

If F is increasing, then for a given value of $F(z)$, we can always find a unique value of z. But for a non-decreasing F, for instance, in the case of a discrete distribution, z may not exist. Equation (15.5) ensures the existence of a value of z for a non-decreasing distribution function also. For any q in the range of F, $F^{-1}(q)$ is the minimum value of the return on the asset with the distribution function F such that $F^{-1}(q) \geq v$. Since F is a non-decreasing function, F^{-1} is also a non-decreasing function (see Gastwirth 1971).

The Lorenz curve associated with the distribution of the rate of return on an asset having the distribution function F and the mean $\Xi(F) = \int_l^u v \, dF(v)$ is defined as

$$LC(F,p) = \frac{1}{\Xi(F)} \int_0^p F^{-1}(q) \, dq, \tag{15.6}$$

where $0 \le p \le 1$. For any given rate of return distribution function F, its Lorenz curve $LC(F, p)$ represents the cumulative proportions of the returns against the cumulative probabilities $p(0 \le p \le 1)$ starting from the bottom. This definition of the Lorenz curve is quite general in the sense that it applies to both discrete and continuous distributions. In Figure 15.3, we show Lorenz curves of some distributions of rate of return.

Figure 15.3   Lorenz Curve and Lorenz Dominance

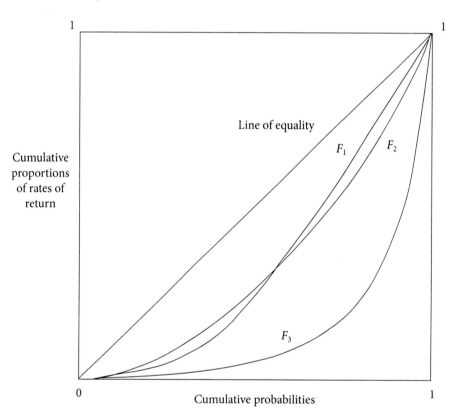

Of two distribution functions F_A and F_B of the rate of return on the assets A and B respectively, we say that F_A Lorenz dominates F_B, which is denoted by $F_A \ge_{LC} F_B$ if and only if

$$LC(F_A, p) \ge LC(F_B, p) \tag{15.7}$$

for all $p \in [0, 1]$. That is, the Lorenz curve of F_A is nowhere below that of F_B. In such a case we also say that F_A is Lorenz superior to F_B. Note that the Lorenz ordering

$\geq_{LC}$ is not complete, that is, if the Lorenz curves of two distributions cross, then neither Lorenz dominates the other. In Figure 15.3, we have neither $F_1 \geq_{LC} F_2$ nor $F_2 \geq_{LC} F_1$, but both $F_1 \geq_{LC} F_3$ and $F_2 \geq_{LC} F_3$ hold. However, the relation is transitive. That is, for any three distribution functions F_4, F_5 and F_6, defined on the same domain, if $F_4 \geq_{LC} F_5$ and $F_5 \geq_{LC} F_6$ hold, then $F_4 \geq_{LC} F_6$ must hold.

The following theorem gives a remarkable consequence of the relation $\geq_{LC}$.

Theorem 15.3: Let F_A, $F_B : [l, u] \rightarrow [0, 1]$ be the distribution functions of the rate of return on the assets A and B respectively, with the same mean. Then the following conditions are equivalent:

(i) $F_A \geq_{LC} F_B$, that is, F_A Lorenz dominates F_B.

(ii) $\int_l^u U(z)dF_A(z) \geq \int_l^u U(z)dF_B(z)$ for all utility functions $U : [l, u] \rightarrow \Re$ that are concave.

This theorem has been proved by Hardy, Littlewood and Polya (1934) and re-interpreted by Atkinson (1970) in the context of welfare ranking of income distributions. What it says is the following: if two assets A and B, with distribution functions F_A and F_B respectively, have the same mean and F_A is Lorenz superior to F_B, then F_A is preferred to F_B by all weakly risk-averse individuals. The converse is also true. This is also same as the condition that under a fixed mean, F_A second order stochastically dominates F_B. However, if the two Lorenz curves cross, then two different weakly risk-averse individuals may have different directional preferences between F_A and F_B. That is, in the case of crossing curves, we may get two weakly risk-averse individuals with different utility functions, say $\hat{U}$ and $\bar{U}$ respectively, such that $\Xi\left(\hat{U}(F_A)\right) \geq \Xi\left(\hat{U}(F_B)\right)$ but $\Xi\left(\bar{U}(F_B)\right) > \Xi\left(\bar{U}(F_A)\right)$, where $\Xi\left(\hat{U}(F_A)\right) = \int_l^u \hat{U}(z)dF_A(z)$ and so on. We omit the proof of this theorem and prove the next theorem, which is more general.

The scope of Theorem 15.3 is quite limited in the sense that it cannot rank rate of return distributions with unequal means. In practice, we often face assets with different means. In such a case the relevant criterion is based on the generalized Lorenz curve (Shorrocks 1973). The generalized Lorenz curve $GL(F, p)$ of the rate of return distribution F is produced by scaling up its Lorenz curve $L(F, p)$ by the mean, so that

$$GL(F,p) = \Xi(F)L(F,p) = \int_0^p F^{-1}(q)dq, \qquad (15.8)$$

where $0 \leq p \leq 1$. Thus, $GL(F, p)$ shows the cumulative returns corresponding to the bottom cumulative probabilities $p(0 \leq p \leq 1)$ (see Figure 15.4).

Given the inverse distribution functions F_A^{-1} and F_B^{-1} associated with the

Figure 15.4   Generalized Lorenz Curve and Generalized Lorenz Dominance

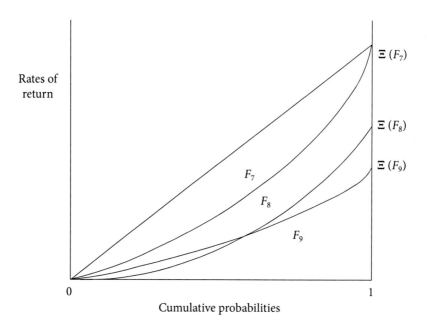

distribution functions F_A and F_B, defined on the same domain, we say that F_A dominates F_B by the generalized Lorenz criterion, or F_A is generalized Lorenz superior to F_B, what we write $F_A \geq_{GL} F_B$ if and only if

$$\int_0^p \left(F_A^{-1}(q) - F_B^{-1}(q)\right) dq \geq 0 \qquad (15.9)$$

for all $p \in [0, 1]$. This means that the generalized Lorenz curve of F_A is nowhere below that of F_B. Note that the higher curve has higher average return. Thus, in Figure 15.4 for the distribution functions F_7, F_8 and F_9, defined on the common domain, we have both $F_7 \geq_{GL} F_8$ and $F_7 \geq_{GL} F_9$, but neither $F_9 \geq_{GL} F_8$ nor $F_8 \geq_{GL} F_9$ is true. Thus, the generalized Lorenz ordering $\geq_{GL}$ is also an incomplete relation.

Theorem 15.4: Let the distribution functions F_A and F_B of the rate of return on the assets A and B respectively be defined on the same domain $[l, u]$. Then the following conditions are equivalent:

(i) $F_A \geq_{GL} F_B$, that is, F_A generalized Lorenz dominates F_B.

(ii) $F_A \geq_{SSD} F_B$, that is, F_A second order stochastic dominates F_B.

(iii) $\int_l^u U \, dF_A(z) \geq \int_l^u U \, dF_B(z)$ for all utility functions $U: [l, u] \to \Re$ that are non-decreasing and concave.

Proof: See Appendix

Theorem 15.4 says that F_A is generalized Lorenz superior to F_B if and only if F_A dominates F_B by the criterion of second order stochastic dominance, which in turn is equivalent to the requirement that all weakly risk-averse individuals who do not prefer less to more will have preference for F_A over F_B. If the mean returns of the two assets are identical, then Theorems 15.3 and 15.4 coincide and in this case we only need concavity of the utility function. (For further discussion on the Lorenz and generalized Lorenz orderings, see Kakwani 1980, Chakravarty 1990 and 2009, and Foster and Sen 1997.)

15.5 RANKING PORTFOLIOS

The objective of this section is to rank portfolios in terms of expected return using the generalized Lorenz curve. Consider a portfolio Λ with n assets and let r_i^Λ be the return on asset i in the portfolio Λ. Return on each asset is assumed to be a random variable. Let $\Xi(\Lambda) = \left(\Xi(r_1^\Lambda), \Xi(r_2^\Lambda), ..., \Xi(r_n^\Lambda) \right)$ be the vector of expected returns, where $\Xi(r_i^\Lambda)$ is the expected return on asset i. It is assumed throughout the section that the elements of vectors of the type $\Xi(\Lambda)$ are non-decreasingly ordered. Then using the definition given in (15.8), we can construct the generalized Lorenz curve of $\Xi(\Lambda)$. Alternatively, the generalized Lorenz curve can be constructed by combining the ordinates at consecutive cumulative probabilities linearly as follows. Given that the elements of $\Xi(\Lambda)$'s are non-decreasingly ordered, the ordinate of the generalized Lorenz curve of $\Xi(\Lambda)$, at the cumulative proportion j/n of the number of assets, is given by $GL\left(\Xi(\Lambda), j/n \right) = \sum_{i=1}^{j} \Xi(r_i^\Lambda) \Big/ n$.

The generalized Lorenz curve of Λ, $GL\left(\Xi(\Lambda), p \right), p \in [0,1]$, is then completed by setting $GL\left(\Xi(\Lambda), 0 \right) = 0$ and defining

$$GL\left(\Xi(\Lambda), \frac{i+\tau}{n} \right) = (1-\tau) GL\left(\Xi(\Lambda), \frac{i}{n} \right) + \tau GL\left(\Xi(\Lambda), \frac{i+1}{n} \right), \quad (15.10)$$

where $1 \le i \le (n-1)$ and $0 \le \tau \le 1$. The convex combination of $GL\left(\Xi(\Lambda), i/n \right)$ and $GL\left(\Xi(\Lambda), (i+1)/n \right)$ considered in (15.10) defines the segments of the curve between the consecutive proportions i/n and $(i+1)/n$ in a continuous manner. The generalized Lorenz curve of $\Xi(\Lambda)$ represents the normalized expected rates of return $GL\left(\Xi(\Lambda), j/n \right) = \sum_{i=1}^{j} \Xi(r_i^\Lambda) \Big/ n$ against the cumulative proportions of number of assets j/n, $1 \le j \le n$.

Now, given two portfolios Π and Ω with n and m assets respectively, we may consider the problem of ranking the corresponding expected return vectors $\Xi(\Lambda)=\left(\Xi\left(r_1^\Lambda\right),\Xi\left(r_2^\Lambda\right),...,\Xi\left(r_n^\Lambda\right)\right)$ and $\Xi(\Omega)=\left(\Xi\left(r_1^\Omega\right),\Xi\left(r_2^\Omega\right),...,\Xi\left(r_m^\Omega\right)\right)$. For $\Xi(\Lambda)\geq_{GL}\Xi(\Omega)$ to hold, it is necessary and sufficient that the average utility of $\Xi(\Pi)$ is not less than that of $\Xi(\Omega)$ for all utility functions that are non-decreasing and concave, that is, $\left(\sum_{i=1}^{n}U\left(\Xi\left(r_i^\Lambda\right)\right)/n\right)\geq\left(\sum_{i=1}^{m}U\left(\Xi\left(r^\Omega{}_i\right)\right)/m\right)$, where U is non-decreasing and concave. Note that we do not need equality of numbers of assets across portfolios for this general result to hold.

For the discrete distribution $\Xi(\Pi)$ we can approximate $F^j(z)$ by

$$F^j(z)=\frac{1}{(j-1)!n}\sum_{i=1}^{n(z,\Lambda)}\left(z-\Xi\left(r_i^\Lambda\right)\right)^{j-1} \qquad (15.11)$$

for all $z\in[l,u]$, where $n(z,\Lambda)$ is the number of expected returns less than or equal to $z\in[l,u]$ in the distribution Λ and $j\geq 2$ is an integer. For $j=1$, $F^j(z)=F(z)$, which is equal to the cumulative proportion of the number of assets with expected return not exceeding z. This expression enables us to talk about the stochastic dominance of different degrees of one vector of expected returns over another.

We now take an example to illustrate the ordering $\geq_{GL}$.

Example 15.3: Let $\hat{\Lambda}$ and $\hat{\Omega}$ be two portfolios with the number of assets being 3 and 4 respectively, where $\Xi\left(\hat{\Lambda}\right)=(2,7,9)$ and $\Xi\left(\hat{\Omega}\right)=(1,2,4,7)$. Then

$$GL\left(\Xi\left(\hat{\Lambda}\right),p\right)=\begin{cases}2p,\ 0\leq p<\dfrac{1}{3},\\[2mm]\dfrac{2}{3}+7\left(p-\dfrac{1}{3}\right),\ \dfrac{1}{3}\leq p<\dfrac{2}{3},\\[2mm]\dfrac{2}{3}+\dfrac{7}{3}+9\left(p-\dfrac{2}{3}\right),\ \dfrac{2}{3}\leq p\leq 1.\end{cases}$$

Since $GL\left(\Xi\left(\hat{\Lambda}\right),p\right)$ is a plot of the normalized cumulative expected returns under $\hat{\Lambda}$ against the cumulative proportions of the number of assets, the first segment of the curve is obtained by integrating $F^{-1}(q)=2$ over $[0,p]$, where $p<(1/3)$. The value of the curve at $p=(1/3)$ is obtained by taking the limit of the integral $\int_0^p 2dq$ as $p\to(1/3)$. Given that we already determined the segment of the curve up to the cumulative proportion $(1/3)$ of the number of assets, the next segment is obtained by integrating $F^{-1}(q)=7$ over $[1/3,p]$, where $p<(2/3)$, and then adding the term $(2/3)$, the value of $GL\left(\Xi\left(\hat{\Lambda}\right),p\right)$, at $p=(1/3)$. The last segment can be determined in a similar manner. Note continuity of the curve at $p = (1/3)$, $(2/3)$.

By a similar argument, we have:

$$GL\left(\Xi\left(\hat{\Omega}\right), p\right) = \begin{cases} p, \; 0 \le p < \dfrac{1}{4}, \\[2mm] \dfrac{1}{4} + 2\left(p - \dfrac{1}{4}\right), \; \dfrac{1}{4} \le p < \dfrac{2}{4}, \\[2mm] \dfrac{1}{4} + \dfrac{2}{4} + 4\left(p - \dfrac{2}{4}\right), \; \dfrac{2}{4} \le p < \dfrac{3}{4}, \\[2mm] \dfrac{1}{4} + \dfrac{2}{4} + \dfrac{4}{4} + 7\left(p - \dfrac{3}{4}\right), \; \dfrac{3}{4} \le p \le 1. \end{cases}$$

It can be easily seen that $\Xi\left(\hat{\Lambda}\right) \ge_{GL} \Xi\left(\hat{\Omega}\right)$. Thus, the average utility value of $\Xi\left(\hat{\Lambda}\right)$ is not less than that of $\Xi\left(\hat{\Omega}\right)$ for all non-decreasing and concave utility functions.

Applied Example 15.1: Porter and Gaumnitz (1972) used monthly rate of return on 140 stocks for the period 1960–63 to generate a mean-variance efficient set of portfolios (see Chapter 14). The stocks were chosen from the 200 largest firms (measured by total assets or total sales) listed in the Fortune 500 as of December 31, 1964. Six portfolios were selected on an *a priori* basis. In order to illustrate the stochastic dominance criteria the same data set was used to develop necessary frequency distributions. Observed returns were classified into frequency intervals of equal length using computationally efficient procedures. It was verified that the number and length of the intervals did not influence the results. Out of six portfolios, the first order rule retained only three portfolios. Out of these three, one was eliminated by the second and third order principles. The example also illustrates incompletes of the stochastic dominance desiderata.

APPENDIX

Proof of Theorem 15.1: $(i) \Rightarrow (ii)$: Letting $\int_l^u U(z) dF_A(z) = \Xi\left(U(F_A)\right)$ and $\int_l^u U(z) dF_B(z) = \Xi\left(U(F_B)\right)$, we have $\Xi\left(U(F_A)\right) - \Xi\left(U(F_B)\right) = \int_l^u U(z) d\left(F_A(z) - F_B(z)\right)$. Using integration by parts, where we treat U as the first function and $(F_A(z) - F_B(z))$ as the second function, we get $\int_l^u U(z) dF_A(z) - \int_l^u U(z) dF_B(z)$ $= U(z)\left(F_A(z) - F_B(z)\right)\Big|_l^u - \int_l^u U'(z)\left(F_A(z) - F_B(z)\right) dz$. Since $F_A(l) = F_B(l) = 0$ and

$F_A(u) = F_B(u) = 1$, $\Xi\left(U(F_A)\right) - \Xi\left(U(F_B)\right) = -\int_l^u U'(z)\left(F_A(z) - F_B(z)\right)dz \geq 0$, where

the last inequality follows from the hypothesis $F_A \geq_{FSD} F_B$ (see inequality 15.1) and the fact that $U'(z) \geq 0$.

(ii) $\Rightarrow$ (i): The proof is by contradiction. It is shown that if (i) does not hold, then there exists a utility function U with non-negative marginal such that $\int_l^u U(z)dF_A(z) < \int_l^u U(z)dF_B(z)$. For this purpose assume that there exists $l < \hat{z} < u$ such that $F_A(z) \geq F_B(z)$ for all $l \leq z \leq \hat{z}$, with $>$ for some $l \leq z \leq \hat{z}$, and $F_A(z) \leq F_B(z)$ for all $z \geq \hat{z}$.

Now, consider the utility function

$$\hat{U}(z) = \begin{cases} \dfrac{(b-a)\hat{z}}{2} + az + \dfrac{(b-a)z^2}{2\hat{z}}, & l \leq z \leq \hat{z}, \\ bz & , z \geq \hat{z}, \end{cases} \tag{15.12}$$

where $0 < b < a$ are arbitrary constants. Then

$$\hat{U}'(z) = \begin{cases} a + \dfrac{(b-a)z}{\hat{z}}, & l \leq z \leq \hat{z}, \\ b & , z \geq \hat{z}. \end{cases}$$

Note positivity of the marginal utility function $\hat{U}$.

For the utility function given by (15.12), we have

$$\int_l^u \hat{U}(z)dF_A(z) - \int_l^u \hat{U}(z)dF_B(z) = -\int_l^u \hat{U}'(z)\left(F_A(z) - F_B(z)\right)dz$$

$$-\int_l^{\hat{z}}\left[\left(a(\hat{z}-z)+bz\right)/\hat{z}\right]\left(F_A(z)-F_B(z)\right)dz - \int_{\hat{z}}^u b\left(F_A(z) - F_B(z)\right)dz. \tag{15.13}$$

By our assumption, the first term of the above expression is negative and the second term is non-negative. The function $\left[\left(a(\hat{z}-z)+bz\right)/\hat{z}\right]$ is positive valued and an increasing function of the parameter a over the interval $[l,\hat{z}]$. Therefore, the magnitude of the first term in (15.13) can be made arbitrarily negatively large by choosing the free parameter a sufficiently high. This in turn will make the sign of the expression negative. That is, there exists a non-decreasing utility function $\hat{U}$ such that $\int_l^u \hat{U}(z)dF_A(z) - \int_l^u \hat{U}(z)dF_B(z) < 0$. Hence not (i) implies not (ii). This completes the proof of the theorem.

Proof of Theorem 15.2: (i) $\Rightarrow$ (ii). From the part (i) $\Rightarrow$ (ii) of the proof of Theorem 15.1 we know that

$$\int_l^u U(z)dF_A(z) - \int_l^u U(z)dF_B(z) = \Xi\big(U(F_A)\big) - \Xi\big(U(F_B)\big) = -\int_l^u U'(z)\big(F_A(z) - F_B(z)\big)dz.$$

In the last integral use integration by parts, where U' is taken as the first function and the second function is $(F_A(z) - F_B(z))$. This gives

$$\Xi\big(U(F_A)\big) - \Xi\big(U(F_B)\big) = -\int_l^u U'(z)\big(F_A(z) - F_B(z)\big)dz =$$

$$-U'(z)\int_l^z [F_A(v) - F_B(v)]dv \Big|_l^u + \int_l^u U''(z)\int_l^z [F_A(v) - F_B(v)]dv\, dz. \quad (15.14)$$

Non-negativity of the first term of (15.14) follows from the hypothesis that $F_A \geq_{SSD} F_B$ (see inequality 15.2) and the fact that U is non-decreasing ($U' \geq 0$). The second term of the expression is also non-negative since U is concave ($U'' \leq 0$) and $F_A \geq_{SSD} F_B$ holds. Thus, $\Xi\big(U(F_A)\big) - \Xi\big(U(F_B)\big)$, given by (15.14), is non-negative.

(ii) $\Rightarrow$ (i): The proof is by contradiction. It is shown that if (i) does not hold, then there exists a non-decreasing, concave utility function U such that $\int_l^u U(z)dF_A(z) < \int_l^u U(z)dF_B(z)$. For this purpose, define the function $H(z) = \int_l^z [F_A(v) - F_B(v)]dv$. Suppose there exists $l < \hat{z} < u$ such that $H(z) \geq 0$ for all $l \leq z \leq \hat{z}$, with $>$ for some $l \leq z \leq \hat{z}$, and $H(z) \leq 0$ for all $z \geq \hat{z}$.

Now, consider the utility function

$$\hat{U}(z) = \begin{cases} -\dfrac{a\hat{z}^2}{6} + \left[\dfrac{a\hat{z}}{2} + b\right]z - \dfrac{az^2}{2} + \dfrac{az^3}{6\hat{z}}, & l \leq z \leq \hat{z}, \\ bz & , z \geq \hat{z}, \end{cases} \quad (15.15)$$

where $0 < b < a$ are arbitrary constants. Then

$$\hat{U}'(z) = \begin{cases} \dfrac{a\hat{z}}{2} + b - az + \dfrac{az^2}{2\hat{z}}, & l \leq z \leq \hat{z}, \\ b & , z \geq \hat{z}, \end{cases}$$

and

$$\hat{U}''(z) = \begin{cases} -a + \dfrac{az}{\hat{z}}, & l \leq z \leq \hat{z}, \\ 0 & , z \geq \hat{z}. \end{cases}$$

Note positivity of the marginal utility function $\hat{U}'$ and non-positivity of $\hat{U}''$. Then for the utility function given by (15.15), by virtue of (15.14), we have

$$\Xi\big(\hat{U}(F_A)\big)-\Xi\big(\hat{U}(F_B)\big)=-\hat{U}'(z)H(z)\Big|_l^u+\int_l^u\hat{U}''(z)H(z)dz=-\hat{U}'(u)H(u)+\hat{U}'(l)H(l)$$

$$-\int_l^{\hat{z}}\big[(a(\hat{z}-z))/\hat{z}\big]H(z)dz-\int_{\hat{z}}^u 0.H(z)dz$$

$$=-bH(u)-\int_l^{\hat{z}}\big[(a(\hat{z}-z))/\hat{z}\big]H(z)dz, \tag{15.16}$$

since $H(l) = 0$.

Note that $H(u) \le 0$ and the function $\big[(a(\hat{z}-z))/\hat{z}\big]$ is positively valued and an increasing function of a over the interval $[l,\hat{z}]$. Therefore, by choosing the value of the free parameter a sufficiently high we can make the second term in (15.16) negatively as large as desired so that $\Xi\big(\hat{U}(F_A)\big)-\Xi\big(\hat{U}(F_B)\big)$ becomes negative. Thus, not (*i*) implies not (*ii*). This completes the proof of the theorem.

In order to prove Theorem 15.4, we first make the following observation. If we write $v = F^{-1}(q)$, then $q = F(v)$, from which we get $dq = dF(v)$. Then

$$\int_0^{F(z)}\big(z-F^{-1}(q)\big)dq=\int_l^z(z-v)dF(v)=zF(z)-\int_l^z vdF(v). \tag{15.17}$$

Using integration by parts in the second term of the final expression of (15.17), where we treat v as the first function and $F(v)$ as the second function, we have

$$-\int_l^z v\,dF(v)=-vF(v)\Big]_l^z+\int_l^z F(v)dv=-zF(z)+\int_l^z F(v)dv. \text{ Hence}$$

$$\int_0^{F(z)}\big(z-F^{-1}(q)\big)dq=\int_l^z F(v)dv. \tag{15.18}$$

Proof of Theorem 15.4: (*i*) $\Rightarrow$ (*ii*): The idea of the proof is taken from Foster and Shorrocks (1988). Define the function $h(z)=\int_l^z\big(F_A(v)-F_B(v)\big)dv$ for $z\in[l,u]$. Evidently, h is continuous on its domain and $h(l) = 0$. Then

$$h(u)=\int_l^u\big(\big(1-F_B(v)\big)-\big(1-F_A(v)\big)\big)dv.$$

Now, we show that $\Xi(F_A)=l+\int_l^u\big(1-F_A(v)\big)\,dv$. We use integration by parts, where we treat $(1 - F_A(v))$ as the first function and 1 as the second function. Then

$$\int_l^u\big(1-F_A(v)\big)\,dv=\big(1-F_A(v)\big)v\Big|_l^u+\int_l^u v\,dF_A(v). \text{ Since } F_A(l) = 0 \text{ and } F_A(u) = 1, \text{ it}$$

follows that $\int_l^u\big(1-F_A(v)\big)\,dv=-l+\int_l^u v\,dF_A(v)=-l+\Xi(F_A).$ Hence

$$h(u) = \int_l^u \left(F_A(v) - F_B(v)\right)dv = \Xi(F_A) - \Xi(F_B).$$ (15.19)

Note also that $\int_0^1 F_A^{-1}(q)dq = \Xi(F_A)$. To see this formally, let $F_A^{-1}(q) = v$, which

gives $F_a(v) = q$. Hence $dF_A(v) = dq$. Thus, $\int_0^1 F_A^{-1}(q)dq = \int_l^u v \, dF_A(v) = \Xi(F_A)$.

We can, therefore, rewrite $\Xi(F_A) - \Xi(F_B)$ in (15.19) as $\int_0^1 \left(F_B^{-1}(q) - F_A^{-1}(q)\right)dq$,

which, in view of (15.9), is non-positive. Hence if all the interior local maxima of h
are non-positive, $h(z) \le 0$ for all $z \in [l, u]$. Suppose a local maximum of h occurs at
$\hat{z} \in (l, u)$. Then either $F_A(\hat{z}) = F_B(\hat{z})$ or, by continuity of F_A and F_B, $F_A(\hat{z}) < F_B(\hat{z})$
and $F_B^{-1}(q) = \hat{z}$ for all $q \in \left(F_A(\hat{z}), F_B(\hat{z})\right)$. Hence

$$h(\hat{z}) = \int_l^{\hat{z}} \left(F_A(v) - F_B(v)\right)dv = \int_l^{\hat{z}} F_A(v)dv - \int_l^{\hat{z}} F_B(v)dv,$$

which, in view of (15.18), becomes

$$\int_0^{F_A(\hat{z})} \left(\hat{z} - F_A^{-1}(q)\right)dq - \int_0^{F_B(\hat{z})} \left(\hat{z} - F_B^{-1}(q)\right)dq$$

$$= \int_0^{F_A(\hat{z})} \left(\hat{z} - F_A^{-1}(q)\right)dq - \int_0^{F_A(\hat{z})} \left(\hat{z} - F_B^{-1}(q)\right)dq - \int_{F_A(\hat{z})}^{F_B(\hat{z})} \left(\hat{z} - F_B^{-1}(q)\right)dq$$

$$= \int_0^{F_A(\hat{z})} \left[\left(\hat{z} - F_A^{-1}(q)\right) - \left(\hat{z} - F_B^{-1}(q)\right)\right]dq - \int_{F_A(\hat{z})}^{F_B(\hat{z})} \left(\hat{z} - F_B^{-1}(q)\right)dq$$

$$= \int_0^{F_A(\hat{z})} \left(F_B^{-1}(q) - F_A^{-1}(q)\right)dq - \int_{F_A(\hat{z})}^{F_B(\hat{z})} \left(\hat{z} - F_B^{-1}(q)\right)dq.$$ (15.20)

Since the second term of the expression in (15.20) is zero, we have
$$h(\hat{z}) = \int_0^{F_A(\hat{z})} \left(F_B^{-1}(q) - F_A^{-1}(q)\right)dq \le 0 \text{ (by (15.9)). It then follows that } h(z) \le 0 \text{ for all}$$

$z \in [l, u]$. Hence (*i*) $\Rightarrow$ (*ii*). By a similar argument we can establish that (*ii*) $\Rightarrow$ (*i*).
Since in Theorem 15.2 we have already shown that conditions (*i*) and (*iii*) are
equivalent, it follows that all of the three conditions (*i*), (*ii*) and (*iii*) are equivalent.
This completes the proof of the theorem.

BIBLIOGRAPHICAL NOTES

A classic reference for first and second order stochastic dominance conditions is Hadar and Russell (1969). Two recent references for comprehensive discussion on these issues are the books by Levy (2006) and Shaked and Shanthikumar (2006). Davidson (2008) is also an appropriate reference for intuitive discussions on the stochastic dominance desiderata. Chakravarty and Zoli (2012) developed stochastic dominance rules for integer variables. Kakwani (1980) and Chakravarty (1990) discussed properties of the Lorenz curve for a continuum of population. Discussions on the Lorenz and generalized Lorenz orderings can be found in Foster and Sen (1997) and Chakravarty (2009).

EXERCISES

1. Each of the following statements is either true or false. If the statement is true, prove it. If it is false, give a counter-example or justify your answer by logical reasoning.

   (a) First order stochastic dominance entails second order stochastic dominance, but the converse is not true.

   (b) Second order stochastic dominance is a reflexive, transitive and incomplete relation.

   (c) Suppose the distribution function of an asset dominates that of another asset by the third order stochastic dominance criterion. Then the implied expected utility dominance remains invariant under any increasing transformation of the utility function.

   (d) Strong second order stochastic dominance is an irreflexive, transitive and incomplete relation.

   (e) Pareto dominance is necessary and sufficient for generalized Lorenz dominance of the expected return vector of a portfolio over that of another portfolio.

2. Let $F_A, F_B : [l, M] \to [0,1]$ be the distribution functions of two assets A and B respectively, where $M > 0$. Now, consider the following set of utility functions:

$$L^* = \{U_1(z) = \ln(z), U_2(z) = z^2, U_3(z) = z^{.5}, U_4(z) = z, U_5 = M^2 z - z^3/3, U_6(z) = 1 - \exp(-z)\}$$

Let L_j^* be the subset of L^* whose utility functions imply that the expected utility value under F_A is at least as much as that under F_B when F_A dominates F_B by the jth order stochastic dominance criterion. Show that $L_3^* \subset L_2^* \subset L_1^*$. Explain the reasoning why L_3^* is a proper subset of L_2^*, which in turn is a proper subset of L_1^*.

3. Demonstrate rigorously that stochastic dominance of order j implies that of order $(j + 1)$, where $j \geq 1$ is an integer.

4. For the rate of return distribution functions $F_I(v)$ and $F_{II}(v)$, considered in Example 15.1, show diagrammatically that F_I first order stochastic dominates F_{II}.

5. Let Ω and Π be two portfolios whose vectors of expected returns on the three assets are respectively $(2, 3, 6)$ and $(1, 5, 5)$. Show that second order stochastic dominance fails to rank these two vectors.

6. Demonstrate diagrammatically that F_{III} second order stochastic dominates F_{IV}, where F_{III} and F_{IV} are the rate of return distribution functions considered in Example 15.2.

7. Suppose there are two assets I and II with random returns r_I and r_{II} respectively. Assume that $r_{II} \overset{d}{=} r_I + \varepsilon$ with $\Xi\left[\varepsilon | r_I\right] = 0$, where Ξ stands for the expectation operator. That is, the return on asset II is equal in distribution to the return on I plus a noise term ε. Show that $I \geq_{SSD} II$ holds.

8. Show that for the portfolios $\hat{\Pi}$ and $\hat{\Omega}$, considered in Example 15.3, the ordering of the expected return vectors $\Xi\left(\hat{\Pi}\right)$ and $\Xi\left(\hat{\Omega}\right)$ by the Lorenz criterion turns out to be inconclusive.

9. It is known that F_A dominates F_B by the jth degree stochastic dominance criterion if and only if the expected utility under F_A is at least as large as that under F_B, where $(-1)^{i+1} U^i \geq 0$ (U' being the ith order derivative of the utility function U) and $1 \leq i \leq j$ (Fishburn 1976). Construct a set of three utility functions for which this condition holds.

10. Let $F_A \geq_{SD}^{\infty} F_B$ denote infinite degree stochastic dominance of F_A over F_B and this is defined by letting $j \to \infty$ in the definition of jth degree stochastic dominance (see inequality (15.4)). Then show that the following conditions are equivalent:

    (i) $F_A \geq_{SD}^{\infty} F_B$.

    (ii) For some j, F_A is dominant over F_B by the jth degree stochastic dominance criterion.

CHAPTER 16

Portfolio Management: The Mean-Gini Approach

16.1 INTRODUCTION

One of the most frequently used methods for ranking uncertain rates of return on assets is the mean-variance approach. The essential idea is to represent the distribution of the rate of return (or return, for short) on an asset by two summary statistics: the mean (indicating the reward) and the variance (indicating variability). The use of summary statistics definitely simplifies the ranking problem. However, the mean-variance analysis may lead to unjustified conclusions. Two assets may have the same mean return and the corresponding variance for one may be higher than that of the other, yet the former may be preferred to the latter by some risk-averse individuals (see Rothschild and Stiglitz 1970; see also Giora and Levy 1969). The stochastic dominance approach does not lead to such unwarranted conclusions. It then becomes worthwhile to develop an alternative approach that summarizes the distributions in terms of two statistics and that retains stochastic dominance efficiency.

In this chapter, we present an alternative approach for comparing returns on assets, building on the theory of stochastic dominance. It uses the mean and the Gini evaluation function as the summary statistics of the distribution of the return. The Gini evaluation function is based on the well-known Gini index, which is used extensively as a measure of income inequality. Use of the Gini evaluation function as a summary statistic of a risky investment allows the derivation of necessary conditions for stochastic dominances (Yitzhaki 1982; Shalit and Yitzhaki 1984). This, therefore, enables us to discard the assets that are stochastically dominated by others. We refer to this approach to portfolio analysis as the mean-Gini approach.

For uncertain assets with continuous type distributions of the rate of return, the mean-variance analysis requires the perfect knowledge of the probability distributions of the returns on all assets. Hence it may fail as a ranking criterion when some distributions, or the distribution of the entire portfolio, are not known. For instance, if all the returns on the assets in a portfolio are lognormally distributed, then the portfolio distribution is not lognormal. Then if the optimal portfolio is chosen according to the mean-variance criterion, assuming lognormality of the asset return distributions, it may be possible to get an alternative portfolio, which will be preferred by all risk-averse individuals. But the stochastic dominance analysis does not rely on such knowledge.

In the next section, we establish relationship between the Gini evaluation function and stochastic dominance criterion. Section 16.3 presents the efficient sets resulting from the mean-variance and the mean-Gini approaches and makes a comparison between them. The mean-Gini portfolio analysis and the capital asset pricing model are presented in Sections 16.4 and 16.5 respectively. Proofs of all the results stated in the main text are relegated to the Appendix.

16.2 GINI EVALUATION FUNCTION AND STOCHASTIC DOMINANCE

The Gini index is the most well-known index of inequality. In addition to its use for measuring income or wealth inequality, it has been employed to study inequality in the distributions of several other attributes, such as land ownership, calorie or energy consumption, health, and school enrollment (see Russett 1964, Addo 1976, Kakwani et al. 1997). In this section, following Yitzhaki (1982) and Shalit and Yitzhaki (1984), we show an application of the Gini index to portfolio analysis.

Let $F : [l, u] \rightarrow [0, 1]$ be the cumulative distribution function of the rate of return (return, for short) on the asset under consideration (see Chapter 15). Unless specified, we assume that all assets are risky. Now, the area enclosed between the line of equality and the Lorenz curve of F, expressed as a proportion of the area under the line of equality, has been considered as an index of inequality. This index is known as the Lorenz ratio (see Lorenz 1905). Incidentally, the Gini index equals the Lorenz ratio, although it was proposed independently as a measure of inequality by Gini (1936).

One can find at least twelve different formulations of the Gini index in the literature (Yitzhaki 1998). For our purpose it will be useful to deal with the following two formulations.

Theorem 16.1: For any asset return with distribution function F and mean $\Xi(F) > 0$, the Gini index $G(F)$ is given by

$$G(F) = 1 - \frac{\left[l + \int_l^u \left(1 - F(z)\right)^2 dz \right]}{\Xi(F)}.$$ (16.1)

Proof: The proof of this theorem can be found in Donaldson and Weymark (1983).

Formula (16.1) has a clear advantage. We do not need continuous differentiability of the distribution function for calculating the Gini index when using this formula. It applies to both continuous and discrete distributions. Moreover, it is easy to compute.

Theorem 16.2: For any asset return X, represented by the distribution function F, the Gini index $G(F)$ can be written as

$$G(F) = \frac{2 \, (\text{Covariance between } X \text{ and } F(X))}{\Xi(F)}, \qquad (16.2)$$

where $\Xi(F) > 0$ is the mean return on the asset.

Proof: See Appendix.

For a discrete distribution, if the asset takes n values then (rank of v)/n becomes the representation of $F(v)$. Note that this method requires no grouping of data to economize on computation. The calculation of the Gini index, using this method, is quite easy.

The Gini index $G(F)$ is a relative index, scaling the return levels on an asset proportionally does not alter its value. It is a compromise index in the sense that when multiplied by the mean return, the resulting index becomes an absolute index. The value of an absolute index remains invariant under equal absolute addition to all return levels. Therefore, the absolute version of $G(F)$ in (16.1) is given by

$$\gamma(F) = \Xi(F) - \left[l + \int_{l}^{u} \left(1 - F(v)\right)^2 dv \right]. \qquad (16.3)$$

Given the mean return, G and γ will rank two assets in the same way.

The Gini, the absolute Gini indices, and the variance are all indicators of dispersion in the return levels of the asset. However, while the first is a relative index, the second and the third are absolute indices. The Gini asset evaluation function is an inverse indicator of dispersion and is defined as

$$\Psi(F) = \Xi(F) - \gamma(F) = l + \int_{l}^{u} \left(1 - F(v)\right)^2 dv. \qquad (16.4)$$

Given the mean return, an increase in Ψ is equivalent to a reduction in γ and vice versa. Since for a risk-averse individual high dispersion in the return on an asset is undesirable, high values of Ψ may be regarded as a good characteristic of the asset. We may regard Ψ as the net reward, where $\Xi(F) = \mu$ represents the reward and γ gives the amount by which reward should be reduced because of variability. The Gini asset evaluation function is financial counterpart to the Gini welfare function employed in welfare economics for ranking alternative distributions of income. (See Chakravarty 2009 for a discussion on the Gini welfare function.)

In order to demonstrate the role of Ψ in ranking uncertain returns on assets, for any two assets with return distribution functions F_A and F_B respectively, let us define

$$e_j(F_A, F_B) = \int_l^u \left(1 - F_A(v)\right)^j dv - \int_l^u \left(1 - F_B(v)\right)^j dv, \tag{16.5}$$

where $j \geq 1$ is an integer. Note that while $e_2(F_A, F_B) = \Psi(F_A) - \Psi(F_B)$, $e_1(F) = \Xi(F_A) - \Xi(F_B)$, which is the difference between the mean returns (see appendix to Chapter 15).

The following theorems, which present the necessary conditions for stochastic dominance, provide the relationship between the mean-Gini analysis and the stochastic dominance criteria.

Theorem 16.3: Let F_A, $F_B : [l, u] \rightarrow [0, 1]$ be the distribution functions of the returns on the assets A and B respectively. Then the conditions $\Xi(F_A) \geq \Xi(F_B)$ and $\Psi(F_A) \geq \Psi(F_B)$ are necessary for F_A to dominate F_B with respect to first and second order stochastic dominance rules respectively.

Proof: See Appendix.

Theorem 16.3 is quite important since it enables us to discard the stochastically inferior alternatives from the set of efficient assets using the summary statistics μ (mean return) and Ψ. In other words, the theorem shows that two statistics (the mean return and the Gini evaluation function), based on the distribution, summarize the entire distribution and they can be applied successfully for efficient ranking of assets. We discuss this issue in the next section in detail.

The condition $\Psi(F_A) - \Psi(F_B)$ parallels Baumol's (1963) expected gain-confidence limit $\mu - \delta\sigma$, where $\delta > 0$ is a constant and σ is the standard deviation. The Baumol condition shows how a distribution with greater mean and greater variance can be preferred. An advantage of the mean-Gini criterion over the Baumol rule is its stochastic dominance efficiency.

The conditions provided in Theorem 16.3 are only necessary. They are not sufficient. While the necessary conditions can be used for any distribution, the sufficient conditions are weaker in the sense that they can be applied for ranking assets whose return distribution functions intersect at most once.

Definition 16.1: Let F_A, $F_B : [0, \infty] \rightarrow [0, 1]$ be the distribution functions of the returns on the assets A and B respectively. Then F_A is said to intersect F_B once from below if and only if there exist $l < v_0 < u$ and intervals $[l, v_0]$ and $[v_0, u]$ such that

$$F_A(v) \leq F_B(v) \text{ for all } v \in [l, v_0], \text{ with } < \text{ for some } v \in [l, v_0],$$
$$F_A(v) \geq F_B(v) \text{ for all } v \in [v_0, u], \text{ with } > \text{ for some } v \in [v_0, u].$$

That is, up to v_0, the graph of F_A lies nowhere above and at some points (at least) below that of F_B. After v_0, the graph of F_A lies nowhere below and at some points (at least) above that of F_B. For instance, from Figure 15.2, it follows that F_A intersects F_B once from below. Equivalently, we say that F_B intersects F_A once from above. When we say that F_A and F_B intersect at most once, intersection can be from below or above.

We can now state the following theorem.

Theorem 16.4: Let F_A, $F_B : [l, u] \to [0, 1]$ be the distribution functions of the returns on the assets A and B respectively. Assume that F_A intersects F_B at most once. Then $e_j(F_A, F_B) \geq 0$ for all $j = 1, 2,\ldots\ldots$, with strict inequality for some j, are sufficient for F_A to dominate F_B with respect to second order stochastic dominance rule.

Proof: See Appendix.

Therefore, an investigator who is interested in isolating a stochastically dominant and efficient set must check whether the distribution functions intersect at most once. For a wide range of distribution functions the sufficient conditions laid down in the theorem are satisfied. For non-intersecting asset distribution functions if all the relevant conditions are satisfied, the former is preferred to the latter by the expected utility criterion, where the utility function is non-decreasing and concave.

16.3 EFFICIENT SET

We begin by considering a set of assets. An efficient set associated with a criterion is defined as the set of assets that are undominated by the appropriate criterion. Let ES_V be the efficient set associated with the mean-variance criterion. Of the two assets, A and B with the distribution functions F_A and F_B respectively, F_A is said to dominate F_B by the mean-variance criterion if $\Xi(F_A) \geq \Xi(F_B)$ but $\sigma(F_A) \leq \sigma(F_B)$, with at least one strict inequality, where $\sigma(F_A)(\sigma(F_B))$ is the standard deviation of the asset whose return distribution function is $F_A(F_B)$. In order to make the comparison of the mean-Gini approach with the mean-variance approach meaningful, the dispersion (or risk) measure we use for the latter is the standard deviation (the positive square root of the variance).

Using the Gini index, we can develop two efficient sets. The first is denoted by ES_G and F_A dominates F_B by this criterion if $\Xi(F_A) \geq \Xi(F_B)$ but $\gamma(F_A) \leq \gamma(F_B)$, with at least one strict inequality. We call this mean-absolute Gini index criterion. According to the second rule, which is the mean-Gini criterion and whose efficient set is denoted by ES_Ψ, F_A dominates F_B if $\Xi(F_A) \geq \Xi(F_B)$ and $\Psi(F_A) \geq \Psi(F_B)$, with at least one strict inequality. Thus, while the former involves comparison of the mean and the absolute Gini index, the latter is defined in terms of comparability of the mean and Gini evaluation function. The former is simply a mean-variance type approach in the sense that we replace the standard deviation, the dispersion measure, by an alternative measure—the absolute Gini index. Further, in this case we also do not have any results that parallel Theorems 16.3 and 16.4.

Now, $\Xi(F_A) \geq \Xi(F_B)$ and $\gamma(F_A) \leq \gamma(F_B)$ imply $\Psi(F_A) \geq \Psi(F_B)$. That is, $\Xi(F_A) \geq \Xi(F_B)$ and $\gamma(F_A) \leq \gamma(F_B)$ are sufficient for $\Xi(F_A) \geq \Xi(F_B)$ and $\Psi(F_A) \geq \Psi(F_B)$. But the converse is not true. Hence it is clear that $ES_\Psi \subseteq ES_G$. Next, note that $\Xi(F_A) \geq \Xi(F_B)$ and $\Psi(F_A) \geq \Psi(F_B)$ are necessary for stochastic dominance, while the elements in ES_V are not subject to any such restriction. Hence $ES_\Psi \subseteq ES_V$.

The advantage of ES_Ψ over ES_V and ES_G is the use of the evaluation function Ψ. As Hanoch and Levy (1969) pointed out, an increase in risk may not be undesirable if it is the result of a shift of some part of the distribution to the right. Non-negativity of e_2 states the minimum increase in the mean return that must accompany an increase in dispersion if the resulting distribution is to be preferred. We may illustrate this by an example.

Example 16.1: Consider two assets A and B whose return distribution functions are given respectively by

$$F_A(v) = \frac{v}{2}, 0 \leq v \leq 2 \text{ and } F_B(v) = v, 0 \leq v \leq 1.$$

A and B are uniformly distributed over the intervals $[0, 2]$ and $[0, 1]$ respectively. Clearly, the former is obtained from the latter by a rightward shift. In order to make the domains of the definition same, we assume that for $1 \leq v \leq 2, F_B(v) = 1$. Then for these two uniform distributions the vectors of mean return, standard deviation and the absolute Gini index are given respectively by $\left(\Xi(F_A) = 1, \sigma(F_A) = \left(1/\sqrt{3}\right), \gamma(F_A) = (1/3) \right)$ and $\left(\Xi(F_B) = (1/2), \sigma(F_B) = \left(1/\sqrt{12}\right), \gamma(F_B) = (1/6) \right)$. In this two-asset world, neither of the two assets dominates the other by mean-variance nor the mean-absolute Gini index criteria. This shows that both the assets A and B are in the efficient sets ES_V and ES_G. But while $\Xi(F_A) = 1 > \Xi(F_B) = (1/2)$, it is also true that $\Psi(F_A) = (2/3) > \Psi(F_B)$ $= (1/3)$. Thus, A dominates B and hence $B \notin ES_\Psi$. An application of Theorem 16.3 enables us to discard asset B from the efficient set ES_Ψ. Thus, although the former has a longer upper tail than the latter, increase in mean return is sufficient to offset any increase in dispersion (as characterized by higher standard deviation or higher absolute Gini index), so that the former distribution becomes more efficient in terms of stochastic dominance.

We may now consider a second example to illustrate the issue.

Example 16.2: Suppose that distribution functions of the returns on the assets A and B are given respectively by

$$F_A(v) = \begin{cases} 0 & ,0 \leq v < b \\ 1-\left(\dfrac{b}{v}\right)^3 & ,v \geq b, \end{cases} \text{ and } F_B(v) = \begin{cases} 0 & ,0 \leq v < b \\ 1-\left(\dfrac{b}{v}\right)^4 & ,v \geq b. \end{cases}$$

The probability that the return on asset A is greater than v is higher than the corresponding probability for asset B. The two distribution functions, presented in this example, are the Pareto distribution functions with parameters 3 and 4 respectively. We assume that the threshold return level b takes on the value 1. Then the mean return, the standard deviation and the absolute Gini index for the two assets A and B are given respectively by the vectors $\left(\Xi(F_A) = (3/2), \sigma(F_A) = \left(\sqrt{3}/2\right), \gamma(F_A) = (3/10) \right)$ and $\left(\Xi(F_B) = (4/3), \sigma(F_B) = \left(\sqrt{2}/3\right), \gamma(F_B) = (4/21) \right)$. Since asset A has a higher mean, higher standard deviation and higher absolute Gini index than asset B, we cannot rank the two assets by the mean-variance and the mean-Gini index criteria. The value of the Gini evaluation function Ψ for asset A is $(6/5)$, which is higher than $(8/7)$, the value of Ψ for asset B. Hence asset A has both higher mean return and a higher Gini evaluation function than asset B. Therefore, the necessary condition, stipulated in Theorem 16.3, excludes asset B from the efficient set ES_ψ. That is, asset A is preferred to asset B by the mean-Gini rule. Clearly, in this case the higher mean is also sufficient to balance out the higher dispersion, as measured by the absolute Gini index or the standard deviation, so that the net reward from asset A is preferred to that from asset B.

The construction of the efficient set ES_ψ is quite simple. We first calculate the mean return and the absolute Gini index for return on every asset, find the efficient set ES_G, and then find $\mu^* = \max(\mu - \gamma)$ where μ is the expected return. This will enable us to discard from the efficient set ES_G all assets with $\mu < \mu^*$, in order to get ES_ψ. We may repeat this procedure for assets with $\mu > \mu^*$ in the efficient set ES_G.

We can also construct the efficient set associated with Baumol's (1963) expected gain-confidence limit criterion. According to this rule, F_A is dominant over F_B if $\Xi(F_A) \geq \Xi(F_B)$ and $\Xi(F_A) - \delta\sigma(F_A) \geq \Xi(F_B) - \delta\sigma(F_B)$, with at least one strict inequality.

16.4 PORTFOLIO ANALYSIS

As in the Markowitz mean-variance analysis, we treat the returns on assets as random variables. The goal then is to choose weights for different assets in the portfolio optimally. In the Markowitz model the optimal set of weights is one that corresponds to minimum dispersion. The variance of the return on an asset is taken as an indicator for its dispersion. In this case we take absolute Gini index of an instrument as the surrogate for its dispersion.

To understand the issue let us consider a portfolio Λ that consists of two assets A and B, that is, $\Lambda = (A, B)$. The return on the portfolio is given by $r_\Pi = x r_A + (1 - x) r_B$, where x is the share of wealth invested in asset A, and r_A and r_B are returns from assets A and B respectively. As in the Markowitz model, the performance of the portfolio depends on the correlation between the assets. If one asset has a positive, linear relationship with the other, then the coefficient of correlation ρ_{AB} is 1. In this case the line *ECH* in Figure 16.1 will represent all possible portfolios that are mixtures of assets *A* and *B*. (This statement and all similar statements of this section parallel the corresponding statements for the mean-variance case and therefore their proofs are omitted.) For independent assets, $\rho_{AB} = 0$ and the corresponding risk–reward curve will be of the type *EDH*, showing that diversification improves performance. If the two assets are perfectly negatively correlated, that is, ρ_{AB} is –1, the curve *EJH* indicates the performance of the portfolio, showing that there will be much improvement in performance. A perpendicular from the midpoint of *JH* on the axis representing the absolute Gini index indicates that the risk is the same corresponding to the cases $\rho_{AB} = 1$ and 0. But return in the former case is lower than that in the latter one. The point *J* represents the case where we have positive reward without any risk. (We can certainly allow short selling and have analogous risk–reward diagrams. Since the diagrams will be similar to the corresponding expositions in the mean-variance case, we are not presenting the case here. For a presentation of this, see Chapter 14.)

Now, suppose a portfolio Ω consists of k assets and return on asset i is represented by r_i, $1 \leq i \leq k$. Then the return from portfolio r_Ω is given by $r_\Omega = \sum_{i=1}^{k} x_i r_i$, where x_i is

Figure 16.1   Portfolio Construction in the Mean Absolute Gini Index Space

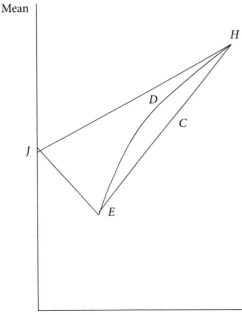

the share of wealth invested in asset i, $\sum_{i=1}^{k} x_i = 1$. Let F_Ω be the distribution function of the portfolio. From Theorem 16.2 it follows that the absolute Gini index of the portfolio is given by

$$\gamma_\Omega = 2\sum_{i=1}^{k} x_i \operatorname{cov}\left(r_i, F_\Omega\left(r_\Omega\right)\right). \qquad (16.6)$$

Formula (16.6) explicitly shows that the risk of the portfolio can be decomposed into a weighted average of the covariance between the variables r_i and the distribution function of the portfolio Ω.

We may note here that the variance of the portfolio Ω can be written as

$$\sigma_\Omega^2 = \sum_{i=1}^{k} x_i \operatorname{cov}\left(r_i, r_\Omega\right). \qquad (16.7)$$

The difference between the two decompositions is that in (16.6) we use the distribution function of the portfolio and in (16.7) the appropriate component is return from the portfolio.

16.5 GINI CAPITAL ASSET PRICING MODEL

In this section we present the valuation result for investors holding portfolios that are mean-Gini efficient. It retains all the assumptions of the classic capital pricing model (CAPM). However, instead of holding mean-variance efficient portfolios, investors now use mean-Gini efficient portfolios. The approach is based on Theorem 16.3. It assumes that the investors maximize their expected utility of returns but the analyst does not know the utility function. Therefore, the investigator uses the mean-Gini rule to summarize the decisions of the investors. Minimization of a portfolio's absolute Gini index for each mean will determine the mean-Gini efficient set. Applying Theorem 16.3, we can now define an efficient subset of the stochastic dominance efficient set. Consequently, every member of this set satisfies the expected utility maximization conditions.

Each investor determines his optimum portfolio by choosing a mixture of assets that minimizes the absolute Gini index of the portfolio given its expected return. Investors can borrow and lend at a risk-free rate λ. The return that investor j receives from his portfolio is given by $\sum_{i=1}^{k} x_i^j r_i + \left(1 - \sum_{i=1}^{k} x_i^j\right)\lambda, \sum_{i=1}^{k} x_i^j \leq 1$, where k is the number of risky assets, x_i^j is share of person j's wealth invested in asset i. The mean-Gini efficiency frontier is shown in Figure 16.2. Because of similarity between the relationships (16.6) and (16.7), the CAPM valuation relationship for a market of investors using the mean-Gini approach will be

$$\Xi(r_i) = \lambda + \left(\Xi(r_m) - \lambda\right)\frac{2\,\mathrm{cov}\left(r_i, F_m(r_m)\right)}{\gamma_m}, \qquad (16.8)$$

where, as before, $\Xi(r_i)$ is the expected value of return on asset i, r_m is the return from the market portfolio, F_m is its distribution function, $\Xi(r_m)$ is its expected value and γ_m is the corresponding absolute Gini index. We refer to this as the Gini CAPM. (Note similarity of this with the mean-variance CAPM

$$\Xi(r_i) = \lambda + \left(\Xi(r_m) - \lambda\right)\frac{\mathrm{cov}\left(r_i, r_m\right)}{\sigma_m^2}$$, where σ_m^2 is the variance of the market return.

See Chapter 14.)

Figure 16.2   The Mean-Gini Efficiency Frontier

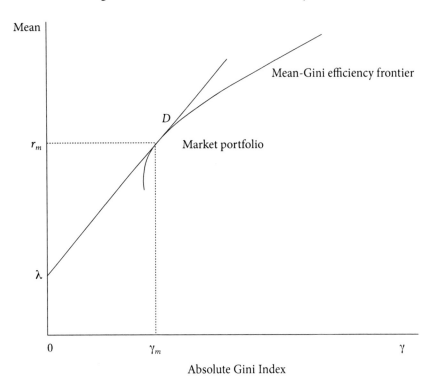

Absolute Gini Index

To understand the relationship between expected return and systematic or non-diversifiable risk—the part of asset $i's$ total risk that cannot be reduced without reducing its expected return—we rewrite $\mathrm{cov}(r_i, F_m(r_m))$ as $\theta_{im}\gamma_i$, where

$$\theta_{im} = \frac{\text{cov}\left(r_i, F_m\left(r_m\right)\right)}{\text{cov}\left(r_i, F_i\left(r_i\right)\right)}, \tag{16.9}$$

F_i being the distribution function of return on asset i. Thus, we can rewrite (16.8) as

$$\Xi\left(r_i\right) = \lambda + \left(\Xi\left(r_m\right) - \lambda\right)\frac{\theta_{im}\gamma_i}{\gamma_m}. \tag{16.10}$$

Therefore, the (Gini) beta of asset i is

$$\beta_{Gi} = \frac{\theta_{im}\gamma_i}{\gamma_m}. \tag{16.11}$$

β_{Gi} is a measure of the degree of responsiveness of the return on asset i to changes in the market. On the other hand, θ_{im} gives the proportion of total risk associated with investment on asset i that cannot be eliminated by the market without reducing expected return.

Applied Example 16.1: Porter and Gaumnitz (1972) investigated whether the stochastic dominance rules to portfolio choice would yield results that differ significantly from the results that would arise if the mean-variance analysis was invoked. For the same data set, considered in Applied Example 15.1, it is noted that the application of stochastic dominance rules reduces significantly the size of the efficient set as compared with the corresponding set in the mean-variance case. Except for highly risk-averse investors, the choice between the mean-variance model and the stochastic dominance model for selecting portfolios was not critical. However, for strong risk aversion, second and third order stochastic dominance rules turned out to be more consistent with maximization of expected utility.

APPENDIX

Proof of Theorem 16.2: From Theorem 16.1 we have

$$G(F) = \frac{\Xi(F) - l - \int_l^u \left(1 - F(X)\right)^2 dX}{\Xi(F)}$$

$$= \frac{\int_l^u \left(1 - F(X) - \left(1 - F(X)\right)^2\right) dX}{\Xi(F)}$$

$$= \frac{\int_l^u F(X)\left(1 - F(X)\right) dX}{\Xi(F)} \tag{16.12}$$

Using integration by parts in (16.12), where we take $F(X)(1 - F(X))$ as the first function, and 1 as the second function, we get

$$G(F) = \frac{1}{\Xi(F)} F(X)(1 - F(X)) X \Big|_l^u - \frac{1}{\Xi(F)} \int_l^u (dF(X) - 2F(X)dF(X))X. \quad (16.13)$$

Since $F(l) = 0$ and $F(u) = 1$ the first term of the right-hand side of (16.13) is 0. Hence $G(F)$ in (16.13) becomes

$$G(F) = -\frac{1}{\Xi(F)} \int_l^u X(dF(X) - 2F(X)dF(X))$$

$$= \frac{1}{\Xi(F)} \int_l^u 2XF(X)dF(X) - \frac{1}{\Xi(F)} \int_l^u X\,dF(X)$$

$$= \frac{1}{\Xi(F)} \int_l^u 2XF(X)dF(X) - \frac{\Xi(F)}{\Xi(F)}$$

$$= \frac{2}{\Xi(F)} \int_l^u X F(X)d F(X) - 1$$

$$= \frac{2}{\Xi(F)} \left[\int_l^u XF(X)dF(X) - \frac{\Xi(F)}{2} \right]. \quad (16.14)$$

Note that F is uniformly distributed between $[0, 1]$, so that its mean is

$\frac{1}{2} \left(\int_0^1 F\,dF = \frac{F^2}{2} \Big|_0^1 = \frac{1}{2} \right)$. This means that (16.14) can be written as

$$G(F) = \frac{2\,(\text{Covariance between } X \text{ and } F(X))}{\Xi(F)}.$$

This completes the proof of the theorem.

The proof of Theorem 16.3 relies on the following lemma.

Lemma 16.1: Let $\varphi : [l, u] \to \Re_+$ be non-increasing and $\psi : [l, u] \to \Re_+$ be a function with the property that $\int_l^z \psi(v)dv \geq 0$ for all $z \in [l, u]$, where $\Re_+$ is the non-negative part of the set of real numbers $\Re$. Then $\int_l^z \varphi(v)\psi(v)dv \geq 0$ for all $z \in [l, u]$.

Proof: Suppose the function ψ changes sign n times over the interval $[l, u]$ at $l < z_1 < z_2 < .. < z_n < u$. Then $\psi(v) > 0$ for $l < v < z_1$, $\psi(v) < 0$ for $z_1 < v < z_2$ and so on. Now, $\int_l^{z_2} \varphi(v)\psi(v)dv = \int_l^{z_1} \varphi(v)\psi(v)dv + \int_{z_1}^{z_2} \varphi(v)\psi(v)dv$. Since the function φ is non-negative and non-increasing, and $\psi(v) > 0$ for $0 < v < z_1$,

$$\int_l^{z_1} \varphi(v)\psi(v)dv \geq \varphi(z_1)\int_l^{z_1} \psi(v)dv. \text{ Since } \psi(v) < 0 \text{ for } z_1 < v < z_2, \text{ we have}$$

$$\int_{z_1}^{z_2} \varphi(v)\psi(v)dv \geq \varphi(z_1)\int_{z_1}^{z_2} \psi(v)dv. \text{ Thus, } \int_l^{z_2} \varphi(v)\psi(v)dv \geq \varphi(z_1)\int_l^{z_2} \psi(v)dv$$

and it is clear that $\int_l^z \varphi(v)\psi(v)dv \geq 0$ for all $l < z < z_2$. This argument can be repeated to demonstrate that $\int_l^{z_{2n}} \varphi(v)\psi(v)dv \geq \varphi(z_{2n-1})\int_l^{z_{2n}} \psi(v)dv$. Therefore,

$$\int_l^z \varphi(v)\psi(v)dv \geq 0 \text{ for all } z \in [l, u]. \text{ This completes the proof of the lemma.}$$

Proof of Theorem 16.3: We have first order stochastic dominance of F_A over F_B if and only if $F_A(z) \leq F_B(z)$, that is, $1 - F_A(z) \geq 1 - F_B(z)$ for all $z \in [l, u]$. Hence a necessary condition for first order dominance of F_A over F_B is that

$$\int_l^u (1 - F_A(v))\, dv - \int_l^u (1 - F_B(v))dv \geq 0, \text{ that is, } e_1(F_A, F_B) = \Xi(F_A) - \Xi(F_A) \geq 0.$$

To prove that $\Psi(F_A) - \Psi(F_B) \geq 0$ is necessary for second order dominance, recall that

$$\Psi(F_A) - \Psi(F_B) = e_2(F_A, F_B) = \int_l^u (1 - F_A(v))^2\, dv - \int_l^u (1 - F_B(v))^2\, dv$$

$$= \int_l^u (F_B(v) - F_A(v))(2 - F_B(v) - F_A(v))dv. \tag{16.15}$$

In (16.15) we take $\varphi(v) = (2 - F_B(v) - F_A(v))$ and $\psi(v) = (F_b(v) - F_A(v))$. By second order stochastic dominance of F_A over F_B for this form of ψ we have $\int_l^z \psi(v)dv \geq 0$ for all $z \in [l, u]$. Also the particular form of φ considered here is non-increasing and non-negative. Hence Lemma 16.1 applies. Consequently, $e_2(F_A, F_B) = \int_l^u (F_B(v) - F_A(v))(2 - F_B(v) - F_A(v))dv \geq 0$. Thus, non-negativity of $e_2(F_A, F_B)$ is a necessary condition for second order dominance of F_A over F_B.

Proof of Theorem 16.4: The first condition is

$$e_1(F_A, F_B) = \Xi(F_A) - \Xi(F_A) \geq 0. \tag{16.16}$$

If F_A and F_B do not intersect, we have either $F_A(z) \geq F_B(z)$ or $F_A(z) \leq F_B(z)$ for all $z \in [l, u]$. The inequality in (16.16) ensures that F_A first order dominates F_B.

Suppose F_A and F_B intersect F_B once. Let $a = \inf_v [F_A(v) \neq F_B(v)]$.
Then $[1 - F_A(a)] = \sup_v [1 - F_A(v) | F_A(v) \neq F_B(v)]$ and $[1 - F_B(a)] =$
$\sup_v [1 - F_B(v) | F_A(v) \neq F_B(v)]$.

Now, $\int_l^u (1 - F_A(v))^j \, dv \geq \int_l^u (1 - F_B(v))^j \, dv$ for all j implies that

$\left[\int_l^u (1 - F_A(v))^j \, dv\right]^{\frac{1}{j}} \geq \left[\int_l^u (1 - F_B(v))^j \, dv\right]^{\frac{1}{j}}$. Therefore, $\lim_{j \to \infty} \left[\int_l^u (1 - F_A(v))^j\right]^{\frac{1}{j}} -$

$\lim_{j \to \infty} \left[\int_l^u (1 - F_B(v))^j\right]^{\frac{1}{j}} = [1 - F_A(a)] - [1 - F_B(a)] = [F_B(a) - F_A(a)] > 0$ (see Roberts

and Varberg 1973, 199).

Thus, $e_j(F_A, F_B) \geq 0$ for all j, with strict inequality for some j, ensures that $[F_B(a) - F_A(a)] > 0$ while $j \to \infty$. Thus, if v_0 stands for the point of intersection, we have $F_A(v) \leq F_B(v)$ for all $v \in [l, v_0]$, with strict inequality for some $v \in [l, v_0]$. On the other hand, $F_A(v) \geq F_B(v)$ for all $v \in [v_0, u]$, with strict inequality for some $v \in [v_0,$

$u]$. This ensures that $\int_l^z F_A(v) \, dv \leq \int_l^z F_B(v) \, dv$ for all $z \leq v_0$ with $<$ for some $z \leq v_0$.

Suppose $\int_l^z F_A(v) \, dv > \int_l^z F_B(v) \, dv$, that is, $\int_l^z (1 - F_A(v)) \, dv < \int_l^z (1 - F_B(v)) \, dv$ holds

for some $z > v_0$. Then given that $F_A(v) \geq F_B(v)$ for all $v \in [v_0, u]$, with $>$ for some $v \in [v_0, u]$, this inequality continues to hold for all $z \in [v_0, u]$. Consequently, we

must have $\int_l^u (1 - F_A(v)) \, dv < \int_l^u (1 - F_B(v)) \, dv$. This contradicts the condition

$e_1(F_A, F_B) \geq 0$. Thus, F_A second order stochastic dominates F_B. This completes the proof of the theorem.

BIBLIOGRAPHICAL NOTES

The Gini evaluation function is analyzed in details in Donaldson and Weymark (1980) and Chakravarty (1990, 2009). A good discussion on the efficient set is available in Yitzhaki (1982). A recent reference for Baumol's (1963) expected gain-confidence limit criterion is Levy (2006). The Gini portfolio analysis and capital asset pricing model are presented and discussed extensively in Shalit and Yitzhaki (1984).

EXERCISES

1. Each of the following statements is either true or false. If the statement is true, prove it. If it is false, give a counter-example or justify your answer by logical reasoning.

    (a) Suppose the distribution function of asset A intersects that of B once. Then since first order stochastic dominance does not hold, second order stochastic dominance also does not hold.

    (b) The efficient sets of the mean-variance and mean-Gini criteria can never coincide.

    (c) Suppose the distribution function of asset A intersects that of B, first from below and then from above. Then third order stochastic dominance cannot be used to rank the assets.

    (d) Baumol's expected gain-confidence limit and the mean-variance criteria will rank two assets in the same way.

2. Assume that assets A and B are lognormally distributed with respective parameters. Derive the conditions for one asset to be preferred over the other by the mean-Gini criterion.

3. Suppose $F_A^j(z)$ intersects $F_B^j(z)$ once, where the definition of $F_A^j(z)$ and $F_B^j(z)$ are given in inequality (16.3). Show that $F_A^i(z)$ and $F_B^i(z)$ cannot be compared by the stochastic dominance rule, where $1 \leq i \leq j - 1$.

4. Assume that intersection of the distribution functions in Theorem 16.4 is not allowable, then show that the set of assets comparable under this condition will be a subset of the comparable set of assets when at most one intersection is allowed.

5. Clearly explain the intuitive reasoning why the conditions laid down in Theorem 16.3 enable us to discard inefficient assets.

6. Consider two investments that are uniformly distributed over $[0, 1]$ and $[2, 4]$ respectively. Apply Theorem 16.3 to show how the mean-Gini criterion becomes helpful in eliminating the first asset from an investor's efficient choice set.

7. If the distribution function F of an asset is continuously differentiable, then the continuous function f, the derivative of F, is called the density function of the asset. An asset return is said to follow the gamma distribution with parameters (c, η), $c, \eta > 0$ if it has the following density function, $f(v) = (gamma(\eta))^{-1} e^{-cv}(cv)^{\eta-1}$, $v \geq 0$,

    where $\left(gamma(\eta) \right) = \int_0^\infty e^{-t} t^{\eta-1} dt$ is the gamma function. Suppose A and B are two gamma distributed assets with $\eta = 2$ and $\eta = 4$ respectively. What can you say about the efficient set here?

8. Give examples of two asset distribution functions that intersect at most once.

9. If assets A and B are uniformly distributed over $[a_1, a_2]$ and $[b_1, b_2]$ respectively, show that $ES_\psi \subseteq ES_V$.

Bibliography

Abidin, N. S. Z. 2008. "Valuation Accuracy: An Empirical Study of Price-Earnings Ratio (PER), Price-Book Ratio (PBR) and Combined PER and PBR Benchmark Multiples in Malaysia." MBA dissertation, University of Malaya.

Aczel J. 1966. *Lectures on Functional Equations and Their Applications*. London: Academic Press.

Addo, H. 1976. "Trends in International Value-Inequality 1969–1970: An Empirical Study." *Journal of Peace Research* 13: 13–34.

Aitchison J. and J. A. C. Brown. 1957. *The Lognormal Distribution*. Cambridge: Cambridge University Press.

Alford, A. W. 1992. "The Effect of the Set of Comparable Firms on the Accuracy of the Price-Earnings Valuation Method." *Journal of Accounting Research* 30: 94–108.

An, Y. and W. Suo. 2009. "An Empirical Comparison of Option-Pricing Models in Hedging Exotic Options." *Financial Management* 38: 889–914.

Anderson, N. H. and J. C. Shanteau. 1970. "Information Integration in Risky Decision Making." *Journal of Experimental Psychology* 84: 441–51.

Apostol, T. M. 1973. *Mathematical Analysis*. London: Addison Wesley.

Arrow, K. J. 1965. *Aspects of the Theory of Risk Bearing*. Helsinki: Yrjo Jahnssonin Saatio.

———. 1970. *Essays in the Theory of Risk Bearing*. Amsterdam: North Holland.

Atkinson, A. B. 1970. "On the Measurement of Inequality." *Journal of Economic Theory* 2: 244–63.

Bailey, R. E. 2005. *The Economics of Financial Markets*. Cambridge: Cambridge University Press.

Baumol, W. J. 1969. "An Expected Gain-Confidence Limit Criterion for Portfolio Selection." *Management Science* 10: 174–82.

Baz, J. and G. Chacko. 2008. *Financial Derivatives: Pricing, Applications and Mathematics*. Cambridge: Cambridge University Press.

Beaver, W. and D. Morse. 1978. "What Determines Price Earnings Ratio?" *Financial Analyst Journal* 34: 65–76.

Berger, A. N. and E. B. Patti. 2002. "Capital Structure and Firm Performance: A New Approach to Testing Agency Theory and an Application to the Banking Industry." Wharton Financial Institutions Center.

Bierwag, G. O. 1987. *Duration Analysis: Managing Interest Rate Risk.* Cambridge: Cambridge University Press.

Bjork, T. 2004. *Arbitrage Theory in Continuous Time,* 2nd ed. New York: Oxford University Press.

Black, F. and M. Scholes. 1973. "The Pricing of Options and Corporate Liabilities." *Journal of Political Economy* 81: 637–59.

Boadway, R. and D. Wildasin. 1984. *Public Sector Economics,* 2nd ed. Boston: Little and Brown.

Bodie, Z., A. Kane and A. J. Marcus. 2008. *Investments,* 7th ed. New York: McGraw-Hill.

Bouzoubaa, M. and A. Osseiran. 2010. *Exotic Options and Hybrids: A Guide to Structuring, Pricing and Trading.* London: John Wiley.

Brav, A., C. R. Harvey, S. Gray and E. Maug. 1999a. "Global Financial Management: Bond Valuation." Mimeographed.

_____. 1999b. "Global Financial Management: Valuation of Stocks." Mimeographed.

Brav, A. and E. Maug. 1999. "Global Financial Management: Debt Policy, Capital Structure and Capital Budgeting." Mimeo.

Brealey, R. A. and S. C. Myers. 2003. *Principles of Corporate Finance,* third reprint. London: McGraw-Hill.

Brigo, D. and F. Mercurio. 2006. *Interest Rate Models-Theory and Practice with Smile, Inflation and Credit,* 2nd ed. New York: Springer.

Broadie, M., J. Detemple, E. Ghysels and O. Torres. 1996. "Nonparametric Estimation of American Options Exercise Boundaries and Call Prices." Montreal: CIRANO.

Cass, D. and J. E. Stiglitz. 1970. "The Structure of Investor Preferences and Asset Returns, and Separability in Portfolio Allocation: A Contribution to the Pure Theory of Mutual Funds." *Journal of Economic Theory* 2: 122–60.

Chakravarty S. R. 1990. *Ethical Social Index Numbers.* New York: Springer.

_____. 2009. *Inequality, Polarization and Poverty: Advances in Distributional Analysis.* New York: Springer.

_____. 2010. *Microeconomics,* Fourth Reprint. New Delhi: Allied.

Chakravarty, S. R. and D. Chakrabarti. 2010. "The Von Neumann–Morgernstern Utility Functions with Constant Risk Aversions." In A. Abergel, B. K. Chakrabarti, A. Chakraborti and M. Mitra (eds), *Econophysics of Order-driven Markets.* Milan: Springer Italia.

Chakravarty, S. R. and C. Zoli. 2012. "Stochastic Dominance Relations for Integer Variables." *Journal of Economic Theory* 147: 1331–41.

Constantinides, G. M. and A. G. Malliaris. 1995. "Portfolio Theory." In R. A. Jarrow, V. Maksimovic and W. T. Ziemba (eds), *Handbooks in Operations Research and Management Science,* vol. 9. Amsterdam: North-Holland.

Cox, J., S. Ross and M. Rubinstein. 1979. "Option Pricing: A Simplified Approach." *Journal of Financial Economics* 7: 229–64.

Damoradan, A. 2010. *The Dark Side of Valuation: Valuing Young, Distressed, and Complex Business*, 2nd ed. Upper Saddle River, NJ: Pearson Education.

Davidson, D., P. Suppes and S. Siegel. 1957. *Decision Making: An Experimental Approach*. Stanford, CA: Stanford University Press.

Davidson, R. 2008. "Stochastic Dominance." In S. N. Durlauf and L. E. Blume (eds), *The New Palgrave Dictionary of Economics*, 2nd ed. London: Palgrave Macmillan.

Demange, G. and G. Laroque. 2006. *Finance and the Economics of Uncertainty*. London: Blackwell.

Dimakos, X. K., L. R Neef and K. Aas. 2006. "Net Present Value with Uncertainty." Norwegian Computer Center.

Donaldson, D. and J. A. Weymark. 1983. "Ethically Flexible Gini Indices of Inequality for Income Distributions in the Continuum." *Journal of Economic Theory* 29: 353–8.

Duan, J.-C. and J.-G. Simonato. 1998. "Empirical Martingale Simulation for Asset Prices." *Management Science* 44: 1218–33.

Duffe, D. 1989. *Futures Markets*. Englewood Cliffs, NJ: Prentice Hall.

———. 1996. *Dynamic Asset Pricing*. Princeton: Princeton University Press.

Edwards, W. 1962. "Subjective Probabilities Inferred from Decisions." *Psychological Review* 69: 109–35.

Eichberger, J. and I. R. Harper. 1997. *Financial Economics*. New York: Oxford University Press.

Fisher, I. 1930. *The Theory of Interest*. New York: McMillan.

Foster J. E. and A. K. Sen. 1997. *On Economic Inequality: After a Quarter Century, Annex to Enlarged Edition of On Economic Inequality by A. K. Sen*. Oxford: Clarendon Press.

Foster, J. E. and A. F. Shorrocks. 1988. "Poverty Orderings and Welfare Dominance." *Social Choice and Welfare* 5: 179–98.

Gastwirth, J. L. 1971. "A General Definition of the Lorenz Curve." *Econometrica* 39: 1037–9.

Gini, C. 1936. "On the Measure of Concentration with Especial Reference to Income and Wealth." New Haven: Cowles Commission.

Giora, H and H. Levy. 1969. "The Efficiency Analysis of Choices Involving Risk." *Review of Economic Studies* 36: 335–46.

Graham, B., D. L. Dodd and S. Cottle with the collaboration of C. Tatham. 1962. *Security Analysis: Principles and Technique*, 4th ed. New York: McGraw-Hill.

Gordon, M. J. 1959. "Dividends, Earnings and Stock Prices." *Review of Economics and Statistics* 41: 351–60.

———. 1962. *The Investment, Financing, and Valuation of the Corporation*. Homewood, IL: R. D. Irwin.

Gravelle, H. and R. Rees. 2004. *Microeconomics*. Englewood Cliffs, NJ: Prentice Hall.

Hadar, J. and W. R. Russell. 1969. "Rules for Ordering Uncertain Prospects." *American Economic Review* 59: 25–34.

Hardy G. H., J. Littlewood and G. Polya. 1934. *Inequalities*. Cambridge: Cambridge University Press.

Hastie, R. and R. M. Dawes. 2001. *Rational Choice in an Uncertain World: The Psychology of Judgment and Decision Making*. London: Sage.

Huang, C.-F. and R. H. Litzenberger. 1988. *Foundations for Financial Economics*. Amsterdam: North Holland.

Hull, J. C. and S. Basu. 2010. *Options, Futures and Other Derivatives*. Delhi: Pearson.

Jarrow, R. and S. Turnbull. 2000. *Derivative Securities*. 2nd ed. Singapore: South Western College Publishing.

Joshi, M. S. 2003. *The Concepts and Practice of Mathematical Finance*. Cambridge: Cambridge University Press.

Kahnemann, D. and A. Tversky. 1979. "Prospect Theory: An Analysis of Decision Under Risk." *Economterica* 47: 263–92.

Kakwani, N. C. 1980. *Income Inequality and Poverty: Methods of Estimation and Policy Applications*. Oxford: Oxford University Press.

Kakwani, N. C., A. Wagstaff, and E. van Doorslaer. 1997. "Socioeconomic Inequalities in Health: Measurement, Computation and Statistical Inference." *Journal of Econometrics* 77: 87–103

Karlin, S. and H. E. Taylor. 1975. *A First Course in Stochastic Process*. New York: Academic Press.

Kim, I. J. 1990. "The Analytic Valuation of American Options." *Review of Financial Studies* 3: 547–72.

Kohn, M. 2003. *Financial Institutions and Markets*, 2nd ed. Oxford: Oxford University Press.

Kwok, Y. K. 2008. *Mathematical Models of Financial Derivatives*. New York: Springer.

Laitinen, E. K. 1997. "Estimation of Internal Rate of Return under Non-steady Conditions." *Journal of Business, Finance and Accounting* 24: 1217–51.

Lintner, J. 1965. "The Valuation of Risk Assets and the Selection of Risky Investments in Stock Portfolios and Capital Budgets." *Review of Economics and Statistics* 47: 13–37.

Levy, H. 2006. *Stochastic Dominance, Investment Decisions Making under Uncertainty*, 2nd ed. New York: Springer.

Lorenz, M. O. 1905. "Methods of Measuring the Concentration of Wealth." *Journal of the American Statistical Association* 9: 209–219.

Lyuu, Y.-D. 2002. *Financial Engineering and Computation: Principles, Martingales and Algorithms*. Cambridge: Cambridge University Press.

Macbeth, J. D. and L. J. Merville. 1979. "An Empirical Examination of the Black–Scholes Call Option Pricing Model." *Journal of Finance* 34: 1173–86.

Markowitz, H. 1952. "The Utility of Wealth." *Journal of Political Economy* 60: 151–8.

_____. 1959. *Portfolio Selection*. New York: Wiley.

Mas-Colell, A., M. D. Whinston and J. R. Green. 1995. *Microeconomic Theory*. New York: Oxford University Press.

Merton, R. C. 1973. "Theory of Rational Option Pricing." *Bell Journal of Economics and Management Sciences* 4: 141–83.

Modigliani, F. and M. H. Miller. 1958. "The Cost of Capital, Corporation Finance and the Theory of Investment." *American Economic Review* 48: 261–97.

_____. 1961. "Dividend Policy, Growth and the Valuation of Shares." *Journal of Business* 34: 411–33.

_____. 1963. "Corporate Income Taxes and the Cost of Capital: A Correction." *American Economic Review* 53: 433–43.

Mosteller, F. and P. Nogee. 1951. "An Experimental Measurement of Utility." *Journal of Political Economy* 59: 371–404.

Oksendal, B. 2003. *Stochastic Differential Equations: An Introduction with Applications*, 6th ed. New York: Springer.

Penman, S. H. 2001. *Financial Statement Analysis and Security Valuation*. New York: McGraw-Hill.

Perold, A. F. 2004. "The Capital Asset Pricing Model." *Journal of Economic Perspectives* 18: 3–24.

Porter, R. B. and J. E. Gaumnitz. 1972. "Stochastic Dominance vs. Mean-Variance Portfolio Analysis: An Empirical Evaluation." *American Economic Review* 62: 438–46.

Pratt, J. W. 1964. "Risk Aversion in the Small and the Large." *Econometrica* 32: 122–36.

Quirk, J. P. 1986. *Intermediate Microeconomics*. Chicago: Science Research Associates.

Reisinger, M. 2008. "Mean-Variance Analysis and the CAPM." University of Munich.

Roman, S. 2004. *Introduction to the Mathematics of Finance: From Risk Management to Option Pricing*. New York: Springer.

Roberts, A. W. and D. E. Verberg. 1973. *Convex Functions*. London: Academic Press.

Ross, S. A. 1976a. "Risk, Return and Arbitrage." In I. Friend and J. Bicksler (eds), *Risk and Return in Finance*. Cambridge: Ballinger.

———. 1976b. "Options and Efficiency." *Quarterly Journal of Economics* 90: 75–87.

———. 1978a. "A Simple Approach to the Valuation of Risky Streams." *Journal of Business* 51: 453–475.

———. 1978b. "Mutual Fund Separation in Financial Theory – The Separating Distributions." *Journal of Economic Theory* 17: 254–86.

———. 1981. "Some Stronger Measures of Risk Aversion in the Small and the Large with Applications." *Econometrica* 49: 621–79.

Rothschild, M. and J. E. Stiglitz. 1970. "Increasing Risk I: A Definition." *Journal of Economic Theory* 2: 225–43.

Rudin, W. 1976. *Principles of Mathematical Analysis*. McGraw-Hill: New York.

Russett, B. M. 1964. "Inequality and Instability: The Relation of Land Tenure to Politics." *World Politics* 16: 442–54.

Samuelson, P. A. 1983. *Foundations of Economic Analysis, Enlarged Edition*. Cambridge, MA: Harvard University Press.

Saunders, A. and M. M. Cornett. 2001. *Financial Markets and Institutions: A Modern Perspective*. New York: McGraw-Hill.

Seydel, R. 2004. *Tools for Computational Finance*, 3rd ed. New York: Springer.

Shaked, M. and G. Shanthikumar. 2006. *Stochastic Orders*. New York: Springer.

Shalit, H. and S. Yitzhaki. 1984. "Mean-Gini, Portfolio Theory and the Pricing of Risky Assets." *Journal of Finance* 39: 1449–68.

Sharpe, W. F. 1964. "Capital Asset Prices: A Theory of Market Equilibrium under Conditions of Risk." *Journal of Finance* 19: 425–42.

Shorrocks, A. F. 1983. "Ranking Income Distributions." *Economica* 50: 3–17.

Smith, C. W. Jr. 1976. "Option Pricing-A Review." *Journal of Financial Economics* 3: 3–51.

Stiglitz, J. E. 1969. "A Re-examination of the Modigliani-Miller Theorem." *American Economic Review* 59: 784–93.

Sundaram, R. K. 1997. "Equivalent Martingale Measures and Risk-Neutral Pricing: An Expository Note." *Journal of Derivatives* 5: 85–98.

Tobin, J. 1958. "Liquidity Preference as Behavior Toward Risk." *Review of Economic Studies* 25: 65–86.

———. 1965. "The Theory of Portfolio Selection." In F. H. Hahn and F. P. R. Brechling (eds), *The Theory of Interest Rates*. London: Macmillan.

Tversky, A. 1967. "Additivity, Utility and Subjective Probability." *Journal of Mathematical Psychology* 4: 175–201.

Vander Weide, J. H. and W. T. Carleton. 1988. "Investor Growth Expectations: Analysis vs. History." *Journal of Portfolio Management* 14: 78–83.

Varian, H. 1992. *Microeconomic Analysis*, 3rd ed. New York: W. W. Norton.

Villamil, A. 2008. "Modigliani–Miller Theorem." In S. N. Durlauf and L. Blume (eds), *The New Palgrave Dictionary of Economics*, 2nd ed. London: Palgrave Macmillan.

von Neumann, J. and O. Morgenstern. 1944. *Theory of Games and Economic Behavior*. Princeton: Princeton University Press.

Whitmore, G. A. 1970. "Third Degree Stochastic Dominance." *American Economic Review* 60: 457–9.

Williams, D. 1991. *Probability with Martingales*. Cambridge: Cambridge University Press.

Wilmott, P., S. Howison and J. Dewynne. 1995. The Mathematics of Financial Derivatives: A Student Introduction. Cambridge: Cambridge University Press.

Yitzhaki, S. 1982. "Stochastic Dominance, Mean Variance and Gini's Mean Difference." *American Economic Review* 72: 178–85.

———. 1998. "More Than a Dozen Alternative Ways of Spelling Gini." *Research on Economic Inequality* 8: 13–30.

Yusuf, M. and B. Randy. 2007. "Risk Aversion in Low Income Countries: Experimental Evidence from Ethiopia." International Food Policy Research Institute.

Zarowin, P. 1990. "What Determines Earnings-Price Ratios: Revisited." *Journal of Accounting, Auditing and Finance* 5: 439–57.

Index

A

affine transformation 22, 24, 28, 46, 48
agency cost 81–2
almost risk-free 171
American Telephone and Telegraph 176
annual equivalent 71–2, 74
annuity 60, 71–3, 87–8, 103–4
arbitrage 5, 13, 15, 76–7, 81, 105, 114, 118, 120–23, 127, 129, 132, 135–41, 143, 151–3, 165–7, 169, 204, 207, 217
arbitrageur 127, 129, 136, 166
Arrow–Debreu security 204–8, 218
asset 4–7, 13, 17, 27, 34–5, 37, 46, 51, 75, 79, 80–82, 98, 105–12, 115–50, 152–3, 155, 158, 160, 164–77, 179–90, 193, 210–12, 215, 217, 221–7, 229–33, 236–45, 251–6, 258–65, 270–82, 285
attainable claim 142, 152
at-the-money 109–10, 179
auxiliary conditions 167
Avon Products 176

B

bank account 213
Bank of England Base Rate 12
barrier: lower 186–7, 194; upper 186–9
Baumol rule 275, 278, 285–6

bearish: calendar-spread strategy 110, 112; price-spread strategy 110–12, 132; positions 108
benefit–cost ratio 63, 67, 73–4
beta: Gini 282, market 240–42; of an asset 240–42, 244, 252; of a portfolio 240–43, 252
binomial: distribution 148; model (one-step) 134–5, 137, 143, 145–7, 150, 152–3, 164, 210, 218; tree 144, 147–9
Black–Scholes–Merton partial differential equation 164–9, 171, 179–80
Black–Scholes pricing formula 107, 164, 167, 170–71, 175–7, 180
bond: at par 90, 102–3; corporate 5, 88, 91; discount 90, 94, 98, 102, 123, 125, 208;
  fixed coupon 89; premium 90, 94; pure prospect 214; semiannual 90, 245; zero-coupon 90, 92, 95, 103, 117, 127, 140–42, 210–11, 214
Brownian motion: arithmetic 162; geometric 158, 160–61, 163, 165, 168, 177, 180, 183, 189
bullish: calendar-spread strategy 112, 132; price-spread strategy 111–12, 132; positions 108

butterfly: hedging 112; price-spread strategy 111, 132

C

calendar-spread strategy 110, 112
call: money rate 12; rate 12
call option: American 117–20, 122, 125, 132; digital 182–4, 189, 191–4, 202; down-and-in 187; down-and-out 186, 202; European 81, 106–7, 109–15, 119–25, 130–2, 152–3, 167, 170–71, 173–4, 176–7, 179, 182, 190–93; foreign currency 109, 183; gap 190–91, 202–3; in-the-money 106, 109, 132; look-back 193, 202; out-of-the money 106, 132; pay-later 192; shout 192, 203; up-and-in 189–90; up-and-out 188–90, 194, 202
capital gain 52, 54
capital market: line 237, 240, 242, 252; perfect 13, 64, 67, 74–5
capital structure 75–7, 82
CAPM 7, 222, 240–41, 243–4, 252, 280–81
certainty equivalent 17, 28–31, 46, 48, 134, 137
Chicago Board of Trade Options 107, 131, 176
closed 18, 44, 141, 166
coin-tossing game 161
common knowledge 81
combination: bottom straddle 112–13; bottom vertical 113; convex 236, 263; linear 28, 140, 151, 231, 235–6, 239, 250; strangle 113, 131–3; strap 113, 132; strip 113, 131
compact set 44
comparative statics 171
complete: asset market 135, 142, 152; ordering 233; relation 19, 69, 262
composite: consumption 205–6; good 8–10
concave 10, 22–9, 31–2, 37, 39, 41, 44, 47, 205, 218, 244, 254, 257–8, 261–2, 264–5, 267, 276
consol 55, 88–9

context independence 21
contingent claim 141–2, 152, 205
continuous: compounding 90–91, 117, 135, 180, 212; random variable 156; rebalancing 168
contract: forward 6, 105–6, 126–33, 160, 180, 214; function 214; futures 6, 105–6, 127–31, 133, 216; legal 4; non-obligatory 130; obligatory 105, 126; spot 126
convenience yield 130
convex: combination 236, 263; function 23, 27, 89, 122
convexity of a bond 87, 97–8, 103
corporate: bonds 91; finance 75, 81; tax 79–80, 82–3; tax rate 80, 82
correlation coefficient 7, 224, 243, 245, 252
cost of: borrowing 166; capital 78–9; carry 130, 133; debt 79, 83; equity 79–80, 82; risk 17, 30–32, 45–6, 243
coupon 5, 88–95, 98–9, 102–4, 117, 127, 140–41, 183, 204, 210–11, 214
covariance 7, 221, 224 – 5, 231, 238, 241, 244, 280
covariance matrix 231, 244
covered call 115
credit derivative 6
CREST 52

D

date of maturity 89, 92, 94, 105–6, 108–9, 119, 123, 125, 127–8, 139, 176
debt-to-equity ratio 78–82
default risk 76
Delta: -hedging 166–7, 180; -neutral 172
delivery: date 126, 216; price 105–6, 126, 128
density function 158, 160, 170, 177–78, 184, 195–6, 286
derivative: over-the-counter 181; security 106, 168–9, 171, 173–4
discount rate 12, 64–5, 67, 89
discounted: asset price 210; present value 9, 12–15, 51, 54, 63–5, 67–8, 71, 76, 80, 82, 87, 96, 99, 103–4, 117, 121, 123–5,

127, 137, 140, 150, 171, 173–4, 208; stock price 211–12, 218

discrete: distribution 259, 264, 274; model 143, 204, 210, 218; -time 113, 134, 150, 154– 6, 161, 208, 215, 217

distribution function 170, 174, 176–8, 194–5, 254, 256–62, 270–71, 273–8, 280–82, 286

diversifiable risk 225, 241, 281

dividend: historical 54, 59; payout ratio 58–9, 61; yield (prospective) 54, 56, 59–61, 149

dominance: relation 233; stochastic (first order, second order, third order) 253–9, 263–5, 270–73, 275–7, 280, 282, 284, 286; strong 254; weak 254

Dow Jones Industrial Average 53

drift parameter 168

duration 87, 94–9, 102–4, 205

dynamic: hedging 166

E

Eastman Kodak 176

efficient: frontier 233–5, 237–8, 241, 252; portfolio 233–6, 238, 240, 243; set 265, 273, 276–8, 280, 282, 285–6

elasticity 28, 43, 46, 48, 95, 174–5, 179

equity 5, 16, 62, 75–83, 190

equivalent: martingale measure 204, 210, 212–13, 215, 218; probability measure 209

European call 81, 106–7, 109–15, 118, 120–24, 130–32, 148, 152–3, 164, 167, 170, 171–4, 176–7, 179, 182, 190–93

European put 108, 110, 112–16, 119, 123–5, 131–3, 153, 167, 170–75, 177, 179–80, 183, 190–93

event 6

exercise price 105

expectation operator 136, 144, 155, 223, 239, 244, 271

expected: rate of return 54–6, 78–9, 137, 157, 165, 168, 213; expected utility 16–19, 21–2, 24, 28–30, 33, 35–7, 40, 45–7, 137,

221, 253–9, 264–5, 270–71, 276, 280, 282; value 19, 22–4, 26–7, 136–7, 140, 144, 155, 168, 170, 183, 189, 205, 208–11, 215, 217, 223, 281

expiry period 144, 148

exponential transformation 26, 91, 117, 144, 170

extension 137

Exxon 176

F

face value 81, 88–90, 95, 98, 102–4, 117, 123, 125, 127

Farkas' Lemma 151

feasible portfolio 221

final: payoff 120; wealth 128–9; value 186

financial: derivative 5, 105; economics 4, 6–7, 76, 134, 204, 253; institution 3–4, 7, 106, 127, 181, 202; instruments 3, 5, 87, 165; markets 3–5, 7, 176; products 4; ratio 54, 58; risks 5; securities 5–6, 26

first fundamental theorem 140

Fisher's proposition 12, 13, 89

foreign currency option 6, 108

forward: contract 6, 105, 126–30, 133, 160, 180, 214; price 105, 126, 128–30, 161, 214–15; interest rate 87, 99–100, 102; rate agreement 87, 101–2

frictionless market 53

frontier portfolio 232, 234, 238–9

futures: contract 6, 105–6, 126–31, 133, 216; process 216, 218

G

gambling: fair 217; sequential 20, 217

gamma 172, 180

gamma distribution 286

geometric Brownian motion 158, 160–61, 163, 165, 168, 177, 180, 183, 189

Gini: absolute 274, 276–81; beta 282; CAPM 281; evaluation function 272–5, 277–8, 285; index 7, 272–4, 276–81

Girsanov Theorem 212

good: inferior 27, 33, 259; normal 27

Greek letters 171, 179

H

hedging: continuous 7; delta- 166, 180; riskless 113, 165; strategy 167
homogeneous expectation 222

I

immunization 87, 98–9, 204
impatient consumer 10
implied volatility 175–7, 179
in-the-money 106, 109–10, 112, 132, 172–4, 182–3, 188, 192
income effect 11
indifference curve 10–11, 29–30, 32–3, 35–6, 47–8
induced probability 17
initiation 126–8, 160, 165, 186, 215
instantaneous: drift 161, 212; interest rate 214; rate of return 157, 168, 183
interaction 7, 17, 22, 225
integral kernel 170, 184, 199
integrand 170, 184
interest rate: floating 14, 204; forward 87, 99–100, 102; risk-free 26, 77, 88, 117, 127–30, 133, 141, 144, 150, 152–3, 165, 168, 171, 174–6, 180, 193, 202, 208, 210; stochastic 129, 204, 213–15, 217; swap 6
interest tax shield 80
internal rate of return 63–6, 70, 73
International Business Machines 176
intertemporal: budget constraint 9; marginal rate of substitution 207–8, 210; preference 9
initial: endowment 10, 206; value 126, 136, 141, 144, 171, 212, 257
intrinsic value 119–20
invariance: scale 32, 45; translation 31–2, 44–5
investment strategy 115, 168, 222
iso-expected output line 30
Itô process 154, 159–60, 163
Itô's Lemma 154, 158–9, 161–2, 165, 180

J

Jensen's inequality 41, 44

L

law of: conservation of value 76
leverage 76, 78–80, 82
levered firm 76–80, 82–3
LIBOR 12, 101, 194
line of certainty 30
linearly independent 231
loan repayment factor 71
logarithmic growth 158
lognormal distribution 145, 160, 163, 177
long position 52, 106–17, 120, 125–7, 129, 131–3, 135, 139, 165, 176, 216, 222

M

Macaulay duration 95–7, 102–4
margin account 128
market: beta 241; capital 4–5, 13, 64, 67, 69, 74–5, 81, 237, 240, 242, 252; commodity 5–6; currency 4; derivatives 4–6; financial 3–5, 7, 176; foreign exchange 5–6; futures 5–6; insurance 5–6, 17, 39; money 5, 12, 213; premium 34; portfolio 237–44, 252; stock 5, 51–3, 55, 106, 131, 241, 245
marking to market 128–9, 216
Markovian process 155, 158
Markowitz: bullet 233–4, 237, 252; curve 232; efficient frontier 233–5, 237, 238
martingale: continuous-time 212–13, 218; discrete-time 208, 210, 217; measure 141, 204, 210, 212–13, 215–18; sub- 209, 218; super- 209, 218
maturity date 92, 94, 106, 108, 123, 125, 127, 176
maturity period 88, 91–2, 98, 101, 126–7, 129–30, 132–3, 172, 179, 192
mean: absolute deviation model 245; -Gini analysis 275; -standard deviation frontier 232; -variance model 221, 282
measure of cost of risk: absolute 30–32, 45; relative 32, 45

minimum-risk weight line 232, 248–9
Modigliani–Miller theorem 76–80, 82–3
money: account process 213, 218; market account 213
mutually exclusive 64–5, 67, 72, 74

N

net present value 63–5, 69–70, 72–4
non: -arbitrage principle 13, 134, 136, 139, 141, 151–2, 169, 207; -dividend paying stock 123, 125, 130, 132–3, 167, 170, 180; -satiation 19, 33
normal distribution 33, 156, 158, 160, 163, 176–8, 183–4, 189, 194–6, 199, 212
numéraire 211–12, 216

O

opposite positions 108, 165
optimistic (bullish) position 108
option: American 106, 108, 117–20, 122, 126, 132, 143, 149, 152, 181, 186, 192; Asian 181–2, 184–5, 218; as-you-like 192; at-the-money 179; barrier 182, 185–6, 190, 203; basket 181; Bermudan 192; binary 182, 202; call 6, 81, 106–25, 130–33, 152–3, 167, 170–77, 179, 181–4, 186–94, 202–3; cash-or-nothing (call, put) 182–3; chooser 192; contingent premium 192; covered 115; digital 181–3; down-and-in 187; down-and-out 186; European 106, 108, 110–11, 119, 124, 132, 149, 164, 167, 175, 180, 185–6, 192–3; exchange-traded 107–8, 181; exotic 6, 181–2, 192, 194, 202; extinguishable 186; foreign currency 6, 108; futures 130, 133; gap 182, 190–91; index 109; in-the-money 106, 109–11, 174, 176, 182–3, 188, 192; intermediate 192; intrinsic value 119–20; knock-in 186; knock-out 186; ladder 181; lightable 186; look-back 193; nonstandard 181, 202; out-of-the-money 106, 109–11, 132, 174, 176, 192; over-the-counter 108, 181; path-dependent 148, 186, 192–3,

202; pay-later 192; plain vanilla 106; preference 192; protective 116–17; put 6, 106–10, 112–19, 121–5, 131–3, 148–9, 153, 164, 167, 170–75, 177, 179–81, 183, 185, 187–93, 202–3; shout 192, 203; standard 107, 181, 192; time value of 119–20, 173, 179; up-and-in 189; up-and-out 187–8; weather 181
ordering: generalized Lorenz 254, 259, 262–3, 270; Lorenz 259–60, 262–3, 270

P

Pareto: distribution 278; dominance principle 69
patient consumer 10
payoff 6, 8, 20, 22–3, 26, 81, 101–2, 106–16, 120–23, 126, 128, 131–3, 142, 148–9, 168, 170–72, 174, 180–93, 202–3, 205, 207–8, 217, 254
perfect: hedging 108, 227; capital market 10, 13, 64, 67, 74–5
perfectly: negatively correlated 224, 226–7, 252, 279; positively correlated 76, 224, 226–7
period of expiration 174, 182–3
perpetuity 55, 88, 103, 119
pessimistic (bearish) position 108
portfolio: diversified 7, 33; dynamic 168–9; efficient 233–6, 238, 240, 243, 280; minimum-variance 234–5, 244, 249; of combination 112; self-financing 166
positive: definite 231, 246; reward 227, 279; premium 242
predetermined: delivery price 105–6; future time 105
premium 4, 6, 17, 24–5, 31–2, 34, 39, 47–8, 90–91, 94, 105, 107–8, 111–17, 119, 126, 130, 188, 192, 240–42
price: forward 105, 126, 128–30, 161, 214–15; futures 129, 204, 216–17; of risk 35, 46, 213, 243; -to-earnings ratio 51, 58, 61
principal: amount 5, 87; –agent problem 81

profitability index 63, 67–8, 73–4
prospect: compound 20–21, 40; even 22, 24–5, 48; theory 17, 36–7, 39, 46, 48
prospective dividend yield 54, 56, 60–61
pseudo-probability 210
psychological discount factor 10
purchasing power 205–6
put option: American 106, 118–19, 121, 125; European 108, 110, 112–16, 119, 123–5, 131–3, 153, 167, 170–75, 177, 179–80, 183, 190–93
put–call parity 123–5, 132–3, 172–4, 179

Q
quadratic utility function 17, 33, 46, 221, 253

R
random variable 7, 21, 41, 117, 141, 148, 152, 154–6, 160, 163, 170, 177–8, 208, 217, 223, 263, 278
random walk 143, 145, 154–5, 161
Radon–Nikodym derivative 210
rate of return 213, 223, 231, 253–5, 258–62, 271–3
rational expectations equilibrium 53
re-hedging 167
replicating portfolio 142
replication 142, 169, 180
representative utility 18
Reserve Bank of India 12
return: gross 161; net 231; rate of 213, 223, 231, 253–5, 258–62, 271–3
rho 174, 179
risk: -adjusted return 243; aversion (Arrow–Pratt measures) 17, 24–7, 31–2, 46–8, 259; diversifiable 225, 241; -free (asset, bond, rate of return, prospect) 26–8, 77, 79, 88, 102, 117, 120, 122, 127–30, 133–5, 140–41, 144, 145, 150, 152–3, 160, 165–6, 168–71, 174–7, 180, 193, 202, 207–8, 210, 212–13, 222, 224, 230–31, 236–8, 241, 244, 252, 280;

market 166, 222, 225, 240–41, 243; -minimizing (portfolios, weights) 221, 226, 229, 232, 244–5, 252; neutral (pricing, probability, valuation) 24, 27, 31, 33, 134, 136–8, 141, 144–5, 149–50, 152–3, 168, 170, 177, 179, 183, 189–90, 194–6, 204, 207, 210–12, 215, 217–18, 256; non-diversifiable 281; of asset 5, 223, 241; premium 31, 48, 240; -reward curve 227, 229, 231, 279; systematic 225; tolerance 24, 28, 47; transfer 4; unsystematic 225, 252
risky prospect 26–8, 30–31, 33–5, 42–3, 46

S
sample space 140
security market line 242, 252
self-financing 166, 180
separable utility 205
Sharpe ratio 243, 252
short: position 106, 108, 109–12, 114–17, 120, 126–9, 131–3, 135, 139, 151, 165–6, 176, 216, 222, 228; selling 52–3, 127, 135, 165, 226–7, 229–31, 252, 279
spot price 128, 130, 187–8, 216
spread strategy: bearish price- 111–12; bullish price- 111–12; box- 112; butterfly price- 111; calendar- 110, 112; diagonal- 112; neutral calendar- 112; price- 110–11; reverse calendar- 112; time- 110
standard: deviation 34–6, 46, 155–6, 177, 223, 232–4, 252, 275–8; normal distribution 170, 176–8, 184, 195; prospect (equivalent) 19–21, 39–40
state: -contingent (claim, price, return, security) 113, 139, 141, 205, 207–8, 210–11; of nature 138–9, 141–2, 208
stochastic: asset price 165; calculus 154; differential equation 145, 158–9, 168, 212; discount factor 214–15; dominance (first order, second order, third order) 253–9, 263–5, 270–73, 275–7, 280, 282,

284, 286; interest rate 129, 204, 213–15, 217; process (continuous-time, discrete-time) 156, 158, 208–9, 218
stock: exchange (Chicago, London, New York, Mumbai, Tokyo) 5, 12, 52–4, 72, 107, 131; index (Amsterdam Exchange, Dow Jones Industrial Average, Nasdaq 100, Sensex, Swiss Market, Toronto Stock Exchange 300) 53
storage cost 129
strike price 81, 105–13, 116–22, 124–5, 130–33, 148, 152, 165, 167, 171, 173–7, 179–83, 185–93, 202
sub-martingale 209, 218
substitution effect 11
super-martingale 209, 218
swap 6, 190
symmetric 79, 132, 146, 174, 231, 246
symmetry 39, 81, 132, 146, 148
systematic risk 225

T
Taylor's formula 162
terminal period 88, 170–71, 182–3, 193
theta 173, 180
time: decay 173; to expiry 118–19, 121–2, 167, 172–3, 175, 177; value 8, 119–20, 125, 173, 179
trading strategy 105, 122, 128–9, 141–2, 166, 168, 176
transactions costs 76, 135, 165, 222
transitivity 19
transpose 114, 116, 126, 222–3, 231, 246
treasury: bonds 102; rate (US, Japanese) 102
trigger price 190–91, 202
trinomial model 137–8, 152, 218
two: -fund (monetary separation, separation theorem) 47, 235, 251; -mutual fund separation 244, 249

U
uncorrelated 163, 224, 242, 252

underlying asset 6, 105–12, 115–19, 121, 123, 126–8, 131–3, 145, 148–9, 160, 165–6, 168–9, 171–2, 175–7, 179, 181, 183–6, 190, 193, 217
uniform distributions 277
US Treasury Bills 177
utility: isoelastic 48; maximization 10, 206, 280; ranking 255

V
value: function 37–9; of strategy 222
vanilla option 106, 171, 186–8, 218
variance 7, 33–4, 36, 46–7, 145–6, 155–61, 163, 170, 173, 177–8, 183, 189, 194, 196, 199, 212, 221–6, 228, 231–2, 234–6, 238–41, 244–5, 247, 249–53, 265, 273–82, 286
vega 173–5, 179, 188
volatility smile 175–6
von Neumann–Morgenstern utility 16–18, 22, 24, 28, 40, 47, 253

W
Wall Street Journal 177
weighting function 37
Weiner: increment 158; process (generalized, standard) 145, 154, 157, 160, 163, 169, 212
writer 108–9, 214

X
Xerox 176

Y
yield: curve 87, 91, 98–9; to maturity 89–92, 102–3

Z
zero: coupon bonds 90, 92, 95, 103, 117, 127, 140–42, 210–11, 214; risk 165, 227, 244

Lightning Source UK Ltd.
Milton Keynes UK
UKOW04n1536300114

225567UK00001B/11/P